ROYAL HISTORICAL SOCIETY

STUDIES IN HISTORY

New Series

BENJAMIN WORSLEY (1618–1677)

TRADE, INTEREST AND THE SPIRIT IN REVOLUTIONARY ENGLAND

BENJAMIN WORSLEY (1618–1677)

TRADE, INTEREST AND THE SPIRIT IN REVOLUTIONARY ENGLAND

Thomas Leng

THE ROYAL HISTORICAL SOCIETY
THE BOYDELL PRESS

First published 2008

A Royal Historical Society publication
Published by The Boydell Press
an imprint of Boydell & Brewer Ltd
PO Box 9, Woodbridge, Suffolk IP12 3DF, UK
and of Boydell & Brewer Inc.
668 Mt Hope Avenue, Rochester, NY 14620, USA
website: www.boydellandbrewer.com

ISBN 978-0-86193-296-2

ISSN 0269-2244

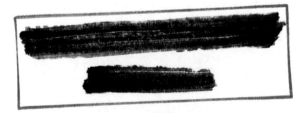

A CIP catalogue record for this book is available
from the British Library

This publication is printed on acid-free paper

Printed in Great Britain by
CPI Antony Rowe, Chippenham, Wiltshire

Contents

Acknowledgements

The setting for the conception and writing of this monograph, has been the History Department of the University of Sheffield, current resting place of the Hartlib papers. I owe my acquaintance with the Hartlib circle as an undergraduate to Mike Braddick and Mark Greengrass, who later became doctoral supervisors and then colleagues; they have been a continued source of support and inspiration throughout. I must also thank my doctoral examiners, Anthony Milton and Mark Goldie, for their useful suggestions which have helped enormously in turning the thesis into a monograph. Antonio Clericuzio, Michael Hunter and John Young kindly read and commented on sections of the book. John Morrill as editor has been the guiding force behind its transformation into something fit for public consumption. I have also benefited from suggestions, correspondence and conversations with many scholars: special thanks to David Armitage, Toby Barnard, Ben Coates, David Como, David Haycock, Ariel Hessayon, Sarah Mortimer, William Newman, David Ormrod, Jason Peacey, Margaret Pelling, Steven Pincus, Lawrence Principe and Charles Webster. Bettina Weichert provided me with translations of German letters. Christine Linehan has been extremely helpful in providing editorial guidance. Jacky Hodgson of the University of Sheffield Library granted permission for the use of the images that appear on the front cover, whilst James Pearson provided advice on their digitisation. Having been undergraduate, postgraduate and lecturer in the History Department at Sheffield, there are many friends, students and colleagues who deserve my thanks, particularly Geoff Little, John Tanner, Kevin Watson and my fellow early modernists Ben Lake and Catherine Marshall. My family and especially my parents Gwynne and Paul Leng have been a source of support throughout. Above all I would like to thank Miriam Dobson for her comments on the manuscript and her unfailing support. I dedicate this book to her, and to my parents.

Thomas Leng,
Sheffield,
April 2008

Abbreviations

A&O	*Acts and ordinances of the Interregnum*, ed. C. H. Firth and R. S. Rait, London 1911
BL	British Library, London
Bodl. Lib.	Bodleian Library, Oxford
Catalogus	J. Dunmore and R. Chiswell, *Catalogus librorum … instructissimarum bibliothecarum tum clarissimi doctissimique viri D. Doctoris Benjaminis Worsley*, London 1678
CJ	*The journals of the House of Commons*
CSPC	*Calendars of state papers, colonial series (1574–1676)*, ed. W. N. Sainsbury, London 1869–96
CSPD	*Calendar of state papers, domestic series (1651–73)*, ed. M. A. Everett Green, F. H. Blackburne Daniell and F. Bickley, London 1877–1939
CSPI	*Calendar of state papers relating to Ireland (1633–65)*, ed. H. Mahaffy, London 1901–7
CTB	*Calendar of treasury books (1669–89)*, ed. W. Shaw, London 1908–23
EcHR	*Economic History Review*
EHR	*English Historical Review*
HJ	*Historical Journal*
HMC	Historical Manuscripts Commission
HP	*The Hartlib papers: electronic edition*, 2nd edn (Sheffield: HR Online, 2002)
HPT	*History of Political Thought*
HR	*Historical Research*
IHS	*Irish Historical Studies*
JBS	*Journal of British Studies*
LJ	*The journals of the House of Lords*
ODNB	*Oxford dictionary of national biography*
P&P	*Past and Present*
SHUR	M. Greengrass, M. Leslie and T. Raylor (eds), *Samuel Hartlib and universal reformation*, Cambridge 1994
T&C	J. Thirsk and J. P. Cooper (eds), *Seventeenth century economic documents*, Oxford 1972
TNA	The National Archives, London
TRHS	*Transactions of the Royal Historical Society*
WMQ	*William and Mary Quarterly*

Notes on the Text

Hartlib papers electronic edition

Documents prefixed by the abbreviation HP are taken from the transcriptions of the Hartlib papers electronic edition (2nd edn). These include both the Hartlib papers held at Sheffield University Library, and relevant additional material, from other archives, included with the second edition. The former are noted as follows:

'Propositions in the behalfe of the kingdome', HP 71/11/8B.

References from additional material include the original archive reference, with the prefix HP added to denote that they are taken from the transcriptions provided by the Hartlib papers electronic edition, as the following examples demonstrate:

Worsley to Hartlib, 18 May 1649, HP (Royal Society, Boyle letters 7.1, fo. 2r.)

Petty to Worsley, 14 Mar. 1649, HP (James Marshal and Marie-Louise Osborn Collection, Beinecke Rare Book and Manuscript Library, Yale University, doc. 36, fo. 1r.)

Dating and transcription conventions

Dates are given old style, with the exception that the new year is dated from 1 January. The original spelling has been retained in manuscript transcriptions, with the exception that abbreviations and contractions have been expanded, with the expanded letters italicised, following the Hartlib papers electronic edition convention (e.g. ye becomes *the*).

Preface

The middle decades of the seventeenth century have attracted perhaps more attention than any other era in English history. The civil war and its revolutionary aftermath, of course, have borne the brunt of this scrutiny, but this is a period remarkable for the convergence of at least two further developments which have been termed revolutionary. Alongside the political revolution, we see the undermining of scholastic natural philosophy and the enthroning of a 'new science' based on experimental and mechanistic principles, and embodied by the foundation of the Royal Society in 1660. And accompanying these intellectual and political revolutions, shifts in the structure of England's overseas trade paved the way for future economic success in what has been termed a commercial revolution. The concurrence of these three 'revolutions' guarantees the enduring interest of these climactic years, and those individuals who lived through them. Such a person was Benjamin Worsley, a figure whose life can illuminate all three.

Born circa 1618, Benjamin Worsley was one of many of his generation who rose from relatively humble origins to prominence thanks largely to the turbulence of the 1640s. Trained as a surgeon in 1630s London, Worsley served the English army in Ireland in the early 1640s but he left his vocation to embark on a career in state service in the employ of the Commonwealth. If the political revolution opened doors for him, then it was the commercial one which secured his invitation inside. In 1650 Worsley gained his first major official appointment as an expert advisor on commercial affairs, becoming secretary to the Commonwealth's Council of Trade, and in the following year played a significant role in the passage of the Navigation Act. Continuing in state service, this time less successfully, Worsley next featured as surveyor-general of the Cromwellian survey of Ireland, only to be overshadowed by his enemy William Petty, who eventually took custody of the celebrated 'Down Survey'. Somewhat estranged from Cromwellian rule, Worsley participated in its destruction in 1659 as a supporter of the leading republican Sir Henry Vane, but his expertise in commercial and, increasingly, colonial matters allowed him to weather the Restoration fairly well. He returned to state employment in 1668 on Charles II's trade council, and went on to enjoy five years of ascendancy on various trade and plantation councils. His career, then, tells us much of the relationship between the political and commercial revolutions over a period spanning the supposed watershed of 1660, which has been seen as laying the foundations of the 'navigation system' that governed the empire for a century to come. It reveals how the motif of commercial advancement became an attractive one to two very different regimes both seeking to establish their legitimacy, the Commonwealth and the restored monarchy, something which Worsley was able to capitalise on by inhabiting the space between Whitehall and the Exchange, advising statesmen on mercantile affairs from a supposedly impartial standpoint.

Alongside this, Worsley was a participant in the century's intellectual revolution, particularly the unseating of scholastic natural philosophy by the experimental method. From 1645 onwards he was in close contact with Samuel Hartlib, a German Calvinist *émigré* committed to the advancement of knowledge through the promotion of communication and intellectual exchange. It is through the papers left by Hartlib and his 'circle' that we know much of Worsley's interest in Baconian experimental science and especially chemistry or 'chymistry'. Thanks to his role in the oft-written about 'Invisible College', he is linked to the celebrated scientist Robert Boyle, his supposed collaborator in this apparently pioneering effort to institutionalise science. But the practical and utilitarian ethos of his early engagements with experimental science increasingly transmuted into a spiritually introspective alchemical quest for spiritual enlightenment as well as mastery over nature. Influenced by the religious enthusiasts of the 1650s, Worsley's piety also took a decidedly unorthodox turn. This tendency becomes hard to detect after Hartlib's death in 1662, which removes the major source, Hartlib's papers, but its persistence is suggested by the fact that Worsley refused to take the Test Act in 1673 as a dissenter from the Church of England, thus bringing his civil service career to its final end four years before his death.

Thanks to his bureaucratic career and intellectual exploits Worsley has attracted attention from a surprising variety of historians, but by far the most influential portrait was that which appeared in the works of the major historian of the Hartlib circle, Charles Webster, especially his momentous work of 1975 *The great instauration*. For Webster, Worsley epitomised the practical utopianism of the Puritan social and intellectual reformers who came to the fore thanks to the political revolution, his economic planning complimenting the scientific, medical and educational reforms of his Hartlibian collaborators. Revolution was thus a motor of progress, and one need only read the closing line of *The great instauration* to see that Webster was writing in a positivist mode fitting to more optimistic times.[1] Essentially, Webster's work was a contribution to the history of science, part of a movement which sought to question the traditional grand narrative of that discipline by identifying previously neglected contributors to the story of the scientific revolution. Worsley, principally through his association with Boyle, was one such figure, showing that idealistic social planning and reform could be a force for intellectual progress, that the intellectual and political revolutions were

---

[1] 'It may turn out that in the scale of values of a future age the utopianism and humanitarianism of puritan science may come to be held in high esteem': C. Webster, *The great instauration: science, medicine and reform, 1626–1660*, London 1975, 520.

indeed connected. But still these new tributaries fed into the same great river of progress towards modernity, an image with which historians are less easy today.

One critique of the 'enlightenment project' of modernity is to see it as a dimension of the European domination of subjected colonial populations, and a sort of 'postcolonial Worsley' has appeared in one recent account as embodying the colonialist ethos of dominion over nature and humanity alike.[2] But in essence this Worsley is identical with the one created, with greater sympathy, by Webster: the self-confident, hard-headed Baconian mercantilist whose spiritual goals were comfortably externalised into the 'universal reform' of the world.

The Worsley who appears in this monograph is perhaps also a child of the times in which it was written, a much less confident figure characterised by doubt and uncertainty, who struggled to resolve competing forces in his life (the 'interest and spirit' of the title), and whose activities are marked by frustration as much as by achievement. For it is the contention of this book that, however revolutionary the political, intellectual and commercial developments of the mid seventeenth century, they produced in those people living through them a great deal of unease. The idea of the 'seventeenth century crisis' is perhaps hackneyed now, but no other term conveys the sense of uncertainty which the breakdown in political, religious, social and intellectual authority produced, to which can be added the commercial crisis which began in the 1620s and only much later could be seen as the beginnings of English ascendancy. But it was precisely in responding to these crises, in seeking solutions to the problems that they created, that innovation, adaptation, even revolutionary change can be seen. To borrow from Aesop a cliché popular in the early modern period, 'necessity is the mother of invention', and so the Worsley presented here is also an opportunist, a survivor, a consequence, not cause, of revolution.

And it is in the twists and turns of a life that we see this character emerge. Biography is of course the most old-fashioned form of history and can be criticised for seeking to 'essentialise' a person, to locate a consistent core of selfhood, a world view or philosophy underpinning each utterance, guiding the individual through the journey of life. But self exists in motion, and only biography can convey the sense of self as formed by transition, by the struggle to maintain coherence in the face of mutability, itself a very seventeenth-century trope. Furthermore, biography can bring out some of the subtle differences, indeed tensions, submerged in collective accounts such as Webster's, acting as case study for the interrelationship between different contexts and discourses. Under such scrutiny some of the cohesiveness of the so-called spiritual brotherhood can be seen to dissolve, revealing tension and disso-

---

2 R. Drayton, *Nature's government: science, imperial Britain, and the 'improvement' of the world*, New Haven–London 2000, 57–8.

nance beneath an apparently common vision as well as problematising its Puritan identity. This account then is unashamedly biographical, using narrative as a means to illuminate the contexts in which this life is set and the tensions at the heart of England's revolutionary crisis.

Introduction

Universal reform in revolutionary England

On 13 May 1678 at a house 'against the Hen and Chickens' in Paternoster Row, close by the building site that was St Paul's cathedral, an auction of the library collections of three gentlemen opened for business. This had been preceded by the publication of a sale catalogue with a title page carrying the name of only one of the collectors in question. It was the first time that the name had appeared in such a place; it would not do so again for over three hundred years.[1]

The name in question was that of Benjamin Worsley, who had died in the previous year and whose life is the subject of this book. The fact that Worsley's name appeared in full public view so fleetingly helps to explain why he has not been the subject of a monograph until now, and perhaps this is fitting for obscurity if not anonymity seems to have been a condition that he cultivated. But in his time, Benjamin Worsley appeared at many important historical junctures, assuming some interesting roles. Although he has only emerged as a fully-fledged historical character relatively recently, the name will be familiar to a wide range of historians of the period. It is the principal aim of this book to bring Worsley in his many guises into the public glare from which he shied.

Those attending the auction of his library would most likely know of Benjamin Worsley, if at all, as the late secretary to the king's Council for Trade and Plantations. Worsley had held this post from 1672 to 1673, the summit of over twenty years of sporadic service to the state as an expert in colonial and commercial affairs, which stretched back to the Council of Trade founded by the Commonwealth in 1650. If they were well informed on intellectual matters, the name might ring a bell as that of an acquaintance of the famed natural philosopher Robert Boyle, or as an enemy of the political economist and surveyor of Ireland William Petty. Accordingly, on the occasions that his name attracted the attentions of historians, at least until the 1960s, it has generally been in connection with either his bureaucratic career or his relations with those two more celebrated names.

In terms of the former, Worsley has been of interest to historians charting the course of commercial policy in the so-called 'mercantilist' era, when England's expanding colonies were subjected to an ever tighter regime of

---

1   J. Dunmore and R. Chiswell, *Catalogus librorum … instructissimarum bibliothecarum tum clarissimi doctissimique viri D. Doctoris Benjaminis Worsley*, London 1678.

1

commercial control beginning with the 1651 Navigation Act, which Worsley had a hand in producing.[2] In fact, it has been known since 1959 that Worsley authored the printed defence of this act, an anonymous pamphlet entitled *The advocate*, as well as another anonymous publication connected to Commonwealth commercial policy, entitled *Free ports*.[3] Worsley resurfaced in the 1660s as a commercial advisor to statesmen such as Sir Anthony Ashley Cooper, the first earl of Shaftesbury, in whose circle he came into contact with another celebrated figure, John Locke, who succeeded him as secretary to the Council of Trade and Plantations.[4] Worsley's potential influence on Locke's economic thought was considered by Peter Laslett, before being firmly demonstrated by Patrick Hyde Kelly, who found that Locke copied five of Worsley's Restoration papers on trade and colonies into his own journal.[5]

In intellectual terms Worsley has been known to Boyle biographers ever since a letter of his appeared in Thomas Birch's eighteenth-century edition of Boyle's works.[6] His name also cropped up in the letters in these volumes written to Boyle by Samuel Hartlib, a relatively obscure German publisher and intellectual communicator based in London from the late 1620s to his death in 1662. Although he did not join the Royal Society or publish any scientific works himself, Worsley thus occasionally appeared as a minor member of the generation that advanced experimental science in England in the middle decades of the seventeenth century.[7] His relations with Petty set Worsley in less favourable light for, as surveyor-general of Ireland in the 1650s, Worsley was the apparently incompetent and intransigent figure whom Petty had to triumph over in order to complete his own celebrated

---

[2] C. Andrews, *British committees, commissions, and councils of trade and plantations, 1622–1675*, Baltimore 1908, 24, and *The colonial period of American history*, IV: *England's commercial and colonial policy*, New Haven 1938, 11, 59–60; G. Beer, *The old colonial system, 1660–1754*, New York 1912, 382; R. P. Bieber, 'The British plantation councils of 1670–4', *EHR* xl (1925), 100.

[3] R. W. K. Hinton, *The Eastland trade and the common weal in the seventeenth century*, Cambridge 1959, 89–94, reprinted in appendix B.

[4] L. F. Brown, *The first earl of Shaftesbury*, New York–London 1933, 129, 140–2; E. E. Rich, 'The first earl of Shaftesbury's colonial policy', *TRHS* 5th ser. vii (1957), 53–4, 61; K. H. D. Haley, *The first earl of Shaftesbury*, Oxford 1968, 255.

[5] P. Laslett, 'John Locke, the great recoinage, and the origins of the Board of Trade, 1695–1698', *WMQ* 3rd ser. xiv (1957), 377; P. H. Kelly, 'Locke on money: an edition of John Locke's three pamphlets on money published in the 1690s', unpubl. PhD diss. Cambridge 1975, 30–2, 334–8, and 'Introduction', to *Locke on money*, ed. P. H. Kelly, Oxford 1991, 6–7. The papers are to be found in 'The 1661 [sic] notebook of John Locke', Bodleian Library, Oxford, microfilm 77. My thanks to David Armitage for originally alerting me to these documents.

[6] *The works of the honourable Robert Boyle*, ed. T. Birch, 2nd edn, London 1772, vi. 635–6.

[7] R. E. W. Maddison, *The life of the honourable Robert Boyle*, London 1969, 63; M. Boas, *Robert Boyle and seventeenth-century chemistry*, Cambridge 1948, 23.

Down Survey of Ireland.[8] Together with some fragmentary references in the calendars of state papers and elsewhere, referring to such episodes in his life as Worsley's employment as surgeon-general to the English army in Ireland in the early 1640s, and his projects to cultivate saltpetre and senna in the 1640s and '60s respectively, this meant that a biography of sorts could be assembled, 'the picture of a bureaucratic careerist' who dabbled in the intellectual affairs of his age.[9] And doubtless he would have remained in such obscurity, had not the discovery of the papers of Samuel Hartlib by G. H. Turnbull opened our eyes to the existence of a whole 'circle' of intellectuals, reformers and projectors surrounding this remarkable figure, with Benjamin Worsley prominent amongst them.[10]

Worsley appeared only sporadically in Turnbull's works, leaving it to another historian to produce the first real portrait of Worsley to incorporate the evidence of the Hartlib papers, which include several of Worsley's letters and papers, as well as numerous references to him elsewhere in the archive. This was Charles Webster, whose 1975 work *The great instauration* still stands as the finest account of the ideals and aspirations of the Hartlib circle.[11] This was a powerful argument for the importance of Puritanism to the 'intellectual revolution' of seventeenth-century England that saw experimental, Baconian science overthrow its scholastic predecessor, something long obscured by the royalist rhetoric of the defenders of the Royal Society. And in Worsley Webster found an ideal figure with which to demonstrate his thesis: not just a neglected figure but a near 'empty vessel' unencumbered by historiographical baggage, whom he could show to have been at the heart of intellectual and public affairs of his day. Worsley was the subject of Webster's last major writing on the Hartlib circle, and by authoring his entry in the *Dictionary of national biography* he symbolically inducted Worsley into the cast of recognised actors in British history.[12] The Benjamin Worsley we know is, more than anything, the creation of Charles Webster.

His importance to Webster can best be seen in an article written in 1974 and heralding *The great instauration*, which considered 'the social rela-

---

8   Y. M. Goblet, *La Transformation de la géographie politique de l'Irlande au XVIIe siècle*, Paris 1930, i. 214–15.
9   J. E. Farnell, 'The Navigation Act of 1651, the first Dutch war, and the London merchant community', *EcHR* 2nd ser. xvi (1961–2), 441. The printed evidence is summarised in J. B. Whitmore, 'Dr. Worsley being dead', *Notes and Queries*, 28 Aug. 1943, 123–8. For a more up-to-date summary see G. Aylmer, *The state's servants: the civil servants of the English Republic, 1649–1660*, London–Boston 1973, 272.
10 G. Turnbull, *Hartlib, Dury and Comenius: gleanings from Hartlib's papers*, London 1947.
11 Webster, *Great instauration*.
12 Idem, 'Benjamin Worsley: engineering for universal reform from the Invisible College to the Navigation Act', in *SHUR*, 213–33, and 'Worsley, Benjamin', in C. S. Nicholls (ed.), *Dictionary of national biography: missing persons*, Oxford 1993, 722–3.

tions of English science in the mid-seventeenth century'.[13] This reassessed an organisation known as the 'Invisible College', which had long been seen as providing the occasion for introducing the young Robert Boyle to experimental science in the mid-1640s. By identifying Worsley as the recipient of two letters written by the juvenile Boyle and published by Birch, Webster was able to argue that he was the leading figure in the London-based Invisible College, and an enduring influence on this major scientist. With Worsley, Webster was able to identify a new 'centre of intellectual organization' in 1640s London, which was centred much more on the practical, utilitarian benefits of experimental science than those contemporary natural philosophers led by John Wilkins whose meetings prefigured the foundation of the Royal Society.[14] Furthermore, the milieu to which Worsley belonged absorbed the revolutionary energy of the period: individuals inspired by their eschatology to hope for a future age of learning, peace and plenty, a worldly utopia achieved through advancing knowledge and restoring humanity to its pre-lapsarian 'dominion over nature'. In particular, Worsley's career exemplified the application of knowledge to the amelioration of the human condition and the perfection of human society through social and economic planning. Thus Webster wedded the two aspects of Worsley's biography which previous historians had considered separately: the administrator and the intellectual, 'from the Invisible College to the Navigation Act'. And these apparently disparate activities were now subsumed to an overarching goal, the 'universal reform' of society and knowledge, in accordance with an ultimately millenarian goal. The political and intellectual revolutions could no longer be considered separately.[15]

Since the publication of *The great instauration*, other historians have cast light on aspects of Worsley's life: T. C. Barnard on his career in Ireland in the 1650s, John Young on a visit he paid to the Netherlands from 1648 to 1649, Antonio Clericuzio on Worsley's authorship of a discussion of astrology once attributed to Boyle, and William Newman and Laurence Principe on his alchemy, for example.[16] Michael Hunter has presented a more critical assessment of Webster's account of the Invisible College, downplaying Worsley's influence on Boyle's intellectual development.[17] However,

---

[13] Idem, 'New light on the Invisible College: the social relations of English science in the mid-seventeenth century', *TRHS* 5th ser. xxiv (1974), 19–42.

[14] Ibid. 25.

[15] Idem (ed.), *The intellectual revolution of the seventeenth century*, London–Boston 1974.

[16] T. C. Barnard, *Cromwellian Ireland: English government and reform in Ireland, 1649–1660*, 2nd edn, Oxford 2000, 219–22, 230–3; J. T. Young, *Faith, medical alchemy and natural philosophy: Johann Moriaen, reformed intelligencer, and the Hartlib circle*, Aldershot 1998, 217–46; A. Clericuzio, 'New light on Benjamin Worsley's natural philosophy', in *SHUR*, 236–46; W. Newman and L. Principe, *Alchemy tried in the fire: Starkey, Boyle, and the fate of Helmontian chymistry*, Chicago–London 2002, 236–56.

[17] M. Hunter, *Robert Boyle, 1627–1691: scrupulosity and science*, Woodbridge 2000, 22–3.

Webster restated his case for the importance of the millenarian world-view in the second edition of *The great instauration*, asserting that Worsley's 'role as the midwife to the Navigation Act demonstrates this puritan ideologue's confidence in the ability to advance towards rule of the saints on earth by means of economic and political will'.[18]

There is no doubt that Webster's work is the starting point for any study of Benjamin Worsley, as it is for the Hartlib circle in general. His encyclopaedic knowledge of the Hartlib papers makes *The great instauration* a treasure-trove of information, especially impressive as it predates the digitisation of the Hartlib archive.[19] But just as is the case with the Harlib circle, Webster has by no means provided the last word on Worsley. For a start, his studies focus on a fairly narrow although crucial period of his life, 1645–51: Worsley's fascinating Restoration career, for example, was largely beyond Webster's scope. Equally important are the ways in which the historiography has moved on in the last thirty years. Historians of science have questioned Webster's account of the role of Puritanism in the rise of science, positing the influence of other groups, although none has uncovered a more convincing 'missing link' between religion and science.[20] Perhaps because of the indecisiveness of such debate, the focus has shifted from uncovering the 'origins' of the scientific revolution, towards issues such as the social construction of scientific knowledge.[21] Other historians have sought to place the scientific revolution within a more comprehensive intellectual history, with epistemology providing the common ground between science and religion.[22] Particularly influential is Richard Popkin's account of the post-Reformation 'sceptical crisis', which provoked many seventeenth-century intellectuals to seek new bases for certain knowledge.[23] Popkin saw the Hartlib circle as belonging to a 'third force' in seventeenth-century philosophy, intellectuals who sought to defend Christian orthodoxy from the sceptical challenge with a characteristic blend of biblicism, millenarianism and natural philosophy.[24] Others too have stressed how the universalism of the Hartlib circle was fashioned in response to a period of 'unprecedented division and diversity of opinions and ideologies in all fields, the religious, the political, the philosophical and the scientific'.[25]

---

[18] C. Webster, 'Introduction to the second edition', *Great instauration*, 2nd edn, Oxford 2002, p. xxxii.

[19] *The Hartlib papers: electronic edition*, 2nd edn, Sheffield 2002.

[20] B. Shapiro, 'Latitudinarianism and science in seventeenth-century England', in Webster, *Intellectual revolution*, 286–316; P. Elmer, 'Medicine, religion and the Puritan Revolution', in R. French and A. Wear (eds), *The medical revolution of the seventeenth century*, Cambridge 1989, 10–45.

[21] See especially S. Shapin and S. Schaffer, *Leviathan and the air-pump: Hobbes, Boyle, and the experimental life*, Princeton–Oxford 1985.

[22] See, for example, J. Wojcik, *Robert Boyle and the limits of reason*, Cambridge 1997.

[23] R. Popkin, *The history of scepticism from Savonarola to Bayle* (1960), Oxford 2003.

[24] Idem, *The third force in seventeenth-century thought*, Leiden 1992.

[25] Young, *Faith*, 250.

Another approach, exemplified by Michael Hunter, is based on constructing nuanced case studies, a biographical antidote to Webster's collective treatment.[26] Similar studies of supposed 'members' of the Hartlib circle have uncovered more variety than Webster, understandably, conveyed.[27] Some of the most interesting work has stressed the European dimensions of the Hartlib circle, for example John Young's discussion of Hartlib's Amsterdam-based German correspondent, Johann Moriaen, whilst studies of figures such as the irenicist John Dury and the mathematician John Pell have told us more about their membership of multi-national intellectual and religious communities.[28] Similarly, Howard Hotson's work on the intellectual background to the 'three foreigners' Hartlib, Dury and the Czech educationalist Jan Amos Comenius, has described how they arrived in England as 'alien influences from beyond the margins of orthodoxy'.[29] His study of Comenius' teacher, the encyclopaedist J. H. Alsted, has shown that beneath a veneer of Calvinist orthodoxy, Alsted absorbed a range of influences including renaissance humanism, hermeticism and the heady dreams of intellectual and moral rebirth of the Rosicrucians. Such work has, if anything, restated the universalism which the Hartlib circle transmitted to England, but whereas Webster saw the goals of 'universal reform' as generally focused outwards, intending to transform the world, Hotson has shown this equally to have been about the transformation of the self: restoring in man the fractured image of God through an encyclopaedic programme of education.[30] Such work implicitly distances the Hartlib circle from the Anglocentric religious identity of Puritanism, suggesting instead an exotic foreign contribution to the Puritan Revolution.

Of course, the 1640s and '50s are no longer as commonly described under this heading. Although historiography has increasingly emphasised the religious nature of the civil war, the 'revolutionary' aspect has been questioned, and even those happy to retain the term nowadays tend to stress how this revolution was solvent of Puritanism, rather than its culmination.[31] The identification of Worsley as a Puritan is the aspect of Webster's account with which this work differs the most. In fact Worsley was open to heterodox spir-

---

[26] M. Hunter, *Science and the shape of orthodoxy: intellectual change in late seventeenth-century Britain*, Woodbridge 1995.

[27] See especially the articles in *SHUR*.

[28] Young, *Faith*; A. Milton, '"The unchanged peacemaker"? John Dury and the politics of irenicism in England, 1628–1643', in *SHUR*, 95–117; N. Malcolm and J. Stedall, *John Pell (1611–1685) and his correspondence with Sir Charles Cavendish: the mental world of an early modern mathematician*, Oxford 2005.

[29] H. Hotson, *Johann Heinrich Alsted, 1588–1638: between Renaissance, Reformation, and universal reform*, Oxford 2000, 233. For the 'three foreigners' see H. Trevor-Roper, *Religion, the Reformation and social change*, London 1967, 237–93.

[30] Hotson, *Johann Heinrich Alsted*, 66–74.

[31] For an emphasis on the revolutionary dimension see J. Scott, *England's troubles: seventeenth-century English political instability in European context*, Cambridge 2000.

itualistic influences, perhaps reflecting how the programme of inner transformation of Alsted, Comenius and the like, could merge with the subjective
piety of radical religion in revolutionary England. Webster's definition of
Puritanism is admittedly broad, and yet once this aspect of Worsley's piety
is brought into question, the coherence of his account of 'universal reform'
is destabilised, and with it the relationship between Worsley's spiritual
and secular goals. Attempt will still be made to relate Worsley's disparate
activities, but this will reveal tension between the forces of 'interest' and
'spirit', two terms which continually appear in his writings and which seem
to represent contradictory world-views or understandings of the self. This
book is therefore an account of Worsley's conscience as much as his intellect, something given a new depth by the discovery of a third anonymous
publication almost certainly written by Worsley, but previously unnoticed
by historians, this time discussing the government of religion rather than of
trade.[32] Thus we shall see how the universal ideals transmitted by the Hartlib
circle fared in the crucible of the English Revolution, and its aftermath, the
Restoration.

The other context of particular importance for Worsley is that of commercial transformation, beginning in his youth with the 1620s crisis in England's
cloth trade to Europe.[33] However, crisis ultimately brought opportunity, and
over the course of Worsley's lifetime the structure of English international
trade would undergo what has been described as a commercial revolution,
as markets were diversified and re-exports grew.[34] Perhaps most striking to
contemporaries was the development of the Atlantic as a major commercial
arena, fuelled by exports from English colonies in the West Indies and north
America, which emerged as viable settlements in this period.[35] Eventually
commercial transformation would elevate England to a position of leadership
in world trade, but for much of Worsley's lifetime the prevailing sense was
one of instability, with English commerce potential prey for the era's major
commercial predator, the Hollander. Dutch trade and shipping provided
both inspiration and warning to those keen to harness the benefits of trade,
in an age of intense international competition over markets in which mutability was the defining condition.[36] As Sir Thomas Roe warned in 1641,
England's apparent commercial success at that time was 'changeable and
depending more upon the iniquity or misery of the times, than upon our

---

32 *The third part of naked truth*, London 1681 (discussed in chapter 8 below).

33 B. Supple, *Commercial crisis and change in England, 1600–1642: a study in the instability
of a mercantile economy*, Cambridge 1959.

34 R. Davis, 'English foreign trade, 1660–1700', in W. E. Minchinton (ed.), *The growth
of English trade in the seventeenth and eighteenth centuries*, London 1969, 78–98; C. Wilson,
England's apprenticeship, 1603–1763, 2nd edn, London–New York 1984, 160–84.

35 R. Bliss, *Revolution and empire: English politics and the American colonies in the seventeenth century*, Manchester 1990, 17–44.

36 J. I. Israel, *Dutch primacy in world trade, 1585–1740*, Oxford 1989.

own foundation and industry ... for nothing stands secure but upon its own foundation'.[37] The search for security would produce the Navigation Act of 1651, and for decades afterwards the fortunes of English trade would be closely entwined with those of the Dutch.[38]

Worsley belonged to a generation of writers and advisors who presented the Dutch as a model commercial nation to be imitated, by making trade the public interest. The language of interest, pioneered in the Dutch republic, focused on surviving in a world of shifting circumstances which outweighed universal values, and as such provided the ideal language for a burgeoning commercial literature in England.[39] Nevertheless private interest continued to be suspected as 'that many-headed Monster', reflecting tensions about economic change which were rooted in an earlier rise in domestic market transactions.[40] Craig Muldrew has described how a shortage of circulating currency made these transactions dependent on insecure credit arrangements, generating a new sense of the competitive nature of society 'as the cumulative unity of the millions of interpersonal obligations which were continually being exchanged and negotiated'.[41] Similarly the debate about international commerce which emerged from the 1620s depression focused upon divining the public good amidst this multiplicity of private transactions, a 'discourse of trade' which considered the appropriate relationship between merchants and the state.[42] Authors jostled to present the state with those maxims necessary to manage private interest for the public good. Of course overseas trade had long been considered to fall under the state's remit, based on a 'time-honoured concept of the proper relationship between trade

---

[37] T&C, 43–4.

[38] D. Ormrod, *The rise of commercial empires: England and the Netherlands in the age of mercantilism, 1650–1770*, Cambridge 2003. See also C. Wilson, *Profit and power: a study of England and the Dutch Wars*, 2nd edn, The Hague 1978; J. I. Israel, 'England's mercantilist response to Dutch world trade primacy, 1647–1674', in S. Groenveld and M. Wintle (eds), *State and trade: government and the economy in Britain and the Netherlands since the Middle Ages*, Zutphen 1992, 50–61.

[39] See, for example, S. Bethel, *The present interest of England stated*, London 1671; S. Fortrey, *Englands interest and improvement*, 2nd edn, London 1673; and W. Carter, *Englands interest by trade asserted*, London 1671. For the intellectual background see R. Tuck, *Philosophy and government, 1572–1651*, Cambridge 1993; J. A. W. Gunn, *Politics and the public interest in the seventeenth century*, London–Toronto 1969; and J. Scott, *Algernon Sidney and the English Republic, 1623–1677*, Cambridge 1988, 207–21. Worsley owned the classic statement of interest theory, Henri, duc du Rohan, *A treatise of the interest of the princes and states of Christendome*, London 1641.

[40] [W. Petyt], *Britannia languens, or a discourse of trade*, in *Early English tracts on commerce*, ed. J. R. McCulloch, Cambridge 1856, 287.

[41] C. Muldrew, *The economy of obligation: the culture of credit and social relations in early modern Europe*, London–Hampshire 1998, 123.

[42] T. Leng, 'Commercial conflict and regulation in the discourse of trade in seventeenth-century England', *HJ* xlviii (2005), 933–54; J. Appleby, *Economic thought and ideology in seventeenth-century England*, Princeton 1978.

and the public interest'.[43] However, commercial crisis and transformation meant that the traditional, indirect means of governing trade, via companies, was increasingly seen as inadequate.

In Worsley's lifetime, the debate over the nature of the state's responsibility over trade came to focus on the foundation of councils and committees of trade, with the Council of Trade formed in 1650 particularly important.[44] On such councils, the ideals of public good and social order, which had long underlain the state's approach to economic change, were to be reconciled with an increasingly complex commercial world, 'redefining the commonwealth', in Wrightson's words.[45] This was also a dimension of state formation, extending state power over trade, although in a way that was often halting and ineffective.[46] Throughout his career, Worsley was able to capitalise on this uncertainty by acting as an intermediary between the political and commercial worlds, neither a politician nor a privately interested merchant, identifying his interests with the state. In a sense this helped to create the 'functional space' which later, more permanent bureaucrats would fill. Thus Worsley's career may serve as a sort of 'microhistory' of the conduct of commercial policy.

In older, especially Marxist, accounts the English Revolution was seen as a crucial stage in the long-term history of commercial policy, as the state increasingly upheld the individualistic interests of that class which had triumphed over the economically conservative royalists, undermining the commercial monopolies favoured by the Stuarts with a programme of 'free trade', and deploying state power to defend commercial interests overseas.[47] This teleology, however, has been undermined as historians have argued for a greater degree of continuity in commercial policy over this period, concluding for example that 'the Civil War was not fought between rival economic schools'.[48] Reflecting the revisionist trend, commercial conflict has been reinterpreted in terms of factionalism rather than prin-

---

[43] B. Worden, *The Rump Parliament, 1648–1653*, Cambridge 1974, 258.

[44] Andrews, *Committees*; P. Gauci, *The politics of trade: the overseas merchant in state and society, 1660–1720*, Oxford 2001, 180–93.

[45] K. Wrightson, *Earthly necessities: economic lives in early modern Britain, 1470–1750*, London 2002, 202–26.

[46] For state formation see M. Braddick, *State formation in early modern England*, Cambridge 2000.

[47] C. Hill, *The century of revolution, 1603–1714*, 2nd edn, London 1980; R. Brenner, 'The civil war politics of London's merchant community', *P&P* lviii (1973), 53–107. See also C. B. Macpherson, *The political theory of possessive individualism*, Oxford 1962. For an analysis of the historiography see A. Hughes, *The causes of the English Civil War*, Basingstoke–London 1991, 117–54.

[48] P. Corfield, 'Economic issues and ideologies', in C. Russell (ed.), *The origins of the English Civil War*, London–Basingstoke 1973, 198. See also J. P. Cooper, 'Social and economic policies under the Commonwealth', in G. Aylmer (ed.), *The Interregnum: the quest for settlement, 1646–1660*, London 1972, 121–42.

ciple.[49] Despite the efforts of Robert Brenner to resurrect the importance of mercantile conflicts in his 'new social interpretation' of the Revolution, revisionism has rendered commercial policy something of a historical backwater, exacerbated by a tendency amongst economic historians to downplay the relevance of state policy to economic change.[50] Focusing on Benjamin Worsley's career, this book seeks to argue that the commercial policy of the Commonwealth was indeed of lasting importance, although this will be charted in terms of changes in political culture, rather than hard economic facts: the emphasis will not just be on assessing the effectiveness of the Commonwealth's commercial policies, but on the successful propagation of the image of a regime committed to defending commerce.[51] This success can be seen in the emulation of certain Commonwealth policies, notably the Navigation Act, by the restored monarchy, something illustrated by Benjamin Worsley's career under both regimes.

Thus this study seeks to relate Worsley's life to larger historical developments, intellectual, political and commercial. None the less it is a biography, and the structure will largely reflect that. Chapter 1 takes us from Worsley's early years as a surgeon's apprentice to his employment as army surgeon in Ireland in the early 1640s, and his return to London and original acquaintance with the Hartlib circle. This chapter also discusses Worsley's relationship with Robert Boyle in the Invisible College years. Chapter 2 looks at Worsley's visit to Amsterdam from 1648 to 1649, an important episode given the significance of the Dutch commercial example. The legacy of this visit can be seen in chapter 3, which considers Worsley's employment on the Commonwealth's Council of Trade, and his role in the Navigation Act. In chapter 4 Worsley continues to be employed by the state, this time as surveyor-general of Ireland in the 1650s, the occasion for his bitter contest with William Petty. The next two chapters are rather more thematic, with chapter 5 considering the nature of Worsley's natural philosophy in the 1650s, and chapter 6 looking at his religious beliefs, as well as picking up the biographical thread to 1660. Chapter 7 sees how Worsley adapted to the Restoration, rebuilding his reputation as an expert in commercial and, increasingly, colonial affairs, and ultimately returning to state employment. Finally chapter 8 considers why this employment came to an end, as Worsley resigned his post on a matter of conscience, presented in new light through a discussion of his long-neglected pamphlet, *The third part of naked truth.*

[49] R. Ashton, *The city and the court, 1603–1643*, Cambridge 1979.

[50] R. Brenner, *Merchants and revolution: commercial change, political conflict, and London's overseas traders, 1550–1653*, Cambridge 1993; C. Clay, *Economic expansion and social change: England, 1500–1700*, II: *Industry, trade and government*, Cambridge 1984, 239–40.

[51] See S. Pincus, 'Neither Machiavellian moment not possessive individualism: commercial society and the defenders of the English Commonwealth', *American Historical Review* ciii (1998), 705–36.

This pamphlet is perhaps the major new source which this study deploys. In the absence of Worsley's own papers, and given that he did not publish extensively, any study of him must rely heavily on the Hartlib papers. A list of Worsley's surviving writings is found in the bibliography; this shows that over half of the total number of items derive from the Hartlib papers. We are comparatively well provided for in terms of Worsley's Restoration career, thanks to the survival of a number of lengthy and highly significant papers he drafted on commercial and colonial policy for statesmen such as Shaftesbury, several of which were collected by John Locke. Another useful, although problematic source, is the catalogue of Worsley's library (the *Catalogus*): useful for the breadth of information which it gives us of his book ownership, but problematic due to the unspecific nature of much of the information given therein. Use will be made of this source throughout the book, to suggest what Worsley may have been reading at particular junctures, but such suggestions can only ever be tentative.[52]

Thus in terms of Worsley's religious and scientific beliefs, for example, the Hartlib papers are undoubtedly the major source, and this of course can create problems. The validity of the term 'Hartlib circle' itself can be challenged as merely the product of a chance survival of his papers. In its defence, the term does successfully describe what was a deliberate effort on Hartlib's part to assemble a network of like-minded intellectuals and reformers, and to harmonise their disparate goals into some sort of common enterprise. Similarly, associates such as Worsley seem to have been conscious that they were participating in such a circle, expecting their opinions to be circulated along the networks which Hartlib assembled and maintained. However, it is important to remember that participation in this circle does not necessarily convey 'membership', much less identity in outlook.[53] Furthermore, those letters Worsley wrote to Hartlib and other associates would have been tailored to their anticipated audience: they are not a transparent reflection of that biographical chimera, an author's 'essential' intellectual personality. In a sense the Worsley who appears in the context of the Hartlib circle is just one of many possible Worsley's, most of whom can be glimpsed only fleetingly, if at all.

If part of the justification for this study is to understand Benjamin Worsley independently of the Hartlib circle, however, it is also hoped that this will add to our awareness of that amorphous body. In seeking to delineate a collective intellectual movement and mentality, Charles Webster understandably stressed the shared ethos and purpose of the 'spiritual brotherhood', sometimes at the expense of their individuality. But what is so interesting about the Hartlib circle is its very diversity, and we can perhaps learn most by examining how it acted as a crucible for various different and sometimes

---

[52] Titles are included in references throughout the text. Only those which have been specifically consulted are included in the bibliography, however.
[53] M. Greengrass, M. Leslie and T. Raylor, 'Introduction', in *SHUR*, 1–26.

conflicting attitudes, which could be transformed by the experience of inter-action. This study therefore seeks to contribute to our understanding of the workings of the Hartlib circle as a forum for intellectual exchange, in terms of the collision of various influences, events and experiences, acted out in a single life. For Benjamin Worsley this story begins with the experience of growing up in the dynamic environment of early Stuart London.

1

London and Dublin, 1618–1647

The apprentice surgeon

'And of all others I am I confesse most tender & yearning towards young persons, Not only their temper but sometimes their very reasons & curiousity sometimes not only their unexperience but their desire of selfe experience, putting them upon tryalls & courses, & conclusions, that they themselves afterwards espy to be destructive to them.'[1]

Whether these reflections on the troubles of youth were born of experience is hard to say, for Benjamin Worsley's own formative years are almost lost to us. By the time that he begins to emerge as a historical character in the papers of Samuel Hartlib, Worsley was in his late twenties with a career already behind him, but it is possible none the less to piece together an impressionistic picture of his life before then. His father Francis originated from gentry farming stock in the Warwickshire village of Kineton, nearby where the battle of Edgehill would later be fought, and throughout his life Worsley claimed the title gentleman.[2] Worsley also described himself as a Londoner, although whether he was born in the capital is unknown.[3] But Worsley must have been in London by the early 1630s, for at the close of that decade he was admitted to the freedom of the Worshipful Company of Barber-Surgeons, having presumably served a conventional seven-year apprenticeship.[4] Their ability to afford the indenture to this reputable trade suggests that Worsley's parents were not poor, although perhaps without a landed estate to pass on to their eldest son.[5]

---

[1]   B. Worsley to Lady [Ranelagh?], 29 July 1653, BL, MS Add. 4106, fo. 224r.
[2]   Worsley's inclusion in the 1664 London visitation records listed his parents as Francis Worseley of Kineton, Warwickshire, and Mary, daughter of Shipman Hopkins of Coventry, gent.: *London visitation pedigrees, 1664*, ed. J. B. Whitmore and A. W. Hughes Clarke (Harleian Society xcii, 1940), 154 (listing the family arms as 'a chief gules, a crescent on the field'). The wills of Worsley's uncle and great-grandfather are included in *London will abstracts*, ed. J. B. Whitmore, London 1961, p. xiii.
[3]   On entering university in 1643, Worsley described himself as an eldest son aged twenty-five from London: *Alumni dublinenses: a register of the students, graduates, professors and provosts of Trinity College in the University of Dublin (1593–1860)*, ed. G. D. Burtchaeli and T. U. Sadlier, Dublin 1935, 895.
[4]   Company of Barber-Surgeons, register of admissions, Guildhall Library, London, MS 5265/1, fo 94r (copy held on microfilm).
[5]   For the social basis of apprenticeship see C. Brooks, 'Apprenticeship, social mobility and the middling sort, 1550–1800', in J. Barry and C. Brooks (eds), *The middling sort*

Whether London was his birth or adopted city, throughout the 1630s Worsley resided in an expanding metropolis, where the authorities struggled with 'overcrowding, epidemics, building control, crime and disorder, unregulated crafts and industries'.[6] The apprentices of London, although famed for their unruliness, were too diverse a group to talk of a single apprentice experience.[7] For most, however, the dominant figure in their life was the master to whom they were bound by law, in Worsley's case one Thomas Cooke, a surgeon and liveryman of the Company. Cooke's shop appears to have been in Fetter Lane in the ward of Farringdon Without, beyond the city walls although still within civic jurisdiction, perhaps serving the lawyers of the nearby Inner Temple. In December 1632 a Cooke of Fetter Lane was mentioned in the censorial proceedings of the College of Physicians, accused of transgressing the boundaries between surgery and physic by furnishing his customers with 'mercury pills'.[8] Apparently Cooke had something of a track record, having in 1631 been warned about prescribing medicines to the poor (a practice he claimed to have learned from his master, Mr Mullins), and later charged with 'salivating' the wife of a plumber from nearby Shoe Lane with a fatal cocktail of drinks and mercury pills.[9] For this Cooke was fined and imprisoned, and perhaps it was with the intention of restoring some of his credit that he next turned informer for the physicians, reporting the empiric William Trigge for unlicensed practice.[10]

We might dismiss Thomas Cooke as a disreputable figure, a quack even, operating amongst a credulous populace. But perhaps what these examples evoke is the intensively competitive nature of the 'medical marketplace' of early modern London, which belied the ordered hierarchy which the physi-

---

of people: culture, society and politics in England, 1550–1800, Basingstoke–London 1994, 52–83.

[6] R. Weinstein, 'London at the outbreak of the Civil War', in S. Porter (ed.), London and the Civil War, Basingstoke–London 1996, 32.

[7] P. Griffiths, Youth and authority: formative experiences in England, 1560–1640, Oxford 1996, 161–9. For apprentice surgeons see S. Young, The annals of the Barber-Surgeons of London, London 1890, 259–60.

[8] 'COOKE, Thomas': Physicians and irregular medical practitioners in London, 1550–1640: database (2004): URL: http://www.british-history.ac.uk/ date accessed, 29 June 2005; M. Pelling, Medical conflicts in early modern London: patronage, physicians, and irregular practitioners, Oxford 2003, 310. The issue is confused by a Thomas Cooke, surgeon, being listed as living in Lombard Street in 1641, although of course the Fetter Lane Cooke may have moved by then: S. R. James, 'A list of surgeons in practice in London and its suburbs in 1641', Bulletin of the History of Medicine xix (1946), 284. A Thomas Cooke of the parish of St Andrew Holborn was rated at £12 in the tithe assessment of 1638: The inhabitants of London in 1638 (1931), 187–91; URL: http://www.british-history.ac.uk/ date accessed, 22 Sept. 2006. Worsley had acquaintances in Holborn: Worsley to S. Hartlib, c. Sept. 1648, HP 46/9/22B.

[9] Mullins was probably James Molins, the celebrated surgeon of St Bartholomew's, also based in Farringdon Without.

[10] For Trigge see Pelling, Medical conflicts, 149–50.

cians sought to maintain.[11] Apparently his transgressions did not prevent Cooke from treating some distinguished patients, for his next summons by the Physicians was regarding the death from the flux of the countess of Bohun, to whom he had given cassia, manna and 'mercurius dulcis', and for which he was forced to pay a bond of £100.

It was in the confines of Cooke's shop that Benjamin Worsley would have learned his trade: dressing and treating wounds and burns, setting bones and performing amputations, alongside routine tasks like pulling teeth, letting blood and tending the body's appearance.[12] It seems that Cooke had an enthusiasm for those chemical remedies that had been promoted as an alternative to Galenic medicine by several sixteenth-century surgical authors.[13] Perhaps this is how Worsley was introduced to the principles of Paracelsian iatro- (medical) chemistry. A later record of his medical preferences betrayed antipathy towards certain elements of Galenic orthodoxy:

> Mr Worsley likes of 1. Abstersifs or depurations that the blood may bee kept pure. 2. of all diuretick's to drive out of sweate and vrin. 3. Cordials. 4. furthering of digestions. 5. outward Applications 6. in chronical diseases a continued good dyet. 7. specifiques of simples. 8. or vniversal Medecins. vtterly rejecting vomiting, Purging, bloodletting.[14]

Worsley continued to practise medicine from time to time throughout his life, but it seems that the surgeon's garb did not appeal. His master's treatment by the College of Physicians would have brought home the relative inferiority of his trade, but this is not to say that surgery was of no value: without the benefits of a university education, the surgeon's shop was where Worsley would have learned a range of skills and specialist knowledge which crossed into the territory of the apothecary and physician, and could be transferred to more supposedly 'intellectual' pursuits.[15] Additionally, surgeons often diversified into enterprises such as producing drugs and cordials for sale to patients, brewing alcoholic drinks and preparing perfumes.[16] But the surgeon's shop was principally a business enterprise, and the vending of its

[11] H. Cook, *The decline of the old medical regime in Stuart London*, Ithaca–London 1986, 28–69.
[12] A. Wear, *Knowledge and practice in English medicine, 1550–1680*, Cambridge 2000, 210–74; M. Pelling and C. Webster, 'Medical practitioners', in C. Webster (ed.), *Health, medicine and mortality in the sixteenth century*, Cambridge 1979, 173–7.
[13] C. Webster, 'Alchemical and Paracelsan medicine', in Webster, *Health, medicine and mortality*, 319.
[14] 'Ephemerides', 1651, pt II, HP 28/2/15A.
[15] M. Pelling, 'Medical practice in early modern England: trade or profession?', in W. Prest (ed.), *The professions in early modern England*, London 1987, 102–3; Wear, *Knowledge and practice*, 212, 225–8.
[16] M. Pelling, *The common lot: sickness, medical occupations and the urban poor in early modern England*, London–New York 1998, 203–29; Wear, *Knowledge and practice*, 214–15, 233–6.

exotic pharmacopoeia identified surgery with the city's burgeoning consumer culture.[17] The competitive environment of surgery seems to have fostered in Worsley an entrepreneurial ethos, which, in combination with the technical skills and knowledge he had acquired, enabled him to leave the trade and pursue a number of other projects.

Urban shops were also gateways between the domestic and the public, conduits for the transmission of a growing phenomenon in early Stuart London, the news.[18] In late 1630s London the circulation of the news was escalating, in pamphlets, woodcuts, ballads, sermons and conversation, a barrage of opinion which the authorities struggled to contain.[19] Through these media Worsley would likely have been well informed of local, national, even international events. His birth roughly corresponded with the Bohemian revolt and the Synod of Dort, events which traumatised a generation of English Protestants, although Worsley belonged to one which grew up with the Thirty Years War and perhaps felt the shock of its outbreak less keenly, particularly by the time it reached its final, confessionally confused, stages.[20] Still, the strength of anti-Catholicism in the English Protestant identity meant that in Worsley's youth many of his countrymen still wished for military intervention on the continent, making the relative international weakness of the nation under Charles I hard to stomach.[21] Commercially, however, Charles's peace with Spain brought success as English trade with southern Europe and the Levant prospered in the 1630s, which was also the decade when England's colonial empire began to take firm root, repairing some of the effects of the disastrous depression in the cloth trade of the 1620s.[22]

If in the 1630s many zealous English Protestants wished for their state to be more potent on the international stage, domestically their fear was of a king holding too much power, as Charles's personal rule was criticised over the presence of Catholics at court, his use of arbitrary taxation and fiscal expediencies, and the reissuing of the Book of Sports.[23] The latter was

[17] G. K. Paster, 'Purgation as the allure of mastery: early modern medicine and the technology of the self', in L. C. Orwin (ed.), *Material London, ca. 1600*, Philadelphia 2000, 193–205. For London's material culture see I. Archer, 'Material Londoners?', ibid. 174–92.
[18] K. Lindley, *Popular politics and religion in civil war London*, London 1997, 6.
[19] D. Freist, *Governed by opinion: politics, religion and the dynamics of communication in Stuart London, 1637–1645*, London 1997.
[20] T. Cogswell, 'England and the Spanish match', in R. Cust and A. Hughes (eds), *Conflict in early Stuart England: studies in religion and politics, 1603–1642*, London–New York 1989, 107–33; Scott, *English political instability*, 89–112.
[21] For the former see P. Lake, 'Anti-popery: the structure of a prejudice', in Cust and Hughes, *Conflict in early Stuart England*, 72–106. For the sense of national humiliation see C. Carlton, *Going to the wars: the experience of the English Civil Wars, 1638–1651*, London 1992, 14–19.
[22] Clay, *Economic expansion*, 187.
[23] For a summary of Charles's reign up to 1638 see A. Woolrych, *Britain in revolution, 1625–1660*, Oxford 2002, 49–84.

part of a wider contest over the direction of the Church of England under Archbishop Laud, which had its most dramatic episode in 1637 with the trial of Bastwick, Burton and Prynne, who became popular martyrs of an increasingly unpopular church hierarchy.[24] But if perceptions of episcopacy had been tarnished, Worsley would also have been exposed to a popular stereotype of their godly opponents as divisive, antisocial and hypocritical.[25] Little wonder with these contradictory currents of opinion that speech was widely seen as inherently dangerous, in need of regulation.

The most contentious discourse, of course, was religious, and in Worsley's London the direction of England's Reformation was fiercely contested by different groups claiming the status of orthodoxy within a culture which reviled separatism and idealised unity.[26] Most of all, contests were fought over individual souls, in appeals to the conscience directed from the pulpit and in print. Young men such as Worsley were the target of special efforts to shape the conscience, catechise and socialise through religion.[27] Perhaps he had occasion to taste the peculiar appeal of the doctrine of election and the 'experimental' approach to religion it demanded.[28] Perhaps he even came across the unorthodox religious alternatives available in London, if not actually encountering the 'separate churches' in person then at least via the negative image of the sects evoked in sermons and print.[29] We can imagine, then, how this city might have shaped the young Worsley's beliefs, as he grew up amongst 'its parish churches crushed in on one another, its lively and scarcely regulated lecturing scene, its complex network of ecclesiastical jurisdictions and peculiars, its variegated godly community spread widely across both the city itself and the social order'.[30] Here in London, Worsley would have experienced the slide of his country towards civil war. But by its outbreak he had left this capital city for another: Dublin.

[24] A. Foster, 'Church policies of the 1630s', in Cust and Hughes, *Conflict in early Stuart England*, 193–223; D. Como, 'Predestination and political conflict in Laud's London', *HJ* xlvi (2003), 263–94.

[25] P. Lake, '"A charitable Christian hatred": the godly and their enemies in the 1630s', in C. Durston and J. Eales (eds), *The culture of English Puritanism, 1560–1700*, Basingstoke 1996, 145–83.

[26] For parish contests in early Stuart London, with a particular focus on the godly, see P. Lake, *The boxmaker's revenge: 'orthodoxy', 'heterodoxy' and the politics of the parish in early Stuart London*, Stanford 2001.

[27] Griffiths, *Youth and authority*, 54–61, 81–96.

[28] Lake, *Boxmaker's revenge*, 35. Worsley owned six works by the Elizabethan Puritan William Perkins, alongside authors such as Robert Bolton, William Ames, William Pembles and John Preston.

[29] M. Tolmie, *The triumph of the saints: the separate churches of London, 1616–1649*, Cambridge 1977. One separatist work in the *Catalogus* was Henry Ainsworth, *Counter-poyson*, Amsterdam 1608.

[30] Lake, *Boxmaker's revenge*, 395.

Ireland and the saltpetre project

Worsley's account of this period of his life was written after the Restoration, by which time it had become expedient to stress his royalist credentials. The letter in question, written to the wife of the earl of Clarendon, thus explained how he had first gone to Ireland at the behest of the lord lieutenant, Strafford, whose household he entered in 1640, although the reasons for this are not given.[31] Strafford left Ireland for the last time that April, but Worsley perhaps had lasting connections with the family for in 1645, he wrote a letter on behalf of Strafford's younger brother Sir George Wentworth, who was facing the sequestration of his estates.[32] However, any allegiance to Strafford did not stop Worsley from accepting an offer from his opponents, the lords justices, to run 'an Hospitall ... for the receiving the weake and wounded men of the whole Army', following the outbreak of the Ulster rising in October 1641.[33] Service in the army was a common way for surgeons to serve as journeymen before setting up shop, and Worsley perhaps showed some aptitude as by January 1642 he had become surgeon-general of the English army based in Dublin, presiding over the surgeon-majors of three regiments.[34]

The war in which Worsley was involved for the next eighteen months soon became famed for its atrocities.[35] The peacetime royalist army, numbering nearly 3,000 and mostly garrisoned at Dublin, was doubled by English reinforcements in March 1642, allowing the king's lord deputy Ormond to achieve several victories which would have delivered Worsley his first wartime patients. However, the outbreak of civil war in England robbed Ormond of external support, and by March 1643 his mutinous forces were virtually confined to Dublin.[36] Worsley himself was forced to complain to his superiors that 'the army is already very much distressed in the cures of wounded men', pleading for supplies which still had not arrived by May.[37] Unsurprisingly, Ormond arranged a cessation with the Catholics

---

[31] Worsley to Lady Clarendon, 8 Nov. 1661, Bodl. Lib., MS Clarendon 75, fo. 300r.

[32] Certificate on behalf of Sir George Wentworth, 29 May 1645, entered into the Book of Orders for the Kent Committee of Sequestrations, TNA, SP 28/210, fo. 71r. My thanks to Dr Jason Peacey for making me aware of this document.

[33] Worsley to Lady Clarendon, 8 Nov. 1661, MS Clarendon 75, fo. 300r.

[34] CSPI, 1633–47, 216, 780. For journeymen see Young, Annals of the Barber-Surgeons, 119; Wear, Knowledge and practice, 210; and Webster and Pelling, 'Medical practitioners', 174–5.

[35] Carlton, Going to the wars, 33–8.

[36] S. Wheeler, 'Four armies in Ireland', in J. Ohlmeyer (ed.), Ireland from independence to occupation, 1641–1660, Cambridge 1995, 44–7, 50. For wartime wounds see Carlton, Going to the wars, 221–9, and B. Donagan, 'The casualties of war: treatment of the dead and wounded in the English Civil War', in I. Gentles, J. Morrill and B. Worden (eds), Soldiers, writers and statesmen of the English Revolution, Cambridge 1998, 114–32.

[37] HMC, Fourteenth report: manuscripts of the marquis of Ormonde, K.P., at Kilkenny Castle, ii, London 1903, 256–7, 284–5.

in September, a controversial action principally calculated to free up royal troops for service in England, and which provoked a disgruntled Worsley into quitting his post.[38] Instead he hoped to pursue his 'Genius' by entering Trinity College Dublin as a pensioner on 15 October 1643, just as the previous year's reinforcements were heading back to fight for the king in England. However, despite telling Lady Clarendon the contrary, he did not complete his degrees, and by the middle of 1644 he was back in London.[39]

Before then, Worsley had planned to recommence his studies in Flanders, only to be captured by a parliamentary ship *en route* and taken to Portsmouth. Worsley probably owed the idea of studying abroad to a fellow member of the medical corps at Dublin, the Leiden-trained Dutch medic Arnold Boate, who had also served under Wentworth before becoming physician-general to the army there. Together with his brother Gerard, in 1641 Boate had published in Dublin an attack on scholasticism, *Philosophia naturalis reformata*, which Worsley owned.[40] Boate and Worsley were both passengers on the captured ship, and on 25 April petitioned the House of Commons for release together, apparently enlisting the help of one of their old masters from Ireland, Sir John Temple, Worsley having refused to take the covenant, although the nature of his scruple is unknown.[41] Boate was lodging with his brother in London by May, and Worsley probably followed him for by the following summer he was in the city collaborating with an associate of the Boates on a project to supply parliament's forces with salt-petre, a crucial ingredient in gunpowder. The individual in question was Samuel Hartlib, whose papers provide a rich record of the next fifteen years of Worsley's life. Had his ship not been intercepted in the previous year Worsley might have slipped from the historical record entirely.

A combination of ambition and necessity probably encouraged Worsley to change vocation. In May 1645 he was briefly imprisoned in Newgate for failing to repay a bond of £30 taken in Ireland, from which he secured his release by petitioning the House of Lords as surgeon-general, claiming to be owed £400 in arrears.[42] His financial problems might have been connected to a summons from the Barber-Surgeons' Company to 'take the clothing' and become a liveryman, a potentially onerous and costly privilege.[43] The Company meanwhile was facing its own financial problems, not for the

---

[38] For the situation in Ireland see Woolrych, *Britain in revolution*, 268–9, 272–3.

[39] Worsley to Lady Clarendon, 8 Nov. 1661, MS Clarendon 75, fo. 300r. In August 1649 Worsley was still discussing the possibility of finally 'taking of my Degree': Worsley to John Dury, 17 Aug. 1649, HP 33/2/4A.

[40] This was listed in the *Catalogus* along with four other works by Arnold Boate.

[41] *CJ* iii. 469; Worsley to Lady Clarendon, 8 Nov. 1661, MS Clarendon 75, fo. 300r.

[42] *LJ* vii. 401–2.

[43] Company of Barber-Surgeons, court minute books, volume v, MS Guildhall 5257/5, fo. 338r (copy on microfilm). My thanks to Dr Ben Coates for informing me of this reference. On the Livery see Young, *Annals of the Barber-Surgeons*, 253.

first time resorting to the clothing as a fiscal expediency.[44] Worsley was apparently reluctant to return to his original trade, however, and resolved to pay a £5 fine instead, which he finally did in November.[45] These were the inauspicious circumstances in which Worsley embarked on his saltpetre project, his credit 'cracked' in a city at war.

London had changed much in his absence. The tide of discourse building in the 1630s had by then burst forth, flooding the streets with an unprecedented torrent of news and opinion. The gathered churches had also gone overground, and on his return Worsley lived at the heartland of this religious revolution: Coleman Street, an area so famed for its sectarian activity that his friend Robert Boyle knew it as 'your heretical street'.[46] This was where John Goodwin's Independent congregation met, whilst the largest Baptist church of the decade gathered in one of the many crowded alleys cutting across the main street of this socially varied ward.[47] But this was a time of Presbyterian ascendance, and toleration for Protestant dissenters was a contested issue.[48]

In the ongoing civil war, demand for saltpetre (potassium nitrate), had soared.[49] It had long been extracted from artificial 'nitre beds', utilising various waste resources to create nitrous earth, although the chemical basis of saltpetre was still not understood and successful production depended largely on trial and error.[50] The commodity therefore continued to be imported on a large scale, particularly from the East Indies, or extracted from places where it occurred naturally such as pigeon lofts, by the unpopular 'saltpetre men'.[51] This 'stinking businesse' was therefore of obvious attraction to aspiring projectors, although Worsley would have resented being called thus.[52] Since their conception in the sixteenth century as a means to promote domestic manufacturing, 'projects' had become associated with

---

[44] Young, *Annals of the Barber-Surgeons*, 139.

[45] Barber-Surgeons, court minute books, v, MS Guildhall 5257/5, fo. 348r.

[46] R. Boyle to Worsley, c. Dec. 1646, in *The correspondence of Robert Boyle*, ed. M. Hunter, A. Clericuzio and L. Principe, London 2001, i. 43.

[47] Lindley, *Popular politics*, 81, 283, 289; Freist, *Governed by opinion*, 89–90, 141; E. More, 'Congregationalism and the social order: John Goodwin's gathered church, 1640–60', *Journal of Ecclesiastical History* xxxviii (1987), 210–35.

[48] A. Hughes, *Gangreana and the struggle for the English Revolution*, Oxford 2004. Contemporary debates on church government and toleration are covered by a volume of pamphlets in Worsley's *Catalogus*, including works by Sir Simonds D'Ewes, 'Smectymnuus', John Cotton, Nathaniel Holmes, John Sadler, John Goodwin, Richard Lawrence, James Pope and the separatist Robert Coachman.

[49] P. Edwards, *Dealing in death: the arms trade and the British civil wars*, Stroud 2000, 91–115.

[50] A. R. Williams, 'The production of saltpetre in the Middle Ages', *Ambix* xxii (1975), 125–7.

[51] R. W. Stewart, *The English ordnance office: a case-study in bureaucracy*, Woodbridge 1996, 80–95.

[52] This satirical description is from T. Brugis, *The discovery of a projector*, London 1641, 25.

charlatanism and monopoly, as the crown increasingly sold patents as a fiscal remedy.[53] Under the Stuarts projects came to be associated with court corruption, and the early 1640s saw the overturning of several industrial patents by parliament, and the infringement of many commercial monopolies.[54] Some, however, saw this as only the first step towards overturning the political and ecclesiastical monopolies of crown and national Church, amongst them Levellers whose works were printed on Worsley's doorstep.[55] Of a like mind was the Kentish gentleman and associate of Hartlib, Sir Cheney Culpeper, who predicted that 'nowe wee are pullinge downe of such monopolies wee shall starte a greate many which yet ly hid', until finally this would make 'Babilon tumble'.[56] This was no time, then, to be seen as a projector.

Nevertheless, the industrial and mercantile advances which projects offered were of obvious attraction in a city faced by fiscal difficulties and economic dislocation.[57] Projectors sought to legitimise their privileges in terms of the public good, and their commercial benefits to the nation: as Daniel Defoe put it at the end of the century, 'every new Voyage the Merchant contrives, is a Project'.[58] Thus, despite the criticism projectors attracted, many still hoped to harness their talents for public profit. One scheme to achieve this that was being touted in the 1640s involved setting up an 'Office of Address', a state-sponsored 'Center of all Mens satisfactions to gaine their Interest in each other for mutual help'.[59] As well as being a labour exchange, the projected Office would offer support to inventors, so that 'the most profitable Inventions … might be Publikely made use of, as the State should think most expedient', freeing them from the need to seek patronage or patents.[60] The promoter of this ingenious design was, of

---

[53] J. Thirsk, *Economic policy and projects: the development of a consumer society in early modern England*, Oxford 1978; D. H. Sacks, 'Parliament, liberty, and the commonweal', in J. H. Hexter (ed.), *Parliament and liberty from the reign of Elizabeth to the English Civil War*, Stanford 1992, 85–121; D. H. Sacks, 'The countervailing of benefits: monopoly, liberty, and benevolence in Elizabethan England', in D. Hoak (ed.), *Tudor political culture*, Cambridge 1995, 272–91; J. Cramsie, 'Commercial projects and the fiscal policy of James VI and I', *HJ* xliii (2000), 345–64; Braddick, *State formation*, 40–2.

[54] M. James, *Social problems and policy during the Puritan Revolution*, London 1930, 131–57.

[55] Freist, *Governed by opinion*, 89–90; A. Houston, '"A way of settlement": the Levellers, monopolies, and the public interest', *HPT* xiv (1993), 381–420.

[56] 'The letters of Sir Cheney Culpeper (1641–1657)', ed. M. Braddick and M. Greengrass, in *Seventeenth-century political and financial papers* (Camden, 5th ser. vii; Camden miscellany xxiii, 1996), 139.

[57] B. Coates, *The impact of the English Civil War on the economy of London, 1642–1650*, Aldershot 2004, 139–62.

[58] D. Defoe, *An essay upon projects*, London 1697, 8.

[59] [J. Dury], *Considerations tending to the happy accomplishment of Englands reformation*, London 1647, 41.

[60] Ibid. 47.

course, Samuel Hartlib, celebrated advocate of ingenuity and self-proclaimed servant of the public good.

Hartlib's enterprise encompassed a huge range of technological and intellectual projects, to which he acted as 'intelligencer', an identity he had been fashioning since settling permanently in London having left his native Elbing on the Baltic coast in 1628.[61] His diverse interests were subsumed towards a higher goal, the perfection of human society in tune with a religiously inspired vision of harmony, something fashioned in direct response to the Protestant diaspora of which he was part. Hartlib consciously placed himself at the centre of an extensive network of correspondents, and his ethos was informed by the ideals of international Protestantism, but none the less he readily adopted the commonwealth rhetoric of his adopted homeland, recasting the ideal of the public good on a global scale. Although in many ways apolitical, Hartlib's religious convictions ensured that his sympathies were with parliament in civil war, something resting on longstanding ties of patronage with figures such as Lord Brooke, Sir Nathaniel Rich and John Pym, and in 1645 with victory in sight, he was looking to exploit the parliamentary desire for 'further reform' to fulfil his own goals of social and intellectual improvement.[62] He was an ideal figure, then, for Worsley to associate with.[63]

The precise circumstances of their meeting are difficult to ascertain, for unfortunately Hartlib's work-diaries, his 'Ephemerides', are lost for these years, but references in Culpeper's letters to Hartlib suggest that it had taken place by the summer of 1645.[64] Probably the Boates were responsible, and Hartlib had extensive contacts amongst the Anglo-Irish community affording ample opportunities for them to meet. But Hartlib was a well-known London figure in his own right, his home at Duke's Place playing host to a range of inventors and intellectuals. One particularly colourful projector with whom Hartlib had dealings, the engineer William Wheeler, appears to have been a friend of Worsley's, and such individuals were attracted to Hartlib like moths to a flame.[65]

Hartlib was at this time actively promoting many schemes to help with a perennial London problem, the urban poor, turning this wasted resource into profit, and Worsley's project was ideally suited to these designs. One of several documents in Hartlib's possession regarding the project suggests that he hoped to achieve this in a highly literal manner. Here, Worsley outlined a proposed workhouse for 150 people which would be financed by doubling as a living saltpetre factory, yielding ten tonnes annually for a profit of £700, satisfying the 'privat interests' of both the labourers and mercantile

[61] For an up-to-date account see M. Greengrass's entry in the *ODNB*.
[62] Webster, *Great instauration*, 41–4.
[63] Idem, 'Benjamin Worsley', 214–15.
[64] 'Culpeper letters', 226–7, 246–8.
[65] For Wheeler see Webster, *Great instauration*, 372–3. For Worsley's connections with Wheeler see 'Culpeper letters', 247.

investors.[66] This was possible because 'all sublunary things whatsoever are generable & Corruptible & ... doe *the* one terminate/ in *the* other', allowing Worsley to turn 'Coruption into Policy and into action'. In other words, he envisaged using the waste products of the labourers as raw material for saltpetre, collected in a trench situated at the end of the workhouse, where it would be covered in lime and earth, and left for two to three years to turn into nitre, pushing the utilitarian ethos of the Hartlib circle to the limits of good taste.[67]

Whether Worsley used this particular design in his final petitions is uncertain, for many similar memoranda exist in the Hartlib papers outlining the project's potential benefits, ranging from educating and housing poor children to preventing the destruction of corn caused by pigeons presently kept as a source for saltpetre.[68] It appears too that Worsley was originally hoping to secure an act 'prohibiting all others to make the old waye', as well as introducing a charge for those households previously subject to digging for saltpetre.[69] Perhaps Hartlib counselled against such monopolistic behaviour, for the final design stressed that Worsley had no intention of infringing on other privileges, or expending public money.[70] After several months' deliberation, Worsley made the short journey to Guildhall to present his first petition, to the court of the lord mayor and aldermen of London, on 17 February 1646.[71] This began by citing the 'seuerall Complaints' which the saltpetre men provoked, nationwide.[72] Worsley thus offered to 'free the whole Common-wealth of the trouble or injury sustyened in haueing their Houses Cellers yards and other places digged vp and spoiled' through his as yet unspecified, method.[73] For this, Worsley requested the privilege of being chartered as 'the Misterie or Corporation of Salt-Peter-Makers', with

---

[66] Worsley, treatise, 'About the poore advertisements', *c.* 1646, HP 15/2/5A–B.

[67] Paul Slack has called it 'the most striking example of [the] intellectual shift which the Hartlib papers provide': *From reformation to improvement: public welfare in early modern England*, Oxford 1999, 84.

[68] See, for example, Worsley?, untitled treatise, HP 53/26/1; 'A new waie for the making of salt peeter and maintaining the poore', HP 53/26/7; and 'An estimate of the greate quantitie of corne that pigeons doe spoyle and destroye in the countie of Cambridge', HP 25/3/4, all *c.* 1646.

[69] 'A exact discouery of *the* charge & damadge to the kingdome in the making of salt peeter', HP 53/26/3A; 'Divers services involved into one benefitiall to the whole kingdome', HP 53/26/1A, both *c.* 1646. See also untitled treatises, HP 53/26/1; HP 53/26/2B, both *c.* 1646.

[70] Worsley appeared to renounce his desire for a patent and public gratuity in an anonymous note of which Hartlib made a copy: 'A memorandum and caution concerning the observations and animadversions about saltpeter', *c.* 1646, HP 39/1/24.

[71] Corporation of London Record Office, Guildhall, records of the court of aldermen, rep. 58 (1645–7), fo. 65r; *LJ* viii. 574.

[72] 'Propositions in the behalfe of the kingdome concerning salt-peter', *c.* 1646, HP 71/11/8A.

[73] Ibid. HP 71/11/8B; 'Motions to the city', *c.* 1646, HP 71/11/9A.

the exclusive privileges this would guarantee.[74] However, in gratitude for their support he offered the city authorities sixty pounds of saltpetre for every tonne produced, which would be used in employing the poor, thus satisfying 'his Conscience and Duty to the publicke'. Furthermore, he offered to surrender the charter to the city following its expiry, keeping only a sixteenth part for himself or his successors, 'To invest or interest the said City wholly in it'.[75]

At this stage of petitioning, it was arguably more important to demonstrate adherence to the public good than the efficacy of the method itself, the details of which would only be revealed following the granting of a charter. This was a bargaining process: in order to win support Worsley had to show the public benefits of the project, and these were described in commercial terms. It being 'a Maxim ever observed by all, well seene in the Rules and pollityes of State' to introduce any 'new Manufacture, or Invention, serving to the improvement of the Materialls of the Land', his project would employ the poor, and produce 'a Commodity in plenty that is now wanting, and of all others most necessarie in the Common wealth'.[76] This was particularly important given that 'wee have alwayes beene forced, to make vse of the favour of other Countryes, There buying ... at greate prices, and running the hazard of the sea for it'.[77] Suitably impressed, on 7 April a special aldermanic committee reported that the proposals would benefit 'the publique good, and ... the interest of this City'.[78]

Worsley had thus demonstrated his public credentials, but not as yet the efficacy of his method. Apart from the workhouse design, there is little clear evidence of the precise way in which Worsley planned to make saltpetre, and it might be that he was merely planning to adapt existing methods in a fairly haphazard way. Throughout 1646 he was in negotiations with the mistress of a deceased saltpetre projector whose method was based on 'Enriching Earth' with various industrial by-products.[79] This is not to say that Worsley was seeking to defraud his supporters, or that he lacked any real scientific basis, although a more theoretical paper on the subject which Webster attached to this project has been shown to date from the early 1650s.[80] However, the fact that Worsley was continuing to consider various methods of production throughout 1646 perhaps explains why he apparently abandoned the project, despite successfully petitioning the House of Lords on 21 November.[81]

---

[74] 'Motions to the city', HP 71/11/9A.

[75] Ibid. HP 71/11/9B.

[76] Ibid. HP 71/11/9A.

[77] 'Propositions in the behalfe of the kingdome', HP 71/11/8B.

[78] Corporation of London Record Office, records of the court of aldermen, rep. 58 (1645–7), fos 91v–92r; LJ viii. 574. There is a copy of this report at HP 71/11/1.

[79] HP 71/11/5B, 13B; 'Culpeper letters', 261, 263–4, 270–1.

[80] Webster, 'New light', 36; Newman and Principe, Alchemy tried in the fire, 240.

[81] LJ viii. 573. Worsley's petition was supported by a certificate from the committee of

Alternatively, it could be that the saltpetre project had already served its primary purpose, allowing Worsley to establish his credentials to patrons amongst the Hartlib circle and the city. In the economy of the projector, hard cash was not the only currency: it was equally important to build a reputation, raising a reservoir of credit which could later be put to profitable use. But this need not only be spent in economically profitable enterprises: for Worsley, it also allowed him access to one of the foremost intellectual networks of the period, and the different rewards it offered.

'Searching spirits': an Invisible College?

Until now, little has emerged of Worsley's character beyond the self-publicising boasts of the projector, but we have also seen hints of a side to him that was curious of more educational pursuits, which had already encouraged him to enrol at university. Worsley also referred to the 'few Bookes' which he carried from Dublin, the first items of what would eventually be a huge collection.[82] It is impossible to know what precisely he might have been reading at the time, but Worsley did occasionally refer to certain favoured authors in letters from just after this period. Natural history was a favoured subject, for which Worsley mined Samuel Purchas's vast travel anthologies, which might also have awakened his interest in the Americas. The 'learned Verulam' (Francis Bacon) was another preferred author.[83] Worsley reserved similarly high praise for exponents of experimental science, citing three Catholic scientists, the Jesuit Athanasius Kircher and the Frenchmen Nicolas-Claude Fabri de Peiresc and Pierre Gassendi, a particular favourite (it was Worsley who recommend Gassendi's biography of Peiresc to its English translator, William Rand).[84] Although Worsley apparently primarily favoured Gassendi as an experimentalist, in his works he would have encountered a thorough critique of Aristotelian science based on classical atomism.

Worsley would have had ample opportunities to discuss such literature with new associates in London such as Gerard Boate, at that time compiling his natural history of Ireland. Other of Worsley's new acquaintances would have been made through correspondence, amongst them Hartlib's loyal supporter Sir Cheney Culpeper, who was particularly interested in Para-

the court of aldermen which had assessed his project. The Lords ordered that an ordinance be drawn up, but no further evidence for this has been found.

[82] Worsley to Lady Clarendon, 8 Nov. 1661, MS Clarendon 75, fo. 300r.

[83] For Purchas see Worsley to Hartlib, 27 July 1648, HP 42/1/1B. For Bacon see Worsley, 'Proffits humbly presented to this kingdome', c. 1646, HP 15/2/63A.

[84] Worsley to Hartlib, 22 June 1648, HP 42/1/1A; P. Gassendi, *The mirrour of true nobility & gentility: being the life of the renowned Nicolaus Claudius Fabricius Lord Peiresk*, trans. W. Rand, London 1657, 'Epistle dedicatory'. For Rand see C. Webster, 'English medical reformers of the Puritan Revolution: a background to the "Society of Chymical Physicians"', *Ambix* xiv (1967), 16–42. Worsley's *Catalogus* listed ten works by Gassendi.

celsian chymical writers such as Jacques de Nuysement, Blaise de Vigenère and Michael Sendivogius.[85] This school of thought had high hopes about the fertilising qualities of saltpetre, and saw salt as the active principle in vegetation, even the spirit of life itself.[86] The idealistic Culpeper was an early convert to Worsley's cause (despite some suspicions he harboured about the militarism of the saltpetre project), and hoped that 'yf saltepeeter be not that very spirit it selfe of the worlde, yet I am confidente from the harmony of chymicall writers that the ayre is that by which the spirite of the worlde begets & manifestes itselfe'.[87] Another 'chymist' with similar opinions whose works were interesting the Hartlib circle was the German Johann Rudolph Glauber, a figure whom Worsley would soon visit with support from Culpeper and Hartlib.

Another sign of Worsley's rising stock within the Hartlib circle was the several designs which Hartlib drew up for his latest protégé, running 'an Office of Agriculture and Traffique' alongside Culpeper, or pursuing experimental philosophy, physics or medicine in a redesigned Winchester academy, for example.[88] Many of his new acquaintances also had connections with Ireland, and they met at the Pall Mall house of another Irish exile, Katherine Jones, Viscountess Ranelagh, the daughter of the Anglo-Irish magnate and earl of Cork, Richard Boyle. Lady Ranelagh was known not just as a hostess, but as a formidable intellect in her own right, interested in such matters as education and natural philosophy: she would be Worsley's lifelong friend. Lady Ranelagh's aunt, Dorothy, was married to the irenicist John Dury, and Worsley too soon became close to the couple.[89] Also close to Lady Ranelagh was John Sadler, lawyer, scholar, parliamentary propagandist and supporter of Hartlib's schemes. Sadler and his patron Lord Brooke represented a neoplatonic strand within English Puritanism which lent itself well to the universalist goals of the Hartlib circle. From his Kent home, Culpeper looked enviously at the 'noble spirits' of the town.[90]

This was also the milieu which excited the imagination of Lady Ranelagh's young brother, who had just returned from his grand tour, only to be impressed by these

> men of so capacious and searching spirits, that school-philosophy is but the lowest region of their knowledge; and yet, though ambitious to lead the way to any generous design, of so humble and teachable genius, as they

---

[85] 'Culpeper letters', 135–6; S. Clucas, 'The correspondence of a XVII-century "chymicall gentleman": Sir Cheney Culpeper and the chemical interests of the Hartlib circle', *Ambix* xl (1993), 147–70.

[86] For more details on this school see chapter 5 below.

[87] 'Culpeper letters', 239.

[88] See Hartlib's various notes: HP 47/9/16–17; HP 47/9/27–30; HP 47/9/33; HP 47/9/37; HP 62/37/1–2.

[89] Worsley to Hartlib, 22 June 1649, HP 26/33/1B; Dury to Hartlib, 25 Aug. 1646, HP 3/3/30–1.

[90] C. Culpeper to Hartlib, c. Dec. 1645, HP 13/279–83.

disdain not to be directed to the meanest, so he can but plead reason for his opinion; ... And indeed they are so apprehensive of the want of good employment, that they take the whole body of mankind for their care.[91]

Much has already been written about the Invisible College, and its supposed role in the intellectual development of Robert Boyle, who had just turned twenty in February 1647 when he wrote the above letter to his former tutor mentioning 'the *invisible*, or (as they term themselves) the *philosophical college*'. Boyle had already used the phrase in a letter from the previous October, in connection with his studies of 'natural philosophy, the mechanics, and husbandry', conducted under the supervision of 'our new philosophical college, that values no knowledge, but as it hath a tendency to use'.[92] A final reference to the elusive Invisible College came in a letter to Hartlib from May 1647, which also noted that the 'society is so highly concerned in all the accidents of your life, that you can send me no intelligence of your own affairs, that does not (at least rationally) assume the nature of *Utopian*'.[93]

Rarely in the history of science can such scattered lines have produced so much debate, regarding the membership of this putative institution and its roles in Boyle's intellectual development and the foundation of the Royal Society. Charles Webster's contribution was to throw Worsley's name into the ring, drawing on two letters written by Boyle to Worsley in late 1646 and early 1647, which suggested a shared interest in experimental science.[94] In the first, Boyle congratulated Worsley on the successful passage of his salt-petre project through the Lords, proclaiming it 'a very justifiable avarice, that wishes not the possession of riches, but the employment'.[95] Boyle complained of the infringements of those 'two-legged moles' the saltpetre-men on his estate in Stalybridge, Dorset, and promised at the next opportunity to send his 'thoughts or experiments' which would aid Worsley's own 'great design'. In the second, Boyle noted the 'Time & Paines I have spent in Chimistry, tho I had never deriv'd from them any other Benefit, then their having thus early radicated my Acquaintance with you', although he hoped in future to contribute more positively to their 'Philosophicall Trafficke'.[96] Boyle claimed that he had been encouraged by these communications to 'court Nature as eagerly as such a disaccomodated Solitude will permit me', particularly in the 'Vulcanian' pursuit of chemistry.[97] However, for the moment Boyle was awaiting the instruments to embark on his chymical career, which would end only in 1649 with his successful erection of a working laboratory.[98]

---

[91] *Boyle correspondence*, i. 46.
[92] Ibid. i. 42.
[93] Ibid. i. 58.
[94] Webster, 'New light'.
[95] Boyle to [Worsley], c. Dec. 1646, *Boyle correspondence*, i. 43.
[96] Boyle to [Worsley], c. Feb. 1647, ibid. i. 48.
[97] Ibid. i. 49.
[98] Hunter, *Robert Boyle: scrupulosity and science*, 22, 24–5.

This, amongst other details, has persuaded Michael Hunter that Boyle's scientific awakening post-dated the lifetime of the Invisible College. Furthermore, he has argued that Webster's evidence for this body is 'much less conclusive than might be supposed', relegating Worsley almost to the position of irrelevant 'background noise' in Boyle's story.[99] Much of this scepticism is well-placed. Even accepting that Worsley is the most likely individual whom Boyle had in mind in his references to the Invisible College, Webster arguably drew a more complete account of this than the evidence allows, endowing it with an organisational coherence conferred by Worsley to maintain contact with his scattered scientific associates, a social basis in the exiled Irish Protestants, a circle of likely members, and a programme of activity based around experimental, Baconian science, 'which differed strikingly from the "new philosophy" of the precursors of the Royal Society'.[100] All of these points can be criticised on some level, making it necessary to reassess Webster's thesis in the light of Hunter's criticisms.

Webster's was the latest in a long line of accounts which interpreted the Invisible College as an early effort to institutionalise science, a precursor to the foundation of the Royal Society, but was this the case? Boyle was certainly enthused by his meetings with Worsley, and the references to the Invisible College may simply be a manifestation of this. His comment to Worsley that 'Chymist's Acquaintance is of age at a Day-old' suggests that their own collaboration was at a similarly juvenile stage.[101] They would have had limited opportunities to meet during Boyle's visits to London, and the term perhaps described their personal correspondence, an informal arrangement rather than an effort at scientific institutionalisation. Or, it might have been a term which Boyle merely used purely for his own reference: it does not appear in Boyle's letters to Worsley, and the truth is that we do not know whether the latter would even have recognised the term 'Invisible College', let alone belonged to it in any formal manner.

If this is to downplay the significance of the Invisible College in the story of the institutionalisation of English science, it is not to deny that Boyle's reflections can tell us much about the activities of Worsley and his milieu at this point. Of particular importance is Boyle's identification of Worsley as a chemist, or 'chymist'. One dimension of this was probably agricultural in nature, involving the sort of speculations which informed the saltpetre project and which were relatively accessible to the part-time practitioner (allowing Boyle to 'catechise my gardener and our ploughmen, concerning the fundamentals of their profession'). Boyle also referred to the experimental findings Worsley was producing in his laboratory, and although Worsley's competence in metallic alchemy has been questioned, this variety of experimentation would have involved distillations and infusions of herbs

---

[99] Ibid. 22.
[100] Webster, 'New light', 34 ff.
[101] Boyle to Worsley, c. Feb. 1647, Boyle correspondence, i. 48.

and spirits in glass alembics, heated in a basin rather than in the alchemist's heavy furnaces.[102] Worsley's letters made extensive reference to distillation and brewing practices, surely the legacy of his time as a surgeon. From Amsterdam, Worsley advised John Dury about the possibility of his wife making a living from distilling spirits, although he doubted whether that 'mechanicke trade' would suit her.[103] Another option was making perfumes, and Worsley had apparently considered retiring to the country to make a living by producing rose spirits and oils. He also drafted a more theoretical paper on the subject of 'the destilling or drawing of spirits'.[104] Although distillations of herbs and simples in wine had been praised by 'Physitians, Chymists, & Phylosophers' for their properties in 'repayring or cherishing our naturall spiritts', they had become corrupted by 'the vulgar, & comon Artists'.[105] Decrying the tendency to still spirits in copper vessels heated by fire, Worsley had developed a way to distil wines in larger glasses and at a lower heat, which produced a purer spirit. Other experiments were oeconomical, to strengthen glasses, to preserve fuel and to recycle unused wine.[106] With typical enterprise Worsley concluded by suggesting how his methods could be practised on a large scale, perhaps in the plantations, with an investment of £50–60 producing an annual profit of £200.[107]

Boyle would later cover similar ground in his book *Of the vsefvlnesse of natural philosophy*.[108] This work also considered the production of distilled medicines, and the first evidence for Boyle's scientific activities in his work diaries was a series of such medical recipes derived mainly from Worsley in 1649.[109] Worsley also contributed other remedies which he perhaps learned as an apprentice: a plaster against toothache, a remedy for 'Breeding of Teeth' in children, an ointment for rickets and an 'oleum febripellens' for use in 'Agues, the Mother, & Small Pox'.[110] In fact Worsley came close to resuming his medical career when he was nominated as surgeon-general to Viscount Lisle's ill-fated Irish expedition, with Gerard Boate as physician general, in July 1647.[111] Later that year Worsley also had his first meet-

---

[102] The negative assessment is in Newman and Principe, *Alchemy tried in the fire*, 236–56.

[103] Worsley to Hartlib, 22 June 1649, HP 26/33/1B.

[104] 'Of the destilling or drawing of spirits some animadversions', *c.* summer 1649, HP 26/33/9–10.

[105] Ibid. HP 26/33/9A.

[106] Ibid. HP 26/33/9B.

[107] Ibid. HP 26/33/9A–10B.

[108] *The works of Robert Boyle*, iii, ed. M. Hunter and E. Davis, London 1999, 395–404.

[109] 'Memorialls philosophicall beginning in the New Year 1649/50', Royal Society, Boyle papers 28, pp. 309–12. Transcription online at http://www.bbk.ac.uk/Boyle/WD6Clean.html, accessed 7 Jan. 2002.

[110] Although Worsley communicated these particular receipts after his return to London in late 1649, Boyle had requested that Worsley send him some remedies against smallpox and the stone in 1647: Boyle to Worsley, *c.* Feb. 1647, *Boyle correspondence*, i. 49.

[111] *CJ* v. 247.

ings with another medically trained intellectual, William Petty, one topic of conversation being Thomas Hobbes, whom Petty had recently met in Paris.[112]

Another possible medical acquaintance was Dr Jonathan Goddard, one of those experimental scientists meeting in London from 1645 to 1648, who in John Wallis's account later went on to form the core of the Royal Society.[113] Thus, although Webster was keen to differentiate the Invisible College from the 1645 group, it seems likely that there was some crossover: Worsley was also in touch with one of the latter's key members, John Wilkins, to whom he intended to 'propose certain Experiments', in order to 'produce a better resolution in some material points of Philosophy and Medicine'.[114] As this indicates, Worsley's scientific interests were less strictly utilitarian than portrayed by Webster, and he willingly delved into speculative and theoretical matters. This is illustrated by a letter he wrote to John Hall, a young Cambridge student whom Hartlib was keen to draw into his orbit.[115] Although only a single exchange of letters between the two survives, it was sufficiently interesting for Hall to suggest it be published.[116] Hall posed to Worsley the question 'Whether the Scripture bee an adæquate Iudge of Physical Controversies or no?', a subject which encapsulated the fraught relationship between the new science and religion, from Galileo to Spinoza and beyond.[117]

Worsley's answer began by considering the capacities required of a judge: full and perfect knowledge of the question at hand, and the ability to 'cleerly and determinately, speake to the thing controverted'.[118] Therefore the question was whether Scripture contained 'all manner of physicall-truths; at least in their primitives', and whether they were 'cleerly or distinctly' shown. Of the first, Worsley had no doubt: given that the Scriptures were the 'immediate efflations of God himselfe', they must therefore 'beare his character, and as lively reflect his Image'.[119] If the human mind was capable of reason, then divine wisdom must be even deeper:

> if I shall find, so much; within the Compasse of humane wisdome (that is
> so inferiour) to be able in their discourses, to weave and intertex, many

112 Worsley to Hartlib, 22 June 1648, HP 42/1/1A.
113 Worsley praised Goddard's adherence to experimental science, particularly 'the Optikes & Chymia', in his letter to Hartlib, 27 July 1648, HP 42/1/1A.
114 Worsley to Hartlib, 1 June 1649, HP (Royal Society, Boyle letters 7.2. fo. 2r).
115 For John Hall see ODNB.
116 John Hall to Hartlib, 17 Dec. [1646], HP 60/14/3–4; 4 Jan. 1647, HP 60/14/9–10; 25 Jan. 1647, HP 60/14/14–15; 7 Feb. 1647, HP 60/14/19–19; c. Mar. 1647, HP 60/14/39A.
117 Hall to Worsley, 5 Feb. 1647, HP 36/6/1A. Galileo considered this issue in his *Letter to Grand Duchess Christina*, in M. Oster (ed.), *Science in Europe, 1500–1800: a primary sources reader*, Basingstoke–New York 2002, 68. For Spinoza see J. Israel, *Radical Enlightenment: philosophy and the making of modernity, 1650–1750*, Oxford 2001, 200–2, 447–9.
118 Worsley to Hall, 16 Feb. 1647, HP 36/6/3A.
119 Ibid. HP 36/6/3B.

rules and precepts belonging even to diverse disciplines without any breath at all, or manifest abruption, either in matter or style; having all notwithstanding but one single respect and conspiring or looking together, at one grand and proper end; why should I not thinke, the wisdome of God able to effect the like, and that after a farr more excellent manner.[120]

Worsley was supremely confident in the 'vniversality of the wisdome of Scripture' and its 'vn-Imaginable dephts', even suggesting that bible study would be a feature of the afterlife.[121] However, this did not mean that it was the most suitable judge in physical controversies: the purpose of the Bible was not to account for natural phenomena, but to impart God's message. Scripture had 'left man a latitude' to investigate nature, and Worsley concluded that

> if any upon a probable phrase of scripture, shall build an axiome in physickes without thinking himselfe afterwards obleiged (for the satisfaction of others) to hold strictly a Correspondency with the rules and lawes of Reason, and experience. I should not conceive my selfe tyed, by any rule, or law in Scripture, to believe or give creditt to his Assertion ... As apprehending it much more safe, to bend the words of Scripture to truth, then to writhe truth so, as it may speake to such or such a sense of Scripture.[122]

Furthermore, Worsley argued that dogmatic interpretations of Scripture had been responsible for dividing Protestants, and so 'a willingness to [bring] Scripture to the Truth', would help to end 'many other controversies amongst vs'.[123]

As Young noted, Worsley was not advocating a secularised natural philosophy, although he distinguished it from scriptural exegesis; rather, the study of nature became an aspect of worship itself, in a way similar to that later advocated by the so-called 'latitudinarians'.[124] Indeed, Worsley at this point seems to have seen no incompatibility between faith and reason, which was the 'law and order, that perfect nature hath planted in vs ...Which in things sensible, desumeth the primordia and certainty of knowledge; First, from the information of the senses, and so ascends by degrees, upwards, till shee terminate in that centre, where all things flow, and to which they all returne'.[125] Such neoplatonic imagery perhaps explains why the letter apparently went down well in the Cambridge of Henry More and Ralph Cudworth, both known to Hall.[126] But Worsley equally demonstrated distaste for the convo-

---

[120] Ibid. HP 36/6/4A.

[121] Ibid. HP 36/6/4A–B.

[122] Ibid. HP 36/3/5B-6A.

[123] Ibid. HP 36/6/6A.

[124] Young, *Faith*, 223–5; Shapiro, 'Latitudinarianism and science, 286–316, and *Probability and certainty in seventeenth-century England*, Princeton 1983.

[125] Worsley to Hall, 16 Feb. 1647, HP 36/6/5A.

[126] Hall noted the favourable response of his tutor, John Pawson, an obscure figure, but

luted religious controversies which were plaguing London and distorting the divine message.

Worsley was by no means alone in yearning for a purer, simpler version of Protestantism: Dury for one hoped to achieve religious pacification by emphasising the fundamental truths of Scripture over divisive forms. But there remained the problem of how to reach the uncontested interpretation of the 'vnimaginable depths' of Scripture on which this would be based. The reformed stress on the word above human customs had left no final arbiter of biblical meaning, severing western Christianity from its clerical anchoring and creating a crisis of authority worsened by Luther's stress on the gulf between man and God. Like Baconian experimental science, which also sought to avoid reliance on custom through inductive reasoning, experimental religion faced the epistemological problem of how to trust human judgements given the unreliability of the senses. Behind Worsley's confidence in the capacity of human reason to relate to God, then, was an ominous climate of metaphysical uncertainty.

This context can also explain the endless exegetical exercises which absorbed so much intellectual energy in the period: painstaking scrutiny of the textual integrity of the Bible in its original languages, expelling human corruptions from the divine text.[127] Such pursuits were of great interest to Worsley's new associates: Arnold Boate was a noted Hebraist, as was Sadler who, along with Lady Ranelagh, patronised the efforts to produce a Hebrew New Testament by the Scottish Presbyterian William Robertson.[128] Worsley too went on to support Robertson and collect an enormous range of Hebraic literature, and he was probably introduced to such matters in this milieu. It is also notable that the linguistic study of Scripture was one of Boyle's early interests, and would be a lifelong preoccupation.[129] Thus, even if we concede with Hunter that Boyle was not actively engaged in experimental science until 1649, this does not exclude him from the activities and interests which Worsley and his associates were pursuing in the preceding years.[130] Nor must we relegate this milieu to the periphery of Boyle's intellectual biography. Certainly Boyle's enduring interest in the ethical dilemmas of the pursuit of science echoed Hartlib's preoccupation with reconciling rewards for scientific or technological innovation with the public good, bridging the divide between the moral issues which initially preoccupied Boyle and his later scientific pursuits. His interaction with the Hartlib circle encouraged Boyle to consider the 'social purpose' of learning in a 'Treatise of publick spiritidness', apparently with Worsley's encouragement, and it is notable

More at least would later take an interest in Worsley (see chapter 2 below): Hall to Hartlib, 5 Apr. 1647, HP 60/14/28A.
[127] D. S. Katz, *Philo-semitism and the readmission of the Jews to England, 1603-1655*, Oxford 1982, 9-13.
[128] W. Robertson, *The second gate, or the inner door to the holy tongue*, London 1654.
[129] Hunter, *Robert Boyle: scrupulosity and science*, 33.
[130] Ibid. 47.

that Boyle's interest in Worsley's 'pious powder-plot', the saltpetre project, was framed in just these terms.[131] Such matters of conscience would later prey much on Boyle's mind, as would his concerns about the potentially atheistic implications of much of the new science, leading him to stress the limits of human reason.[132]

The tension between the competing claims of reason and revelation manifested itself in an interesting episode, which briefly illuminates the activities of Worsley's circle in the Invisible College years. The case in question was that of Sarah Wight, a young woman whose wasting illness and subsequent godly conversion and miraculous recovery attracted much attention in London.[133] Worsley and Boate were sent by a concerned Lady (probably Ranelagh, who visited on 19 May 1647) to examine the fasting Wight, although she refused the cordial they prescribed for her, whilst another of Hartlib's circle, Dr Thomas Coxe, subjected her to a more thorough interrogation regarding her claim to be sustained by divine grace alone.[134] Here, the medics might appear as sceptical rationalists antithetical to the spiritualists who seized upon Wight's case, but they too appear to have been drawn to her as a possible example of providence at work, albeit one which required their learned scrutiny. Wight's case also became linked to the religious conflicts in post-civil-war London, when it was used by the Baptist Henry Jessey as a means to unite the troubled saints.[135] For Jessey, Wight was a symbol of God's activity in this world, which might allow the saints to surmount their formal divisions. Ranelagh too reportedly asked Wight for her opinion on how to reconcile such divisions, and Wight's answer would have been endorsed by many of Worsley's Hartlibian associates: it would be through 'The beholding a reconciled God, seen by all'.[136] By witnessing her Worsley was (perhaps unwittingly) drawn into this cause.

However, such consensus was proving difficult to achieve following the collapse of clerical authority in the 1640s. The Presbyterian settlement put forward by the Westminster Assembly (of which Dury was a member) had failed to re-establish spiritual order, only dividing parliament's supporters

---

[131] 'Ephemerides', 1648, pt II, HP 31/22/8B; *Boyle correspondence*, i. 43. The treatise was apparently eventually published in Hartlib's *Chymical and medicinal addresses*, London 1655. For Boyle's interest in the 'social purpose' of science see J. R. Jacob, *Robert Boyle and the English Revolution: a study in social and intellectual change*, New York 1977, 28–38, and Hunter, *Robert Boyle: scrupulosity and science*, 202–22.

[132] Hunter, *Science and the shape of orthodoxy*, 225–44.

[133] B. R. Dailey, 'The visitation of Sarah Wight: holy carnival and the revolution of the saints in civil war London', *Church History* lv (1986), 438–55; C. Scott-Luckens, 'Propaganda or marks of grace? The impact of the reported ordeals of Sarah Wight in revolutionary London, 1647–52', *Women's Writing* ix (2002), 215–32.

[134] H. Jessey, *The exceeding riches of grace advanced by the spirit of grace*, London 1647, 9, 56, 113–21. Ranelagh is named as 'Lady Renula' in the pamphlet, which is present in Worsley's *Catalogus*.

[135] For religious conflict see Hughes, *Gangreana*.

[136] Jessey, *Exceeding riches*, 88.

further. Unfortunately the letter Worsley wrote in 1647 'concerning the Intereste of the People', which might have given some idea of his perspective on these developments, is lost, although tellingly Culpepper noted that 'hee hathe moste excellently described the Intereste', but was less successful in demonstrating 'the Peoples title to it'.[137] This context of discord was part of the backdrop to the Invisible College, whatever precisely Boyle meant by these words, and there is indeed evidence that Boyle was fascinated if repelled by the sects meeting at Worsley's Coleman Street.[138] But London was a city effectively under military occupation from August 1647, threatened by another civil war. It is no surprise, then, that Worsley was already looking to leave this weary city, for one which pulsed with the intellectual and commercial energies of the time: Amsterdam.

[137] 'Culpeper letters', 311.
[138] The question of whether Boyle was in a 'dialogue with the sects', however, is controversial: Jacob, *Robert Boyle*; Hunter, *Robert Boyle: scrupulosity and science*, 51–7.

2

Amsterdam, 1648–1649

'Proffits humbly presented to this Kingdome'

Benjamin Worsley left his home town at the close of 1647, spending nearly two years in Amsterdam. Why he chose this destination is not hard to grasp: the United Provinces of the Netherlands had loomed large in the English imagination since emerging from their long war of independence from Spain.[1] It was widely believed that this victory was based on the might of Dutch commerce, something which provoked much envy in seventeenth-century England. Worsley himself had played on the fears of Dutch commercial domination to promote his saltpetre project, in a speculative proposal entitled 'Proffits humbly presented to this Kingdome', which he probably drafted shortly before journeying to the republic.

'Proffits' placed the saltpetre project in an ambitious setting derived from an earlier Hartlib-sponsored project of two Huguenots, Hugh l'Amy and Peter le Pruvost, which sought to elevate England to leadership of the international Protestant cause.[2] L'Amy and le Pruvost were in negotiations with parliament from 1645 to 1646, and Worsley apparently considered joining with them in an enterprise, perhaps with merchant backing, although Dury warned him that the two Huguenots were suspicious of those whose 'interest of Profit will carye them astraye from a public good'.[3] Instead, Worsley borrowed their format: agricultural and fishing improvements along with his own saltpetre project financing and being deployed in a new English colony, which would in turn enrich and empower England. Colonial imports, Worsley explained, would preserve 'a vast expence of money within the Commonwealth of this Kingdome'.[4] Prosperity would encourage 'all sorts of Artists & ingenious men' to bring their skills to England, 'by which we may … deprive our neighbour Kingdoms of their rich manufactures or Arts'.[5] This would be at the cost of England's competitors, for 'as wee shall and

---

[1] W. Speck, 'Britain and the Dutch Republic', in K. Davids and J. Lucassen (eds), *A miracle mirrored: the Dutch republic in European perspective*, Cambridge 1995, 173–95.
[2] Webster, *Great instauration*, 221, 371–2, 380.
[3] Dury to Hartlib, *c.* May 1646, HP 3/3/19A.
[4] 'Proffits humbly presented to this kingdome', *c.* 1646, HP 15/2/61B. This may be the 'Discourse' showing 'by plaine ordinary and familiar way's the Crowne or Common-*wealth* of *England* might in few *years* bee made the richest (if that bee the happiest) and the most flourishing Country in the world' which Worsley was still touting in 1649: Worsley to Hartlib, 1 June 1649, HP (Royal Society, Boyle letters 7.2, fo. 2r).
[5] 'Proffits humbly presented', HP 15/2/63B.

may thus daily raise and strengthen ours: so the Kingdoms about us will, and must necessarily as much decay and weaken'.[6] These domestic profits, however, would also revive England's flagging fortunes in foreign trade, a vision of national monopoly that prefigured the Navigation Act:

> Our Nation receiving the wholl benefitt both of the Commodities itselfe and monopolizing also the trading for them into their owne hands, it will be like as but somewhat more, then if Spaine Italy and those Countryes which now vent those Commodities wer ours by Conquest and possesion.[7]

Catholic Spain would be one victim of this commercial imperialism, therefore, but more importantly the project would counterbalance the commercial prowess of the Dutch, and 'prevent the Hollanders overgrowing us'.[8]

To Webster, this discourse 'effectively demonstrated how a co-ordinated programme of innovation and economic reform could be used to guide the nation towards a utopian goal'.[9] Indeed, Worsley concluded the treatise by declaring the many benefits that would arise from commercial dominance, consisting of a prospectus of the aspirations of the Hartlib circle: reformation of laws, propagation of the Gospel, the advancement of education and learning, and finally 'indeavouring an Union and reconciliation throughout all the Christian at least all the Protestant Churches'.[10] But if we accept J. C. Davis's conclusion that early modern utopias were generally situated outside of time, then 'Proffits' ill fits this genre, preoccupied as it was with the process of change which could only be mastered, not transcended.[11] The reunification of the Protestant Churches would come from this hard won hegemony:

> By which meanes as wee shall bee secure from all feare off them soe wee shall bee able to give, and to dictate lawes to them, which advantage may bee turned to a most pious and Christian end in preserving peace Universally amoungst them … and soe wee may sitt as judge and Vmpire of all Christian differences, and may draw and ingross the blessings and promises to ourselves that are made to the Peace makers.[12]

This economic nationalism was somewhat at odds with the Protestant internationalism so important to Hartlib and Dury, who had already called for parliament to continue its crusade on the continent against Spain.[13] Such

---

[6]   Ibid. HP 15/2/63B–64A.
[7]   Ibid. HP 15/2/62A–B.
[8]   Ibid. HP 15/2/62A.
[9]   Webster, *Great instauration*, 381.
[10] 'Proffits humbly presented', HP 15/2/64B.
[11] J. C. Davis, *Utopia and the ideal society: a study of English utopian writing, 1516–1700*, Cambridge 1981, 37–8.
[12] 'Proffits humbly presented', HP 15/2/64A.
[13] S. Hartlib, *The necessity of some nearer conjunction and correspondency amongst evangelicall Protestants*, London 1644.

concerns had motivated their support for l'Amy and le Pruvost, who aimed 'not alone to benefitt us as wee are a state by ourselves, but to make us beneficiall to all the Protestants of Christendome, and to put in our hand the strength of their Cause against there enemies the Papists'.[14] Culpeper for one appeared to notice the discordance between the two visions, and advised that Worsley refashion his proposal to aim for the glorification of God 'throwghout the whole worlde', to the benefit not just of 'this family, Cownty, Nation', but 'whole mankinde'.[15] There was thus an implicit tension between Culpeper and Dury's universal values and Worsley's vision of an amoral world governed by international competition and the force of self interest, which pitted England against Catholic and Protestant nations alike. Such thoughts perhaps were with him as he crossed for the first time onto the continent, and into a state which was at once his nation's most powerful Protestant ally, and its key commercial rival.

The apprentice chymist

Worsley's first port of call in the Netherlands was Rotterdam, where he fulfilled the first of many commissions for his English backers, gathering intelligence on the windmills which his friend Wheeler had patented in the Netherlands ten years earlier.[16] He travelled next to the Hague by way of Delft, to meet one of Wheeler's estranged investors, the royalist ambassador and patron of Hartlib Sir William Boswell, who reported that the discredited projector's 'Interest' in the Netherlands was worthless.[17] Having delivered letters from Dury and Culpeper to Boswell and another supporter on the opposite side of the political spectrum, Sir Robert Honywood, the brother-in-law of Sir Henry Vane the younger, Worsley finally arrived at his destination proper in February.

Worsley had certainly chosen an auspicious time to visit Amsterdam. By then the Münster peace negotiations were bringing thirty years of European war and eighty years of national struggle for the United Provinces to an end, a victory for the mercantile Holland regents against the bellicose Orangists in this complex polity.[18] This was a time of republican ascendancy over the House of Orange, something reflected in the grand building style epitomised

---

[14] Dury to W. Strickland, 6 Nov. 1646, HP 25/7/2A.

[15] Culpeper to Hartlib, c. spring 1646, 'Culpeper letters', 244.

[16] Worsley to Hartlib, 14 Feb. 1648, HP 36/8/1A.

[17] Ibid. HP 36/8/4B. For Worsley's continued support for Wheeler see Worsley to Hartlib, 1 June 1649, HP (Royal Society, Boyle letters 7.2, fo. 1v); 22 June 1649, HP 26/33/3A; 3 Aug. 1649, HP 33/2/2B; Wheeler to Hartlib, 29 Oct. 1649, HP 34/3/3 (drafted by Worsley).

[18] J. I. Israel, *The Dutch Republic: its rise, greatness, and fall, 1477–1806*, Oxford 1995, 595–609.

by Amsterdam's new town hall, then under construction.[19] As well as civic pride, this rebuilding reflected the bounties which peace with Spain had brought for Dutch trade, now entering a new phase of global primacy which spelled disaster for certain sectors of English commerce.[20]

Worsley's host, Johann Moriaen, was a businessman who would have enjoyed some of the fruits of this boom. But, as John Young's study has revealed, Moriaen's eclectic intellectual and scientific interests also made him something of a corollary to Samuel Hartlib, for whom he served as agent in the Netherlands.[21] Like Hartlib, Moriaen was a product of the Germanic Calvinist diaspora, and his associates were similarly international. Prized amongst them was Johann Rudolph Glauber, the German alchemist whose 'new philosophical furnaces' were the chief attraction for Worsley in the Netherlands, having caused a stir amongst Hartlib's circle in the preceding months. Glauber was an experienced practical chemist, and his tutelage was potentially highly lucrative, but there was another side to Worsley's trip. As Young has shown, 'chymistry' was perceived to be an area of sanctified knowledge, offering the chance to 'cure' the fallen material world and to 'rewrite Creation in better accord with the original divine intention', a spiritual as well as technical task.[22] Worsley's visit was clearly intended to set him on the path of the adept, and was tinged throughout with a curious mixture of enterprise and mysticism.

Fittingly, perhaps, for such an exalted venture, Worsley's progress was not straightforward: he was unable to meet Glauber until August, and was thereafter hindered by problems of finance and communication, as well as the reluctance of this rather cantankerous figure to impart his secrets.[23] Worsley faced pressing material concerns throughout his visit, then, leading him to consider many alternative means of support, and he in fact became rather well known for his 'useful suggestions for earning one's bread', as Hartlib's Polish correspondent Cyprian Kinner put it.[24] Moriaen was his partner in many of these, and Worsley demonstrated his chymical credentials to his new host by analysing an 'Alexipharmacum, against stinking Watter' which was being touted by one of Moriaen's associates.[25] Initially Worsley hoped that this remedy against the putrefaction of waters could have medicinal and philosophical uses, but after analysis he found it to be merely 'an infussion upon a hurtfull or unwholesome minerall'.[26] Having shown his competence to Moriaen and another new associate, the Dutchman Adam Boreel, Worsley was able to undertake other experiments with his hosts whilst they waited

[19] Ibid. 863–73.
[20] Ibid. 610–12, and Dutch primacy, 197–202.
[21] Young, Faith, passim.
[22] Ibid. 174.
[23] Ibid. 183–226.
[24] C. Kinner to Hartlib, 23 July 1648, HP 1/33/39–42 (trans. W. J. Hitchens).
[25] Worsley to Hartlib, 4 May 1648, HP 71/15/1B.
[26] Worsley to Hartlib, [18] May 1648, HP 71/15/2B.

for Glauber. An early project of theirs involved various new methods of dyeing.[27] Worsley also hoped to enlist the help of one of Moriaen's kinsmen, Jacob Pergens, in a land drainage venture based on similar technology to Wheeler's mills, although the Dutchman doubted that any of his compatriots would work in England for 'feare of civill warrs, from the Royall or Levelling party'.[28]

Fortunately, similar 'engines of motion' were also being developed by two potentially more willing sources: the Dordrecht-based inventor Caspar Kalthof, and William Petty in England, whom Worsley attempted to unite in an ultimately unsuccessful collaboration.[29] Originally he was concerned that Petty was planning to rival some of his own projects, but in return for vouching not to do so Petty requested that Worsley 'fish out' information about Kalthof's rival machines.[30] Worsley was apparently happy to oblige in this intellectual intrigue, but if Petty hoped he would be a passive informant, he was to be disappointed. In June 1649 Worsley wrote to Petty thanking him in rather exaggerated terms for his 'generous offer' to collaborate with Kalthof, whom he had in the meantime visited and was evidently acting as unofficial agent for.[31] Having manoeuvred himself into the position of go-between, Worsley seems to have been hoping to benefit from whichever invention was the more successful, but unsurprisingly Petty evaded giving out any further details.[32] As it turned out this reservation was wise, for shortly afterwards Kalthof was rumoured to have set fire to his own engine to hide its flaws.[33]

Such problems of communication beset Worsley's first meetings with Glauber in the late summer of 1648.[34] References in Culpeper's letters suggest that Moriean and Worsley had begun work on a 'Menstruum vniversale' independently of Glauber.[35] However, by the following spring Worsley and Moriaen had turned their attention to developing new furnaces, probably from Glauber's designs. On 18 May Worsley asked that Hartlib pass on news of 'the businesse of our new furnace for the melting of Lead Oare without Bellow's' to Boyle, who had visited the Netherlands in the previous year.[36]

---

[27] Worsley to Hartlib, 4 May 1648, HP 71/9/2A; 1 June 1648, HP 71/9/3A.

[28] Worsley to Hartlib, 22 June 1649, HP 26/33/1A; Young, *Faith*, 221.

[29] Young, *Faith*, 221–2.

[30] W. Petty to Worsley, 14 Mar. 1649, HP (James Marshal and Marie-Louise Osborn Collection, Beinecke Rare Book and Manuscript Library, Yale University, doc. 36, fo. 1v).

[31] Worsley to Petty, 15 June 1649, HP 8/50/1A.

[32] Petty to Worsley, 28 [June?] 1649, HP (Marshal and Osborn Collection, doc. 34, fo. 1r).

[33] Young, *Faith*, 221.

[34] Ibid. 220–1.

[35] Culpeper to Hartlib, 16 Aug. 1648, and Culpeper to Worsley, 9 May 1648, 'Culpeper letters', 342, 335–6.

[36] Worsley to Hartlib, 18 May 1649, HP (Royal Society, Boyle letters 7.1, fo. 1r). For Boyle's visit see Hunter, *Robert Boyle: scrupulosity and science*, 44. For Boyle's early interest

Worsley was hopeful that this innovation would 'recompence the charge, waiting and expence' of his journey.[37] Further intelligence of this 'Metallicke Worke' came in the following month, although progress was temporarily halted after Moriaen scalded his legs.[38] Shortly before his departure from Amsterdam Worsley was still noting that 'some thing is still further expected in our metallicke Busynesse'.[39] However by then Moriaen was reporting that Worsley was at last ready to collaborate with Glauber, an ill-fated collaboration discussed in chapter 3.[40]

Worsley's furnace experiments were financially supported by John Sadler, who visited Amsterdam from August to October 1648.[41] Further backing came from John Dury, who sent a letter to Worsley with Hartlib's son Samuel, a rather wayward youth who had been sent to stay with Worsley in January 1649.[42] In return for him running a number of errands, Dury offered to assist Worsley by putting him in touch with his uncle, David Ramsay, who 'had a Patent for all the Mynes of England & Wales'.[43] Worsley responded enthusiastically, and in May Dury revealed that Ramsay was indeed interested in employing Worsley as a technician for their 'operation upon Mars' (i.e. iron).[44] By June he was reportedly offering Worsley use of 'a mine of Antimony and another of Iron in the B. of Durham'.[45] By then, however, Worsley was beginning to tire of the projector's lot, complaining 'of the vanity of proposing any invention to the world of any kind if they see he have not a purse of his owne at least to ioyne in it, eyther wholly sleighting a man, or thinking all he moves is out of selfe designe, or requiring very high Conditions from him'.[46] Soon he was looking for 'a place of settled imployment', either in England or the colonies: Amsterdam had seemingly failed to yield its anticipated rewards.

Worsley's personal frustrations seem to have coloured his perceptions of the place, which, he complained, disagreed 'with my health, & as litle, or lesse, with my affection'.[47] Even Moriaen had reservations about the aloof

in Glauber, which probably 'reflects Worsley's early influence', see Newman and Principe, *Alchemy tried in the fire*, 213.

[37] Worsley to Hartlib, 18 May 1649, HP (Royal Society, Boyle letters 7.1, fo. 2r).
[38] Worsley to Hartlib, 1 June 1649, HP (Royal Society, Boyle letters 7.2, fo. 1r).
[39] Worsley to Dury, 27 July 1649, HP 33/2/19B.
[40] Young, *Faith*, 225.
[41] J. Sadler to Hartlib, 16 Aug. 1648, HP 46/9/4A; Worsley to Hartlib, 1 June 1649, HP (Royal Society, Boyle letters 7.2, fo. 1r). Somewhat confusingly, Worsley frequently referred to Sadler as 'Monsieur Amy', for example in Worsley to Dury, 17 Aug. 1649, HP 33/2/4A.
[42] Dury to [Worsley], 26 Jan. 1649, HP 1/7/1A.
[43] Dury to Worsley, 14 Mar. 1649, HP 1/2/1A; 'A memorandum for Mr Worsley', HP 1/2/2B.
[44] Dury to Worsley, 2 May 1649, HP 4/1/25A.
[45] Dury to Worsley, 12 July 1649, HP 26/33/5A.
[46] Worsley to Hartlib, 22 June 1649, HP 26/33/2B.
[47] Worsley to Dury, 27 July 1649, HP 33/2/19B.

demeanour of his adopted countrymen.[48] However, as a major commercial, religious and intellectual entrepôt, Amsterdam exerted a gravitational pull on Europe and beyond, creating an enormously fertile environment by which, despite his doubts, Worsley can hardly have been untouched.

The triple entrepôt

As a crossroads of intellectual and commercial traffic, Amsterdam was an attractive location for those craftsmen and inventors whose products fuelled the scientific revolution, and during his stay Worsley encountered several of them. Some were friends of Moriaen: the iatrochemist Johann Unmussig and Johann Sibbertus Küffler, whose father-in-law Cornelius Drebbel had run a successful dye-works in pre-war London and was much praised by Worsley.[49] Worsley was probably author of a letter to Hartlib describing a globe witnessed at the house of the printer and geographer Joan Blaeu, another associate of Moriaen, which was destined for an East Indian king.[50] Worsley also sampled the products of the master telescope-maker Johann Wiesel of Augsburg, from whom he purchased a glass costing £50, through which he observed the city of Haarlem, the moon and the satellites of Jupiter.[51] Worsley became a regular customer of Wiesel, propagating his 'tubes' to interested Englishmen such as Henry More and the virtuoso Sir Paul Neile.[52] Other inventions were more unusual, such as a 'sweating chaire' constructed to cure a looking-glass-maker suffering from the effects of mercury poisoning.[53]

Worsley was most inspired, however, by his encounter with Ahasuerus Fromanteel, an Anglo-Dutch clockmaker whom he first met in June 1648, being particularly taken by his microscopes.[54] Worsley already owned a glass bought in London for 25s., but Fromanteel's finer specimens encouraged him to eulogise on the uses of this instrument in demonstrating the 'immensity of the wisedome of God', showing 'that nothing was done by chance or occasion'. Whereas some atomists saw this 'little world' as comprised of identical particles of matter, Worsley was struck by its diversity, which to him proved

[48] Young, *Faith*, 37.
[49] For Drebbel's dye-works see Weinstein, 'London', 23; for Worsley's esteem see Worsley to Hartlib, c. July 1657, HP 26/56/4B.
[50] [Worsley?] to Hartlib, 19 Mar. 1649, HP 53/35/2A.
[51] Worsley to Hartlib, 18 May 1649, HP (Royal Society, Boyle letters 7.1. fos 1v–2r); Worsley to Hartlib, 27 July 1648, HP 42/1/1A–B.
[52] Young, *Faith*, 50–1; H. More to Hartlib, 9 Oct. 1649, HP 18/1/32–3; I. Keil, *Augustanus Opticus: Johann Wiesel (1583–1662) und 200 Jahre Optisches Handwerk in Augsburg*, Berlin 2000, 379, and 'Technology transfer and scientific specialization: Johann Wiesel, optician of Augsburg, and the Hartlib circle', in *SHUR*, 268–78.
[53] Worsley to [Hartlib], 26 May [1648], Royal Society, Boyle letters 7, no. 50, fos 1v–2v.
[54] Worsley to Hartlib, 22 June 1648, HP 42/1/1A.

that 'not every man only but every beast or fowle of the same species, yea, every sand is known by its name'.[55] Noting that these instruments might also be used to investigate the signatures of plants, Worsley observed that 'it would imploy many yeares, & fill a good volume, to discover to the world this little Atlantis, or Vnknowne part of the Creation', a task Robert Hooke would shortly attempt. Meanwhile the microscope prompted Worsley to consider the principles of learning more fundamentally:

> For I now having abdicated much reading of Bookes, vulgare received Traditions & common or Schoole opinions, have divided knowledge into Divine & humane ... For humane knowledge I honour only that which is immediately deduced from, or built vpon Reall, & certayne Experiments; & those so many, as to make an infallible vniversall; seing according to the Schooles science is not of particulars. All men therefore sedulous in Experiments, I honour alike whether they be physicall or naturall, medicinall, Astronomicall Opticall or any way mechanicall or Chymicall, all Knowledge carefully grounded vpon these, beeing not only certaine or Reall but Vsefull.[56]

Divine knowledge, on the other hand, was merely 'what the spiritt of god hath sett doune plainely, in symple & univocall tearmes & easy to the vnderstanding of any, looking vpon the points controverted, as the opinions but at best, if not the Inventions & pryde of men'. In both science and religion, then, Worsley sought to avoid a reliance on human 'customs' by embracing experimentation, and for the former natural history was ideally suited, revealing as it did the variety of God's creation which no human philosophy could capture in full.

One novel anti-scholastic philosophical system in particular was frequently accused of attempting to do just that, and in Amsterdam Worsley may have briefly crossed paths with its author, René Descartes, to whom he promised to deliver a letter from Hartlib shortly before the Frenchman left the Netherlands.[57] Cartesianism had caused a great stir in Dutch intellectual life, already fraught by confessional conflicts, and Worsley's *Catalogus* contained contemporary Cartesian works by Henricus Regius and Cornelis van Hogelande.[58] More mainstream was the final flowering of Dutch humanism epitomised by Gerard Johann Vossius, whose works encompassed history, chronology, linguistics and biblical study.[59] With thirteen entries Vossius was one of the best represented authors in the *Catalogus*, which clearly bears the impact of Dutch intellectual life, with notable collections of the works

[55] Worsley to Hartlib, 27 July 1648, ibid.
[56] Ibid. HP 42/1/1B.
[57] Worsley to [Hartlib], 3 Aug. 1649, HP 33/2/2B.
[58] Namely Henricus Regius' *Fundamenta physices*, Amsterdam 1646, and *Fundamenta medica*, Utrecht 1647, and Cornelius van Hogelande's *Cogitationes*, Amsterdam 1646. For this context see Israel, *Dutch Republic*, 565–91.
[59] Israel, *Dutch Republic*, 577–81.

of Erasmus (six works), Hugo Grotius (ten), the Arabist Thomas Erpenius (five) and the chiliast James Brocard (four). Even more numerous were works published in the Netherlands, and on this visit Worsley may have picked up such contemporary Dutch publications as Johannes Baptista Van Helmont's *Opera omnia*, Jan Jonston's *Idea universae medicinae practicae* and Willem Piso and Georg Marcgraff's *Historia naturalis Brasiliae* (all published in Amsterdam in 1648).[60] The latter belonged to a rich Dutch school of colonial natural history and medicine, and Worsley also commended Johann de Laet's *Americae utriusq; description* (Leiden 1633), alongside Johann Eusebius Norimbergius' *Historia naturae* (Antwerp 1635).[61] This was an enduing interest: in 1657 Hartlib noted that Worsley recommended the *Geographia generalis* (Amsterdam 1650) of Bernard Varenius, as 'one of the best that ever hath beene written for a true Method … being Geographical and Natural History together'.[62] Worsley's interest in natural history, as well as his critical engagement with Cartesian mechanics (which later chapters will document), were thus likely cradled in Amsterdam, and its continuing intellectual pull may be gauged by the number of Dutch publications in the *Catalogus*.[63] Also very well represented in this were Dutch works of theology, reflecting another side to Amsterdam's flourishing entrepôt.

One aspect of Dutch society which struck seventeenth-century English observers was its reputed liberty of conscience. Indeed Amsterdam was a city where many religious groups could worship more openly than anywhere else. However, toleration was neither universal nor uncontested, and the Calvinist 'public church' fought hard to maintain its hold on religious orthodoxy, often in alliance with the House of Orange.[64] Toleration was thus linked to the republic's political contests, and was most keenly supported by the mercantile oligarchs of Holland who also favoured peace with Spain. To such republicans as Johann de Witt, trade and toleration were natural partners, and the Dutch state should cultivate both as its 'interest'.[65]

During Worsley's stay in Amsterdam, his homeland had of course

---

[60] Worsley cited the latter as an exemplary work of natural history in a letter to Hartlib, c. July 1657, HP 26/56/2B.

[61] Worsley to Hartlib, 27 July 1648, HP 42/1/1B. To these names might be added the Netherlands-based physicians Jacobus Bontius (who specialised in tropical medicine), Pieter van Foreest, Nicolaas Tulp and Franciscus Sylvius, all listed in the *Catalogus*. For these authors see D. Struik, *The land of Stevin and Huygens*, Dordrecht 1981, 102–31.

[62] 'Ephemerides', 1657, pt II, HP 29/6/4A. This work is listed in Worsley's *Catalogus*.

[63] At least 124 from Amsterdam, 147 from Leiden, 21 from The Hague and several from other cities.

[64] H. Schilling, *Religion, political culture and the emergence of early modern society: essays in German and Dutch history*, Leiden 1992, 353–81.

[65] Israel, *Dutch Republic*, 499–505, 637–45. For the importance of Dutch interest theory as represented by de Witt, Pensionary of Holland from 1653 to 1672, see Scott, *Algernon Sidney, 1623–1677*, 210–13, and 'John de Wit and other Great Men in Holland' [i.e. Pieter de la Court], *The interest and political maxims of the Republick of Holland and West-Friesland*, London 1702.

become a republic, and Worsley's own sympathy with the regicide (if not a doctrinaire republicanism) was shown by his response to a letter written to Moriaen from the Calvinist Prince Augustus of Anhalt. This letter had reportedly observed that 'it should bee a warning to all Princes and Persons in chiefe Authority, that they bee Fathers not mere Rulers and Tyrants over their People And that God had called them to an opportunity of doing good, and providing for the happines and blessing of their subjects'. Worsley considered that 'from a Prince' this judgement was 'not more excellently divine then rare'.[66] Other reactions to the regicide that he encountered were less sympathetic, however, and Worsley reported that many Dutchmen 'did disfavour our proceedings, and were rather inclinable to thinke iust the Princes Interest'.[67]

Despite this hostility, several supporters of the Commonwealth looked to the United Provinces as a model Protestant republic to emulate, particularly those who admired its supposedly tolerant religious situation. Indeed, Worsley's new associates in Amsterdam were eclectic in their religious tastes. Despite being a sometime Calvinist minister, Moriaen's faith was hardly orthodox, instead being broadly irenic or 'impartial', and open to the influence of such mystics as Jacob Böhme.[68] Less conventional still was Adam Boreel, who in 1646 had founded the Amsterdam congregation of the Collegiants, a sect which had originated in 1620 from the confessional disputes then raging in the public Church.[69] Originally separating from the latter after the contra-Remonstrant victory, this group blended Erasmian humanism, pacific Mennonite anabaptism and the mystical chiliasm of the radical reformation, meeting in 'colleges' to discuss Scripture free from clerical supervision.[70] Boreel himself leaned towards the spiritualist wing, scorning the visible Churches in preference for the 'inner light' which connected the believer to God, a concept which explains why English Quakers later found common ground with the Collegiants. However, this did not mean that Boreel relied on personal revelation alone: in fact he was also a noted scholar of Scripture, indeed a biblical literalist who saw the creeds and confessions of the visible churches as human corruptions. In contrast, Boreel's college did not claim to be a divinely inspired institution, merely a place for believers to discuss Scripture and wait for God to inaugurate the true Church on earth.[71] Boreel's reading of Scripture was infused with millenarian expectations, and we know that in Amsterdam Worsley was reading chiliastic

---

[66] Worsley to Hartlib, 18 May 1649, HP (Royal Society, Boyle letters 7.1, fo. 2v).

[67] Worsley to Hartlib, 22 June 1649, HP 26/33/1A.

[68] Young, Faith, 16–21, 81–92.

[69] A. Fix, Prophecy and reason: the Dutch Collegiants in the early enlightenment, Princeton 1991, 44.

[70] Ibid. 23–52.

[71] Ibid. 90–4; R. Iliffe, '"Jesus Nazarenus legislator": Adam Boreel's defence of Christianity', in S. Berti, F. Charles-Daubert and R. Popkin (eds), Heterodoxy, Spinozism, and free thought in early-eighteenth-century Europe, Dordrecht–Boston–London 1996, 375–96.

literature of the sort popular amongst the Collegiants.[72] Had he attended their meetings, then, Worsley would have found amongst the Collegiants a vibrant, egalitarian and anti-confessional religious environment of apocalyptic anticipation whose tolerance contrasted with the dogmatic disputes he had left behind in London.

Boreel was also an active Hebrew scholar, and Worsley directed a number of Dury's queries to him regarding Jewish demonstrations of the 'falshood of the Mahumetan Religion'.[73] Boreel and Moriaen had several acquaintances amongst Amsterdam's Jews, another religious group which Worsley would presumably have first encountered in these years.[74] It is not known whether he fulfilled Dury's request to canvass this group for their opinion about the possibility that the American natives were in fact a lost tribe of Jews.[75] But he did make the acquaintance of the messianist Rabbi Menassah ben Israel, with whom Dury was negotiating regarding the readmission of the Jews to England.[76] Chapter 1 discussed how Hebrew language, culture and religion were of interest to biblical scholars wishing to gain a full understanding of Scripture, but this was not the only reason to communicate with this usually despised group. Dury's interest in readmission was motivated by the desire to achieve the conversion of the Jews, which was believed to be a precursor to the commencement of the millennium.[77] Worsley too had specified one of the goals of 'Proffits humbly presented' as being 'the Conversion of the Iewes a worke as most Divines conceave shortly to be expected and without doubt at hand'.[78] Study of Hebrew was also of interest to those seeking to restore or recreate the lost, Adamic language, or to create a new universal language, which interested many amongst the Hartlib circle.[79] This fascination with Hebrew led scholars to take an interest in the Jewish 'mystical interpretation of language', kabbalah, which hoped to explain how 'the infinite and transcendent God ... makes Himself known in the material world'.[80] Christian

---

[72] A letter from Moriaen's associate Appelius mentioned that he and Worsley had been reading a commentary by the millenarian von Frankenberg (perhaps the discourse published by Hartlib in 1651 under the title *Clavis apocalyptica*), which might be 'a key of many mysteries of God, which doubtlesse eere long are to be revealed': HP 45/1/47. For Collegiant chiliasm see Fix, *Prophecy*, 57–83.

[73] Dury to Worsley, 2 May 1649, HP 4/2/26B.

[74] Young, *Faith*, 41–8.

[75] Dury to Worsley, 12 July 1649, HP 26/33/5A. For this debate see Katz, *Philo-semitism*, 127–57.

[76] Dury to Worsley, 14 Mar. 1649, HP 1/2/1A. For the Hartlib circle's interest in Jewish conversion see R. Popkin, 'Hartlib, Dury and the Jews', in *SHUR*, 118–36.

[77] Katz, *Philo-semitism*, 89–126.

[78] 'Proffits humbly presented', HP 15/2/64A–B.

[79] Katz, *Philo-semitism*, 43–88. See also J. Bono, *The word of God and the languages of man: interpreting nature in early modern science and medicine*, I: *Ficino to Descartes*, London–Madison 1995.

[80] Katz, *Philo-semitism*, 71; Y. Petry, *Gender, Kabbalah and the Reformation: the mystical theology of Guillaume Postel (1510–1581)*, Brill 2004, 73; F. Yates, *Giordano Bruno and the hermetic tradition*, London 1964.

kabbalah was pioneered by the Renaissance neoplatonists Ficino and Pico, and continued to be pursued by authors such as the sixteenth-century Catholic universalist Guillaume Postel and the heterodox philosopher Giordano Bruno, all names well represented in Worsley's *Catalogus*.[81] Worsley referred approvingly to kabbalah in a letter written a decade after this visit.[82]

In Amsterdam, Worsley was therefore exposed to a whole new range of religious opinions. Not that he would necessarily have welcomed this: his letters often registered distaste for sectarianism, abhorring controversialists who wrote 'volumes in this kind, & every man proclayming his darknesse to be light: by which we come to be divided into sects & Schismes', and claiming that it was no shame to be ignorant of certain passages of Scripture, 'The Spirit of god being wee know but one & must alwayes [be] the same'.[83] Worsley's hostility to schism, however, was perhaps directed more against those who insisted on dogmatically asserting points of doctrine and were thus responsible for causing division, rather than 'impartial' Christians such as Boreel and Moriaen, whose irenic, simplified piety was apparently close to his own. Worsley's religion was also ethical, as when he reflected on the death of Cyprian Kinner, that we must 'break ourselves of this custome to take care only to get estates for ourselves, or our mere families, and meditate more of our privat Interest, then of the Interest of God's Church, and of Mankind in the general'.[84] On the subject of morality he wrote that 'there is nothing lesse or worse taught in the Vniversitys', recommending instead the classical Stoics Epictetus and Marcus Aurelius Antoninus.[85]

None the less, from a strict Calvinist point of view Worsley's irenic piety could itself be construed as unorthodox, and it certainly drew him to taste some extremely heterodox waters in the form of Socinianism, the anti-Trinitarian sect whose illicit works were available in Amsterdam.[86] Worsley commended the writings of the Socinian Johann Crell, who had 'collected all the commands and precepts almost in Scripture that concerne the doing of any moral duty, or abstaining from any moral evil' in a book

---

[81] Worsley owned six of Postel's and eight of Bruno's works, as well as important kabbalistic works by Pico, Jean Pistorius, Petrus Galatinus and Jacques Gaffarel, and an edition of the kabbalistic 'Book of Creation', the *Liber jezirah*, Amsterdam 1642, by Hartlib's associate Johann Stephan Rittangel.

[82] [Worsley] to [Boyle], *c.* late 1658–early 1659, HP 42/1/32B.

[83] Worsley to Hartlib, 27 July 1648, HP 42/1/1B.

[84] Worsley to Hartlib, 18 May 1649, HP (Royal Society, Boyle letters 7.1, fo. 1r).

[85] Ibid. Two editions of Meric Causabon's translation of the Emperor Marcus Aurelius Antoninus' *Meditations*, as well as three editions of the stoic Epictetus' *Enchiridion*, were included in the *Catalogus*, along with Salmasius' edition of Simplicius' *Comment in Epictetum*, Leiden 1640, and Justus Lipsius' *Philosophia and physiologia stoica*, Leiden 1644.

[86] For Socinianism see H. John McLachlan, *Socinianism in seventeenth-century England*, Oxford 1951, and J. Champion, *The pillars of priestcraft shaken*, Cambridge 1992. The forthcoming work of Sarah Mortimer will uncover much about the influence of Socinianism in England.

which gave Worsley 'much pleasure'.[87] Although not necessarily subscribing to these views himself, the number of Socinian works in Worsley's *Catalogus* attests to a serious exploration of their ideas.[88] Worsley was possibly introduced to these by the Amsterdam-based physician William Rand. When back in London Worsley wrote to Rand about their doctrines, perhaps with his own scruples, and Rand replied that whilst he did not count himself a Socinian, 'yet I see no reason but one, why, the men or their doctrine should disturbe the mind of your selfe or any rationall ingenuous christian; & that is the Inchantment & Sorcery of the reverend Clergie, who being movd by their Interest to make a lamentable noise of heresy blasphemy & what not, doe terrifie the minds of men'.[89] Perhaps Worsley was also attracted by the tolerant, ethical and anti-clerical dimensions of this controversial creed.

The Socinians were also noted for their precise reading of Scripture, something which attracted the interest of many Collegiants.[90] Despite his early distaste for religious controversy, at some point in his life Worsley was drawn into intensively reading works of scriptural exegesis and theology, at least if the number of works on those subjects in his *Catalogus* can be relied upon. The Netherlands provided many of these, and Worsley collected several Remonstrant authors including Grotius and Vossius, as well as Petrus Bertius, Johannes Drusius and the *Opera* of Simon Episcopius and of Jacobus Arminius himself. Similarly, and perhaps surprisingly for someone who has been termed a Puritan, Worsley owned certain works by Arminian-leaning English theologians including John Cosin, Richard Montague and Thomas Jackson, as well as Henry Hammond, William Chappell, George Sandys, John Hales and Sir Thomas Browne, and Thomas Lushington's translations of Crell. An enduring interest in the liberal wing of Dutch theology is suggested by Worsley's ownership of a 1675 edition of the *Opera theologica* of the Remonstrant Stephan Courcelles, as well as six works by the Leiden theologian and philologist Johann Cocceius.[91] Conspicuous by their absence are many key contra-Remonstrant authors, allowing us to summarise this side of the collection as strong in the works of Vossius, Vorstius and Volkelius, but entirely lacking in Voetius.[92]

---

[87] Worsley to Hartlib, 18 May 1649, HP (Royal Society, Boyle letters 7.1, fo. 1v).

[88] Worsley's catalogue listed thirteen works bearing the name of Faustus Socinus himself as well as Przipcovius' biography of him (making him one of six best represented authors in the whole library), eight by Crell, two by Jonas Schliting and single works by Valentin Schmaltz, Adam Goslavius and Joachim Stegmann, as well as works by the major English anti-Trinitarians John Biddle and John Knowles.

[89] W. Rand to Worsley, 11 Aug. 1651, HP 62/21/1A–B.

[90] Fix, *Prophecy*, 135–60.

[91] For the 'Cocceians' see Israel, *Dutch Republic*, 660–9. Worsley also owned several works by antecedents of this liberal tradition, such as Jacobus Acontius, Mino Celsi and Sebastian Castellio, alongside Erasmus and Grotius.

[92] Worsley owned two works by the Socinian Johannes Volkelius, and five works by Conradus Vorstius (1569–1622), who was often accused of Socinianism. Gisbertus Voetius was a key counter-Remonstrant theologian. See Israel, *Dutch Republic*, 428–30.

However, it would be wrong to deduce therefore that Worsley was a closet religious rationalist, for the *Catalogus* is equally strong in mystical or 'enthusiastic' works supposedly from the opposite end of the religious spectrum, although the complex religious identity of the Collegiants, for example, belies the apparent dichotomy between 'rational' and 'enthusiast'. For spiritual counsel concerning the 'true aims of a Christian', Worsley turned to a figure whose piety is similarly elusive, the irenicist John Dury, who advised that 'till we learne the ways of Christ experimentally, and be inabled to utter them demonstratiuely and rationally, we are not sufficiently taught in the mystery of his life within us'.[93] Such an experimental approach to religion had the advantage of avoiding clerical intermediaries, and scriptural exegesis was thus central to it, but equally the desire to experience Christ internally encouraged a radically subjective piety tinged with antinomianism, a direction in which Worsley was perhaps already heading in Amsterdam.

Intellectually and religiously, then, Amsterdam was a fertile environment, but the most famed feature of its entrepôt was of course commercial. This had been a consistent theme of the discourse of trade in England, and 'Dutch commercial prowess acted more forcefully upon the English imagination than any other economic development in the seventeenth century'.[94] Typical was the Jacobean projector John Keymer's diagnosis of how the Dutch had become 'powerful & rich in all kinds of all Merchandizing, Manufacture, & fulnesse of Trade, and yet have no Commodities in their own Country growing'.[95] This was achieved by trading in the goods of other nations, including England, 'out of which they draine and still covet to exhaust our wealth and coyn, and with our own Commodities weaken us'.[96] It was with this model in mind that Henry Robinson advised parliament, on the eve of the Civil War, to make England 'the *Emporium* or Warehouse from whence other Nations may bee furnished with forraine commodities of all sorts'.[97]

If Dutch commercial prowess could provoke such envy in the early 1640s, when it was relatively sluggish, then by the time that Worsley arrived in Amsterdam this was turning into positive alarm. By then Dutch trade was returning to the unrivalled position it enjoyed when Keymer was writing, as freight rates tumbled in the aftermath of the Treaty of Münster of 1648. Worsley was able to see the fruits of this first hand in the warehouses of Amsterdam, which teemed with goods unloaded off Dutch ships arriving from markets which English merchants had previously dominated. English trade to Italy and the Levant, which had benefited from Spanish-Dutch war, suddenly collapsed under the challenge of returning Dutch competition.[98]

---

[93] Dury to Worsley, 2 May 1649, HP 4/1/27A.
[94] Appleby, *Economic thought*, 73.
[95] J. Keymer, *A cleare and evident way for enriching the nations of England and Ireland*, London 1650, 1.
[96] Ibid. 2.
[97] H. Robinson, *Englands safetie in trades encrease*, London 1641, 20.
[98] Israel, *Dutch supremacy*, 203–4.

1649 was the first year of the century in which more cloth was exported eastwards into the Baltic Sound in foreign than English ships.[99] Keymer's depiction of Holland's design 'to get the whole Trade of Christendome into their hands, not only for Transportation, but also the Command of the Seas', seemed to be truer than ever.[100]

This success was attributed to the actions of the Dutch state in encouraging and defending trade, a course Worsley advised the new English republic to take by making 'Merchandise and Trading and the incouragement of it the Great Interest of the State, as many Commonwealths (j say not Kingdoms) haue lately done. As of Venice Florence (when it was a *Common Wealth*) Genoa and Holland'.[101] One way to achieve this was to have a 'New *East India* Company erected, and the Authoritie of Par*liament* to countenance it encourage it and settle it with fit Priviledges'. This would encourage many Dutch investors to take their cash to England, particularly those who resented being excluded from investing in the Dutch East India Company, the VOC, due to its high rate of stock, a grievance which Worsley regarded as a 'great Secret of State' in Amsterdam. Worsley considered that 'the very flourishing of Amster*dam* is made or kept vp at least by the *East India* Company', and this great joint stock company offered one model of commercial govern-ance.[102] However, this method was currently having far less success in the Americas, as the Dutch West India Company was languishing having lost its Brazilian territories to the Portuguese in 1646.[103]

At the same time, however, non-company Dutch commerce with the Americas was flourishing, in particular at the expense of English merchants who were suffering from the effects of civil war. By the late 1640s Dutch merchants were dominating the carrying trade between the English colonies and Europe, virtually monopolising exports of Virginian tobacco and kick-starting the sugar industry in the West Indies. These infringements caused consternation amongst English merchants who previously dominated these trades, and it was his acquaintance with a group of these that provided Worsley with the opportunity to gain favour with the new regime back home. Worsley had of course already considered some sort of colonial career in alliance with the Huguenots l'Amy and le Pruvost, the latter of whom Hartlib was attempting to tempt back to England from his Netherlands base in 1648.[104] In early 1649 Worsley had also considered setting up a sugar grinding business in Barbados.[105] But another sort of opportunity arose when, in summer 1649, he reported being approached by 'Diverse Merchants' from

[99] Hinton, *Eastland trade*, 85.
[100] Keymer, *Cleare and evident way*, 17.
[101] [Worsley] to Hartlib, 10 Aug. 1649, HP 43/35B.
[102] Ibid. HP 42/35A.
[103] Israel, *Dutch supremacy*, 163–9.
[104] Worsley to [Hartlib], 3 Aug. 1649, HP 33/2/2B.
[105] 'Ephemerides', 1649, pt II, HP 28/1/7B.

England, who told him of their concerns about recent developments in Virginia.[106] As well as complaining about Dutch competition, they reported how the royalist governor of that colony, Sir William Berkeley, had recently launched a crackdown on supporters of parliament in Virginia. Thus Worsley conveyed to his allies in England the situation in Virginia:

> not only Civill, & Industrous men, but good men, began to increase There./ And a church 2 or 3 of the Independent, & Presbyterian way, were gathered./ some coming thither from the Bermudas, or sommers Island, some from new=England./ And very great Expectation that Debaushery, & sensuality, so reigning, there./ would quickly in a great measure have beene discountenanced, might they have beene countenanced, or at least permitted to stay there./ But some of the ministers, & some other heads of Churches, were Banished, as men schismaticke & factious./ And an oath or Covenant pressed to mainteyne the Governour and the Interest of the Crowne, against the parliament./[107]

Worsley claimed that his mercantile contacts were willing to advance 'A very considerable stock', on the condition that Virginia's government was placed into a commission able to represent their interests. For his own 'future settlement & Relation to the World' Worsley envisaged employment in Virginia, presenting himself as one who 'may assist in the furtherance of Trading incourage Industry & may contribute to the flowrishing of the plantation'.[108] Meanwhile a new Virginian administration would encourage investment and commerce, and the introduction of a plethora of new commodities (aniseed, sweet fennel, rice, flax, woad, hogs and beef) and industries (leather and soap, distilling, flax-spinning, linen and dyes). Virginia would follow Barbados, which 'hath within 10 yeares raysed its land from almost nothing; to be as deare … or dearer then in England'.[109] With these ends in mind, Worsley exhorted Dury, Hartlib and Sadler to pass on his suggestions to their political patrons.

Accordingly, Dury approached John Bradshaw, the president of the recently constituted Council of State, its Latin secretary John Milton and Walter Frost, the principal secretary, who responded favourably.[110] However, given 'the natural slownes of the Parliament', Dury suggested that more concrete plans were needed.[111] Worsley had already written to Hartlib explaining the proposal in more detail, allowing Dury to draw up a memorandum which he probably used to promote the project.[112]

---

106 Worsley to Dury, 27 July 1649, HP 33/2/18A.
107 Ibid.
108 Ibid. HP 33/2/18A–B.
109 Ibid. HP 33/2/19A.
110 Dury to [Hartlib], 30 July 1649, HP 1/2/9A.
111 Ibid. HP 1/2/9B.
112 Worsley to [Hartlib], 3 Aug. 1649, HP 33/2/1–2; Dury's adaptation is at HP 33/2/22, 61/5/1–2.

The details of Worsley's proposal for a new administration for Virginia will be considered in chapter 3, but here it is worth considering the identity of Worsley's unnamed mercantile contacts. Part of his plans involved assembling a council to govern Virginia, and in the weeks before he returned to England in November 1649, Worsley was corresponding with Hartlib and Dury about the choice of commissioners, 'the main hinge and ... great strength of the thing'.[113] Worsley was relatively flexible as long as it comprised 'men well interessed and related well affected to the imploiment', suggesting Nicolas Corsellis, an Anglo-Dutch merchant associated with Hartlib, the prominent colonial merchants Maurice Thomson and William Pennoyer, the London alderman Thomas Andrews, and Martin Noell, 'a great Plantation and Parliament-man', who would attain prominence as an advisor to Cromwell in the 1650s.[114] However, it appears that at this point Worsley knew these merchants, many of whom were also active in London politics, by reputation only, and they were unlikely therefore to have been the ones who approached him in summer 1649. Further uncertainty is introduced by Worsley's alarmed response to Dury's earlier suggestion that he 'get Propositions Authentically drawn vp by the Adventurers', in order to allow the Council of State to offer them a commission.[115] This provoked Worsley to backtrack, explaining to Dury that the merchants were willing to invest their money only as 'a secondary motive ... which would follow, if the Parl*iament* would please in altering that present Governement (which did concerne them for their owne Interest)'.[116] It seems at least possible then that Worsley was deliberately exaggerating his mercantile contacts in order to promote his own suitability for an official post. This may seem an insignificant detail, but it becomes more important given that Thomson, Pennoyer and Andrews were three of the leading colonial interloping 'new merchants' whom the historian Robert Brenner has claimed would soon be directing the Commonwealth's commercial policy, with Worsley acting as their cipher.[117]

If he had suspicions of Worsley's credentials, however, Dury kept them quiet, and assuaged Worsley by agreeing that 'if the State will not owne their owne Interest, it cannot bee expected that Privat men should engage for them without some assurance ... and protection'.[118] Following Dury's advice, Worsley wrote to enlist the support of Walter Strickland, parliament's envoy in The Hague.[119] In turn, Strickland wrote to a leading Commonwealth politician, Sir Henry Vane the younger, arguing that Worsley's plans had 'the same Reason which goeth through the change of Goverment established

---

113 Worsley to [Hartlib?], *c*. Sept. 1649, HP 33/2/20A.

114 Ibid. HP 33/2/20A–B.

115 Dury to Worsley, 8 Aug. 1649, HP 1/2/12A–B.

116 Worsley to Dury, 17 Aug. 1649, HP 33/2/3B.

117 Brenner, *Merchants and revolution*, 589.

118 Dury to Worsley, 31 Aug. 1649, HP 1/2/14A–B.

119 Worsley to Strickland, *c*. Aug./Sept. 1649, HP 61/8/1–3.

in England'.[120] By the time he departed for England, in November 1649, all was ready for his plans to be put into action, and for Worsley to gain the employment he so sought.

In some senses Worsley left the Netherlands much as he had arrived there, still seeking a vocation to fulfil his intellectual and material ambitions, but his time in Amsterdam had certainly left its mark. From now on Worsley would focus his energies on making a living through office-holding rather than projecting, and although from time to time he sought to profit from such ventures, Worsley's scientific explorations thereafter were increasingly speculative, and in fact spiritual, in nature. More and more he came to identify his material interests with those of the state, meanwhile. How Worsley came to balance the competing claims of interest and the spirit, having finally achieved some of the success he strove for in government service, will be considered in the following chapters, when the proclamation of a republic in England opened new opportunities for an ambitious man like him.

---

[120] Strickland to Sir Henry Vane, 2 Sept. 1649, HP 61/9A.

3

The Council of Trade and the Commonwealth, 1650–1651

Historiography

Worsley returned to London in November 1649 with an invitation to Whitehall, where the new republican regime was struggling to establish its legitimacy domestically and internationally. For the next two years Worsley would contribute to this, firstly by helping to fashion the Commonwealth's response to the royalist rebellions in many of England's overseas colonies, and then by becoming secretary to the body created to revive the nation's commerce, the Council of Trade. This has been central to interpretations of the Commonwealth's commercial policy, particularly the Navigation Act of 1651, and the relationship between political and economic change in an era once seen as marking the beginnings of modernity.

Older studies had a clear place for commercial change and conflict in accounting for the revolution, which for Marxists such as Christopher Hill had ramifications for the emergence of capitalism in England.[1] The Commonwealth's aggressive promotion of commerce and perceived hostility to paternalistic or monopolistic regulation were thus seen as the fruits of parliament's victory over the traditionalist royalists, paving the way for England's ascent to commercial and imperial glory. But under the revisionist microscope, political conflict appeared contingent, local and personal, rather than based on clear ideological, much less social or economic, differences. In terms of commercial policy, this trend is summed up by Blair Worden's conclusion that 'the Rump's preoccupation with commerce reflected rather than created a trend. The government's economic concerns remained traditional'.[2]

As these quotations suggest, accounts of the Council of Trade and the Commonwealth's commercial policy have focused on whether its goals were traditional or progressive, in particular regarding 'free trade'. Thus, J. P. Cooper showed that the Commonwealth was not attempting to forge

---

[1] For statements of the importance this historian attached to the Rump's commercial policies see C. Hill, 'A bourgeois revolution?', in J. G. A. Pocock (ed.), *Three British revolutions: 1641, 1688, 1776*, Princeton 1980, 109–39, and 'The place of the seventeenth-century revolution in English history', in C. Hill, *A nation of change and novelty: radical politics, religion and literature in seventeenth-century England*, London–Chicago–Melbourne 1993, 19–37.
[2] Worden, *Rump Parliament*, 299.

a modern capitalist order through *laissez-faire* policies in poor relief or industrial regulation, for example. The failure of the Rump to abolish the trading companies has been seen as particularly important, and Cooper found 'no evidence of doctrinaire hostility to chartered companies' on the Council of Trade.[3] Cooper and others therefore saw considerable continuity in pre- and post-civil war commercial policy.[4] Furthermore, even if the Council of Trade did have a clear agenda (which Cooper doubted) it had a brief lifespan, and overall 'the Rump's conservatism and reluctance to override corporate privileges or vested interests appear in prolonged failures to act'.[5]

A critical issue here has been the relationship between the state and merchants, company or interloping, particularly in the passage of the Navigation Act. Building on the work of J. E. Farnell, Brenner argued that this was a victory for the 'new merchants', a closely integrated group of colonial interloping traders whom he saw as coming to power with the Commonwealth, at the expense of the generally royalist company merchants.[6] Mercantile conflict is at the centre of Brenner's attempt to construct a 'new social interpretation' of the revolution, and because its members included some of the leading new merchants, the Council of Trade assumes an elevated importance in his argument. Pre-eminent amongst these was Maurice Thomson, one of those names which Worsley put forward as a commissioner for Virginia, and both Farnell and Brenner highlighted the apparent connection between Thomson and Worsley as demonstrating the mercantile-political alliances which underpinned the new regime. Thus for Brenner the new merchants 'sought to influence the government so as to further their own immediate interests', whilst the republican politicians aimed 'to make commercial policy serve the goal of enhancing English world power, especially in order to validate their own leadership, to give legitimacy to the Commonwealth, to prove the superiority of the republican form of rule and, not least, to protect the republic from its many enemies abroad'.[7]

Of course republicanism and commerce were often associated in the early modern imagination, and some historians have seen this as informing the rhetoric of the English republic. For Pincus, its defenders invented 'a new ideology applicable to a commercial society, an ideology that valued wealth but also the common good'.[8] Worsley's name figured prominently in Pincus' account, thanks principally to his authorship of two official pamphlets promoting the Commonwealth's commercial policies, *The advocate* and *Free ports*. His role as a bureaucrat and propagandist, with both political and

3   Cooper, 'Social and economic policies', 132.
4   Ibid. 124; Clay, *Economic expansion*, 239–40.
5   Cooper, 'Social and economic policies', 139.
6   Brenner, *Merchants and revolution*.
7   Ibid. 580. See also Farnell, 'Navigation Act of 1651', 439–54.
8   Pincus, 'Neither Machiavellian moment not possessive individualism', 708. See also B. Hoxby, *Mammon's music: literature and economics in the age of Milton*, New Haven–London 2002, 62–90.

mercantile contacts, therefore makes him an important figure in examining the various debates surrounding the Council of Trade.

There is a pervasive tendency in these debates to conclude that the Commonwealth's failure to abolish the trading companies signifies its essential conservatism, a conclusion which arguably endorses the teleological framework which it purports to debunk. By contrast, Sean Kelsey's recent account of the political culture of the Commonwealth has sought to transcend the dichotomy between traditional and progressive, by showing it to have been 'a regime animated by a genius for conserving order in a radically imaginative way'.[9] Presented with the task of establishing its legitimacy following civil war, an unpopular military coup and the regicide, the Commonwealth 'not only successfully restored the norms of civil government, but also invented novel means for its expression'.[10] The Rump's commercial policy fits in with this account, for although its aims were primarily defensive, based on restoring and reviving flagging trade after the dislocation caused by the civil war and bolstering an insecure regime, this none the less could elicit a novel approach. An important dimension of this was responding to the revival of Dutch shipping, which Worsley had witnessed in Amsterdam, something which became entwined with the complex relations between the two republics, encompassing the proposal for a union, the Navigation Act, and the subsequent descent into war.[11] More pressing at the time of Worsley's return to England, however, was the state of colonial trade, and his path to the Council of Trade began with the parliamentary settlement of royalist Virginia.

No state or politick body: the reduction of Virginia

Even before he had left Amsterdam, Worsley's eager lobbying had encouraged the Council of State to take Virginia into consideration, on 13 October 1649.[12] Then, on 29 November, Sir Henry Vane's Committee of the Admiralty ordered that Maurice Thomson and other colonial merchants present their ideas for the settlement of the colony. In the meantime Worsley, having finally arrived in London, was given permission to search in the state records for information about Virginia.[13] The eventual meeting, on

[9] S. Kelsey, *Inventing a republic: the political culture of the English Commonwealth, 1649–1653*, Manchester 1997, 11.
[10] Ibid. 1.
[11] S. Pincus, *Protestantism and patriotism: ideologies and the making of English foreign policy, 1650–1668*, Cambridge 1996, pt I; Wilson, *Profit and power*; Ormrod, *Commercial empires*.
[12] CSPC, 1574–1660, 331.
[13] Ibid. 331–2. Copies of some of the records seem to have come into Hartlib's hands: a speech to the Virginia committee, HP 61/2/1–14; a treatise on the development of Virginia, HP 61/3/1–25; 'A breviat of the records of Virginia', HP 61/4/1–2.

9 January 1650, largely endorsed Worsley's proposals for the reduction of Virginia, although it was not until May that he was ordered to help draw up a commission putting this into effect.[14]

The details of this plan were geared to the twin needs of securing political and commercial control over the errant colony, at a point when its royalist sympathies and preference for trading with Dutch merchants threatened to cut it adrift from the motherland. The government was certainly aware of these problems before Worsley surfaced, but he helped nudge it into action by supplying a vigorous argument for the importance of Virginia to the Commonwealth's political and commercial fortunes, a defence of parliament's right to dispose of the colony, and a plan for how to achieve this with mercantile support. Initially Worsley argued that parliament's sovereignty over Virginia derived from the colony's strategic importance to England: 'It being if not simply & positively Theirs; yett at least Relatively, As the good or harme of that plantation, & manner of the Government There; may reflect at present or futurely vpon the Commonwealth of England; vpon the good of Trading, vpon merchants, & vpon the freinds & Interest of the Parliament'.[15] Sir William Berkeley's commission as governor meanwhile had been invalidated by the regicide, and parliament was therefore free to dispose of his office. Worsley's letters described how Berkeley had taken power in alliance with a faction of planters, whom he had persuaded to trade with the Dutch.[16] But Berkeley had a hidden agenda: 'To Bring the Planter to a lesse dependance vpon London & her Merchants' and to 'tye them with the lesse Trouble to his Intrest'.[17] Ultimately his aim was to preserve Virginia for the Stuarts, and destroy the parliamentarian interest.

In order to bring Virginia back under parliamentary control, Worsley suggested the creation of a London commission comprising two parliamentarians and two merchants, which would be responsible for appointing a government resident in Virginia. As well as being able to license those departing for Virginia, these commissioners would have power 'To debar the Trading of the Hollander and of all strangers There'. The Virginian council would be chosen from amongst the planters, ensuring that by 'ioyning these Gentlemen their power interest, & Relations to the former Comissioners, The Governour might be made yet the more vnable to make any considerable Party There'.[18] Naming Thomson as one of the possible commissioners, Worsley thus suggested delivering to these merchants a share of power not only in governing Virginia, but in licensing its trade. In doing so, Worsley was intervening in a deeply rooted contest for the political and commercial control of the colony and its trade.

[14] CSPC, 1574–1660, 332, 339.
[15] Worsley to [Hartlib], 3 Aug. 1649, HP 33/2/1A.
[16] Ibid.
[17] Ibid. HP 33/2/1B.
[18] Ibid. HP 33/2/2A.

Merchants had been involved in Virginia since its foundation, but the collapse of the Virginia Company in 1622 ended any possibility of it being a privately governed colony, and thereafter the crown ruled through an appointed governor and council with an assembly representing the planters.[19] In the following years, however, a fissure had opened between the majority of colonists and a small group of landowners who dominated the emerging tobacco trade in conjunction with certain unincorporated English traders, namely Brenner's 'new merchants'.[20] As well as coming from relatively humble origins, these merchants were often involved in colonial settlement themselves. Pre-eminent were a group of planter-traders led by Maurice Thomson, connected by a series of business and familial ties linking merchants and ship-owners in England and Virginia with tobacco-producing colonists. These individuals came to dominate Virginian society and politics, promoting expanded production, opposing price regulation, excluding Dutch merchants and seeking to monopolise the tobacco trade. There thus emerged a 'merchant-councilor interest distinct from, and in important ways directly opposed to, the interest of the generality of planters', who had most to gain from a more open trade.[21]

In the 1640s these commercial-factional conflicts became politicised. In 1642 Berkeley had been appointed as governor by the crown, with particular instructions to counter Puritanism in Virginia, which had been promoted by many of the leading councillors and new merchants.[22] In order to achieve this, Berkeley empowered the smaller planters, undermining the political supremacy of the new merchants and their allies.[23] Measures were also taken against their dominance over colonial trade, with the passage of an 'Act against the Company' to ensure there would be no return to regulation of trade from London, and legislation opening trade to Dutch merchants.[24] Worsley had seen the consequences of these measures in Amsterdam, and they were precisely what his plans hoped to reverse.

By the time that he was readying to put these plans into action, in May 1650, news of Virginia's formal proclamation of Charles II of October 1649 had arrived in England, only to be followed by further royalist declarations from Barbados, Bermuda, Antigua and Maryland.[25] This escalation of the

[19] Y. Man, 'English colonization and the formation of Anglo-American polities, 1606–1664', unpubl. PhD diss. Johns Hopkins 1994, 17–72.

[20] Brenner, *Merchants and revolution*, 116–20.

[21] Ibid. 117.

[22] Ibid. See also K. Butterfield, 'Puritans and religious strife in the early Chesapeake', *Virginia Magazine of History and Biography* cix (2001), 17–19, and C. G. Pestana, *The English Atlantic in an age of revolution, 1640–1661*, Cambridge MA. 2004, 65.

[23] Man, 'English colonization', 268–81; J. Kukla, 'Order and chaos in early America: political and social stability in pre-Restoration Virginia', *American Historical Review* xc (1985), 289.

[24] Bliss, *Revolution and empire*, 30; Brenner, *Merchants and revolution*, 586.

[25] Pestana, *English Atlantic*, 86–122; Bliss, *Revolution and empire*, 86–8.

problem of colonial rebellion perhaps explains the delay in producing a legislative response, which finally arrived on 3 October 1650, when 'An Act for prohibiting Trade with the Barbadoes, Virginia, Bermuda and Antego' was passed, having been ferried through parliament by Maurice Thomson's brother George. Another cause of delay might have been domestic criticism, however. Agents representing Virginia were an obvious source of complaint, but Worsley's plans also threatened to deliver control of the tobacco trade into the hands of a mercantile clique, and this seems to have created resentment amongst their competitors. Worsley wrote a paper arguing that 'The merchants of London cannot Blame or wonder at the parlaiment, for affirming their iust Right & Authority to governe forraigne plantations, & dispose of outer Colonies of English'.[26] Warning its critics that 'Parlaiment may command their owne merchants to forbeare Trading There', Worsley derided Virginia's claims to independence:

> They of Virginia are no more then an English Colony./ They are no State/, or politick Body/, & consequently in no Capacity of being received into Protection by any forreigne nation,/ or of making a Confederacy or Alliance with any other state, or Prince/, nor of contracting any League with Any eyther for their defence; or for their being supplyed with things necessary; or for having their Commodityes taken from them.

Parliament was the undisputed 'supreame Authority of the English nation', whilst the colonies were 'but a Branch of our owne nation', an argument similar to that officially adopted by the Commonwealth.[27] With such aggressively imperialistic rhetoric being voiced, unsurprisingly many colonists felt that their rights were under threat by the new regime, and given the content of the 1650 Act they had good reason. This raised a fleet to suppress the rebellions, whilst trade to the colonies, especially in foreign ships, was to be licensed from England. It also threatened to introduce a single, centralised oversight of the colonies, overriding the local systems which had emerged over recent decades.[28] For Brenner this 'gave the colonial merchants just about everything they had requested', namely 'the restoration of English merchant hegemony throughout the British empire'.[29]

However, even by then there appears to have been some retreat from the more aggressively imperialistic dimensions of Worsley's original plans. Worsley had already softened his rhetoric, claiming that parliament sought 'no more then their owne Right of super-intendency', and had no intention of undermining the Virginian's 'iust Libertyes'.[30] Principally this meant offering them freedom to 'choose Those who shall Immediately governe

---

[26] 'Further animadversions about Virginia', c. 1650, HP 61/6/1A.
[27] Pestana, *English Atlantic*, 162–3.
[28] Ibid. 100.
[29] Brenner, *Merchants and revolution*, 592.
[30] 'Further animadversions about Virginia', HP 61/6/1A.

Them', and Worsley hoped that the plantation 'will be settled without Bloodshed', so that 'the Assembly and the Richer, soberer, & perhap the greater part of the Plantation; will be glad of the friendshyp, & Goverment of Parliament'.[31] This attitude seems to have been shared by the regime generally: in return for political and commercial loyalty the Commonwealth was apparently ready to allow Virginia a measure of self-government, and there would be no attempt to govern through a London-based council.

Thus when the two Commonwealth fleets empowered to bring the colonies to obedience left England, in August and September of 1651, there was already some room for compromise. This in fact was generally the course taken, as the various colonies were guaranteed 'free trade' in return for their surrender.[32] Primarily this meant that trade would not be subject to regulation by any English merchants, denying the new merchants their goal of reintroducing an exclusive trading company dealing in tobacco.[33] In any case the Navigation Act had by then superseded the commercial terms of the 1650 Act, and although it excluded the Dutch from the import trade into the colonies, it did allow the export trade to remain open.[34] Thus, although the four-man commission sent to Virginia was dominated by new merchants, two of whom were made governor and secretary respectively after Berkeley's surrender in 1652, this faction did not regain hegemony within Virginia, and the political rights won by the planters in the 1640s were not overturned.[35] Despite occasional crises, for the rest of the 1650s Virginian society was relatively harmonious.[36] The political reduction of this and the other rebellious colonies had indeed been achieved with little bloodshed.

All this, of course, was happening far beyond the direct reach of the English state, which could not realistically institute Worsley's original plans for imperial centralisation against the wishes of so many inhabitants of this distant colony.[37] Instead, the Commonwealth was reliant on those merchants who in effect connected England with its empire. That it chose to work with the new merchants reflects their status as the most politically sympathetic commercial faction, but beyond this it is hard to see them as significant enough to support the entire edifice of Brenner's 'new social interpretation' of the revolution. Influential they may have been, but the Commonwealth

---

[31] Ibid. HP 61/6/2A.

[32] Pestana, *English Atlantic*, 103–20; Bliss, *Revolution and empire*, 90–1; W. F. Craven, *The southern colonies in the seventeenth century, 1607–1689*, Baton Rouge 1949, 256.

[33] Brenner, *Merchants and revolution*, 131; Bliss, *Revolution and empire*, 61–2.

[34] Cooper, 'Social and economic policies', 135.

[35] Bliss, *Revolution and empire*, 89; Craven, *Southern colonies*, 255–7; W. M. Billings, *Sir William Berkeley and the forging of colonial Virginia*, Baton Rouge 2004, 106–12.

[36] Craven, *Southern colonies*, 265–7; Kukla, 'Order and chaos', 293; Bliss, *Revolution and empire*, 92–3; Pestana, *English Atlantic*, 157–212.

[37] For the wider context see J. P. Greene, *Peripheries and center: constitutional development in the extended polities of the British empire and the United States, 1607–1788*, Athens, GA–London 1986.

never ceded control of Virginia to Thomson and his faction, and although the Navigation Act instituted the protection against Dutch competition demanded by Worsley's mercantile contacts, it did so within a national monopoly transcending any particular commercial interest. Similarly, despite the membership of Thomson and some of his allies, the Council of Trade never followed a purely new merchant programme. This reluctance to allow merchants direct control of commercial regulation created room for intermediaries able to bridge the political and commercial worlds, precisely the situation Benjamin Worsley was able to exploit by becoming secretary to the Commonwealth's Council of Trade.

The Council of Trade

The Rump Parliament first discussed the possibility of founding a council to regulate the nation's trade on 11 January 1650, following petitions to the Council of State from various trading companies requesting that their privileges be confirmed.[38] None the less the meeting on Virginia that Worsley had attended two days before at Vane's Admiralty committee probably had some effect on the decision to found a council. Worsley was named secretary as early as 16 March, in the act's second parliamentary reading, and it seems likely that he had been consulted over its drafting by the MPs responsible, Thomas Challoner and Richard Salwey.[39] On the same day the number of commissioners was fixed at fifteen, including Challoner, Salway and Vane. Later in the summer Sir Cheney Culpeper was chosen as a member, although John Sadler was rejected.[40] Finally, on 1 August 1650, the Rump Parliament passed 'An Act for the Advancing and Regulating of the Trade of this Commonwealth', creating a Council of Trade of fifteen commissioners, with Worsley's salary specified as £200 plus £300 to employ clerks and messengers.[41]

As well as the individuals named above, the council included some of Brenner's new merchants, namely Thomson, the Dartmouth merchant and East Indian interloper Thomas Boone, and another opponent of the East India Company, Alderman John Fowke.[42] But this was not a majority, and in fact it seems to have deliberately included representatives from the whole commercial nation, ranging from Somerset (the clothier MP John Ashe), to Yarmouth (William Greenwood) and York (Henry Thompson). Currency issues were a speciality of Sir Ralph Maddison, an old ally of Gerald de

---

[38] Brenner, *Merchants and revolution*, 602–3; Cooper, 'Social and economic policies', 131.
[39] *CJ* vi. 383.
[40] Ibid. vi .425–6.
[41] *A&O* ii. 403–6.
[42] Brenner, *Merchants and revolution*, 607.

Malynes, whilst the established leadership of the East India Company was represented by William Methwold. Vane's brother-in-law Sir Robert Hony-wood was also summoned, ensuring that Hartlib's circle was well represented, whilst Worsley took on Samuel Hartlib junior as a clerk.[43]

The idea of founding a council to supervise trade was not new, having been amongst the proposals put forward by two pamphleteers, Hartlib's associate Henry Robinson, and the merchant Lewes Roberts, a decade earlier.[44] Both authors called on the newly assembled parliament to promote commercial revival through a 'Commission, ... advising and consulting all advantages of commerce, amongst which some understanding Merchants will be necessarie' (Robinson), or a body of 'able and discreet Merchants, with power and sufficient priviledge, to examine the disorders of trafficke, and irregular Traders ... entituled as States-merchants' (Roberts).[45] A precedent was the 1622 commission, founded to consider the decay of the cloth trade, but with a broader remit which reflected awareness that the traditional means by which the state had governed trade, via the chartered companies, was insufficient to meet the crisis which English trade was then entering.[46] Furthermore, this commission's debates were taken onto a public stage, via several pamphlets debating the relative merits of fixing the exchange rate. By the time of the publishing boom of the 1640s, this 'discourse of trade' was well established.

This was in part a literature of complaint, as authors lamented the commercial dislocation caused by civil war. Thus the merchant John Battie diagnosed how, 'as the fire that's kindled within doores, and in the bed-straw, as it were, rageth more violently: so *civill* War ruines *Trade* faster than any other, and makes poverty and desolation post in one after the other, wheresoever it is kindled'.[47] Similar were those 'free trade' assaults on the exclusive privileges of the merchant companies, such as Thomas Johnson's attack on the Merchant Adventurers, who 'like Incubusses doe suck the very vitall spirits, and drive into one veine that masse of blood which should cherish the whole body'.[48] Partly such authors capitalised on the perceived association between monopolies and Stuart corruption, but they also presented commercial arguments in favour of their abolition. Thus Johnson argued that the Merchant Adventurers' cloth monopoly had restricted the market, depressing prices and diverting wealth into privileged hands: 'were this Trade enlarged, it would tend to the multiplying of able

[43] Cooper, 'Social and economic policies', 133. Captain John Limbrey was added in April 1651, along with the master of the mint Dr Aaron Guerden.
[44] Robinson, *Englands safetie*; L. Roberts, *The treasure of trafficke, or a discourse of forraigne trade*, London 1641. See Webster, *Great instauration*, 355–8.
[45] Robinson, *Englands safetie*, 46; Roberts, *Treasure*, 65.
[46] See the instructions, printed in T&C, 16–27; Andrews, *Committees*, 11–12.
[47] [J. Battie], *The merchants remonstrance*, London 1644, 2–3.
[48] T. Johnson, *A discourse consisting of motives for the enlargement and freedome of trade*, London 1645, 4.

and wealthy Merchants, it would disperse it to a greater latitude'.[49] Nor were these empty words, for the 1640s saw the privileges of the companies under threat from interloping merchants.

However, few if any writers advocated a genuinely '*laissez-faire*' approach to commercial regulation. Even Johnson believed that 'there bee Generall Lawes to regulate trade, and to preserve it from confusion; we desire still a government, but not a Monopoly'.[50] This allowed Henry Parker to defend the Merchant Adventurers by asserting that '*Freedome* and *restraint* are things opposite ... yet both admitting of severall degrees, and limitations, they are not so opposite but that some kinde of restraint may be reconciled to some kinde of freedome'.[51] Similarly Robinson supported 'free trade', but defined this as a relaxation of the customs regime.[52] However, he was willing to concede that it might be expedient that 'both the setting open at liberty all Trad free alike to all men, and the inclosing of it by Charter and Corporations, may be seriously debated and agreed on, that it may neither be quite ruined, for want of good Government, nor yet obstructed, no less then if monopolized, by colour of a Corporation'.[53]

The foundation of the Commonwealth saw a new crop of commercial pamphlets offering numerous projects of economic diversification. Alongside legal and electoral reform, one anonymous author demanded that 'care be taken for the encouragement and encrease of Trade throughout the Commonwealth'.[54] The time-honoured project to promote an English fishery was revived as a solution to London poverty.[55] Samuel Hartlib responded similarly by increasingly focusing his publications on agricultural improvement.[56] Hugh Peter synthesised many of these proposals, arguing that the '*Increas of Merchandise*' was 'a special means to inrich anie Nation'.[57]

The twelve instructions issued to the Council of Trade reflected this resurgent discourse, with three dealing with domestic trade, and the next seven focusing on foreign.[58] Final instructions covered fishing and the plantations, although the latter was in practice neglected, presumably because the council expired before the royalist colonies had surrendered. Currency and the exchange rate were also covered, but more important were those

---

[49] Ibid. 22–3.
[50] Ibid 25.
[51] H. Parker, *Of a free trade*, London 1648, 7.
[52] Robinson, *Englands safetie*, 2, 6.
[53] Idem, *Briefe considerations, concerning the advancement of trade and navigation*, London 1650, 9.
[54] *Severall proposals for the generall good of the Commonwealth*, London 1651, 8.
[55] T. Jenner, *Londons blame, if not its shame*, London 1651.
[56] T. Raylor, 'Samuel Hartlib and the commonwealth of bees', in M. Leslie and T. Raylor (eds), *Culture and cultivation in early modern England: writing and the land*, Leicester 1992, 94–5.
[57] H. Peter, *Good work for a good magistrate*, London 1651, 82.
[58] *A&O* ii. 404–5.

instructions concerning the fate of the merchant companies, and the possibility of stimulating re-exports through manipulating the customs regime: free trade and free ports.[59]

Although it was empowered to summon officers of the exchequer, mint and excise, and consult all official records, the Council of Trade was not an executive body and was initially commissioned only until 29 September 1651. The intention of the regime in founding this council can best be gauged by the preamble to the act, announcing that parliament was 'taking into their care the maintenance and advance of the Traffick Trade, and several Manufactures of this Nation' so that 'ye poore people of this Land may be set on work, and their Families preserved from Beggary and Ruine, and that the Commonwealth might be enriched thereby'.[60] This was based on the principle that 'the Trade of this Nation both at home and abroad, being rightly driven and regularly managed, doth exceedingly conduce to the Strength, Wealth, Honour and Prosperity thereof'. Security was therefore a key aim: as *The Impartial Scout* reported, 'the Parliament of *Englands* actions and results are both swift and effectual, leaving no means unattempted for the preservation of the Commonwealth'.[61] The Council of Trade was therefore intended initially to restore commerce after the dislocation of civil war and to buttress the legitimacy of the republic, but it had the potential to go further.

The latter is suggested by a memorandum from Hartlib's papers apparently written by Worsley for the council's benefit, setting out 'The ends of Forraigne or Outland Trade'.[62] These began with the provision of a market for domestic labour through exports. However, the import trade was also important, 'that wee may be the more plentifully supplied & stored with such Commodities as we want from other Countries and that at the best & cheapest hand, ... Whether they be Commodities for pleasure or necessitie'.[63] Meanwhile the state should use diplomatic means to ensure that no nation became dominant. Further 'ends' were to gain bullion and to increase shipping (vital to 'the power, strength and repute abroad of this nation').[64] Only then did customs come into consideration. All commercial laws and charters should be framed with these ends in mind.[65]

In the absence of a full set of its papers, it is difficult to determine whether the Council of Trade followed these principles for its seventeen months of

---

[59] Brenner, *Merchants and revolution*, 603.

[60] A&O ii. 403.

[61] *The Impartial Scout*, no. 59 (2–9 Aug. 1650), 265.

[62] 'The ends of forraigne or outland trade state and asserted', c. 1650–1, HP 66/1/1/2. The copy is in a secretary hand, but with corrections by Worsley. Its tone and content suggests that it was intended to be addressed to a deliberative body like the Council of Trade.

[63] Ibid. HP 66/1/1A.

[64] Ibid. HP 66/1/1B.

[65] Ibid. HP 66/1/2A.

existence.[66] A list of reports made on the eve of its dissolution tells us that it reported eight times to the Council of State and seven to parliament.[67] Having had its initial commission extended until the end of 1651, the council prepared six further reports, making 'great progress' on eight more issues. For convenience its work can be divided into three areas: internal trade and manufacturing, reform of the merchant companies, and commercial relations with the Dutch, which will be dealt with separately. Worsley appears to have been busily employed in preparing its business, whilst his authorship of the two pamphlets arising indirectly from the council's deliberations suggests that his role went beyond administration.[68]

One of the first issues which the council considered was sending convoys to protect merchant shipping, something made possible by the naval build up of the previous decade.[69] It had been prompted by complaints from the Levant Company to the Council of State regarding French attacks. The regicide had made the Commonwealth an international pariah, and English merchants were considered fair game for foreign and royalist privateers, precipitating a crisis in London shipping.[70] Presenting the Council of Trade's report to parliament on 31 October, Thomas Challoner described how the injuries inflicted by the French were injurious to the honour, strength, wealth and trade of the nation, and thus proposed establishing a regular convoy which would be financed by increased customs.[71] Parliament responded quickly with an act to this effect.[72]

This was a clear instance of state resources being used to defend trade in a manner which would become increasingly common.[73] The council responded similarly to a mercantile petition calling for protection for foreign merchants importing bullion into England, by advising parliament to offer convoy protection, which was the subject of another quickly passed act.[74]

---

[66] No journal of the council's proceedings survives, and only fragments of its work have been found. Undoubtedly it did collect much important material however, which, according to Thomas Violet, Worsley left in the hands of Hartlib, Jr: *Mysteries and secrets of trade and mint-affairs*, London 1653, 178.

[67] SP 18/16, no. 138, printed in T&C, 64–5. An almost identical list is also printed in Violet, *Mysteries*, 177–9. These, however, are not entirely consistent with information from CJ, cited below.

[68] Rand to Hartlib, 29 July 1651, HP 62/30/4A; W. Wheeler to Worsley, 25 Aug. 1650, HP 34/3/5A.

[69] Brenner, *Merchants and revolution*, 607.

[70] Coates, *Impact*, 117–38.

[71] CJ vi. 488–90.

[72] A&O ii. 444. The council also reported on establishing a convoy for trade to Holland, Zealand and Flanders: T&C, 64.

[73] R. Conquest, 'The state and commercial expansion: England in the years 1642–1688', *Journal of European Economic History* xiv (1985), 155–72; Brenner, *Merchants and revolution*, 580–4; Braddick, *State formation*, 213–21; D. Loades, *England's maritime empire: seapower, commerce and policy, 1490–1690*, Harlow 2000.

[74] CJ vi. 520–2; A&O ii. 495. Thomas Violet claimed to have made this report: *Mysteries*,

This was a rare instance of the council fulfilling its instruction to consider controversial monetary issues, another being the draft report on 'the assignation of bills and court merchant'.[75] The latter was intended to resolve business disputes quickly so as to avoid clogging trade, whilst bills of debt were a way to overcome currency shortages, enabling a merchant to trade 'with the debts that others owe him'.[76] Generally, however, the council seems to have left these 'mysteries' to the Committee of the Mint, concentrating instead on ways to encourage trade besides currency manipulation or regulating the exchange. Therefore Ralph Maddison probably had little opportunity to promote his policies for legally fixing the exchange rate at the council table.[77]

Its responses to these petitions show the council to have been willing to lend a sympathetic ear to various commercial parties, including merchant companies: after all, given the embattled state of commerce, it made little sense to pursue policies deliberately harmful to merchants. The companies certainly used this argument in defence of their privileges in their petitions to the Council of State. The Eastland Company, for example, argued that it had been formed to 'vindicate the trade out of the usurped power of strangers', specifically by encouraging English shipping.[78] However, this had been undermined 'by the loose trading of unskilful persons, who taking advantage of this liberty and our want of power to restrain them', tended to trade at a loss, leading to a decline in English shipping. A new charter would 'rescue this trade out of the hands of strangers, ... prevent foreign shipping, and promote the English navigation', aims which the Commonwealth would eventually seek to advance not by issuing new charters, but through the Navigation Act.[79]

The failure to issue new charters suggests that the regime was lukewarm about supporting the companies against their interloping rivals, but it was at least listening to their complaints, and did not launch a direct assault. A case in point was the East India Company, which had faced competition throughout the 1640s from interlopers including Thomson and Fowke, who preferred to trade outside of the joint-stock framework and hoped to mimic the Dutch by founding colonial settlements in the east.[80] The failure of the Commonwealth to abolish the East India Company has been interpreted as a sign of its conservatism, but Brenner argued that the settlement it

177. His arguments against the export of bullion are in *The advancement of merchandize*, London 1651, 29–32.
[75] T&C, 65; Violet, *Mysteries*, 180.
[76] Robinson, *Englands safetie*, 37. For court merchant see ibid. 25–6, 33–4, and Violet, *Advancement*, 25–8.
[77] For Maddison's policies see his *Great Britains remembrancer, looking in and out*, London 1654.
[78] Petition dated 10 Dec. 1649, in Hinton, *Eastland trade*, 188–94.
[79] Ibid. 194.
[80] Brenner, *Merchants and revolution*, 168–81; *A calendar of the court minutes etc. of the East India Company, 1644–1649*, ed. E. B. Sainsbury, Oxford 1912, p. xi.

imposed in December 1649 fulfilled the 'free trade' demands of the new merchants.[81] However, this agreement, whereby Thomson's faction joined with members of the company to set up a new United Joint Stock, can be seen as a hostile corporate take-over, following which many members of the old board joined the new company, rather than the victory of one commercial ideology over another.[82] In any case, the matter was settled before the Council of Trade was formed; had it not been, the council probably would have counselled compromise, given that it included William Methwold of the old company. The council also supported the company's argument for being allowed to export bullion, helping to reverse parliament's original negative response.[83] Tellingly, their decision was made in part by scrutinising the previous licences issued to the company, showing a respect for legal precedence which reflected the regime's general attitude to restoring civil norms.

The council had been instructed to respond to calls for free trade on a wider scale, although it seems only to have intervened in those disputes brought before it. The contents of an unfinished report about the Spanish trade are unknown, but its approach in dealing with the Guinea and Greenland trades was pragmatic. In the 1640s Maurice Thomson had forced his way into the Guinea Company, which traded on the African Gold Coast, much as he had done with the East India Company, but the company continued to face competition from interlopers (Thomson amongst them), as well as the Dutch.[84] The council's response, issued in November 1650, was to suggest that an area of the coast be reserved exclusively for the company for fourteen years, with the rest (where the main trade was in slaves) left open.[85] A similar attitude prevailed regarding the Muscovy Company at Hull, which had petitioned against the presence of interlopers fishing for whales in the Greenland sounds. The council decided in the short term to allow the company to fish two sounds exclusively, with the interlopers to fish the others in a joint stock. By November 1651 this deal had still not been put into practice, however, and both parties were negotiating with the Council of Trade. Eventually the issue had to be settled by the Protectorate, which placed the regulation of the trade into the hands of a committee.[86]

Equally contested was the Newcastle coal trade, subject to bitter disputes

---

[81] Brenner, *Merchants and revolution*, 608–9.
[82] Ibid. 608–13. See also Coates, *Impact*, 187.
[83] *CJ* vi. 460–2, 513–14, 530–1.
[84] Brenner, *Merchants and revolution*, 163–5.
[85] W. R. Scott, *The constitution and finance of English, Scottish and Irish joint-stock companies to 1720*, ii, Cambridge 1910, 15–16; P. E. H. Hair and R. Law, 'The English in western Africa', in N. Canny (ed.), *Oxford history of the British empire*, I: *The origins of empire*, Oxford 1998, 253–4.
[86] *The proceedings at the Council for Trade, between the Muscovia Company, monopolizers of the trade to Green-Land, and others, adventurers thither, for a free-trade*, London 1652; Scott, *Joint-stock companies*, 72–4; Cooper, 'Social and economic policies', 132.

between ship-owners and members of the city corporation.[87] The council's final report to parliament, on 26 September 1651, attacked the restrictive practices pursued by the latter, although still in 1655 one opponent of the Newcastle magistracy was complaining that this report had 'lyen dormant ever since, to the great detriment of the Commonwealth in the excessive prizes of Coals'.[88] Such disputes were common in domestic trade and manufacturing, as various corporate interests struggled for precedence, and the council spent considerable time attempting to manage them.[89] As in foreign trade, civil war had disturbed the usual corporate regulation of manufacturing. The cloth trade was particularly contested, and throughout the summer of 1651 the council was attempting to persuade various parties to resolve their differences.[90] From the traditional cloth trade, it turned to the new draperies, issuing a report on dornix weaving in East Anglia. Further reports were drafted on the production of heavy dyed silk and cloth, Colchester bays, tin and gold and silver thread.

The council clearly accepted the established view that manufacturing demanded increased supervision to uphold quality, particularly in order to maintain the credit of English goods in foreign markets. Worsley justified such regulation in *The advocate*, noting 'The singular and prudent care' of the Dutch, 'in preserving the Credit of most of those Commodities which are their own proper Manufactures; By which they keep up the Repute and Sale of them abroad, taking hereby a very great advantage of the contrarie Neglect in us'.[91]

Although there was nothing new in the desire to institute effective regulation of manufacturing, the council's proposed method may have proven more innovative, if put into practice. On 22 September 1651 it reported on abuses in manufacturing, which were 'to the great detriment and cozenage of the Commonwealth', and resulted from companies being 'unskilful and negligent in the managing of the affairs of their government'.[92] It therefore recommended that parliament institute its own regular inspection of the companies. As Cooper concluded, 'The aim was regulation through corporate bodies themselves subject to review and regulation', a domestic version of the Navigation Act.[93] Having already reported to the Council of State on the need for 'reforming and settling all the inland trade and manufactures of

---

[87] R. Howell, *Newcastle Upon Tyne and the Puritan Revolution*, Oxford 1967, 305–7; Cooper, 'Social and economic policies', 138.

[88] R. Gardner, *Englands grievance discovered, in relation to the coal-trade*, London 1655, 59, 55–7.

[89] J. P. Cooper, 'Economic regulation and the cloth industry in seventeenth-century England', *TRHS* 5th ser. xx (1970), 73–99.

[90] Andrews, *Committees*, 26–7.

[91] B. Worsley, *The advocate: or, a narrative of the state and conditions of things between the English and Dutch nation, in relation to trade*, London 1651, 7.

[92] SP 18/16, fo. 54, printed in T&C, 255–6.

[93] Cooper, 'Social and economic policies', 133.

the nation under a certain way of government', Vane and Salwey repeated these pleas on 15 October.[94] However, by then the council's commission was coming to its end and the prospect of these plans being put into effect was declining. In December the council again reported that without such action 'whole trades and multitudes of men depending upon them' would 'be ruined and beggared, and our stock ... more and more lessened', but this was not enough to secure an extension of the council into 1652.[95]

More success was had in the promotion of inland navigation, with the council reporting on cutting the river Wye from Guildford to the Thames, and considered the Derbyshire Derwent amongst other rivers.[96] However, only the former was subject to an act of parliament, reflecting the difficulty of translating proposals into legislation.[97] In fact, it might be argued that the Council of Trade ultimately had little impact: one contemporary observer, the goldsmith and former royalist plotter Thomas Violet, certainly registered dissatisfaction with the regime's response to its reports.[98] However, as Violet's pamphlets show, the council did stimulate interest beyond Whitehall, becoming a focal point to many commercial appeals to the Commonwealth. Violet petitioned the council on several subjects, and claimed to have issued reports on its behalf.[99] He certainly printed some of the council's papers in his pamphlets, alongside his own petitions and arguments for reform of the merchant companies. Directing his proposals to the Council of Trade as 'the Master-workmen ... for the building of the trade of this Common-wealth', Violet launched a broad critique of merchant companies and demanded that foreign merchants be freely allowed to trade in England.[100] These, he argued, were the means by which commercial nations like the Netherlands became 'Warehouses and Shops for all the Merchandizes of the world', and 'by this waie you will make *England* truly *the Empress of the sea, when everie sea-port-town will bee an Amsterdam*'.[101]

Another writer to publish his addresses to the Council of Trade was Samuel Chappel, who petitioned on various matters of commercial and fiscal reform.[102] Amongst these was the idea of founding a national bank, and a similar project was presented to the council by William Potter, an associate of Robinson and Hartlib.[103] His idea was for a group of tradesmen to

[94] SP 18/16, fo. 76r.
[95] Ibid. no. 139, printed in T&C, 257.
[96] A&O ii. 404; CJ vi. 515, 542, 592–3.
[97] A&O ii. 514–17.
[98] Violet, *Mysteries*, 160. Robinson reported that 'the Councel of Trade are sayd to have prepared severall Bills' for the 'Recovery and Advancement of Trade': *Certain proposals in order to the peoples freedome and accomodation*, London 1652, 7.
[99] Violet, *Advancement*, 93–104.
[100] Ibid. 5.
[101] Ibid. 10–11.
[102] S. Chappel, *A diamond or rich jewel*, London 1651.
[103] 'Ephemerides', 1650, pt III, HP 28/1/68A.

pool their credit and issue bills of exchange, which would be accepted by specially designated shops, an 'invention' comparable to a 'MYNE *of* GOLD *discovered in this Land*'.[104] The secret relied on speeding up 'the revolution of commodities' by increasing the stock of money, allowing traders to make quick returns on their purchases.[105] Another way to overcome reliance on bullion was a land bank, a project supported by Culpeper, although Worsley was sceptical.[106] Potter's project did not receive the official support of the Commonwealth, but the following decades saw many similar schemes for land banks and paper credit, culminating in the foundation of the Bank of England in 1694.[107]

This was good publicity for the Council of Trade, and whilst most of its business was referred from the Council of State or parliament, it did receive several petitions directly. Worsley himself was petitioned by two bailiffs of the Corporation of Linne near Scarborough, who requested his aid in securing a more open market in coal, having already experienced his 'fauour in the furtherance of their iust Requests, for the takeing off, the greuious Oppression, and Discouragements of their Coale Trade'.[108] These examples suggest that the council was going some way to fulfilling its remit to represent the commerce of the whole nation. Furthermore, it was not just a reactive body, but sometimes took the initiative in contacting outside parties. The capital's merchant community was obviously important, and when considering the subject of convoys, the council directly consulted mercantile opinion on the exchange.[109] It also regularly summoned parties to attend or give their opinions in writing, for example calling on silk dyers to report on 'their reformation of heavy dyed Silke'.[110] Another body summoned to report on the textile industry was the trade committee of the city of London.[111] The council went further afield in seeking to fulfil its instruction to improve the fishery, writing to the local authorities of Aldeburgh in Suffolk, near Ipswich, for their opinion about 'promoting the ymprovement of the sayd Fishing Trade', in January 1651.[112] The corporation responded by advising

---

[104] W. Potter, *The key of wealth*, London 1650, 21. See also idem, *The trades-man's jewel*, London 1650, and *Humble proposalls to the honorable the Councell for Trade*, London 1651.

[105] Idem, *Key of wealth*, 5, 7, 2.

[106] This project was described in 'An essay upon Mr. W. *Potters* Designe concerning a bank of lands', probably written by Culpeper and published with Cressy Dymock's *A discovery for new divisions, or, setting out of lands*, London 1653. For Culpeper's authorship see M. Braddick and M. Greengrass, 'Introduction' to 'Culpeper letters', 132–3. For Worsley's doubts see 'Ephemerides', 1653, HP 28/2/75A.

[107] J. K. Horsefield, *British monetary experiments, 1650–1710*, London 1960.

[108] J. Harrison and J. Burton to Worsley, 24 Apr. 1651, HP 43/40A.

[109] *CJ* vi. 488–90.

[110] Report of the silkmen to the Council of Trade, HP 53/19A.

[111] *CSPD, 1651*, 270–1.

[112] Answer of the Aldeburgh Corporation to the Council of Trade, Suffolk Record Office, Ipswich, Aldeburgh borough records, EE1/P4/9.

that 'all Forreners may be debarred from bringing into this Common Wealth any kinde of Fishe whatsoever', a measure later included in the Navigation Act.[113] The most notable example of the council reaching out to the commercial nation was in its considerations regarding free ports, discussed below, when it sought opinion from various merchant parties and ports.

Thus, despite its lack of executive power and its relatively short duration, the Council of Trade possessed significance beyond the functional. It can be seen as contributing to the image of the Commonwealth as a regime devoted to the defence of trade, simultaneously restoring commercial normality after the dislocation of war, and advancing national prosperity in a way fitting for this new and flourishing republic.

The fruits of office

For many of Worsley's associates, the declaration of the Commonwealth presented an opportunity to participate in the imaginative creation of a new regime. Already before Worsley's return to England John Sadler had defended it in print, whilst Dury became chief apologist for the Engagement, and Hall was employed on the regime's newspaper, Mercurius Politicus.[114] As the regime became more firmly established, defeating its many enemies at home and abroad, such propaganda increasingly moved from defending the republican regime to celebrating its superiority over monarchy, exemplified in the triumphalist rhetoric of another associate of Hartlib, John Milton, and other classical republicans.[115] In terms of trade, the emphasis shifted somewhat from defence to its aggressive promotion by a state invigorated by fiscal, military and naval transformation. The relationship between trade and republicanism is complex, and the classical roots of the latter is sometimes seen as making it irreconcilable with commercial society, although as Scott has noted commerce was hardly absent from the classical world.[116] However, rather than being inspired by classical examples, those who celebrated the Commonwealth's commercial policy could equally draw inspiration from a vernacular republican tradition, which celebrated commonwealth values, civic self-government and the English nation itself.[117] Another influential political philosophy making an impact in the early 1650s was that of Thomas

---

[113] A&O ii. 560.

[114] J. Peacey, Politicians and pamphleteers: propaganda during the English civil wars and Interregnum, Aldershot 2004, 98, 105–6, 128–9, 186, 198–200.

[115] Worsley's Catalogus listed Milton's first and second Defences of the republic, Sadler's Rights of the kingdom, and a collected run of Mercurius Politicus from June 1650 to September 1653. For this literature see J. Scott, Commonwealth principles: republican writing of the English Revolution, Cambridge 2004.

[116] Scott, Commonwealth principles, 94.

[117] Kelsey, Inventing, 97, 106–7, 202–6. See also P. Withington, The politics of commonwealth: citizens and freemen in early modern England, Cambridge 2005.

Hobbes, an author well represented in Worsley's *Catalogus*, perhaps because he too believed in strong state power. William Rand certainly thought that Worsley would find in *Leviathan* 'many things to your palate, though some which I thinke sufficient to procure a gentle vomit, where the contemplation of royall majesty had dazeld the good Gentlemans senses'.[118]

It seems that some of the regime's growing mood of self-confidence rubbed off on Worsley, as he enjoyed the perks of the job. Signs of this are occasionally recorded in Hartlib's 'Ephemerides', as when the two dined with the Master of the Mint Aaron Guerden, who showed them 'some of the late king's goods', including a red coral salt-cellar worth £1,000, and a 'cup of Vnicorne set in gold of 500. lb. price'.[119] Worsley's personal situation had certainly improved, and he could now afford to dispense patronage, for example to the urban reformer John Lanyon.[120] Another new contact arrived from New England in late 1650, namely the prodigious alchemist George Starkey, who was soon involved in experimental activity with Boyle and others of Hartlib's circle. Worsley attempted to enlist Starkey for his own projects, and the American was nearly swayed by this 'ingenious Gentleman'.[121] The venture which Worsley hoped that Starkey would join was a collaboration involving Moriaen and a consortium from Amsterdam, which had purchased from Glauber details of 'a process of extracting gold from tin scoria'.[122] Serious money was tied up in this venture, about which Moriaen and Worsley were corresponding in 1650–1, although Moriaen became increasingly disillusioned with Worsley's minimal contributions and was eventually forced to withdraw having accrued great losses.[123] Worsley continued to take an interest in scientific experimentation, writing a letter on husbandry at Hartlib's request, and planning to 'make a Club for the perfecting of Mechanical Arts' along with two physicians and future Fellows of the Royal Society, Christopher Merret and Daniel Whistler.[124] But more lucrative opportunities were soon on the horizon.

Through his work Worsley had established various mercantile contacts, and he made at least one attempt to exploit these for material gain. On 10 December 1651, with his salary on the council shortly to expire, Worsley made an offer of £5,600 to the East India Company to purchase its dockyard at Blackwall, which had become a burden ever since the company had begun

---

[118] Rand to Worsley, 11 Aug. 1651, HP 62/21/1A. Worsley's *Catalogus* listed eight works by Hobbes, although not *Leviathan*.

[119] 'Ephemerides', 1650, pt I, HP 28/1/44A.

[120] M. Jenner, '"Another epocha"? Hartlib, John Lanyon and the improvement of London in the 1650s', in *SHUR*, 343–56.

[121] Quoted in W. Newman, 'Newton's *Clavis* as Starkey's *Key*', *Isis* lxxviii (1987), 567. See also Newman and Principe, *Alchemy tried in the fire*, 245–7.

[122] Young, *Faith*, 226.

[123] Ibid. 226–32.

[124] S. Hartlib (ed.), *Samuel Hartlib his legacie of husbandry*, 3rd edn, London 1655, 105–6; 'Ephemerides', 1650, pt I, HP 28/1/77A.

to freight rather than build ships.[125] Worsley requested to move some timber into the yard, suggesting that he planned a ship-building venture (perhaps anticipating a post-Navigation Act boom in the industry).[126] Unfortunately, this project soon ran into problems, and on 28 February 1652 he appeared before the company's court, equivocating about raising the necessary fine.[127] One of his backers had pulled out, ending Worsley's brief foray into business.

Soon Worsley returned to the security of a state salary. It seems that the mercantile contacts he made while working for the Commonwealth were less important than the access this gave him to powerful politicians. Particularly important was Vane, the most illustrious figure on the Council of Trade and a major figure in the regime. Vane is most known for his religious mysticism, which led him to call for the separation of Church and State and toleration for the sects, but he was also an effective politician and administrator of the navy.[128] Religiously, Vane shared a neoplatonic strain within English Puritanism which stressed the status of reason as a divine faculty, and which had the potential to depart from orthodox Calvinism.[129] Perhaps Worsley, who was similarly uncommitted to liturgical forms, was one of those figures who congregated around Vane (he introduced Vane's close ally and fellow council member, Richard Salwey, to Hartlib).[130] A rival for patronage from the likes of Vane was William Petty, who complained about Worsley 'aspersing mee to Sir H. Vane, [and] our frends at St Iames' (the latter no doubt including Lady Ranelagh at Pall Mall).[131] Worsley's existing rivalry with Petty was thus developing into the bitter conflict which would eventually threaten to ruin both men.

But for the time being, Worsley must have felt confident about his prospects, a successful servant of a regime beginning to make its mark on the world. Given its inauspicious beginnings, the military successes of the Commonwealth in 1650 seemed to some of its defenders to prove the superiority of this form of government, and at the end of that year such republicans were given further cause to celebrate. Across the channel, the pro-Stuart

---

[125] *A calendar of the court minutes etc. of the East India Company, 1650–1654*, ed. E. B. Sainsbury, Oxford 1912, pp. xxix, 40.

[126] Ibid. 145.

[127] Ibid. 157, 159.

[128] R. Mayers, 'Real and practicable, not imaginary and notional: Sir Henry Vane, *A healing question*, and the problems of the Protectorate', *Albion* xxvii (1995), 37–72; D. Parnham, 'Politics spun out of theology and prophecy: Sir Henry Vane on the spiritual environment of public power', *HPT* xxii (2001), 53–83.

[129] Scott, *Commonwealth principles*, 44–9, 160–4.

[130] 'Ephemerides', 1650, pt III, HP 28/1/64A. For Worsley's continued association with Vane see chapters 4 and 6 below.

[131] Petty to Hartlib, 23 Oct. 1653, HP (Marshal and Osborn Collection, doc. 23); L. Sharp, 'Sir William Petty and some aspects of seventeenth-century natural philosophy', unpub. DPhil diss. Oxford 1977, 91; Petty to Hartlib, 1 Mar. 1653, HP (Marshal and Osborn Collection, doc. 24).

stadholder of the United Provinces, William II of Orange, had died without an adult heir, leaving the republican regents of Holland in control.[132] This presented the Commonwealth with a providential opportunity to draw closer to its fellow Protestant republic, surmounting the strains of commercial rivalry. The negotiations for an Anglo-Dutch union, and their eventual failure, would have profound impact on the Commonwealth's commercial policy, and would provide the occasion for its most famous piece of legislation.

Trade's advocate: free ports and the Navigation Act

The threat posed to England's commercial independence by Dutch shipping had been clear to Worsley, indeed to most observers, even before the boom which he had witnessed in Amsterdam. The 1650 act for the colonies had imposed some measure of protection against the competition of Dutch merchants in the Americas, but the complaints of the merchant companies had revealed a deeper problem. A regime so soaked in patriotic rhetoric, and obsessed with raising England's reputation internationally, was unlikely to tolerate this state for long. Accordingly the Council of Trade reported on the subject of the 'restraint of goods of foreign growth to be imported in foreign bottoms' to the Council of State, on 4 April 1651.[133]

The situation, however, was complicated by the fact that the Dutch were fellow Protestants, and potential allies against the Catholic Habsburgs, making some sort of union attractive. This was the intended outcome of a Vane-backed parliamentary mission to The Hague, conducted by Oliver St John and Walter Strickland, which was in negotiation in May and June.[134] This was precisely the point when the Council of Trade was considering the possibility of opening free ports, a measure explicitly aimed at imitating the Dutch entrepôt by allowing the storage of goods for re-export at little or no custom, which had been adopted with success at Dover in the 1630s.[135] Commercial union might allow Dutch merchants access to this system without endangering English trade. As Ralph Maddison put it, without such a union the Dutch would 'make our Ports their store houses; and become thereby Huxters amongst us, which were too much unless they were incorporated one Nation with us'.[136]

The most difficult question for the Council of Trade therefore was to decide whether or not to allow foreign ships access to free ports. As Brenner noted, the council considered both positions, suggesting first that foreign goods

[132] Pincus, *Protestantism and patriotism*, 15–17.
[133] T&C, 64.
[134] Pincus, *Protestantism and patriotism*, 24–35.
[135] J. S. Kepler, *The exchange of Christendome: the international entrepôt at Dover, 1622–1651*, Leicester 1976; Violet, *Advancement*, 3.
[136] Maddison, *Great Britains remembrancer*, 38.

should be admitted 'if Imported in English Bottoms', but then concluding 'that all Nations in Amity be admitted the benefit of this Free Scale in their own vessells'.[137] This was amongst the questions which the council posed to three groups of merchants in April 1651, one consisting of leading company merchants, another of foreign merchants trading to England, and a third unnamed group probably representing the new merchants.[138] All three groups responded favourably, although they differed on the point of whether to give access to foreign shipping.[139] Brenner suggested that the new merchants were orchestrating the proposal, but it is surely significant that they were consulted as an external party, rather than as a part of the council itself.[140] The council also called on the expert advice of Trinity House, and invited the outports to petition for free port status. Dover petitioned most vigorously, as the town authorities joined with merchants to argue for its ideal situation for an entrepôt trade, but the council also received petitions from Plymouth, Barnstable, the Isle of Wight, Southampton and Portsmouth.[141]

This seems to have concerned London's authorities, who feared that free port privileges could be used to draw trade away from the capital, and in June the court of aldermen ordered that John Fowke, their representative on the Council of Trade, keep them informed.[142] In December they petitioned to make London a free port. By then, however, union proposals with the Dutch had broken down, and the problem of competition had returned to the fore. On 31 July the council reported again on the need to restrain imports in foreign shipping, with the Navigation Act being put to parliament only a few days later, before being passed on 9 October. No doubt Oliver St John's anger at having been spurned in The Hague hastened its passage, but this act was undoubtedly intended to provide the protection which English shipping had seemed to require long before his failed embassy. Thus it ensured that imports into England and its colonies from outside of Europe were to be made only in English owned and manned ships, whilst European goods were to be imported either in English ships or in ships owned by the country of production.[143] Clearly the main objective was to bar imports in Dutch ships, although the export trade was left open. Whilst the promotion of English shipping had been a long-term goal of commercial policy, this had generally been achieved through company charters rather than national legislative measures, and in this sense the Navigation Act was an important departure.[144]

[137] MS Add. 5138, fo. 145r; Brenner, *Merchants and revolution*, 614.
[138] Brenner, *Merchants and revolution*, 618.
[139] MS Add. 5138, fos 146r–v.
[140] Brenner, *Merchants and revolution*, 618–24.
[141] MS Add. 5138, fos 152r–164r
[142] Andrews, *Committees*, 29.
[143] L. A. Harper, *The English navigation laws: a seventeenth-century experiment in social engineering*, New York 1939, 48. The act is printed in *A&O* ii. 559–62.
[144] Bliss, *Revolution and empire*, 58–9; Cooper, 'Social and economic policies', 135; Braddick, *State formation*, 411–14.

By imposing a simplified framework on a complex commercial situation, the act inevitably attracted criticisms, which the Council of Trade responded to in its final report. Those merchants who had relied on freighting Dutch ships, probably Merchant Adventurers, would have suffered most immediately.[145] Another complaint was that the act favoured London over provincial merchants, 'for most of the out ports not capable of Foreign Trade to Indies and Turkey, the Londoners having the Sole Trade, do sett what price they please upon their Comoditys'.[146] In response, the regime published a brief pamphlet outlining its commercial logic, printed on behalf of the Council of State by its usual printer William Dugard. Although anonymous, the author was in fact Benjamin Worsley, something first noticed by R. W. K. Hinton.[147]

The title page of *The advocate* announced that it was to be sold by Nicholas Bourne at his shop on the Exchange. As such, it was clearly aimed at a mercantile audience, but it can also be seen as part of the regime's broader propaganda drive.[148] Its frontispiece thus bore the same patriotic emblem as Milton's propaganda works, namely the coat of arms of the Council of State which incorporated St George's cross, and was written under the patriotic pseudonym *Philopatris*.[149] The first imprint in early 1652 (with the preface bearing the date 11 February 1651/2) was probably aimed principally at critics of the act, but its republication later that year might have been part of the regime's propaganda campaign against the Dutch in the lead-up to war.

Subtitled 'A narrative of the state and condition of things between the *English* and *Dutch* nation, in relation to trade', the pamphlet comprised a report 'presented in *August* 1651', possibly from the Council of Trade to the Council of State.[150] It began, however, with a preface whose millenarian tone has led it to be described by Pincus as 'apocalyptic economics'.[151] Here, Worsley declared that 'I dare not but own the Belief of the Coming of his Appearance, and the breaking forth, very shortly, of his Glorie', seeming to suggest that the Navigation Act did indeed fit into some apocalyptic scheme.[152] For Webster, too, here was a clear example of millenarian utopianism providing the motivation for practical social policies.[153] However, rather than describing the post-millennial condition, the preface to *The advocate* lingered on the apocalypse itself, 'a sight very strange, and very unexpected to men; ... in som measure even contrarie (and perhaps, very unwelcom) unto the most enlarged and raised thoughts wee have yet

---

[145] Ormrod, *Rise of commercial empires*, 35.
[146] Captain John Limbrey's 'Propositions concerning the Advice of Trade', MS Add. 5138, fo. 165v.
[147] Hinton, *Eastland trade*, 89–94.
[148] Peacey, *Politicians and pamphleteers*, 268.
[149] Kelsey, *Inventing the Republic*, 97.
[150] Worsley, *The advocate*, 1.
[151] Pincus, *Protestantism and patriotism*, 48.
[152] Worsley, *The advocate*, sig. B1r.
[153] Webster, *Great instauration*, 465.

prepared out selvs with, to receiv it'.[154] This 'Coming' would be signified by 'the stripping men of that Honor, Credit, and Repute' which lay behind 'the whole Indeavors, Practice, Studie and Wisdom (if not Religion) of All States, Ages, Nations and Men'.[155] But Worsley found no easy consolation in these expectations, professing uncertainty about the inscrutable will of God:

> not knowing what the Councils of God intend to bring forth for the settlement of this Nation; Nor how hee hath resolved in his Wisdom to dispose of it, (as to its outward Condition,) whether Hee intends wee shall bee oppressed by other Nations about us, that hee may the more manifest his Power and Protection over us: Or that wee shall bee advanced in Prosperitie above others, that so hee may perhaps shew us our vanitie ... not knowing this, I can as little judge what means Providence will pleas to use in order to the bringing to pass these his purposes, whether hee will chuse This, or reject That.[156]

The Commonwealth was unable to see clearly its providential destiny, but this did not preclude it from taking care of its 'outward Condition' through trade. Thus, rather than fitting easily into some apocalyptic schema, the Navigation Act was here presented as a secular expedient fashioned in the absence of clear guidance from above, an act of self-preservation in an amoral world of commercial competition:

> It is by Trade, and the due ordering and governing of it, and by no other means, that Wealth and Shipping can either bee encreased, or upheld; and consequently by no other, that the power of any Nation can bee susteined by Land, or by Sea: It beeing not possible ... according to the Cours of humane affairs, for anie Nation (having no Mines to supplie it self) to make it self powerful in either of these (this is, either Monies or Shipping) without Trade, and the Cours of it.[157]

The pamphlet's main section began by citing the recurring fear of zealous English Protestants before the Civil War, namely 'the Design of *Spain* ... to get the Universal Monarchie of Christendom'.[158] Of equal danger, however, were Dutch designs 'to laie a foundation to themselvs for ingrossing the Universal Trade, not onely of Christendom, but indeed, of the greater part of the known world'. Their hope was to 'poiz the Affairs of any other State about them, and make their own Considerable, if not by the Largeness of their Countrie; yet, however, by the Greatness of their Wealth; and by their potencie at Sea, in strength and multitude of Shipping'.[159] For evidence

[154] Worsley, *The advocate*, sig. B1r.
[155] Ibid. sig. B1v.
[156] Ibid. sig. B2r.
[157] Ibid. 12.
[158] Ibid. 1.
[159] Ibid. 1–2.

of these designs, Worsley drew on the complaints of various commercial interests, for example the Eastland Company, whose shipping had apparently fallen from 200 sail a year to 'scarce twenty' (*The advocate* gave similar figures).[160]

Dutch commercial domination was supported by 'the great number of Shipping they have constantly built; and … the manner of managing their Trade and Shipping, in a conformitie and direction to their Grand End'.[161] Worsley therefore presented an account of the efficiency of Dutch shipping and convoying. By such means, Dutch freight rates undercut English ones by as much as 20 per cent, which had ultimately 'Compelled our Nation … to hire and freight the *Holland* shipping'.[162] Although freighting Dutch ships allowed English merchants to stay afloat, this was at great cost to English shipping, introducing the possibility of an alarming downward spiral to dependency:

> For this method and manner of managing their affairs, daily adding to *their* stock, and answerably diminishing the Stock and Treasure of *this Nation*: and by laying it so, as it *run* thus in a Circle, each part of it … strengthening another part: it would unavoidably have tended to a greater and greater disenabling us to hold anie Trade with them: and to have made themselvs, for Wealth and Shipping, the Masters over us.[163]

Thus the Navigation Act, 'so happily and timely established by the Parliament', was intended to rescue the nation from a dangerous condition of dependency.[164] It took as its model the policies of the Dutch republic itself, which was zealous in '*making this their Care and Protection of Trade abroad in all places their Interest of State*'.[165] However, the Dutch example could be applied in more positive ways, and this was the argument in *The advocate's* sister pamphlet *Free ports*, in which Worsley presented what were probably the Council of Trade's findings on the subject.[166] Although ultimately the free ports project went the same way as Anglo-Dutch union, the publication of this pamphlet in 1652, again bearing the arms of the Council of State, shows that it still had its supporters.

Nations, Worsley began, were divided into those that relied on others for their shipping, and those that provided this service: from this situation 'doth arise the wisdom of som Nations in fetching Commodities from the places of their Growth at that fit and seasonable time, and storing them up till the Necessitie of other Nations to call for them'.[167] By mastering this trade,

---

[160] Hinton, *Eastland trade*, 189, 191; Worsley, *The advocate*, 6.
[161] Worsley, *The advocate*, 3.
[162] Ibid. 4.
[163] Ibid. 6.
[164] Ibid. 13.
[165] Ibid. 9.
[166] B.W[orsley], *Free ports, the nature and necessitie of them stated*, London 1652.
[167] Ibid. 1.

the United Provinces had become 'a rich and general Magazine or Store ... for other Nations'.[168] Carrying the commodities of northern and north-east Europe into England, France and Portugal, and then bringing back goods from southern Europe and the East and West Indies northwards, the Dutch were able to place 'their whole Interest in the encouragement and sagacious Managerie of this Cours and Circle of Traffique'.[169] But the Dutch were no better situated to perform this re-export trade than England, which had the advantage of superior native and colonial commodities, as well as 'the Freedom and Independencie that our Shipping have upon the Ports of any other State, or Nation', and excellent coasts and harbours.[170] Unfortunately, the current basis of English trade was 'onely for Consumption', and therefore 'confined to a Stock, and such a Stock as must not exceed its own expence or Consumption'.[171]

Free ports would therefore 'move this Nation to undertake the like general Mart, as hath the Hollander'.[172] This would have multiple benefits: 'to the Quickning of Trade; to the Imploiment of the poor throughout the whole Common-wealth: to the making of all Forreign Commodities more cheap, and more plentiful ... to the raising the Exchange, and bringing in of Bullion: to the augmenting of the Revenue of the State: and to the making other Nations more dependent upon this'.[173] Like the Navigation Act, free ports would increase 'the Power and Strength of this Nation, both by Land and Sea'. However, Worsley specifically rejected the most literal interpretation of the balance of trade, arguing that trade was more complex than this:

> Wherefore all Consultations whatsoever about Trade if *Free Ports* bee not opened, and this Whole-sale or General Trade bee not incouraged, do still but terminate in som Advice or other about Regulating our Consumption, and have no other good at farthest, but preventional; *that our Balance of Import exceed not our Export*: which to confine our selvs to alone, is, on the other side, a Cours so short, as it will neither serv to rais the Strenght of this Nation in Shipping, or to Govern the Exchange abroad; nor yet to avoid the Damage and Mischief the Subtiltie of the foreign Merchant will hereby bring upon us.[174]

This was no narrow 'mercantilist' orthodoxy, therefore, and for Worsley free ports would introduce a dramatic change in the commercial base of the nation:

> For a Nation to deal or traffique in Wares and Merchandizes for its own expence and consumption, as countrie Gentlemen, or ordinarie Trades-men; And for a Nation to make its self a shop, and to buy and sell for the

168   Ibid. 2.
169   Ibid. 3.
170   Ibid. 5.
171   Ibid. 7.
172   Ibid. 3.
173   Ibid. 4.
174   Ibid. 8.

furnishing and provision of other Nations; as a man that keep's a Ware-hous, or Store-hous; which latter Trade is that wee speak of.[175]

This vision of commercial transformation represents perhaps the height of the ambitions of the Council of Trade: the state taking action not just to defend the nation's trade, but to consciously transform it. However, the Navigation Act rather than free ports would be the commercial legacy of the Commonwealth. This act has recently been described as 'staggeringly ambitious' in its goal to 'create an overarching national monopoly within which English shipping and long-distance trade could develop'.[176] In the immediate term, the Navigation Act contributed to, although did not directly cause, the growing Anglo-Dutch tension which would break out into war in July 1652. This was a blow to Protestant internationalists like Hartlib and Dury who had enthusiastically supported the plans for union, as well as to Vane, although he led the war effort on the admiralty committee once it had begun.[177] Even before then Worsley was on the look-out for a new post, as the Council of Trade was discontinued at the end of 1651, possibly in part because of the deterioration in Anglo-Dutch relations. Fortunately, his work for the previous two years had raised his profile amongst the Commonwealth's leading politicians, and another commission was not far away.

This chapter has sought to understand the Council of Trade in terms of the patriotic, self-confident commonwealth rhetoric cultivated by the regime's defenders. Generally seeking to restore commercial normality and thus buttress the legitimacy of the regime, the Council of Trade none the less had a potentially more assertive agenda based not so much on 'free trade' as 'governed trade', as the state took over some of the governmental functions of the merchant companies in order to advance and transform commerce. The Navigation Act was the major legacy of this proactive approach, free ports its notable failure, and it would be wrong to trumpet the council's significance without acknowledging its limitations. However, it did contribute to a perception, which grew in hindsight, that the Commonwealth era was a time of commercial prosperity, something evoked by critics of the Protectorate and the restored monarchy alike.[178] Although in many senses it was fashioned in a context of insecurity and with a defensive outlook, what was remembered of the Commonwealth's commercial policy therefore tended to be its self-confident and aggressively nationalistic aspect. This dimension is illustrated nowhere better, perhaps, than in the two pamphlets that Benjamin Worsley authored on the republican regime's behalf.

[175] Ibid. 7.

[176] Ormrod, *Rise of commercial empires*, 32.

[177] For Hartlib and Dury's support of Anglo-Dutch union see their prefaces to the apocalyptic tract *Clavis apocalyptica: or, a prophetical key*, London 1651, probably written by Abraham von Frankenburg.

[178] See, for example, S. Bethel, *The world's mistake in Oliver Cromwell*, London 1668.

4

Ireland, 1652–1656

The land survey

When Benjamin Worsley first left Ireland in 1644, he joined an exodus of Protestant settlers fleeing in the face of the Catholic Confederate's advances. But by the time that he was looking for a new commission, eight years later, prospects were much brighter for the aspiring colonist. Worsley was amongst those who descended on Ireland to capitalise on the Cromwellian re-conquest; fatefully, on the same voyage was another ambitious Englishman who would soon become Worsley's intractable rival, William Petty.

Petty and Worsley were both attracted by the potential of Ireland, where (as Petty later recalled), 'many endeavours' were underway 'to regulate, replant, and reduce that countrey to its former flourishing condition'.[1] However, Petty was to prove much the more successful in exploiting this situation, establishing himself as a major landowner with his earnings from the land survey. Intellectually, Petty used the 'Down Survey' to develop what he would later call 'political arithmetic', his Hobbesian science of government, of which Ireland would become a model example.[2] But for Worsley the experience was far less positive. Following the humiliation of being supplanted by his former collaborator, Worsley turned to increasingly mystical reflections, under the influence of those army radicals who would eventually overthrow Henry Cromwell's rule in Dublin in 1659, which Worsley participated in by assisting the attempt to impeach Petty. He became somewhat intellectually isolated in Ireland, distant from his former collaborators in the Hartlib circle and alienated from Petty's circle, who were laying down the roots of the new science in Ireland.[3] Ireland thus brought disappointment for Worsley, and Barnard argued that 'service there was an unimportant episode in his life'.[4] Indeed the experience had little positive impact, but in terms of his intellectual biography, his disillusionment was significant.

Worsley arrived in Ireland, in October 1652, as secretary to the parlia-

---

[1] W. Petty, *History of the Cromwellian survey of Ireland, A.D. 1655–6, commonly called the 'Down Survey'*, ed. T. C. Larcom, Dublin 1851, 1.

[2] Sharp, 'William Petty', 137; Webster, *Great instauration*, 438–42; Goblet, *Transformation*, i; P. Buck, 'Seventeenth-century political arithmetic: civil strife and vital statistics', *Isis* lxviii (1977), 67–84.

[3] The Irish interests of the Hartlib circle Ireland are covered in detail in Barnard, *Cromwellian Ireland*, 213–48, and 'The Hartlib circle and the origins of the Dublin Philosophical Society', *IHS* xix (1974–5), 56–71.

[4] Barnard, *Cromwellian Ireland*, 222.

mentary commissioners led by Fleetwood, with Petty the chief physician.[5] Clearly Worsley had acquitted himself well enough on the Council of Trade to continue his ascent in the state's service, his annual salary now reaching £400.[6] Worsley also retained contacts amongst several leading Irish Protestants, principally through the Boyle family. However, the influence of these 'old Protestants' was momentarily on the wane, although Worsley continued to deal with them as secretary to the commissioners at Dublin Castle.[7] They would have to wait for the rule of Henry Cromwell in the second half of the decade to reverse this, in the face of opposition from the radicals in the army. Petty's association with the former led Worsley naturally to lean to the latter, although he did not sever his links with the Boyles. The land settlement would be one theatre for these factional struggles, and so Worsley and Petty became drawn into a contest over the future of English rule of Ireland.

Before then, however, Worsley nearly left Ireland altogether. In April 1653 he was nominated by the Commonwealth's Committee for Trade and Foreign Affairs for the post of secretary to Viscount Lisle's embassy to Sweden, a commercially important location.[8] This was not his first connection with Lisle, the eldest son of Robert Sidney, the earl of Leicester: six years earlier Worsley had been nominated to serve under him as surgeon-general in Ireland, where Lisle was lord-lieutenant and figurehead of the Irish 'Independents'.[9] However, this appointment proved as stillborn as the last: having returned to London, Worsley found that Lisle had been replaced by Bulstrode Whitelocke, nullifying his commission.[10] In June he was granted £50 as compensation for his wasted journey, but in his absence the post he had left back in Dublin had been filled.[11] Fortunately, a potentially more rewarding opportunity had arisen just as he returned to London.

During summer 1653 Cromwell's nominated parliament was in the process

---

[5] Fleetwood was proclaimed commander in chief of the army in Ireland on 24 August 1652, joining Edmund Ludlow, John Jones, John Weaver and Miles Corbet as a parliamentary commissioner: ibid. 17–18.

[6] The commission appointing Worsley to this role has not been located; he was paid £200 on 20 March 1653, about six months after beginning the job: J. O'Hart, *The Irish and the Anglo-Irish landed gentry*, Dublin 1969, 244.

[7] HMC, *Sixty-third report: manuscripts of the earl of Egmont*, i, ed. S. C. Lomas, London 1905, 515, 522.

[8] *CSPD, 1652–3*, 272.

[9] See chapter 1 above. For the Irish 'Independents' see P. Little, 'The Irish "Independents" and Viscount Lisle's lieutenancy of Ireland', *HJ* xliv (2001), 941–61.

[10] John Dury, however, joined this embassy, carrying copies of Worsley's pamphlets and reporting from Stockholm that 'his Aduocate is here extremely well liked, & … I have imparted it to the Lord Chancelour Oxenstiern who finds it a solid peace; the Queene also spoke of it yesterday unto me; & told me that shee had seene it transcribed into the Swedish tongue': Dury to Hartlib, 14 May 1652, HP 4/2/19A. Hartlib probably circulated translations of these pamphlets around his circle, which would explain the existence of a German translation of *Free ports* in the Hartlib papers (HP 31/23/32–5).

[11] *CSPD, 1652–3*, 395.

of laying down the legislative framework to redistribute land confiscated from Irish rebels. The basis of this settlement stretched back to 1642, when parliament had enlisted private capital to pay for re-conquest by offering a share of Irish land to those 'adventurers' who invested in this venture.[12] Implementation of this finally began in July 1653, when a committee of adventurers at Grocers' Hall in London opened their lottery to determine the distribution of land.[13] The principle that land confiscated from Catholic rebels should pay for re-conquest was extended to the military in June 1653, allowing arrears owed to members of the Irish army to be settled by land grants. On 26 September 1653 it was enacted that confiscated land was to satisfy these two debts, to be divided equally between soldiers and adventurers.[14] Whereas the adventurers were to have considerable freedom in allocating their share, the army's moiety was under the supervision of the parliamentary commissioners, and the act gave further instructions to this effect. Thus the commissioners were empowered to make 'a gross survey' of all available lands, prior to an 'exact and perfect survey and admeasurement', to be conducted by a surveyor-general.[15] This officer was to oversee the measurement of all forfeited lands 'by their qualities, quantities, names, situation, parish or place'. Worsley appears to have taken the post of surveyor-general in October 1653, his £400 salary paid half in lands.

Worsley held this post until January 1658. However, after December 1654 the survey was effectively administered by Petty, although Worsley fought a war of attrition to maintain his influence.[16] Petty was meticulous in documenting his administration of the survey, but this distorts our knowledge of its course under Worsley's stewardship, evidence for which is sparse, a problem exacerbated by confusion between the various 'gross', 'civil' and 'down' surveys. Undoubtedly on taking up his commission Worsley faced a complex task: first it was necessary to determine the extent of confiscated lands available for allocation, which required intelligence from locals.[17] Worsley's main task was to survey the soldiers' lands, but it was necessary first to determine the total amount of forfeited land which would then be divided between the soldiers and adventurers. Only then could the more detailed survey commence, from which individual parcels of land would be allocated. However, the instructions which Worsley was following until April 1654 demonstrate only a partial awareness of these logistical difficulties.[18] The first step was to assemble a register of forfeited lands, which would

---

[12] K. Bottigheimer, *English money and Irish land: the 'Adventurers' in the Cromwellian settlement of Ireland*, Oxford 1971, 40.
[13] Petty, *Cromwellian survey*, 368–70.
[14] Ibid. 353–68.
[15] Ibid. 370.
[16] E. Strauss, *Sir William Petty: portrait of a genius*, London 1954, 58–60.
[17] Petty himself would complain about the complexity of the enterprise: *Cromwellian survey*, 119–25.
[18] Printed ibid. 370–1. See Goblet, *Transformation*, 170–1.

be done by commissioners holding courts throughout the country. Following this there was to be a rough survey of forfeited lands 'mentioning only in gross' the contents of lands, which would then be sent to Worsley in Dublin, who would forward a copy to the adventurers at Grocers' Hall for their lottery. Meanwhile, the surveyor-general was to consider means to produce a 'gross survey', with 'less expence, and in a shorter time', postponing 'a more exact admeasurement' until the 'allotment of each person's respective proportion'.[19]

This emphasis on speed, in fact, led to the initial 'gross survey' being conducted even before proper information about forfeited estates had been gathered. Eventually this would be the subject of a separate survey, the 'civil survey' which was undertaken from June 1654 to 1656. Petty would later complain about delays in being supplied with the 'terriers' of the civil survey, books of information about the proprietorial and economic status of individual baronies. The fact that Worsley's surveyors had to work without this information can explain some of the weaknesses of the gross survey, which was carried out from November 1653 to April 1654, and was intended both to gather information about confiscated lands and to estimate (but not accurately measure or map) their size.[20] Very little information survives of this stage of survey; a rare example suggests that it provided only minimal information.[21] Unsurprisingly, it was soon recognised to be unsatisfactory, although a copy of the survey was sent to the adventurers to use in their allocation.[22] The original instructions had always envisaged a progression from the gross survey to a survey by admeasurement, but these problems hastened the demise of the former as it was realised that no division could take place on such inaccurate grounds.

On 14 April 1654 Worsley was ordered to terminate the gross survey and put the survey by measurement into action.[23] Over the following months he issued payments to his surveyors.[24] Goblet condemned this stage of the survey as a waste of money, but it is harsh to blame Worsley for the flawed instructions he was following.[25] Worsley remained in control of the surveying process throughout spring 1654 as instructions for the next stage were drawn up, working with Petty's friends Sir Anthony Morgan and Miles Symner on

[19] Petty, *Cromwellian survey*, 371.
[20] R. Simmington, 'Introduction' to *The civil survey, AD 1654–1656*, Dublin 1931, pp. iii–x; J. G. Simms, 'The civil survey, 1654–6', *IHS* ix (1955), 257–61.
[21] Printed in W. H. Hardinge, 'On manuscript mapped and other townland surveys in Ireland of a public character, embracing the Gross, Civil, and Down surveys, from 1640 to 1688', *Transactions of the Royal Irish Academy: Antiquities* xxiv (1873), 39–40. For the Gross Survey see Petty, *Cromwellian survey*, 313, and Goblet, *Transformation*, 171.
[22] R. Dunlop, *Ireland under the Commonwealth*, ii, Manchester 1913, 510–11.
[23] Ibid. 418–19.
[24] Hardinge, 'On manuscript mapped and other townland surveys', 11–12; 'Commonwealth state accounts, 1653–56', ed. E. MacLysaght, *Analecta Hibernia* xv (1944), 246.
[25] Goblet, *Transformation*, 173.

planning a new survey throughout the summer.[26] Petty was to reserve his criticisms for the survey that resulted from these deliberations, rather than for the gross survey.

If the nature of the gross survey is obscure, the survey by measurement which followed from May to September 1654 is even more so. It has been confused with the civil survey (which commenced in June 1654), but in fact they were two entirely different enterprises.[27] Following the gross survey it was decided to separate the jobs of reconnaissance and measurement, the former being conducted by commissioners gathering information from local inhabitants, which would then be used by the surveyors conducting the latter.[28] Worsley was to concentrate on organising the survey by measurement, which would provide information detailed enough to allow full allocation of the soldiers' lands, 'the exact and perfect admeasurement' envisaged in the act of September 1653. Worsley was instrumental in ensuring that new, fuller instructions were drawn up on 11 May 1654 by a special committee.[29]

It appears that Worsley administered a full measurement survey on these grounds for the next four months. Again, the evidence is scant, although it seems that several baronies in County Cork had been fully surveyed by the end of August.[30] But the survey was halted prematurely in September when Petty launched his attack. Petty later claimed that he had previously tried to inform Worsley of the faults of his method, only to be dismissed with 'contemptuous smiles'.[31] Perhaps Worsley was right to be wary: already Petty had ruthlessly supplanted a fellow medical officer in the Irish administration, and was ominously practising his surveying along with Morgan.[32]

Petty's criticisms of the 'absurd and insignificant way of Surveying then carrying on by Mr Worsly' focused mainly on weaknesses in organisation and payment.[33] By measuring the boundaries of estates only, the survey was 'a meer vitiation of the Countries estimate'; the 'Grossness' of the survey would make subdivision 'tedious and litigous' with most lands having to be re-surveyed, whilst the system encouraged fraudulent returns.[34] The fact that these criticisms were accepted by the commissioners suggests that they

[26] Petty, *Cromwellian survey*, 6, 54–7.
[27] Goblet appears to make this mistake: *Transformation*, 173–80.
[28] Simmington, 'Introduction', pp. viii–ix.
[29] Although Petty argued that they were 'clogged with unnecessary instructions, things done *pro virili*', he did concede that they were superior to the previous ones: *Cromwellian survey*, 7.
[30] Payment was issued to three surveyors for surveying these territories in that month: 'Commonwealth state accounts', 266–7.
[31] Petty, *Cromwellian survey*, 3.
[32] Goblet, *Transformation*, 218; Sharp, 'William Petty', 114–15, 119–22.
[33] W. Petty, *Reflections on some persons and things in Ireland*, London 1660, 13.
[34] The method of payment encouraged surveyors to falsely return unprofitable lands as profitable, because they were only paid for the latter despite in effect having to measure the former: ibid. 13–14.

84

were accurate, but by the time that Petty repeated them in print in 1660 his 'vituperation for Worsley knew no bounds'.[35] Petty's description of Worsley's progress in Ireland should be understood in this light:

> having been often frustrated as to his many severall great designes and undertakings in England, hoped to improve and repaire himselfe upon a less knowing and more credulous people. To this purpose he exchanged some dangerous opinions in religion for others more merchantable in Ireland, and carries also some magnifieing glasses, through which he shewed, *aux 'espirits mediocres*, his skill in severall arts, soe as at length he got credit to be imployed in managing the Geometrical Survey of Ireland.[36]

Some historians have been too ready to accept this caricature uncritically.[37] In fact Petty had the advantage of being able to watch Worsley's progress from the sidelines and note his mistakes, whilst devising what would undoubtedly be a superior plan of action. Therefore even if Petty made no use at all of the actual results of Worsley's survey, he would have benefited from observing the difficulties it encountered.

No doubt Petty capitalised on this when, on 8 September 1654, he directed his concerns to a specially convened commission of officers, which reported in Petty's favour later in the month.[38] It was becoming increasingly likely that yet another survey would be necessary, and therefore Petty's offer to measure all lands 'according to naturall, artificiall, and civill bounds', by October 1655, was welcomed.[39] Throughout September Worsley engaged in a counter-attack: 'he secretly laboures with severall of the chief officers of the army, and particularly Sir Charles Coote, and such of the members of the councill as he has most interest with, to obstruct the further consideration of the Drs proposalls'.[40] However Coote, a leading Protestant landowner, soon switched his allegiance to Petty, helping his proposals to be accepted on 27 October, when it was agreed that Petty would perform an exact survey of lands in their smallest denominations, paid by acre and employing his own surveyors.[41] What had begun as a state-controlled enterprise was therefore to be contracted out to a private individual, who promised to save time and money, but who would make huge profits from doing so.

The huge wealth and estates that Petty acquired from the Down Survey would attract suspicion throughout the decade, culminating in an attempt to impeach him for corruption. Probably Petty was innocent of this, but the protest of Worsley's surveyors at being 'disposed to the insatiable desire of a covetous monopoler' shows unease at a private individual profiting from

[35] Sharp, 'William Petty', 121.
[36] Petty, *Cromwellian survey*, 2.
[37] For example, Goblet, *Transformation*, 215–16.
[38] Petty, *Cromwellian survey*, 4, 8–10.
[39] Ibid. 9.
[40] Ibid. 10.
[41] Ibid. 13–14.

this public business.[42] Petty himself did little to avoid these criticisms: at the same time as he was negotiating his contract, he made an agreement with one of the officers responsible for deciding in his favour, Sir Hardress Waller, who would take a share of the profits for helping in the surveying of Munster, leading to accusations of bribery.[43] Similarly, as a private individual Petty was not bound by the same rule which forbade the surveyor-general from purchasing the soldiers' land-debentures, which Petty exploited adroitly.[44] Much of his wealth, however, was gained by skilful utilisation of the terms of his contract, settled on 11 December 1654, by which Worsley and Petty agreed that the latter would perform an accurate survey within thirteen months.[45] Having performed the humiliating task of writing to his surveyors to discontinue their work, Worsley then drew up the instructions for his replacement, marking the beginning of the Down Survey.[46]

This survey is justly famous as a landmark in geography, the maps that Petty produced from it providing a lasting and remarkably accurate record. Most innovative was Petty's administration of the survey, a division of labour deploying numerous hands and thus minimising reliance on professionally trained surveyors.[47] Although there is no doubt that Petty had rescued what was looking likely to have been a long-drawn out and expensive process, we can conclude in Worsley's defence that he was acting under imprecise orders and facing much pressure to produce a rapid survey, without the benefit of the civil survey; more positively, he had been instrumental in instituting the first major revision of the survey in spring 1654, whilst his stage of the surveying process was a necessary preliminary to Petty's greater achievements, even if only by exposing problems that the venture would face.

Petty completed his survey by March 1656. He initially faced intractable opposition from the surveyor-general, but over the course of 1655 an uneasy truce emerged between the two men.[48] As surveyor-general Worsley still had a role in co-ordinating the surveying process, and by October 1655 Petty claimed to Hartlib that 'There is not that Distance between us that you may imagine.'[49] Furthermore, Worsley had the chance to repair some of his damaged reputation by being appointed to several administrative committees, to hear complaints from the adventurers and the army, for letting out houses and lands owned by the Commonwealth, and for regulating

---

[42] Ibid. 19.

[43] Ibid. 32–4.

[44] Ibid. 353–68.

[45] Ibid. 23–9.

[46] Ibid. 36–8. Larcom saw these instructions as carefully considered, showing that Worsley was more competent than Petty allowed: ibid. 320.

[47] On Petty's method of administering the survey see ibid. pp. xiv–xvi, 322–3; Barnard, *Cromwellian Ireland*, 226–9; Strauss, *William Petty*, 67–73; Sharp, 'William Petty', 126–33.

[48] On Worsley's obstructions see Petty, *Cromwellian survey*, 43–4.

[49] Petty to Hartlib, 17 Oct. 1655, HP (Marshal and Osborn Collection, doc. 28).

Dublin schools, for example, as well as the Irish Council of Trade founded in February 1656.[50] These seem to have busied Worsley enough to allow Petty to get on with his job relatively unhindered, at least until 1656.

The occasion which reawakened Worsley's animosity was Petty's attempt to submit the final draft of the survey. Of course Worsley's professional pride was at stake, but by then the conflict between the two had become enmeshed with an increasingly factionalised political situation. Initially this was due to the presence of a large army in Ireland, which was being demobilised. Hungry for their lands, the army officers had already begun to pressure Petty into finishing the survey, in July 1655.[51] But also in that month Henry Cromwell, son of the Protector, arrived in Dublin as commander of the Irish army, whilst the lord deputy Fleetwood soon returned to England.[52] Under Fleetwood, the army in Ireland had been the dominant political force, leading to resentment amongst the existing Protestant settlers in Ireland, the old Protestants.[53] This was exacerbated by the rise of Baptists within the army under Fleetwood's indulgent command.[54] As well as dividing the Protestant interest in Ireland, this development was alarming to Oliver Cromwell because several of the leading Baptist officers were also hostile to the Protectorate.[55] Henry Cromwell had been sent to Ireland to counter this, but although Fleetwood left Ireland, he remained 'a convenient and dangerous focus for Henry Cromwell's opponents'.[56] Cromwell increasingly favoured the old Protestants, laying 'the foundation of the Protestant "ascendancy" over Irish land and politics', but this attracted considerable opposition against both him and his allies, notably Roger Boyle, Baron Broghill (Robert Boyle's elder brother), as well as William Petty, who became Cromwell's secretary in 1658: '*politiques* who shared his approach'.[57]

In early 1656, when Petty was seeking to have the Down Survey accepted, this opposition was at its height, and the land settlement was one theatre of conflict. It was then that Worsley began to ally with Petty's most intractable opponent amongst the Baptist officers, Sir Hierome Sankey. Sankey would lead the attempt to impeach Petty in 1659, and had already figured prominently in army discontent about delays in payment.[58] Petty was wary

[50] Dunlop, *Ireland under the Commonwealth*, ii. 487, 529, 538–9; T. Corcoran, *State policy in Irish education, AD 1536 to 1816*, Dublin 1916, 76; 'Gleanings from the Irish Council-Books of the times of the Commonwealth and the Cromwells', in S. Urban, *The Gentleman's Magazine* xxxvi (1851), 572–3.

[51] Petty, *Cromwellian survey*, 66–7.

[52] Barnard, *Cromwellian Ireland*, 20.

[53] Idem, 'Planters and policies in Cromwellian Ireland', *P&P* lxi (1973), 42.

[54] Idem, *Cromwellian Ireland*, 98–106; P. Kilroy, 'Radical religion in Ireland', in Ohlmeyer, *Ireland from independence to occupation*, 201–17.

[55] Barnard, *Cromwellian Ireland*, 105.

[56] Ibid. 21.

[57] Idem, 'Planters and policies', 31, 45.

[58] Idem, *Cromwellian Ireland*, 232. On Sankey see A. Shirren, '"Colonel Zanchy" and Charles Fleetwood', *Notes and Queries* cxcviii (1953), 431–5, 474–7, 519–24, and Petty, *Cromwellian survey*, 78–9.

of an alliance between Worsley and Sankey, writing to his brother in March 1656 that they were 'at work' against him.[59] Petty must have been relieved, then, when on 11 March 1656 Worsley and Sankey were excluded from the committee which had been considering his survey, leaving it dominated by Petty's allies. However, Worsley was presented with another opportunity in May when he was called on formally to examine the survey.[60] He eventually reported on 18 August 1656, a month late, summoning the remnants of his influence to launch an attack on the standards of the Down Survey.[61] Thus Worsley cited numerous minor instances of negligence. Although the survey committee accepted Petty's answers, Worsley had none the less prevented him from finishing his work by several months. Meanwhile, Petty's opponents had been stoking up objections amongst the soldiers who were finally beginning to be granted their estates, which inevitably provoked complaints.[62] This was an uncomfortable situation for Petty, but his supporters amongst the soldiery ensured that his name was put forward to the Irish council as a trustee to oversee distribution of their lands.[63] The creation of a commission comprising Petty, Vincent Gookin and Miles Symner put this process firmly in the hands of Henry Cromwell's supporters, but Cromwell was not yet in absolute control and thus, when the council ordered that the Down Survey be extended to the adventurers' lands, this was jointly entrusted to Worsley and Petty (on 3 September 1656).[64]

The adventurers in London had already begun a disorganised allocation of lands based on the gross survey, which was causing much argument. Accordingly, Worsley was sent over in October to negotiate with them, and Petty exploited his rival's absence to secure his payment and amass the majority of his estates.[65] However, far from rushing back to Ireland, Worsley lingered in London. Oddly, he enlisted the help of Petty's ally Vincent Gookin to write to the Protector and his secretary Thurloe 'to dispense with his longer stay'.[66] His extended visit gave Worsley the chance to renew his acquaintance with members of the Hartlib circle, whilst he claimed in a letter to Henry Cromwell that the continued divisions amongst the adventurers were preventing his return to Dublin.[67] However, Worsley had another reason not to return, as he explained to Cromwell: two-and-a-half years previously he had been granted the estate of one Gerard FitzGyrald in Queen's County, but on an insecure lease. Fearing that 'this may be Prised away from me',

[59] Petty also named one of his surveyors, John Humphreys, as an ally of Sankey and Worsley: W. Petty to J. Petty, 6 Mar. 1656, MS Add. 72850, fo. 1r.
[60] Petty, Cromwellian survey, 111–12.
[61] Ibid. 111–15.
[62] Ibid. 80–102.
[63] Ibid. 85–7.
[64] Ibid. 184–5, 390–2.
[65] Ibid. 126–7, 155, 211–14.
[66] V. Gookin to J. Thurloe, 3 Feb. 1657, in A collection of the state papers of John Thurloe, vi, ed T. Birch, London 1742, 37.
[67] Worsley to H. Cromwell, 17 Mar. 1657, BL, MS Landsdowne 821, fo. 352r.

Worsley explained that without his estate being confirmed, there was little to tempt him back to Ireland.[68]

This petition was evidently successful, for in 1657 Worsley was granted a twenty-one year lease of these lands as arrears for payment as surveyor-general.[69] Meanwhile the matter of the adventurers' lands was the subject of an act dated 9 June 1657 which provided for a re-survey. Fearing that he would be replaced as surveyor-general, Worsley enlisted the help of Lady Ranelagh and Robert Boyle, who apparently used their influence with Broghill to prevent this from happening.[70] This only delayed the inevitable, however: Henry Cromwell's grip on power was strengthened when he became lord deputy in November 1657, and the following January Worsley was replaced by Gookin as surveyor-general.[71] Following the Restoration, when he was keen to show his opposition to Oliver Cromwell, Worsley explained that 'upon *the* passing of *the* Petition and Advise I declared so much dissatisfaction as that upon his sonnes being made Deputy of Ireland ... my place of surveyor generall was given to another privattly, without any Exception brought against me, or any knowledge had of it by *the* Councill'.[72] Worsley still had some supporters, therefore, but when he returned to Ireland at the end of July 1657, he had lost much of his influence, although he still had a sting in his tail, as Petty would find out.[73]

The estate Worsley acquired in Queen's County was in the village of Tymogue, in the barony of Stradbally, convenient for Dublin and allowing him to enjoy something of the life of a landowner.[74] His property was extended during his return to London in October 1656, when Worsley married.[75] His wife was Lucy Cary, the daughter of a Dartmouth merchant whose family had invested much money in the Irish adventure.[76] By marriage, Worsley acquired land in the parish of Churchtown in Rathconrath, County

---

[68] Ibid. fo. 352v.

[69] *CSPI, 1663–5*, 472.

[70] See Ranelagh's letter to Boyle, requesting that he be 'Mr Worsley's advocate to Broghil', in the matter, 5 June 1657, *Boyle correspondence*, i. 216.

[71] T. Barnard, 'Lord Broghill, Vincent Gookin and the Cork elections of 1659', *EHR* lxxxviii (1973), 357. On Cromwell's replacement of Fleetwood see Barnard, *Cromwellian Ireland*, 21–2.

[72] Worsley to Lady Clarendon, 8 Nov. 1661, MS Clarendon 75, fo. 300v.

[73] Worsley remained in contact with Sankey: on 30 May 1657 they were deponents in a Chancery suit regarding a dispute about lands in the barony of Goran, County Kilkenny, supporting the claims of the Irish Protestant politician Sir John Borlase against Isaak Troughton: TNA, C 24/812, pt 2.

[74] *A census of Ireland, circa 1659*, ed. S. Pender, Dublin 1939, 504.

[75] The wedding took place at the Church of St. Mary's in Aldermary, on 9 November: *The parish registers of St Mary Aldermary, London, 1558–1751*, ed. J. S. Chester (Harleian Society Registers v, 1880), 26. The following March banns were published for the marriage in the parish of St Olaves, Hart Street: *Registers of St Olave, Hart Street, London, 1563–1700*, ed. W. Bannerman (Harleian Society Registers xlvi, 1916), 274.

[76] Lucy Cary's name is given in Worsley's entry in the London visitation of 1664: *London visitation pedigrees, 1664*, 154. A total of 143 citizens of Dartmouth had originally invested £2,398 but only 44 were eventually granted land, and the Cary family including Lucy

Westmeath.[77] In addition, Petty alleged that Worsley had unjustly acquired an estate in Balleen in the barony of Galmoy, County Kilkenny, and had also attempted to persuade Petty to withhold a nearby parcel of land from the army's moiety for him, in Clontubbrid.[78] These accusations of corruption were intended to deflect attention from those made against Petty, and there is no additional evidence to support them. However, it does seem that during his time as surveyor-general, Worsley was acquiring land throughout Leinster.

Worsley's estates provided a retreat from Dublin, where he could conduct those experiments and trials in 'agricultural chemistry' which formed the basis of his natural philosophy.[79] In doing so he participated in the 'planting' of Ireland, a colonial endeavour by which English Protestants sought to demonstrate their superiority over the Irish Catholics as the bringers of prosperity to a godforsaken wilderness.[80] Such claims to cultural dominance found their intellectual corollary in the proposals of the Hartlib circle for improving Ireland, epitomised by Gerard Boate's *Irelands natural history*.[81] Worsley's attitude was typically dismissive of the local population: in his letter to Henry Cromwell, he described how he had found his estate 'wholly waste; and without any Tennant save a very few Cabbins of Irish', whom he preceded to 'turne off' before putting in 'a Plough, and some little stocke'.[82] Unsurprisingly he was a keen supporter (along with many of the army radicals) of the attempt to transplant the Catholic population to Connaught, which he claimed to have supported 'with that vigour on *the* behalfe & for *the* security of *the* English Plantations There'. [83] By then he had been made a justice of the peace, and came into conflict with leading old Protestants, notably his old ally Sir Charles Coote, whom he alleged had protected several of the Irish and thus became his 'Avowed and professed Adversary'; on his part, Worsley claimed to have brought several 'Tories' to 'Trayall; ... when some other of the Justices of the peace ... would scarse be seene in it'.[84] Thus he shared the attitude of the radical generals towards the Irish, although like most of them Worsley failed to lay down deep roots in Ireland, and left the nation apparently for good in 1659. The colonial 'expert' proved to have little capability in the actual business of colonisation.

were particularly active in buying up shares: Bottigheimer, *English money and Irish land*, 158; CSPI: *Adventurers, 1642-1659*, 255-6.
[77] *Census of Ireland*, 521.
[78] Petty, *Reflections*, 27, 32.
[79] See chapter 5 below.
[80] See N. Canny, *Making Ireland British, 1580-1650*, Oxford 2001.
[81] Barnard, 'Improvement in Ireland', 281-97; P. Coughlan, 'Natural history and historical nature: the project for a natural history of Ireland', in *SHUR*, 298-317.
[82] Worsley to H. Cromwell, 17 Mar. 1657, MS Landsdowne 821, fo. 352v.
[83] Worsley to Lady Clarendon, 8 Nov. 1661, MS Clarendon 75, fo. 300v.
[84] Ibid. Worsley was keen to remind the Irish Council of 'care for clearing the country of Tories and other dangerous persons' in 1659: Dunlop, *Ireland under the Commonwealth*, ii. 692.

The changeableness of things

If for Worsley the 1650s was a decade of professional disappointment, for many parliamentarians it was one of bewilderment and, ultimately, disillusion. Worsley was by no means unusual, therefore, when he reflected on the unexpected obstacles facing the godly in 'the choice of our happinesse' in a letter to an unnamed lady, dated 24 September 1654.[85] Doubtless Worsley was still reeling from Petty's assault earlier in the month, but his sense of anxiety was exacerbated by an uncertain political climate. He had found prominence under the Rump Parliament, but since its dismissal in April 1653 there had followed the brief rule of Barebone's Parliament and then the proclamation of Cromwell as Lord Protector in December 1653; as he wrote, the Protector's first, toothless, parliament was sitting.[86] Worsley purported to be baffled by 'the changeablenesse of things', leading him to question his political assumptions:

> For though wee were at length convinced there was much willfullnesse arbitrarinesse Injustice, tyranny, partiality, favour oppression in a king. Yet a Parli*ament* how glorious did wee call that Institution; how full, how comprehensive, for power, for wisedome, for authority, & all things reqvisit to make vp A Government It was therefore fitt by so long a continuance of one Parli*ament* & *the* issue of *that* together with *the* qvicke succession & transactings of 2. more. That wee should experimentally see, *that* in Parlia-*ment* may bee selvishnesse, partiality, hight of oppression, vnmercifullnesse, folly & weakenesse, both in Counsell, authority & power.[87]

Perhaps his own personal setbacks contributed to this pessimism, but many others had viewed the foundation of the Protectorate as a betrayal of the parliamentary cause. In the light of these confusions, Worsley had been moved to look more deeply at 'the Principles & foundation of Government ... both from scripture & reason', but this bought little comfort.[88] All Worsley could discern was 'A cleare & wide difference between *the* ends of Government & *the* manner of administration & execution of those ends'. The ends were 'alwaies one & necessary', but there was no 'Rule, Law or Prescript either in scripture or in nature' for any particular form of government.[89] Such a disdain for formality in politics as in religion was a conspicuous feature of the period, and for Worsley this was based on an understanding of the

---

[85] Worsley to [countess of Leicester?], 27 Sept. 1654, HP 65/15/1A. This letter is discussed in Scott, *England's troubles*, 243.
[86] See Woolrych, *Britain in Revolution*, 601–15.
[87] Worsley to [countess of Leicester?], 27 Sept. 1654, HP 65/15/2B.
[88] Ibid. HP 65/15/2B–3A.
[89] Ibid. HP 65/15/3A.

determining force of power, and not principle, in human affairs.[90] The forms of government throughout the ages, he explained, emanated from 'the sole free & arbitrary pleasure of such who laying hold vpon the opportunityes offered them haue in all ages, seazed & assumed the Government', so

> That the formes of Government were all a long in all ages imposed vpon the people with more & lesse of Power from & by which they received their essence: though offerred vnder other consideration. That vnder all formes as well the more eminent as the more subordinate Ministers were constrained to Act according to the mind & intention of those who first calculated & produced that forme. And therefore noe new thing.[91]

Government was beset by 'vnavoideable & almost necessary Tendencies to be corrupted', and the only hope was that it might be exercised by those who held the best 'qvalifications & fittnesse', although even these were prone to 'the temptation of power'.[92] This sceptical perspective informed Worsley's judgement of both Barebone's Parliament (which owed its existence to Cromwell and therefore was 'irrationall & absurd' to challenge him) and the present one, 'seing what they can doe for the people doth not at all appeare'.[93] England under the Protector had yet to emerge from that spiritual darkness which Worsley had described in the preface to The advocate, and he was left wondering 'how ill ... it testifyes our beleefe of the Lords coming'.[94]

Thus to Worsley power dominated politics, but only in the 1650s, when he found himself out of sympathy with the ruling regime, did this become problematic. But if he were sceptical about the course of political affairs, this was not outright opposition, and he would successively serve Strafford, the Long Parliament, the Rump, Barebone's, the Protectorate, the restored Rump and the army-backed regime that expelled it, before resurfacing under Charles II. Worsley's loyalties were split in the 1650s, and he continued to rely on his friendship with Robert Boyle and Lady Ranalegh, members of a leading old Protestant family, even as he was moving towards opposition to Henry Cromwell.[95] Meanwhile many members of the Hartlib circle, notably Dury and Hartlib, were committed supporters of Cromwell, a long-standing patron whom they hoped would reunite the Protestant cause at home and

[90] J. C. Davis, 'Against formality: one aspect of the Puritan Revolution', TRHS 6th ser. iii (1993), 265–88.
[91] Worsley to [countess of Leicester?], 27 Sept. 1654, HP 65/15/3B.
[92] Ibid. HP 65/15/3B–4A.
[93] Ibid. HP 65/15/4A–B.
[94] Ibid. HP 65/15/4B.
[95] For evidence that Worsley was on good terms with Old Protestants such as Sir John Clotworthy and Sir William Parsons in 1653 see a letter, possibly to Lady Ranelagh, 29 July 1653, MS Add. 4106, fos 224–5. His willingness to cross political boundaries is shown by the help he gave to no less a figure than the wife of Ormond, in retaining her Irish estates, in 1655: HMC, Fourteenth report: manuscripts of the marquis of Ormonde, i, London 1902, 322.

abroad. A rift threatened to open between Worsley and his former allies, therefore, but both seemed willing to avoid controversy in the interests of preserving unity.[96] Worsley's standing was not so great that he had to take sides publicly, allowing him to oscillate between various groups, as when he acted, in 1655, as a go-between for Fleetwood and Colonel Edmund Ludlow, an enemy of the Protectorate.[97] Another 'Commonwealthman' for whom Worsley retained some loyalty was Sir Henry Vane, by then a figurehead of opposition to Cromwell. Years later, Petty explained that the enmity between he and Worsley arose because 'I was for a singule person, he for an other forme, or for *the* singule person Sir Hen: Vane'.[98] In early 1656 Worsley drafted a discourse responding to Vane's controversial spiritual reflections, *A retired man's meditations*, and Dury cautioned Worsley to 'walke very warily in giuing it'.[99] Worsley was certainly associated with Vane during the turmoil that followed Cromwell's death.

As well as these groups, during the 1650s Worsley was exposed to the influence of the army, and in particular Baptist officers. Religiously, this was already apparent in the letter discussed above, when Worsley prefaced his discussion of the uncertain state of English politics with a similarly questioning diagnosis of mankind's spiritual condition. Truth, he explained, was obstructed by custom, and man's perceptions were

> like seing of things thorough water or any other cleare & transparent medium; through which *the* light coming refracted to us, though wee see with much clearnesse every thing yet they are in an Inverse posture to us, to *what* they are in themselves; & so is *the* truth of all things to our naturall vunderstandings as long as we are induced to judge of them by *the* dictates of sense. And how few are brought into a higher light. How hard to get *ourselves* above this earth, & *the* corrupt manners & customes of it they can best tell, (& how best also to pitty others) who lye most vnder *the* Burthen of it.[100]

Typically, in resolving this epistemological problem, Worsley veered between confidence, that '*the* Lord hath beene pleased to discover himselfe more neerely to me then ever', and crippling doubt, that 'it is by our Pride only ... & our indulging of it: That wee are kept from discerning him'.[101] Fearing that 'custome doth soe prevail over mee', Worsley found his tongue 'faltering & stammering' from proclaiming the truth, 'that *the* Lord is in us', words

---

[96] It is perhaps telling that the scribe had noted the words 'R.W's canting letter' on Hartlib's copy of the letter discussed above: Worsley to [countess of Leicester?], 27 Sept. 1654, HP 65/15/4B.
[97] *The memoirs of Edmund Ludlow, 1625–72*, i, ed. C. H. Firth, Oxford 1894, 408.
[98] Petty to Tomkins, 7 Dec. 1672, MS Add. 2858, fo. 57v.
[99] Dury to Hartlib, 22 Jan. 1656, HP 4/3/147A.
[100] Worsley to [countess of Leicester?], 27 Sept. 1654, HP 65/15/1A.
[101] Ibid. HP 65/15/1B.

that would have struck a chord with the Quakers who would shortly arrive in Ireland.[102]

The original copy of this letter is now held as part of the Sidney family manuscripts, calendared as being written to Dorothy Sidney, countess of Leicester and mother of Viscount Lisle, and indeed it has a hint of the neoplatonism associated with that family and its most famous member, Lisle's brother Algernon, another Vanist.[103] However Worsley never assumed the public face of a Vane or a Sidney, instead shying from public affairs which offered so much personal disappointment and disillusion. Rather, throughout the 1650s Worsley became increasingly preoccupied with the inner tribulations of the spirit. This shift can be seen most clearly, perhaps, in the direction that his natural philosophy took in Ireland.

---

[102] Ibid. HP 65/15/2A.

[103] HMC, *Seventy-seventh report: manuscripts of Lord de L'Isle and Dudley preserved at Penshurst Place, Kent*, VI: *Sidney papers, 1626–1698*, ed. W. A. Shaw, London 1966, 496–8; Scott, *Algernon Sidney, 1623–1677*, 17. Both Philip and Algernon served in the Irish army in the early 1640s when Worsley was surgeon-general: ibid. 82.

5

Natural Philosophy: The Search for Energy

Utopian designs

On 8 May 1654 Benjamin Worsley was granted £250 by the Irish Council in Dublin, allowing him to conduct a trial in the production of saltpetre, in return for eventually supplying the army with a total of 10,000 lb.[1] This was a reprise of the project which had been his first step away from the career of surgeon, nearly ten years earlier. Despite his frustrations as a projector, Worsley had maintained an interest in natural philosophy, and during his visit to Amsterdam from 1648 to 1649 he was experimenting fairly intensively. Although his ambitions to master Glauber's alchemical techniques were frustrated, Worsley had learned enough of the 'chemical philosophy' to harbour aspirations to complete his training as an adept, despite full-time employment. In 1654, thanks to state sponsorship, this possibility seemed about to be realised.

However, Worsley's reputation as a scientific practitioner fared little better than his professional career in Ireland, and by the time of the founding of the Royal Society in 1660 he was a marginal figure within the scientific community. His political reputation by then was questionable, but neither had Worsley successfully fashioned a secure scientific identity which might allow him to participate successfully in Restoration science. This was a stark contrast with his sometime collaborator, Robert Boyle, who in the years following his immature scientific exploits with Worsley in the late 1640s had been conducting increasingly sophisticated experiments, most famously in the rich intellectual environment of Oxford from 1655 onwards.[2] Even before then, in London, Boyle's experimental sophistication was growing in an area long excluded from the official story of the 'scientific revolution': alchemy. Thanks especially to the works of William Newman and Lawrence Principe, we now know much about intensive laboratory experimentation which this involved.[3] In the early 1650s Boyle was being tutored in this

---

[1] This sum comprised £50 plus an advance of £200: 'Commonwealth state accounts, 1653–56', 249.
[2] For Oxford see R. G. Frank, *Harvey and the Oxford physiologists: a study of scientific ideas and social interaction*, Berkeley–Los Angeles 1980.
[3] Newman and Principe, *Alchemy tried in the fire*; W. Newman, *Gehennical fire: the lives of George Starkey, an American alchemist in the scientific revolution*, Cambridge, MA. 1994; L. Principe, *The aspiring adept: Robert Boyle and his alchemical quest*, Princeton 1998; L. Principe and W. Newman, 'Some problems with the historiography of alchemy', in

pursuit by the American alchemist George Starkey.[4] Along with other figures such as Hartlib's son-in-law Frederick Clodius, these would form the chymical centre of the Hartlib circle.[5] Worsley, however, was far removed from both Oxford and London, and struggled to maintain parity with these more serious practitioners.

As Toby Barnard has shown, Ireland did see a growth in scientific activity in these years, but mainly within William Petty's circle. Another alchemist, Robert Child, arrived in northern Ireland in 1651 and later corresponded with Worsley, but he died in 1654.[6] Boyle visited Ireland from 1652 to 1654 and was apparently in touch with Worsley towards the end of his visit.[7] At this point Hartlib enlisted Worsley into his efforts to complete the natural history of Ireland, which he hoped would be assisted by the land survey.[8] However, the Worsley-Petty schism undoubtedly hindered Hartlib's efforts, despite their early collaboration on 'a physick garden'.[9] Worsley continued to pursue agricultural research on his estate, where he claimed to have planted 'above a thousand young setts of Roses', hoping to become 'the Greatest Master of them of any Man in this Countrey'.[10] On Culpeper's recommendation he and his army associates planted clover-grass seed, but the crop failed, much to Worsley's disrepute.[11] Miles Symner, an ally of Petty and so a hostile witness, later alleged that this was due to Worsley's own negligence, but Worsley himself frequently complained that his public responsibilities were hindering his scientific efforts.[12] Such obstacles limited his experimental success, but none the less Worsley's letters tell us much about the changing scientific climate of the period.

Worsley was encouraged to return to his 'Vtopian designes' for saltpetre having been asked by the Irish Council to examine the proposals of a soldier 'for an Artificiall way of breeding et increasing of Salt-Peter', in summer

---

W. Newman and A. Grafton (eds), *Secrets of nature: astrology and alchemy in early modern Europe*, Cambridge, MA 2001, 385–431.

[4] Newman and Principe, *Alchemy tried in the fire*, 213–36.

[5] Along with Sir Kenelm Digby, Clodius and Boyle were part of the so-called 'Chemical Council', although evidence for this putative body is even sparser than for the Invisible College: ibid. 259.

[6] See, for example, his letters to Hartlib, 9 Oct. 1652, HP 15/5/18–19; 23 Nov. 1652, HP 15/5/16–17; 8 Apr. 1653, HP 15/5/20–1; 28 Oct. 1653, HP 15/5/24–5.

[7] See Hartlib to Boyle, 8/9 May 1654, *Boyle correspondence*, i. 190.

[8] Hartlib reported to Boyle that he was glad that 'Mr. *Worsley* also is like to engage in the prosecution of these affairs, and this kind of surveying of lands': ibid. i.170.

[9] R. Child to Hartlib, 28 Oct. 1653, HP 15/5/25B.

[10] Worsley to Hartlib, 16 May 1654, HP 70/8/1B. Worsley also planted madder: HP 70/7A.

[11] The exchange is printed in Hartlib, *Samuel Hartlib his legacie*, 3rd edn, 248–50. The soldiers in question, 'Col. J', 'Col. H' and 'Capt. V', were perhaps Sankey, Colonel John Hewson and Captain John Vernon, the latter two being prominent Baptists.

[12] R. Wood to Hartlib, 3 Mar. 1657, HP 33/1/12A; [Worsley] to [Boyle], *c.* late 1658– early 1659, HP 42/1/28B.

1653.[13] Without a hint of irony, Worsley described how this soldier 'understood nothing of it further then the Common Projectors of making it, with Dung Vrine and the like stuffe'. Although Worsley's original project had utilised the same noxious substances, now he claimed the ability to produce saltpetre without urine or dung, based on understanding 'the whole mystery of it'. This new-found confidence derived from theories about the life-giving propensities of saltpetre which Worsley owed principally to Glauber's writings.[14]

Although his original interest in saltpetre was not merely utilitarian, now Worsley hoped 'not only to give a very good account of Peter and the nature of it, but something also of vegetation', a subject which preoccupied him for the rest of the decade.[15] This rested on a conviction that 'Salt is the seate of life et vegetation, et so the subject of nutrition', which in turn reflected a well-established tradition in early modern alchemy or chymistry. Although the central goal of alchemy was to transmutate base metals into gold by means of the philosopher's stone, as far back as the thirteenth-century corpus of [pseudo-]Geber, alchemical writings had considered the elemental composition of metals. In order to transmutate metals, it was necessary to alter this composition, something achieved by a 'philosophical', purified mercury which Geber explained in proto-corpuscular terms, referring to two inherent qualities, bearing the characteristics of mercury and sulphur.[16] Another dimension found in many medieval alchemical writings understood the formation of metals in the earth as growing from seeds, culminating in Paracelsus' sexualised and organic cosmology, which added a third principle, salt.[17] Paracelsians tended to elevate the importance of salt as the life-giving principle in all of nature, which allowed the concepts of alchemy to be extended into what Debus termed 'agricultural chemistry'.[18] This tradition was richly represented in Worsley's *Catalogus*, which included three works by Paracelsus, and others by followers of his including Severinus, Burggrav, Duchesne, Beguin, Sala, Hartprecht, d'Espagnet, Nuysement and Blaise de Vigenere (whose *Discourse of fire and salt* was published in English in 1649), as well, of course, as Glauber.[19] A particularly important

---

[13] Worsley to Hartlib, 16 May 1654, HP 66/15/1A. Part of this letter, which discussed the theories underpinning his new saltpetre project, was printed in Hartlib, *Samuel Hartlib his legacie*, 217–19, as 'a Philosophical Letter concerning Vegetation and the Causes of Fruitfulness'.

[14] Newman and Principe, *Alchemy tried in the fire*, 241–2.

[15] Worsley to Hartlib, 16 May 1654, HP 66/15/1B.

[16] Newman, *Gehennical fire*, 95–8. However, see the reservations in A. Clericuzio, *Elements, principles and corpuscules: a study of atomism and chemistry in the seventeenth century*, Dordrecht–Boston–London 2001, 2–3.

[17] Newman, *Gehennical fire*, 106; A. Debus, *The chemical philosophy: Paracelsan science and medicine in the sixteenth and seventeenth centuries*, i, New York 1977, 79–80.

[18] Debus, *Chemical philosophy*, ii. 410–40.

[19] For this literature see Clericuzio, *Elements, principles and corpuscules*, 35–47.

translation appeared in 1650, namely John French's edition of *A new light of alchymie* by Michael Sendivogius. This Polish adept held that saltpetre grew naturally in the earth, containing within itself *semina* (seeds bearing its nature) which penetrated other matter, converting it into nitre. Such ideas were incorporated into a sweeping cosmology, whereby the energising ingredient found in saltpetre, sometimes called *sal nitrum*, combined with sulphurous soil to produce metals and minerals, ultimately nourishing plants on the earth's surface. This 'philosophical' nitre was also found in the atmosphere, where it joined with celestial rays from the sun, becoming an *aerial nitre* which cherished life. This explained the unique qualities of saltpetre, as a fertiliser as well as an ingredient in gunpowder: 'obtained from the heavens and transmitted by rain to the earth, the fertilizing agency was acquired by terrestrial saltpeter to a greater degree than any other substance'.[20]

Worsley's understanding of saltpetre was steeped in this tradition. Thus one paper explained that he had 'found out by Experience a ferment, which mixt among fit Matter, will cause the whole at lenght to turne into the nature of nitrium'.[21] This was simply 'the best and richest earth, that can bee got of Saltpetre, which being impregnated with its owne nitrous Spirit will Multiply & increase it selfe vpon first matter'.[22] To speed up the process, Worsley suggested using grass cuttings mixed with lime and wood-ash, which would also contain 'that nitrous Vniversal spirit'. Together, these would be laid in open pits, bottomed with clay to prevent the nitrous matter being swept away by rain, and would soon ferment into good saltpetre. Thus his method sought to replicate and speed up the conditions by which saltpetre multiplied, forming a 'perpetual mine of salt-Peter' like the one later envisaged by Boyle.[23]

The theory underpinning this method was expanded in another discourse, 'De nitro theses'.[24] This blended Sendivogian ideas with common observations from agriculture in a number of related theses, notably that 'Natures intent in the breeding of Salt-Peter in the Vpper Surface of the Earth is for the generation of Plants and by them for the præservation of Animals'. To demonstrate this, Worsley cited the fertilising properties of 'Seedes steeped in Water mixed with Salt-Peter'.[25] Such observations led Worsley

---

[20] Newman, *Gehennical fire*, 87–9 (quote at p. 89). See also A. Debus, *Man, nature and the Renaissance*, Cambridge 1978, 44–61, and H. Guerlac, 'The poet's nitre', *Isis* xlv (1954), 243–55.

[21] 'Observations about saltpetre', *c*. May 1653, HP 39/1/11A. For the attribution of this document to Worsley see Newman and Principe, *Alchemy tried in the fire*, 240.

[22] Ibid. HP 39/1/11B.

[23] R. Boyle, *The sceptical chymist*, quoted in Webster, *Great instauration*, London 1975, 380.

[24] 'De nitro theses, quædam', *c*. May 1654, HP 39/1/16–20. Newman and Principe have conclusively shown that this paper was written after Worsley visited Amsterdam, as it contains a claim which relied on Glauber's experiments in saltpetre, which were not available before then: *Alchemy tried in the fire*, 241–3.

[25] 'De nitro theses, quædam', HP 39/1/16B–17A.

to conclude (with Glauber) that 'all Plants likewise containe in them a Salt', the elusive *sal nitrum*.[26] One need merely watch nature at work to posit the existence of an energising substance or property found in vegetables and ingested by animals. As well as discovering an effective means to breed saltpetre, Worsley therefore believed that he had identified the life-spirit which nourished living things.[27]

The theoretical dimension allowed Worsley to extend his discussion from vegetation to transmutational alchemy. Following his announcement of the revived saltpetre project, Worsley engaged in a protracted debate about the composition of metals with Clodius, but whereas his earlier discussions about saltpetre were full of confidence, here Worsley's comparative inexperience in laboratory alchemy was exposed.

The vanity of an impostor

Worsley's attitude to alchemy was ambivalent. His experiences in Amsterdam demonstrated the impenetrability of the art, whilst his official employment precluded any serious labour over the furnace, and yet he found it hard to disregard the special status which alchemy held as the 'key to nature'.[28] Whereas Moriaen complained that Worsley had lost faith in transmutation in 1651, by late 1653 this had changed.[29] In a letter which Hartlib quoted to Boyle, Worsley explained that he had 'laid all considerations in chemistry aside, as things not reaching much above common laborants, or strong-water distillers, unless we can arrive at this key, clearly and perfectly to know, how to open, ferment, putrify, corrupt and destroy (if we please) any mineral, or metal'.[30] By breaking down metals into their constituent parts, it would be possible to build up new substances, which would be 'a higher work in nature'. Worsley had written to Clodius about this subject in 1653, hoping 'either to be an assistant towards it, or assisted in it'. The letters they exchanged in the following year were widely circulated around the Hartlib circle, and to Newman and Principe they demonstrate the existence of 'disparate schools, with strong differences of opinion', within alchemy.[31]

The debate was initiated by a treatise in which Worsley applied *sal nitrum* theories to the structure, growth and transmutation of metals. Although this discourse is now lost, three replies exist from July 1654: from Clodius, a correspondent in Hamburg (perhaps Frederick Schlezer), and Culpeper, who

---

[26] Ibid. HP 39/1/17B; Newman and Principe, *Alchemy tried in the fire*, 242.
[27] 'De nitro theses, quædam', HP 39/1/19A.
[28] For chemistry as 'key to nature' see Newman, *Gehennical fire*, 72, and Webster, *Great instauration*, 384–402.
[29] Newman and Principe, *Alchemy tried in the fire*, 247; Young, *Faith*, 232–3.
[30] Hartlib to Boyle, 28 Feb. 1654, *Boyle correspondence*, i. 155.
[31] Newman and Principe, *Alchemy tried in the fire*, 248.

had similar ideas about the 'vegetative Life in Mettals'.[32] However, Clodius' response was less sympathetic, as he accused Worsley of failing to detail his method of producing the philosopher's stone, which Clodius (following Geber) believed should be produced from a *sophic* mercury extracted from quicksilver.[33] Worsley responded by questioning alchemical terminology, asserting that 'names are imposed vpon things, att the meare pleasure and fancye of such whoe first impose them'.[34] Alchemists tended to 'speake doubt-fully, mystically, & enigmatically, for the better clouding their discription of things'. Names such as 'mercury' or 'sulphur' applied only indirectly to the nature of the bodies being described, 'by reason onely of some aptnes or resemblance *that* their matter hath to those other boddyes whose names are improperly transferred to them', and should not be taken literally.[35] Worsley thus denied that the 'philosophical mercury' which alchemists discussed was the same as common quicksilver. Those who laboured to 'torture' this substance out of metals were 'greatly mistaken'. The identity of the philo-sophical mercury was doubly important because, it was commonly claimed, this substance would be identical with the '*prima materia* or basic ingredient of metals in general'.[36] Worsley therefore ventured that '[mercury] currens is not the most simple or proper substance which the metalls are vltimately resolved into by nature, but Nature doth by a proper Colliquation of her owne yeild another simple liquid, pure and spermaticke substance'.[37]

Sendivogius too had posited a seminal quality as 'the Elixir of everything, or Quint-essence, or the most perfect decotion, or digestion of a thing', produced autonomously by 'Nature'.[38] The Sendivogian dimension was even more explicit in Worsley's exposition of his 'spermaticke substance':

> for as mutch as in all minerals & mettalls there is a participation of the same lyfe, blessing vegitatiue & multiplicatiue virtue, as was given in the creation to plants & other seed bearing boddyes by reason the said vigi-tatiue virtue or spiritt is to the outward sence imprisoned, & not to bee diserned vntill brought forth in or by this Mercuriall substance hence the same substance ... is cal'd Sperma or Anima cuiuslibet Mettali.[39]

This would be acquired by means of a 'Phylosophicall putrefaction', which would at once effect 'a totall & erreducible distruction, and att the same

---

[32] Culpeper's notes on Worsley's discourse, 10 July 1654, HP 39/2/14A, 15A. The reply from Hamburg, dated 25 July 1654, is at HP 39/2/131–4.
[33] [F. Clodius] to [Worsley], 4 July 1654, HP 16/1/7. The author and recipient of this letter, which was written in Latin, were identified by Newman and Principe, who have provided an authoritative reading: *Alchemy tried in the fire*, 249.
[34] Worsley to [Clodius], *c.* summer 1654, HP 42/1/26A.
[35] Ibid. HP 42/1/26B.
[36] Newman, *Gehennical fire*, p. xiii.
[37] Worsley to [Clodius], *c.* summer 1654, HP 42/1/26B.
[38] M. Sendivogius, *A new light of alchymie*, trans. John French, London 1650, 6.
[39] Worsley to [Clodius], *c.* summer 1654, HP 42/1/26A. The Latin phrase roughly trans-lates as 'the spirit whose libation is in the metals'.

tyme an Animation' of a substance's spirit.[40] Another letter explained how, in the process of putrefaction, 'the vertue & life of those things which were before shutt, are now not only made manifest, but have a great addition & increase of their energy'.[41] The resulting 'rich Sulphur' would contain not only 'the life of mettals', but also would be 'the same body with the true Mercury & Salt of Mettals'. Worsley's conclusion was overtly Sendivogian: 'you must know the meaning of Sal Centri terræ. I say you are to study to gett Sal centri terræ. for in salt is all energy'.[42]

Clodius knew all too well the source of Worsley's speculations, and demanded that Worsley substantiate them.[43] Worsley's answer is lost, but a letter to Hartlib reveals that he had been stung by Clodius' stance. Already forced to present himself as 'soe great a novice in matters of this nature', now Worsley backed away further, claiming to 'abhorre the vanity of an Impostor, in vaunting myselfe as a master of this, or that rare or great secrett'.[44] He feared that his reputation had been damaged, exhorting Hartlib to 'blaze not my name for a foolosopher'.[45] However, rather than withdrawing his claims, Worsley attempted to re-define the purposes of his 'greate worke' to downplay the importance of transmutation. His interest, by contrast, was in understanding natural operations, so that he might practise a 'further & higher light & direction in nature'.[46] Rather than being a 'Master of any particular great secrett', Worsley claimed his skill was in 'putting nature on worke by other kinde of media, & after another manner then common operators dreame of'. Most audaciously, Worsley argued that although he had little practice in laboratory alchemy, yet 'if I should apply my selfe to it my error can not be great in it'.[47]

Newman and Principe have scorned this 'armchair' alchemy, and indeed Worsley's chymical ambitions far outstripped his capabilities.[48] This was apparent to his correspondents, and Hartlib's 'Ephemerides' for 1655 noted an anonymous scholar known to Boyle, well 'versed in all Chymical Writings', who was 'more vsed in the practical part then Mr Worsley'.[49] However, this does not necessarily mean that Worsley was 'content to rest assured in the superiority of theory and let others descend to the harsh world of laboratory practice', although his letters sometimes give that impression.[50]

---

[40] Ibid. HP 42/1/27A.
[41] Worsley to Hartlib, c. autumn 1654, HP 42/1/38B.
[42] Ibid. HP 42/1/39A.
[43] Clodius to Worsley, c. Aug. 1654, HP 42/1/36–37. For which see Newman and Principe, *Alchemy tried in the fire*, 251.
[44] Worsley to [Clodius], c. summer 1654, HP 42/1/26A; Worsley to [Hartlib], 31 Oct. 1654, HP 42/1/3A.
[45] [Worsley] to [Hartlib], c. autumn 1654, HP 42/1/39A.
[46] Worsley to [Hartlib], 31 Oct. 1654, HP 42/1/3A.
[47] Ibid. HP 42/1/3B.
[48] Newman and Principe, *Alchemy tried in the fire*, 250.
[49] 'Ephemerides', 1655, pt IV, HP 29/5/52A-B.
[50] Newman and Principe, *Alchemy tried in the fire*, 251.

Rather, the rhetorical stance of the outsider was defensive: by denying that he claimed the full status of an adept, Worsley hoped to preserve the integrity of his ideas and his capability to pursue his own 'great work'. Worsley consistently advocated an experimental approach to natural philosophy, but he lacked the time and resources to follow the intensive labour demanded by alchemy. But he seems to have been far from 'content' with this situation, which bred a degree of self-doubt beneath his veneer of intellectual arrogance. On the subject of alchemy, he claimed 'to prefer it before any other natural knowledge, or, perhaps, employment; yet I can find nothing very valuable or very desirable, either in myself, or others. And when I have once a while considered things, I find myself as much inclined to fear or suspect them, as I do to wish them'.[51]

Plants and stars

One reason why Newman and Principe highlighted Worsley's relative inexperience in practical alchemy appears to have been to show that his branch of alchemy – the *sal nitrum* 'school' – was 'antithetical to the highly technical operations' which characterised the work of George Starkey, whom they see as Robert Boyle's key chemical tutor.[52] The example of Glauber perhaps suggests that the two were not necessarily incompatible, but Worsley's own practice of metallic alchemy was undoubtedly limited, although one letter almost certainly written by him to Hartlib provides evidence that he was producing chemical medicines in Dublin deploying antimony, and used to induce sweating.[53] The letter also mentioned the 'stupendious effects' of medicines produced by the 'common Antimonycall Cup', and Worsley had described such a receipt, for use on horses, in a letter written from Amsterdam.[54] Worsley described antimony as a 'great a restorer of the Liver, or so great a purifier or refiner of the masse of Blood', and even repeated this receipt in a letter to Boyle of 1659.[55] Thus it would be unfair to conclude that Worsley's furnaces were unlit during the 1650s, but none the less the occasional production of chemical medicines was a long way from his lofty ambition to discover the 'philosophical putrefaction' of metals.

Instead, Worsley's scientific experimentation in the 1650s took him out of the laboratory and into the field and garden, as he delved more deeply into the question of vegetation. Although they did not encourage much

---

[51] Worsley to Hartlib, c. late 1653, quoted in Hartlib to Boyle, 28 Feb. 1654, Boyle, *Correspondence*, i, 155.

[52] Newman and Principe, *Alchemy tried in the fire*, 238.

[53] [Worsley] to [Hartlib], 1656, HP 26/58/1B.

[54] Worsley to Hartlib, 18 May 1649, HP (Royal Society, Boyle letters 7.1, fo. 1r). This remedy, which involved stewing ale and spices in the antimony cup, was published in Hartlib, *Samuel Hartlib his legacie*, 267.

[55] [Worsley] to [Boyle], c. late 1658–early 1659, HP 42/1/29B.

serious practice in metallic alchemy, Worsley's *sal nitrum* ideas did provide a framework for investigations into organic chemistry which were much more suitable for the part-time practitioner. Before he arrived in Ireland, Worsley had already taken an active interest in the science of agriculture; for example in 1651 Hartlib reported that he had 'an Experiment of the highest Philosophy viz How to make out of Apples very good sugar which would bee to turne England into Barbados'.[56] His circumstances in Ireland meant that Worsley increasingly turned to this area as an outlet for his scientific aspirations, and during his stay from 1652–3, he was studying fruit preservation.[57] As well as its practical uses, this might cast light on the processes of growth and decay in nature in general and therefore deserved more philosophical consideration, and Worsley also noted how fermented mother of saltpetre could be used to preserve and cool water.[58] When he returned to the subject of saltpetre in 1654, this was likewise subordinated to 'higher' questions about vegetation. However, Worsley recognised that his claims had to be grounded in experiment and observation, and so he set out a programme to investigate the effects of different salts on plants, to discover if 'any salt doth vniversally nowrish all Plants ande make them thrive'.[59] It was first necessary however to consider the other variables: 'water to dissolve et make fluid the particles of Salt, whereby the pores of the Plant or seed may … admitt it' and 'Earth as a fitt Vterus or matrix to keepe the thing planted steady'.[60] Thus Worsley's considerations turned to the composition of earth, 'For my imbitions signify nothing if my Earth bee before hand impregnated with an other Salt'. Similarly, Worsley considered whether 'raine-water hath life in it selfe', something suggested by the apparently spontaneous appearance of minute insects in putrefied water.[61]

Although he was only able to return to science at intervals, it appears that Worsley followed this framework throughout the decade. During the 1650s members of the Hartlib circle had become increasingly interested in the subject of husbandry, for both practical and speculative reasons. The centrepiece of Hartlib's agricultural publications was his *Legacie of husbandry*, the third edition of which included Worsley's letter of 16 May 1654, as 'A philosophical letter concerning vegetation or the causes of fruitfulness'.[62] As well as much practical information concerning agricultural techniques (including a letter by Worsley on the technique of 'rowling' to spread roots), the *Legacie* included several other 'philosophical' enquiries, notably Robert Child's long letter on defects in the practice of husbandry.[63] Like Worsley,

[56] 'Ephemerides', 1651, pt I, HP 28/2/2B.
[57] Ibid. 1653, pt II, HP 28/2/57A.
[58] Ibid. 1653, pt III, HP 28/2/63B.
[59] Worsley to Hartlib, 16 May 1654, HP 66/15/1B.
[60] Ibid. HP 66/1/2A.
[61] Ibid. HP 66/1/2B.
[62] Hartlib, *Samuel Hartlib his legacie*, 217–19.
[63] Worsley's letter is printed ibid. 105–7. References in Hartlib's 'Ephemerides' suggest that this letter dated to spring 1651: HP 28/1/7B, 8B, 9A.

Child was concerned to base his knowledge on sound principles, to which end he posed the questions 'whether all things are nourished by Vapours, Fumes, Atoms, Effluvia? or by Salt, as Urine, Embrionate, or *Non specificate*? or by Ferments, Odours, Acidities?'[64] Worsley was evidently inspired by Child's enquiries, for he later explained that his thoughts 'vpon the whole subject of vegetation' were merely 'a Comment' on these 'ingenious, large, & comprehensive Qveries'.[65]

Worsley became acquainted with one likeminded correspondent of Hartlib, the 'philosophical gardener' of Herefordshire John Beale, during his extended visit to England from 1656 to 1657.[66] At the author's request, Hartlib sent Worsley a copy of Beale's chapter headings for his planned work on gardening, 'A physiqve garden'.[67] Worsley responded favourably to this 'Treasure', replying with his own methodical programme of agricultural research, based on observations such as that 'all Earth, that had a competent vigor & lust, was perpetually conceiving & spawning, though noe way assisted, sollicited, or imprægnated, by the care ... of Man'.[68] Worsley next turned his attentions to the natural properties of plants, and their 'improvement or alteration' by artificial means. Each plant would be analysed to compare fertility in a range of climates and different soils. These findings would provide the 'Substrata to the intended discourse', on 'the true causes of vegetation'.[69] A second branch of enquiry would consider the 'Oeconomicall' uses of plants, in manufacturing, dying, food and medicine. Thus Worsley posited a thorough Baconian natural history of plants, although his exemplar was another natural historian, the botanist Petrus Lauremberg.[70] Beale went on to tailor his research in horticulture, sylviculture and fruit preservation, to Worsley's 'acute enquyryes & proposalls'.[71]

Worsley's planned natural history of vegetation was also the occasion for his most well-known scientific treatise. One part of the research programme would consider experiments to preserve fruits, and his 'Phytologicall letter' to Hartlib recounted a trial to conserve gooseberries which, after nine months, were found to be fully restored to their original colour and taste

---

[64] Ibid. 38, discussed in Debus, *Chemical philosophy*, ii. 422–3.

[65] [Worsley] to Hartlib, *c.* Apr. 1657, HP 8/22/1A.

[66] On Beale see M. Stubbs, 'John Beale, philosophical gardener of Herefordshire', *Annals of Science* xxxix (1982), 463–89 (pt I); xlvi (1989), 323–63 (pt II), and M. Leslie, 'The spiritual husbandry of John Beale', in Leslie and Rayler, *Culture and cultivation*, 151–72.

[67] J. Beale to Hartlib, HP 55/21/3–4.

[68] [Worsley] to Hartlib, *c.* Apr. 1657, HP 8/22/1B. Hartlib entitled this 'a Phytologicall Letter'.

[69] Ibid. HP 8/22/2B.

[70] Lauremberg, coiner of the term *Pansophia*, was author of an *Apparatus plantarius*, Frankfurt 1632, on bulbous and tuberose plants, listed in Worsley's *Catalogus*: L. Thorndike, *A history of magic and experimental science*, VIII: *The seventeenth century*, New York 1958, 7.

[71] Beale to Hartlib, 18 Apr. 1657, HP 52/15/1A. See also his letters of 4 May 1657, HP 62/23/1–4, and 9 Apr. 1658, HP 52/73–85.

when immersed in hot water.[72] This appears to have been the 'strange way of preserving Fruits, whereby even *Goos-berries* have been kept for many Moneths', based on 'a new and artificial way of keeping them from the Air', which was included in part two of Boyle's *Of the vsefulesse of natural philosophy*.[73] Worsley had certainly been passing on to Boyle his experiments 'about a more perfect way of conserving of green flowers and fruit' at this time.[74] Physical corruption, Worsley recognised, depended in some way on atmospheric conditions, and so his enquiries into vegetation led him to consider the effects of meteorological events such as thunder and rain, and their relationship with 'The Operation & influence of the Sun … the Moone', and 'the other Coelestiall bodyes'.[75] Consideration of these astral influences led Worsley to the controversial subject of astrology, and he hoped that experimentation might establish 'a greater Certainty in these Principles'. Having returned to Ireland in summer 1657, Worsley wrote a long 'Physico-astrological letter' which, as Antonio Clericuzio discovered, was eventually published anonymously in Boyle's posthumous *The general history of the air* (1692), entitled 'Of celestial influences or effluviums in the air'.[76]

Worsley's original premise was that the decay of organic bodies was related to atmospheric conditions, which in turn relied on planetary motions. Whilst he never claimed to be an astronomer himself, Worsley had become an enthusiastic purchaser of telescopes in Amsterdam, and later procured information from Boyle about the three 'systems of Saturn' of Huygens, Gassendi and Hevelius, as well as the telescopes of Boyle's fellow Oxonian, Christopher Wren.[77] Of the current astronomers, Worsley hoped that Thomas Street and the German Nicolas Mercator, both known to Hartlib, might together perfect the 'Theory of the Plannetts' and surmount those 'Errors and disagreements in opinion' which had plagued the discipline.[78] Worsley however saw little value in calculating the motions of the plancts for their own sake, unless 'Wee cann propound noe end benefitt vse or Advantage,

[72] [Worsley] to Hartlib, *c.* Apr. 1657, HP 8/22/3B.
[73] Boyle described this method as being from an 'eminent Naturalist': printed in *Works of Robert Boyle*, iii. 358.
[74] Worsley to Boyle, 14 Oct. 1657, *Boyle correspondence*, i. 242.
[75] [Worsley] to Hartlib, *c.* Apr. 1657, HP 8/22/2B–3A.
[76] Worsley to Hartlib, *c.* July 1657, HP 26/56/1–4. See Clericuzio, 'New light', 236–46.
[77] [Worsley] to [Boyle], *c.* late 1658–early 1659, HP 42/1/28A. Hartlib recorded the names of Worsley's favourite 'optical Workemen' in his 'Ephemerides' of 1657: Baily, Smethwick and Straitter, HP 28/6/16A, 16B, 17A. Works on astronomy in Worsley's *Catalogus* included Johann Hevelius' *Selenographia* (1647) and *Dissertatio de nativa Saturni facie* (1656), two editions of Christian Huygens's *Systema Saturnium* (1659), as well as works by Galileo, Christoph Scheiner, Gassendi, Thomas Lydiat and contemporary English astronomers including Thomas Street, Vincent Wing, Thomas Williford, Seth Ward and Joseph Moxon.
[78] Worsley to Hartlib, *c.* July 1657, HP 26/56/1B.

That may recompence *the* Trouble & pains bestowed vpon them', and the particular end he had in mind was to test astrological predictions. Worsley was wary of being accused of the same 'superstition & Paganisme' as astrologers, who were often persons of 'Imposture, ignorance and want of Learning'. However, he remained convinced that the stars exercised great powers:

> these Cælestiall bodyes (according to *the* Angles they make one vpon another but especially with *the* Sunn or with *the* Earth in our Meridian or with such and such other points in *the* Heauens) may haue a power to cause such & such Motions Changes and alterations (stronger or weaker according to *the* Nature of *the* Angle) as *the* Extremityes of which shall at Length be felt in every one of vs, And this may be evidenced first by vndeniable experiments not only from things inanimate & vegitate but from *the* vndoubted observations of Physitians as well in seuerall Chronicall as Acute distempers & more eminently in all Lunaticke Epilepticke Paraliticke or Lethargicke Persons.[79]

In order to reform astrology, Worsley suggested a Baconian natural history based on observing and recording various meteorological and atmospheric conditions as they related to the position of the stars. By accurately recording these variables, it would be possible to test planetary influence on the weather.[80]

Worsley attached particular importance to air-pressure, which he understood as determined by two opposite 'motions', rarefaction and condensation, which were related to the 'Extreame Motions' of generation and corruption.[81] Whereas Cartesian philosophy reduced natural phenomena to mechanistic matter and motion, Worsley's understanding of motion was biological, something which he shared with many alchemical authors.[82] This perspective avoided the apparently materialistic implications of Cartesian physics, as the final cause of all movement was determined by an inherent biological force, which could be identified with *sal nitrum* or, as Worsley increasingly termed it, energy. Worsley's ideas about celestial influences were steeped in the cosmologies of Paracelsus' followers, and Clericuzio has identified Jean d'Espagnet's *Enchiridion phisicae restitutae*, which was in fact listed in his *Catalogus*, as a possible source.[83] Thus, the planets and the sun and moon had their 'owne Proper light', which was 'accompanied further with some power virtue or Tincture that is proper to it'.[84] Together these planetary bodies transmitted their lights to earth, exerting powerful effects on the planet and its atmosphere. Weather conditions were one product of

[79] Ibid.
[80] Ibid. For this, and other, attempts to 'reform' astrology see P. Curry, *Prophecy and power: astrology in early modern England*, Cambridge–London 1989, 61–7.
[81] Worsley to Hartlib, *c.* July 1657, HP 26/56/2B.
[82] Debus, *Chemical philosophy*, ii. 316.
[83] Clericuzio, 'New light', 241.
[84] Worsley to Hartlib, *c.* July 1657, HP 26/56/3A.

these astral influences, but the sun's rays also awakened forces latent in the earth:

> Not only the Ayre by reason of its Thynnes & subtlety is capable of being thus penetrated moved and altered by these planatary virtues and Lights. But for asmuch alsoe as our spirits and the spiritts likewise of all mixt bodyes are really of an Aerious ætheriall Luminous production & Composition these spiritts therefore of ours and the spiritts of all other Bodyes must necessarily noe Less suffer an impression from the same Lights and Cannot be Lesse subject to an Alteration, Motion, Agitation, and infection through them and by them … these spiritts being the only Principles of Energy, power, force, & life in all bodyes wherein they are, and the immediate Causes through which all alteration Comes to the bodyes themselves.[85]

The earth was thus 'enlightened, warmed, Cherished and Frucified by the power vertue and Influence of the Sunn'.[86] Worsley explained how solar rays awoke the 'seminall dispositions, Odors and ferments' residing in terrestrial bodies. Just as the philosopher's stone penetrated base metals to act on their inward 'spirits', or the *semina* in saltpetre transmitted its virtues into neighbouring matter, interplanetary rays penetrated the atmosphere, stimulating growth and decay. These were the astral effects which Worsley hoped to analyse with the methods and instruments of the new science.

Hartlib went on to circulate copies of the treatise around his circle, procuring a Latin translation from Mercator so that it might be sent overseas.[87] Beale gave a favourable response, and this encouraged Worsley to seek the opinions of other learned authorities such as Elias Ashmole, but particularly from 'our frinds & correspondents at Oxford'.[88] He also wrote a shorter 'Problema physico-astrologicum' which considered the influence of the moon, 'the Laboratory workehouse or shop of the rest of the Planets'.[89] Unfortunately, Worsley found the Oxford academics to be unsympathetic, sadly noting that 'our vniverity Professors are resolved to stand to the Doctrine & Tradition of their Fathers, without further doubt or question'.[90] Just as was the case in his debate with Clodius, Worsley was forced onto the defensive, denying that he intended 'a positive proofe or assertion of the Planetts Influences', although he reaffirmed his belief that astrology was 'an antient, a great, a vsefull, a necessary, & a certaine truth' without which 'noe man shall ever vnderstand the Antient Philosophers', or 'finde out their great secret'.[91] But the response from Oxford persuaded Worsley to have his

---

[85] Ibid. HP 26/56/3B.
[86] Ibid. HP 26/56/2A.
[87] Clericuzio, 'New light', 238. The Latin copy is at HP 42/1/18–25.
[88] Worsley to Hartlib, 14 Oct. 1657, HP 42/1/9A. For Beale's response see his letter to Hartlib, 15 Sept. 1657, HP 31/5/51–60.
[89] HP 42/1/16A.
[90] Worsley to Hartlib, 20 Oct. 1657, HP 42/1/11A.
[91] Ibid. HP 42/2/11B.

name removed from Mercator's translation, and once again he retreated into scientific anonymity.[92]

Principia sub alterna

This episode seems to emphasise Worsley's intellectual distance from Boyle and his Oxford milieu. However, Boyle evidently valued the letter enough to include it amongst the material for his *General history of the air*, and Clericuzio and Henry have suggested that he probably agreed with its general approach.[93] Thus it might be that Boyle took seriously some of those speculations about astral influences which Worsley inherited from the *sal nitrum* tradition of Sendivogius and Glauber. Boyle covered this subject in his *Tracts about the cosmical qualities of things* of 1671, which considered the possible existence of effluvia with special properties which were projected by the stars, whilst his eclectic natural philosophy incorporated numerous chemical qualities.[94]

Boyle was consistently wary of mathematical reductionism, and one unpublished essay noted that 'There are a great many things which … cannot with any convenience be immediately deduced from the first and simplest principles; namely matter and motion; but must be derived from subordinate principles; such as gravity, fermentation, springiness, magnetism etc'.[95] Worsley had ventured a similar position during his debate with Clodius. Against Worsley's claims about salt, a friend of Clodius had put forward van Helmont's belief that water was the *prima materia*.[96] In response, Worsley suggested that

> though we must according to this analysis at length determine our thoughts into deCartes principles of not onely of water, but of atomes. yet as these thinges have theire commendation, so the knowledge of other bodyes which may … be principia sub alterna; though Atomes or water maye said to be principia generalissima, are often times very vsefull.[97]

Worsley's 'principia sub alterna' reminds us of Boyle's 'subordinate principles', and Newman and Principe too have noted a similarity with Boyle's

---

[92] Clericuzio, 'New light', 238.
[93] Ibid. 239; J. Henry, 'Boyle and cosmical qualities', in M. Hunter (ed.), *Robert Boyle reconsidered*, Cambridge 1994, 127.
[94] Henry, 'Boyle and cosmical qualities'; A. Clericuzio, 'A redefinition of Boyle's chemistry and corpuscular philosophy', *Annals of Science* xlvii (1990), 561–89, and *Elements, principles and corpuscules*, 103–48.
[95] This is quoted in Henry, 'Boyle and cosmical qualities', 123.
[96] For Helmont on water see Newman, *Gehennical fire*, 111, and C. Webster, 'Water as the ultimate principle of nature: the background to Boyle's Sceptical chymist', *Ambix* xiii (1966), 96–107.
[97] [Worsley] to [Hartlib], c. autumn 1654, HP 42/1/38A.

use of 'intermediate explanations' not immediately reducible to matter and motion.[98] For Worsley, 'vegetation' was one such principle and, although he consented to mechanism, he believed that this did not preclude the existence of other processes in nature. He would have encountered corpuscular theories of matter which posited atoms bearing qualities and powers in many works listed in his *Catalogus*, by both Paracelsian and anti-Paracelsian authors, including Libavius, Sala, Nicholas Hill, Daniel Sennert, William Davidson and indeed Gassendi. In fact several contemporary English natural philosophers listed in the *Catalogus* were publishing similar corpuscular ideas, including Sir Kenelm Digby, Nathaniel Highmore and Walter Charleton.[99] Worsley's own natural philosophy was much more preoccupied with discovering the nature of 'energy', the life-giving force which he believed united all of Creation, than the *minima materia*. In this, he was not so far from contemporary natural philosophers inspired by Harvey's discovery of the circulation of the blood to investigate what ingredients were necessary to sustain life, culminating with John Mayow's conclusions about the role of aerial substances in respiration.[100] Thus, whilst Paracelsian or Sendivogian-style cosmologies were increasingly rejected as systematic explanations, notably by Boyle in *The sceptical chymist*, they had a residual influence which continued to stimulate research.

At about the same time that Worsley was investigating the nature of saltpetre, Boyle himself was researching the same subject, which would eventually be published as his famed 'Physico-chymical essay … touching the differing parts and redintegration of salt-petre'.[101] This essay repeated Glauber's experiment to separate saltpetre into its fixed and volatile parts, which Worsley had included in his own 'De nitro theses', and it may be that Boyle learned of this experiment via Worsley.[102] Although Boyle's 'Essay on nitre' was much more technically sophisticated than Worsley's, it seems possible that he was encouraged to turn to this subject by Worsley's digressions about saltpetre.[103] Similarly, the Worsley-Clodius debate perhaps exerted some influence on Boyle's own attempts to provide a firm corpuscular grounding to chemistry in publications like *The sceptical chymist*.[104] Worsley himself was reluctant to assign a simplistic universal structure to matter, considering instead:

[98] Newman and Principe, *Alchemy tried in the fire*, 254–6.
[99] For corpusclar in distinction to mechanistic atomism see Clericuzio, *Elements, principles and corpuscules*.
[100] Frank, *Harvey and the Oxford physiologists*.
[101] Included in *Certain physiological essays* of 1661: *Works of Robert Boyle*, iii. 93–149.
[102] Newman and Principe, *Alchemy tried in the fire*, 252–3.
[103] Ibid. 254. See also Frank, *Harvey and the Oxford physiologists*, 117–28.
[104] Boyle owned a copy of one of Clodius' letters to Worsley: Newman and Principe, *Alchemy tried in the fire*, 251 n. 149. On *The sceptical chymist* see Principe, *Aspiring adept*, 35–52.

Whether all this may bee sufficiently cleared from Aristotles Hypothesis of the 4. elements: Or from Paracelsus his 3. Principles of salt, Sulphur, & Mercury, or from Dr Cartes Doctrine of body figure or Motion; or whether by some Magnetick or Astrologicall supposition, Or whether without all these, by a plaine, direct, Analyticall Consideration & Examination of all & every particular body, concurring to Vegetation, & of the share, that each of them beareth from the very first Motion or Conception of Vegetation, to its ultimate Maturity or perfection.[105]

Worsley clearly leaned to the last position, but he surely would not have considered himself a doctrinal adherent to any 'school of thought', least of all an 'epigone' of Sendivogius.[106] On the subject of alchemy, Worsley concluded 'That this great worke is like the body of Philosophy, it is distributed into many parts … & many men have talked of Robin hood, that never shott in his Bow', citing Sendivogius as only one influence after Basil Valentine ('as having least Tricks, & most solidity of knowledge'), Paracelsus, Bernard Trevisan and others.[107] Although he certainly relied on Sendivogian ideas, Worsley's usage of them did not prevent him from maintaining the primacy of experiment over theory, which some mechanists seemed to deny.[108] His findings about saltpetre were based on 'common et familiar Experiments'; Helmont's conclusions about water were refuted by 'common experience, which is the Mistresse of Phylosophers'; he submitted his 'Physico-Astrologicall Letter', 'to the Iudgement of Comon experiense', asserting that 'things of the greatest consequence doe oft tymes depend vpon the most Comon observations'.[109] Indeed, he blurred the division between experience and experiment, and introduced his discovery of a luminous piece of wood by explaining that 'here happened a pretty odd Experiment to me'.[110] This providential Baconianism suited his part-time status, justified by the principle that 'God or Nature doth nothing in vaine', something which Boyle would not deny.[111]

Boyle, of course, raised experimentation to a higher level than this, but Worsley too developed a characteristic approach to natural history, whereby 'common experiments' would provide the basis of more 'philosophical' investigations.[112] Both his 'enquiries about Vegetation' and his proposed natural history of astrology took this form. Another example is a proposed investiga-

---

[105] [Worsley] to Hartlib, c. Apr. 1657, HP 8/22/2B.

[106] Newman and Principe, Alchemy tried in the fire, 251.

[107] [Worsley?] to [Hartlib?], 14 Feb. 1655/6?, HP 42/1/5A.

[108] For Descartes see R. M. Sargent, The diffident naturalist: Robert Boyle and the philosophy of experiment, Chicago–London 1995, 27–35.

[109] Worsley to Hartlib, 16 May 1654, HP 66/15/1B; 'De nitro theses', HP 39/1/19A; [Worsley] to [Hartlib], c. autumn 1654, HP 42/1/38A; Worsley to Hartlib, c. July 1657, HP 26/56/2A, 2B.

[110] Worsley to Boyle, 30 Oct. 1665, Boyle correspondence, ii. 569.

[111] 'De nitro theses', HP 39/1/16A.

[112] For Boyle see Sargent, Diffident naturalist.

tion of colours about which he wrote to Beale shortly after the Restoration, partly as a commentary on Boyle's similar enquiries.[113] The seventeenth century of course saw great advances in those technologies which allowed the natural world to be observed with new accuracy, and Worsley afforded these an elevated place in his natural histories, at one point outlining a 'history of Opticall Experiments' to improve telescopes.[114] In the same letter (to Boyle) he posed a series of questions about the new pendulum clocks developed by Christiaan Huygens, considering for example whether they were affected by the weather 'as it is supposed all other motions are'.[115] Elsewhere, Worsley subjected thermometers to similar trials.[116] Although he recognised the value of these instruments, Worsley believed that they offered only an indirect view of nature, which the naturalist should be wary of accepting uncritically. On thermometers, he warned that 'no man must expect another will ever be accurate in mechanical matters, upon a bare direction, without we take pains'. This seems to reflect an underlying unease with the mathematisation of nature, so that even an apparently unproblematic abstraction such as the measurement of time was a human construct. Another time-keeping device upon which Worsley commented, this time a water-clock or clepsydra, aroused similarly ambivalent feelings. Whilst Worsley considered 'that figure weight & motion are *the* affections of all visible quantityes & *that* noe Idea can be conceived rightly of figure without a supposition of commensurablenesse or Proportion', he also believed that no certain standards had been found for motion, weight or size.[117] This was because 'All motions *that* are made', such as those of the clepsydra, were an 'Imitation only of other motions', and failed accurately to match the rhythms of nature. This consideration led Worsley to doubt the principles of the mechanical philosophy more fundamentally:

> though some of our late Philosophers have told us much of Motion, & have beene earnestly desirous to resolve all *the* Phœnomena of nature into it, viz. either into circular hyperbolicall, ellipticall or rectilineall motion, yet they seeme very defective in describing to vs the cheefe Agent or cause ... to this motion. And sometimes *the* very motions *that* they do suppose or imagine to be in bodyes are altogether as intoxicate & absurd as *the* absurdityes they by this new Philosophy strive to avoid. See Hobbs about *the* Magnett. Lett any man also examine Cartes opinion how *the* minde itselfe comes to discerne or perceive colors as he hath deliverd it in his Dioptricks.[118]

Worsley found atomic explanations of colour to be 'deficient, & that which

[113] [Worsley] to [Beale], c. May–June 1660, MS Add. 78685, fos 103–4.
[114] [Worsley] to [Boyle], c. late 1658–early 1659, HP 42/1/28A.
[115] Ibid. HP 42/1/28A.
[116] Worsley to Hartlib, c. July 1657, HP 26/56/4A; Worsley to Hartlib, 14 Apr. 1658, quoted in Hartlib to Boyle, 27 Apr. 1658, *Boyle correspondence*, i. 267.
[117] [Worsley?] to Hartlib, c. Jan. 1658, included in Hartlib to John Pell, HP (MS Add. 4279, fo. 48r).
[118] Ibid.

stands in need of another solution, then that of Cartes', for example noting how the sun and air could change the colour of terrestrial bodies, which 'strickt Cartesians' would not accept.[119] To Worsley, mathematics was a human construction and, as such, could not fully encompass the complexity of God's creation, a perspective rather similar to Boyle's.[120] With typical relativism, Worsley considered that 'all Commerce whatsoever even throughout the whole world & almost all Artes' rested on 'a supposition of something to be certaine in measure bignesse or length, or in weight', standards not 'found in nature. Consent only giving the Being to that certainty there is & this consent growing into a use or law by continuance of time or Custome'. Worsley was reluctant, therefore, to elevate mathematics to the status of natural laws, and this also made him 'exceeding vigilant in all new mechanicall Production'.

Worsley's response to mechanism reflects the transitional nature of this period, as the new science impacted on existing intellectual structures.[121] Descartes's philosophy could appear to relegate the role of God in nature to that of a distant figure, and as an antidote Worsley elevated the importance of natural history, a subject in which he apparently read widely, and which to him demonstrated the full complexity of creation.[122] Similar concerns probably influenced his attachment to *sal nitrum* explanations, which lent themselves particularly well to spiritualistic accounts of the natural world, a tradition going back to Paracelsus' evocation of a chemical universe.[123] Culpeper was attracted to such ideas precisely because they accorded with his religious principles, and surely the same can be said of Worsley.[124] As the principle of life residing in all living things, this 'philosophical salt' could be equated with the neoplatonic *anima mundi* or the world-soul. For Worsley, salt was the source of energy which was necessary to sustain life, a force which united creation from the stars into the depths of the earth, causing all movement. From energy, it was easy to progress to the idea of an iden-

---

[119] [Worsley] to [Beale], c. May–June 1660, MS Add. 78685, fo. 103r
[120] S. Shapin, A *social history of truth: civility and science in seventeenth-century England*, Chicago–London 1994, 336.
[121] J. Schuster, 'The scientific revolution', in R. Olby, G. Cantor, J. Christie and M. Hodge (eds), *Companion to the history of modern science*, London–New York 1990, 217–40.
[122] As well as the authors noted in earlier chapters, Worsley's *Catalogus* included numerous works on natural history, by Francis Bacon (six works of natural history), Conrad Gesner (five), Jan Jonston (four), Georg Agricola and Andrea Baccius (three each). But these are outnumbered by an eclectic range of natural histories on subjects ranging from precious stones (Anselmus Boëtius de Boodt), to roses (Johann Karl Rosenburg), exotic plants (Prospero Alpini), silk worms (Olivier de Serres), insects (Thomas Moffet) and inks (Petro Maria Caneparius' *De atramentis*, Venice 1619, a work Worsley recommended: 'Ephemerides', 1658, HP 29/7/7B–8A).
[123] Debus, *Man, nature and the renaissance*, 52; Young, *Faith*, 169.
[124] See, for example, Culpeper to Hartlib, 4 July 1649, HP 13/254–5. See also Clucas, 'Correspondence of a "Chymicall gentleman"', 152.

tifiable 'spirit of life' itself which showed the presence of God throughout nature much more vividly than the mathematical world-view of Descartes, and indeed, Worsley's natural philosophy became increasingly fixated on the idea of the spirit throughout the 1650s.

Traditionally alchemy has been seen as a mystical art, involving the transformation of the self as well as the material world. However, Newman and Principe have argued that this ignores the strongly practical and scientific dimension to early modern chymistry.[125] Certainly their studies have confirmed this aspect, but Worsley belonged to the vitalistic and illuminist tradition of alchemy which they have downplayed. Writing to Clodius, he concluded by noting that 'A minde willing to bee crucifyed & made wholy conformable to the Lord Christ is ten thousand tymes dearer ... then all this knoweledge of the Lapis'.[126] Perhaps Worsley was hiding behind such pious rhetoric, but even so he was evoking a prevalent sense that the aspiring adept had to possess spiritual gifts as well as practical knowledge in order to perform this most exalted work. Worsley presented himself in this light to Hartlib, when he described his progress in the art. Having considered some of Glauber's writings, 'it pleased god to discover the thing so clearly to me, that I sett downe the very thing in my Adversaria, as a matter further to be weighed & experimented, & yet understood it not, nor was the better for it'. Only since coming to Ireland did Worsley begin to reach a higher understanding:

> nor should [I] have beene ever able to have applyed any of these hynts, so as to have made any vse of them vnlesse God had (as he did) further as it were imposed the consideration of it upon me, by bringing my observation to a non plus, upon a kind of fortuitous experiment made by me, which I speake even to this End to shew; that the Lord hath his seasons, & that it is not of him that wills, or of him that runnes, but of God only who in this as in more higher things enlightens whom he will.[127]

As Young noted, Worsley 'cast his younger self in the role of a competent technician who had not received insight into the hidden mysteries of his own knowledge', until he received divine illumination.[128] Young has perceptively shown that the attraction alchemy held for the Hartlib circle owed much to its ability to 'cure Creation' of its fallen state, by accessing metaphysical truths through the physical world, and mastering the fabric of nature itself.[129] Of course, a mystical appreciation of alchemy did not preclude serious experimental work; however, in order to understand the profound value attached to this 'great work' in the early modern period, it

[125] Newman and Principe, 'Some problems'.
[126] Worsley to Clodius, c. summer 1654, HP 42/1/27A.
[127] Worsley to Hartlib, 14 Feb. 1655/6, HP 42/1/5B.
[128] Young, *Faith*, 233.
[129] Ibid. 151–81.

is necessary to recognise its spiritual significance. To ignore mainly speculative practitioners like Worsley would actually be to underestimate the
contemporary cultural significance of alchemy, which extended far beyond
the laboratory. Even Boyle, we should remember, apparently believed in the
possibility that men could communicate with angels through the workings
of the philosopher's stone (although this concerned, as well as captivated
him).[130]

The reformation of medicine

All the ingredients of Worsley's natural philosophy in the 1650s are apparent
in a remarkable letter which he wrote to Boyle in late 1658 or early 1659.[131]
The recipient has only recently been identified, on the basis that he was
clearly an Oxford-based scientist, and also because the letter mentions a
receipt to cure the 'red water' in cattle which Boyle mentioned elsewhere.[132]
Worsley's authorship is confirmed by a number of factors. As well as fitting
in with the direction of his natural philosophy and theology at the time,
and mentioning a number of individuals in whom he had already taken an
interest (including Fromanteel, Huygens and Gassendi), the author offered
his old remedy for the rot in sheep, based on stewing ale in the antimony
cup.[133] But this letter, the surviving extracts of which amount to nearly
10,000 words, covered a range of subjects.[134] Worsley began by thanking
Boyle for taking care on his behalf of some unidentified business with the
Catholic nobleman Sir Kenelm Digby, another philosopher of salt.[135] In
response to an observation passed on by Hartlib, from the physician Jacob
Bontius, about the ocular benefits of consuming fish liver, Worsley noted

---

[130] Principe, *Aspiring adept*, 191–200; Hunter, *Robert Boyle: scrupulosity and science*,
93–118. In relation to Boyle's interest in angelic communication, Principe cited a letter
which considered the possibility of a 'Lapis Angelicus and Evangelicus', which might
allow communication with angels and spiritual enlightenment, written in the hand of a
Hartlibian scribe and dated 19 Oct. 1660. The tone of this letter is rather reminiscent
of Worsley's own scientific and religious ideas at the time, suggesting that he may have
been the author. Similarly, the author's request that the recipient (probably Hartlib)
communicate the letter anonymously would fit in with Worsley, as he was keeping a low
profile in the aftermath of the Restoration: BL, MS Sloane 648, fos 99–100.

[131] [Worsley] to [Boyle], *c.* late 1658–early 1659, HP 42/1/28–33, 60/2/1–4.

[132] The letter is printed in *Boyle correspondence*, i. 301–18. See also Beale memorandum,
HP 51/74–5, and Beale to Hartlib, 21 Dec. 1658, HP 51/52–4.

[133] [Worsley] to [Boyle], *c.* late 1658–early 1659, HP 42/1/29B.

[134] Two scribal extracts survive in the Hartlib papers: it is likely that at least one section
is missing.

[135] Frank, *Harvey and the Oxford physiologists*, 126–7. Worsley's *Catologus* listed Digby's
Two treatises of the nature of bodies and immortality of the soul, Paris 1644, *Theatrum sympa-
theticum*, Nuremberg 1660, and *Choice receipts in physick and chirurgery*, London 1668.

that his likely source was the Dutchman Petrus Forestus, whose works he had no doubt encountered in Amsterdam.[136]

Whereas twelve years earlier Boyle had requested scientific intelligence from Worsley's laboratory, now their positions were reversed, and Worsley depended on Boyle for the latest news of natural philosophy. In the commerce of ideas, Worsley was struggling to maintain parity with a Boyle intellectually energised by the fertile Oxford environment.[137] Perhaps aware that they were by now distant intellectually as well as physically, Worsley none the less wrote that he hoped that they might some day be 'at a lesse distance then wee are at present', claiming that 'you have the power (if ever the Lord bring us to meete) to challenge from mee the free discovery & plaine demonstration of those principles which I have acquainted you with in generall'.[138] These were his 'medicinall & Philosophicall Principles', and in particular his 'thoughts to begin a solid & practicall foundation of medicine upon'.

Worsley proceeded to outline a characteristically methodical programme of medicinal research, based on 'a diligent inquisition of the nature & essence of Health', and which factors 'may dissolve this naturall & well constituted Oeconomy of nature'. Worsley was open-minded about the 'sects of Physitians', whether 'Galenistarum, IatroAstrologorum, Paracelsitarum, vel IatroCHymicorum, Helmontistarum & Adeptorum', for each contained 'something that is certaine & experimentall'.[139] Thus, although the Galenic explanation for cathartic medicines was absurd, none the less experience had shown their benefits in some cases.

As well as being subordinate to experimental evidence, methods of treatment would have to be based on an understanding of the true causes of distempers, which Galenic explanations failed to do, Worsley citing 'the Plague, ... spotted & pestilentiall fever, ... poisons & venomous bytings of serpents, & ... contagion or Infection'.[140] In order to 'lay true & sure grounds for the reformation or augmentation of the Art of Medicine', Worsley asserted

---

[136] [Worsley] to [Boyle], *c.* late 1658–early 1659, HP 42/1/29A–B.

[137] It is difficult to ascertain the regularity of Worsley's correspondence with Boyle through the 1650s. Clearly sometimes they were communicated via Hartlib, and only two letters from Worsley to Boyle survive for the decade. One of these begins by noting that the latter had recently written two letters to Worsley which he had yet to reply to. Boyle was evidently still communicating his experiments to Worsley for his judgement, in this case some to do with copper and antimony, and another which Worsley cryptically referred to as 'the plot, that was laid at the *Rhenish* wine-house'. Worsley reflected that 'it is in part real experiment; the grounds of it solid; the law of it nature; the method of it certainty, or rather necessity ... a real door, a key, a light to things visible, and to the harmony between them and other things invisible'. This suggests that some of their intimacy from the late 1640s remained, and it would be interesting to know more about this unidentified experiment. However, Worsley could offer little experimental knowledge in return: Worsley to Boyle, 14 Oct. 1657, *Boyle correspondence*, i. 241–2.

[138] [Worsley] to [Boyle], *c.* late 1658–early 1659, HP 42/1/29B.

[139] Ibid. HP 42/1/30A.

[140] Ibid. HP 42/1/30B.

that it would be necessary to submit the progress of diseases to careful examination, through compiling 'Hystoryes' which would 'more purely observe the
course, way & method of nature'. Not all remedies worked for all people,
and Worsley noted the allergic reaction of one Lady of their acquaintance
to honey of roses. Such maladies could be of great value in understanding
physiology, revealing that 'there is a sense not only in the mouth of the
stomack but even in other parts of the body much more subtile'.[141]

Up to this point Worsley's discourse has all that we have come to expect
from his natural philosophy: a methodical outline, an eclectic approach to
competing explanatory systems and a stress on natural history prefiguring
somewhat Thomas Sydenham's approach.[142] At this point, however, the
tone of the discourse changed. Worsley identified the fourth aspect in the
reformation of medicine as understanding 'what is the Roote of death in
every man', meaning not just in individual cases, but the cause of mortality
itself, a subject which might seem to go beyond the compass of the physician.
In fact, it could be argued that this subject was not for mortal consideration at all: given that death had been the divine punishment for the fall, to
question its causes might be seen as blasphemous and beyond human reason.
Worsley acknowledged that death was 'a subject that is barely Physicall',
and perhaps 'that which is necessarily laid upon all men; and that which
wee finde to depend upon a fatality or decree; ... & that therefore all the
Philosophy that can be spent about it ... is but a meere vaine & empty
speculation'.[143] This, however, did not prevent him from venturing 'another
manner or solution then is perhaps commonly given':

> For it may be did wee rightly know all the Gates & Avenues of death wee
> should not thincke it either Enthusiasticke or Ridiculous either to affirme
> or to expect a freedome or Liberation from the common state of mortality
> & corruption: which state there are some perhap in the earth also (though
> not knowne save unto some few) who presume & that not without ground
> they shall see.[144]

By understanding the root of death, it might be possible to overcome death
itself and, even more contentiously, Worsley suggested the existence of some
who were close to achieving this condition.[145] Boyle was likely to need some
convincing about this for, although many alchemical authors had suggested
that the philosopher's stone could be used as a medicine which would greatly
extend the human lifespan, perhaps by hundreds of years, to actually assert

[141] Ibid. HP 42/1/31A.
[142] For connections between Sydenham and the Hartlib circle see A. Cunningham,
'Thomas Sydenham: epidemics, experiment and the "Good Old Cause"', in French and
Wear, *Medical revolution*, 164–90. For Boyle's own unpublished tract on medical reform
see Hunter, *Robert Boyle: scrupulosity and science*, 157–200.
[143] [Worsley] to [Boyle], c. late 1658–early 1659, HP 42/1/32A.
[144] Ibid. HP 42/1/31B.
[145] Ibid. HP 42/1/33A.

that death itself could be avoided was a dramatic statement.[146] One figure
to make a similar claim, the mystic Paul Felgenhauer, in a 'Theosophicall
German treatise' which was included in Hartlib's *Chymical and medicinal
addresses*, enveloped his prophecy of a death-defeating universal medicine
in apocalyptic warnings about the downfall of conventional medicine and
alchemy alike.[147] It would be a short step to collapsing the division of heaven
and earth entirely. For Worsley, too, the claim to immortality was as much
a spiritual as an intellectual one. To understand how Worsley came to make
this claim, it is necessary to consider the direction that his religion had taken
in the 1650s, and speculate about the identity of the 'candidati' whom, he
claimed, were ready to throw off the shackles of mortality and return to the
state of Adam in Eden.

[146] For the history of such aspirations see D. B. Haycock, *Immortal flesh: a modern history
of longevity*, forthcoming 2008.
[147] P. Felgenhauer, 'A translate of the eleventh chapter, taken out of a theosophicall
German treatise, printed in the year 1655', in Hartlib, *Chymical and medicinal addresses*,
n.p.

6

Spiritual and Political Principles, 1657–1659

The upper springs

Benjamin Worsley's religiosity presents certain ambiguities. Although he has been termed a Puritan, in the late 1640s he was pronouncing a theology almost 'latitudinarian', willing to elevate experience above Scripture in accounts of natural phenomena, trusting reason to discern truth, even to the extent that he found succour in Socinian writings. His letters disdained the convoluted spiritual outpourings of the sects, but showed little taste for religious discipline, seemingly preferring an irenic and anti-formal Protestantism. Ethically he expressed hostility to materialism and self-interest, whilst taking a robust stance towards worldly affairs. Indeed, it is sometimes hard to see how Worsley's conscience related to his actions at all.

All this seems to change in the 1650s. Surrounded by religious radicals in the army, Worsley appeared to absorb their mysticism, collapsing the division which he once erected between divine and human learning. Little wonder that William Petty judged that in religion Worsley was 'apt to be any thing that will make him great'.[1] It will be suggested that there was more continuity in Worsley's religion than Petty allowed, centred on a desire directly to access divine truth free of human encumbrances. However, this makes it difficult to directly relate Worsley's religion to any wider enterprise. In Charles Webster's account, Worsley was one of the 'spiritual brotherhood' whose Puritanism and millenarianism, projected externally into numerous projects, became a template for 'universal reform'. However, it is clear from his preface to *The advocate* that the connection between Worsley's religion and his worldly projects was not necessarily so direct. Worsley would indeed eventually base his political stance on the approaching millennium, but this does not mean that for him Revelation offered a consistent guide to public action, much less a manifesto.

In *The advocate*, Worsley had shown an ambivalence towards commerce which, despite its public importance, was a product of corrupt human desires. Worsley betrayed similar sentiments shortly after arriving in Ireland, having been sent a copy of a tract published by Hartlib outlining the means to enrich Virginia through cultivating silkworms and monetarising its economy. Worsley commented that whilst he liked the former, 'their Proposition about Money to be carried to Virginia j vtterly dislike even so much as if it were

---

[1] Petty, *Reflections*, 89.

possible j would banish money from here in Ireland'.[2] Similarly, in his debate with Clodius, Worsley asserted that a humble spirit was 'ten thousand tymes more to bee preferred then even the disposal of a whole commonwealths revennue'.[3] It was in this context, too, that Worsley apparently began to discuss his spiritual principles in writing, and this is no coincidence because the intensive self-examination demanded of the alchemist was similar to the spiritual seeking of the Interregnum. As Nigel Smith has discussed, this centred on the desire to experience the light of God internally through annihilating selfhood, an exercise which paradoxically elevated the self as the medium for spiritual awakening.[4] Worsley's letters at this time became increasingly concerned with 'registering the changing spiritual state of the self' in this manner.[5] To Hartlib he described his realisation that 'I am as dyrt, comtemptible, neyther having in my selfe nor being able to discerne any thing of goodnesse'.[6] God, and not man, was the source of all good and therefore his guide: 'And pray what is Dyrt he should thinke himselfe so good & so great, as to take upon him to iudge, what designes are fitt to be promoted in the world: & at what times & by what meanes?'

The Lord alone was 'the fountaine of good': apparently great men appeared like the bubbles produced by running water, ephemeral and soon replaced by others, a transience which men struggled to accept. 'God brings forth this excellency by this man & we are afraid, o he will dye or he will abuse it, & neglect it! Cannot he bring forth another Bubble, as big as he.'[7] This was a theology of human powerlessness, but not fatalism: purging oneself of human pride was the necessary preparation to becoming an appropriate vessel for Godly perfection, and 'God will never make any man Eminently Instrumentall for him, until he hath shewed him the uselessnesse of himselfe & of all other creatures.' Worsley's spiritual condition was therefore that of waiting on the Lord:

> He hath richly given me the nether springs, but it is the upper springs I wayte also for. He hath shewed me how large, & how bountifull he can be. But it doth not yet appeare to me wherfore he hath done all this, or wherein, or what time, or how farre he will make use of me, now if it be fitt for me, to wayte his will my selfe. … Are not those things that we specially receive from the Lord to be specially disposed of by him?[8]

---

[2] Worsley to Hartlib, 24 Nov. 1652, HP 61/7/9B. The tract in question was Virginia Ferrar's *Glory be to God on high*, London 1652. This extract was published in the second edition, which was re-christened *The reformed Virginian silk-worm* and included in S. Hartlib (ed.), *The reformed commonwealth of bees*, London 1655.

[3] Worsley to Clodius, *c.* summer 1654, HP 42/1/27A.

[4] N. Smith, *Perfection proclaimed: language and literature in English radical religion, 1640–1660*, Oxford 1989.

[5] Ibid. 229.

[6] Worsley to Hartlib, 31 Oct. 1654, HP 42/1/3B.

[7] Ibid. HP 42/1/4A.

[8] Ibid. HP 42/1/4A–B.

There was no comfort in this state. At this time, late 1654, Worsley's personal and public life were in flux, having seen his control of the Irish land survey cruelly snatched away by Petty, whilst suffering something of an intellectual humbling from Clodius. Politically, too, this was an uncertain period, and Worsley had little confidence about what role God had designed for him in these affairs. He would spend much of the rest of the decade thus waiting.

A permanent dream

His new Baptist associates were doubtless partly responsible for Worsley's 'spiritual turn', but his acquaintance with radical religion was also likely to have been partly literary. Worsley's library catalogue listed works from this period by Independents (Jeremiah Burroughs, Nathaniel Holmes), Baptists (Thomas Patient, Richard Everard, Samuel Richardson), Fifth Monarchists (Mary Cary, John Tillinghast) and other unclassifiable figures (John Salt-marsh, Sir Henry Vane). An important source of religious inspiration in these years was non-English in origin, transmitted by translators such as Giles Randall.[9] Worsley owned his edition of Nicolas of Cusa's *Opthalmos, or the single eye, entituled the vision of God* (1646), alongside English editions of Valentin Weigel (*Of the life of Christ*, 1648) and the familist Tobias's biography of Hendrik Niclaes (*Mirabilia opera dei*). Most numerous were the translated works of Jacob Böhme, nine in total (six of which were bound into one volume), although Worsley claimed to prefer the prophetic writings of Böhme's pupil Abraham von Frankenburg, 'whose writings seeme to me, to be much more allied to their Principles, then anything I could ever discerne in Böhmen'.[10]

Most influential, perhaps, was another translator of European mystical and neoplatonic literature, John Everard, represented in Worsley's *Catalogus* by the edition of his sermons published in 1653 as *Some gospel-treasures opened*.[11] When explaining to a (possibly baffled) Hartlib the meaning of his obscure passage on the 'upper springs', Worsley wrote that 'no man was like to do any great matters in this World, for God. That hath not the spiritt of Othniell (which is) to discerne Gods seasonable opportunityes'.[12] This was a reference to the biblical character who captured the city of Kiriathsepher and was given in return Caleb's daughter Achsah, and with her 'the upper springs

[9] For the significance of such translations see Smith, *Perfection proclaimed*, pt II.

[10] [Worsley] to [Hartlib?], 14 Feb. 1655/6, HP 42/1/6A. Despite this statement there are distinct Behemist traces in Worsley's writings on the spirit, as discussed below, particularly in his use of the term 'centre'. The forthcoming publications of Dr Ariel Hessayon on Böhme will no doubt cast more light on this.

[11] For Everard see Smith, *Perfection proclaimed*, 107–36, and D. Como, *Blown by the spirit: Puritanism and the emergence of an antinomian underground in pre-civil-war England*, Stanford 2004, 219–65.

[12] Worsley to Hartlib, 29 Nov. 1654, HP 42/1/4B.

and the nether springs' of her father's land (Joshua xv. 16–17). Everard had used this passage to demonstrate his method of reading Scripture to reveal its true, hidden meaning, taking the Hebew translation of the names to interpret the passage as saying 'whosoever smiteth and taketh the City of the Letter' – meaning the outward sense of Scripture – would enjoy 'the Rending of the vail' – its true meaning. Othniel, from the Hebrew, meant 'Gods good time, or The Lords fit Opportunity'.[13] The sense that Worsley was directly inspired by Everard's interpretation of this obscure passage is strengthened by several affinities between Worsley's self-debasing spirituality and Everard's own idiosyncratic writings, which centred on a six-step programme towards attaining 'deiformity', or oneness with God, involving recognition of one's own worthlessness and utter annihilation of the self: 'When the soul comes *to be awaked*, and to see God thus *filling all in all*, to be *the motion* and *agent* in all things: then he falls *down* before God, and is *ashamed*; and throws down *all his own pride* and *arrogancie*.'[14] When John Dury advised Worsley to seek experimental knowledge of Christ, he surely did not have in mind Everard's conclusion that 'To see Christ to be *all* in all *in us*, this is to know him experimentally'.[15] Worsley's letters, though, are infused with the same desire to experience God's 'inbreathings'.[16]

Interestingly, Everard's opening sermon was on the subject of Mark ix. 50 ('have salt in your selves'), which concluded by saying that 'salt is (for so it is) the central existence of every thing; that is, salt is *the substance, the strength, supporter, and compacter* of every visible and mixt body: So is Christ to every creature'.[17] Everard's insistence on the presence of Christ within all creatures (and not just the elect, for salt 'seasons all alike'), would later be evoked by the Quakers and their 'spirit within'. Worsley owned Quaker works by Nathaniel Rich, five by Isaac Penington, and a volume of tracts by George Fox and others, but he also had personal contact with at least one of those Quakers active in Ireland during his time there. This was John Perrot, who left in 1657 on a mission to convert the sultan of Turkey.[18] Whilst he failed to get that far, he did reach Rome where he turned his attention to the pope, only to be imprisoned as a lunatic. On the way, Perrot had written to his 'Deare Friend' Worsley, explaining his progress and asking that he provide assistance to his ship-captain; his salutation to Worsley was characteristically Quaker, 'Reaching the seed in thee'.[19] Perrot was spurred

---

[13] J. Everard, *Some gospel-treasures opened*, London 1653, 277–8. For a commentary on this sermon see Como, *Blown by the spirit*, 232–3.
[14] Everard, *Gospel-treasures*, 20.
[15] Ibid. 77.
[16] Worsley to Hartlib, 29 Nov. 1654, HP 42/1/4B.
[17] Everard, *Gospel-treasures*, 15.
[18] For Quakers in Ireland see Barnard, *Cromwellian Ireland*, 109–12. For Perrot see N. Smith, 'Exporting enthusiasm: John Perrot and the Quaker epic', in T. Healy and J. Sawday (eds), *Literature and the English Civil War*, Cambridge 1990, 248–64.
[19] J. Perrot to Worsley, 10 Sept. 1657, HP 26/28/2A.

on by a personal revelation in which the Lord had chosen him as his 'sharpe instrument to thresh upon the mountains of turkye'.[20] Worsley sent a copy of this prophecy to Hartlib, along with Perrot's letter and an expanded account of his journey, in his own hand.[21] Thus it is likely that Worsley was personally supporting the Quaker's venture, a conclusion strengthened by his accompanying note, signed 'one who is willing to serve the meanest for Christs sake'.[22]

Worsley apparently accepted the reality of Perrot's prophecy, which had 'hardly beene given to any stranger yett', and looked forward to 'that day which many see not though it be nigh ... when the Mountaines are throwne downe and the valleys exalted'. Perrot sought to make himself the Lord's vehicle, writing to Worsley 'not at a distance, but in the Truth of god, in his power & measure thou mayest feele my presence!'[23] Such sentiments collapsed the division between man and God, who spoke through him, and this was theologically dangerous territory even within the relatively tolerant Hartlib circle. Hartlib would later come to fear the 'sword of the Quakers', whilst to John Beale they were in 'the depthes of Satan. For they are filled with the gall of bitternes, & are ... given to rayling & reviling'.[24]

Indeed there was much to fear from that explosion of radical religion of the 1640s and '50s, marked as it was by 'episodes' of mystical illumination which merged God and the spirit in moments of supernatural inspiration, dreams and visions which were 'genuine intimations of the proximity of the divine'.[25] Despite the spectre of antinomianism, however, Hartlib and his correspondents were hardly free from interest in such inspired prophesies, as long as they derived from a reliable source. In early 1658 Hartlib sent to Worsley the collection of prophecies compiled by Comenius, *Lux in tenebris*, prompting from Worsley some reflections on the validity of prophecy as a medium for divine communication.[26] Although these visions were 'sweet-meates', Worsley was not wholly credulous: those of Nikolaus Drabik (Drabicius), for example, were 'dreames rather then visions', and 'Ordinary & naturall'.[27] However, Worsley also explained that he did not see the gift of prophecy as ceasing with the age of the Apostles. Prophecy was present in all ages, and its ultimate object was to explicate the 'person mystery office

---

[20] Copy of Perrot's prophecy, HP 26/28/4A.

[21] Account of Perrot's journey, in Worsley's hand, HP 26/28/3.

[22] Note from Worsley to Hartlib concerning Perrot, HP 26/28/5A.

[23] Note from Worsley? to Hartlib concerning the prophecy of John Perrot, c. late 1657, HP 26/28/1A.

[24] Hartlib to J. Worthington, 20 July 1659, in *The diary and correspondence of Dr John Worthington*, ed. J. Crossley, i (Chetham Society xiii, 1847), 143; Beale to Hartlib, 6 Aug. 1658, HP 51/4B.

[25] Smith, *Perfection proclaimed*, 102.

[26] On *Lux in tenebris* see F. Yates, *The Rosicrucian enlightenment*, London–New York 1972, 203–8.

[27] Worsley to Hartlib, 20 Jan. 1658, HP 33/2/12A.

Kingdome or Gospell of Christ', the great prophet himself and the 'Alpha & Omega of the whole'. Worsley accepted that there might be more specific prophecies relating to 'privatt or perticular Providences' such as Christopher Kotter's prediction of the restoration of Frederick V to Bohemia in *Lux in tenebris*.[28] But ultimately Scripture was the 'compleat hystory', and Worsley would 'despise & Reiect any Vision, dreame Exstasy Revelation or prophesy, that would pretend to shew vs another way or mystery of God'. Perrot-like revelations had their place in illuminating Scripture, but they were merely 'the very small and young dawnings, The thyn scattering Prodromi … In comparison of that great spirit of glory … that he is about to powre down vpon his church'.[29]

One reason to suspect that apparent prophecies may in fact be dreams was because of the fallibility of the mind and senses of fallen man. The concern of pedagogical reformers such as Alsted and Comenius (both very well represented in Worsley's *Catalogus*) was to build a method which would guide the mind from out of this labyrinth.[30] Worsley was well aware of the obstacles to gaining certain knowledge, hazardous 'Rockes' including 'bare opinion', and 'Prevalency & Authority of Custome'.[31] The fall of man had shattered the divine image of God, and left him in a condition of metaphysical uncertainty:

How will he be more certaine, That he is thereby neerer the truth: or that the Roote of what he so firmely & constantly beleeves rests not in some species of Melancholy: in some abtruse Web of metaphysicall subtility or vnintelligible curiosity. In the height or strength of an Active powerfull, perswasion & fancy. In a permanent dreame or in the shop & wombe of his owne single Imagination & notion or in the dreames & Imaginations of others that are eqvally as mad as he.[32]

The post-Reformation aspiration to transcend the corruptions of papal 'custom' and directly access God's message had left no recognised arbiter in spiritual affairs, which might lead to scepticism that man could ever rise above his fallen senses and reach God.[33] But just as he had affirmed that God would make him instrumental despite his worthlessness, Worsley proclaimed that with God's help truth would overcome doubt:

For I affirme positively that there is a multitude of Truth, yea which is more that Truth is much larger then errour. For error is but finite, weake, inconstant, temporary, & the production only of sleepe & of the night. Truth is

[28] Yates, *Rosicrucian enlightenment*, 203–4.
[29] Worsley to Hartlib, 20 Jan. 1658, HP 33/2/12B.
[30] D. Čapková, 'Comenius and his ideals: escape from the labyrinth', in *SHUR*, 75–91. Worsley's *Catalogus* listed no less than fifteen works by Alsted, and seven by Comenius.
[31] Worsley to Hartlib, 14 Oct. 1657, HP 42/1/7B.
[32] Ibid.
[33] Popkin, *Scepticism*.

infinite, powerful, strong, constant, before all time, & *the* production of necessity vnity light.[34]

Referring perhaps to philosophers like Descartes who sought to deduce their own existence and that of God from first principles, Worsley affirmed that 'a man may be more certaine of Truth then some are now of their owne beings, & that they are not Beasts rather then men'.

For the means to access this truth, Worsley turned to a fusion of reason and the divine reminiscent of Comenius' *Pansophy*.[35] Advocating the holistic study of all disciplines, Worsley warned that 'he that will study Chymistry also & thinke to compleate him*self* in knowledge thereby shall be allwayes in a labyrinth, & a thick wood without being able to institute a series of any experiments rationally sollidly & certainely'.[36] By contrast, Worsley aimed at becoming a 'vniversall Scholler', hoping like Alsted to overcome the fragmented self through 'a reformation of the individual, conceived as the restoration of the image of divine perfection to each of the human faculties through an encyclopaedic education'.[37] Alchemy, too, should 'lead vs to a certaine not imaginary knowledge of simplicity homogeniety clarity, purity, Perfection & *the* solitary & yet distinct waies of nature'.[38] Above all, true knowledge rested on seeing 'harmony, Image & resemblance' between the 'lawes, course, & motions' of nature, and '*the* lawes, mysteryes, Revelations, & discoveryes of things spirituall'. Only through this combination of human and divine learning could man 'see one face, viz. Constancy, simplicity, Identity, Homogeniety, Vnity'.[39]

Seventeenth-century intellectuals were preoccupied with affirming certain knowledge of God in the face of scepticism or atheism, and Worsley's solution was to invoke 'Truth' in an almost mystical sense, evoking the neoplatonic discourse *The nature of truth* (London 1641) by John Sadler's patron Robert Grevelle, Lord Brooke, which he owned. But God's presence could also be discerned in Scripture, in creation and in the rational soul implanted in man. As a divine faculty, reason was a vehicle through which to access holy truths and was thus not necessarily incompatible with revelation. Indeed, it was important to be wary of those who neglected clear thinking: the writings of Ramon Lull were 'darke, as full of Sophistication & corruptions', and Paracelsus, whilst commendable as a 'cleare & Rationall man', was 'intoxicated now & then partly with *the* sight of his owne knowledge'.[40]

---

[34] Worsley to Hartlib, 14 Oct. 1657, HP 42/1/8A.
[35] See Popkin, *Third force*, 104–5.
[36] Worsley to Hartlib, 14 Oct. 1657, HP 42/1/7A.
[37] Hotson, *Johann Heinrich Alsted*, 273.
[38] [Worsley?] to [Hartlib?], 28 July 1658, HP 15/8/19A. Although the author of this letter is not noted on Hartlib's extract, comparison with the following quotation strongly suggests that it was by Worsley.
[39] Worsley to Hartlib, 14 Oct. 1657, HP 42/1/7A–B.
[40] Worsley to Hartlib, 14 Feb. 1655/6, HP 42/1/5–6.

In the case of alchemy, 'the knowledge of that great secret doth correct the wildenesse of the Imagination & depends only upon the sobriety of Truth'.[41] However, thinking perhaps of his dalliance with Socinianism, Worsley was suspicious of those philosophers who sought to elevate human reason above its place, 'the right Reasoned man, the Atheist the formall Professor the luke warme ignorant hypocrite'.[42] Reason clearly had its limits:

> And therefore though I disdaine nothing that is Right & solid Reason, though I know or believe nothing nor can doe in Naturalls but vpon a very strict & severe scrutiny & exploration of Reason. Though I know noe man can have any thing in reality & truth that is not consistent with the highest reason. Yet as I doe make a vast distinction between the power of Reason & the Gifts (graces, goodnesse wisedome) & influence of God soe I doe much more putt a price vpon his Gifts in any man then vpon the consideration of his Reason & Parts.[43]

Knowledge without piety was thus empty, and recognition of this was a necessary step towards God, a journey from the self to the spirit. Worsley's understanding of the spirit was laid out in a series of 'Principles', beginning with the assumption that living things each contained within them a series of three 'centres', evoking neoplatonic as well as Behemist spirituality.[44] However, this equally echoed the scholastic understanding of the soul, which was divided into three sets of 'faculties': vegetative faculties possessed by all living things, including growth and reproduction; emotional faculties, providing for sensation and motion, and shared by humans and animals; and finally, confined to humans alone, the intellectual faculties of the rational mind.[45]

Worsley adopted a similar hierarchy of the spirit, although he included non-living objects in his discussion, perhaps to show that the whole physical world was connected by the same life-force. Worsley's basic unifying principle, shared by all bodies, was not a set of faculties but a 'Magicall Centre', which explained how 'the earth though moveable both annually & diurnally yet standeth with a perpetuall respect in its poles to one constant certaine poynt in the Heavens'.[46] Thus the earth followed a fixed orbit, and equally every terrestrial body contained 'a Center struck: which is the Center of Gravity to it, which Centre doth as constantly move paralell to the Centre of

[41] [Worsley?] to [Hartlib?], 28 July 1658, HP 15/8/19A.
[42] Worsley to Hartlib, 20 Jan. 1658, HP 33/2/12B.
[43] Worsley to W. Potter, 7 Apr. 1658, HP 39/2/62B.
[44] Worsley to Hartlib, 8 Sept. 1658, HP 62/10/1A. For the significance of 'centre' see Smith, Perfection proclaimed, 215, 245. My thanks to Dr Ariel Hessayon for pointing this out to me.
[45] D. Garber, 'Soul and mind: life and thought in the seventeenth century', in D. Garber and M. Ayers (eds), The Cambridge history of seventeenth-century philosophy, i, Cambridge 1998, 760.
[46] Worsley to Hartlib, 8 Sept. 1658, HP 62/10/1A.

the earth'. The second 'centre', found only in living ('or rather progressively moving') beings combined the motions of respiration and circulation of the blood. The constant beating of the heart and 'coveting of Respiration' were necessary for life itself, and Worsley interpreted them as 'paralel with the Light', by which he appears to have meant an external life-force circulated around the body in blood.[47] Although he did not overtly say so, this could clearly be identified with the 'philosophical' or 'central salt', *sal nitrum*.

These centres were distinct, but parallel. This was also true of the third centre in man, 'struck through his spirit or intellectual part (which is that that makes him capable of personality)'.[48] Just as gravity and respiration connected the individual to the cosmos, the spirit itself relied on a communion with the external world. Worsley demonstrated this by noting that 'noe Body Spirit or Soull … can stand or be one moment of time solitary, or by its selfe; but that all things both are in Consortship, & made in a dependance with, & upon some other things'. Just as the heart beat 'constantly in a Communion with ayre light or Anima Mundi', unable to move itself, the human spirit could not bear solitude, but constantly demanded 'a communion of its kinde & with its nature and kinds'.[49] Human sociability therefore demonstrated that the soul was incapable of self-motion, but required external stimulation.

In his preface to *The advocate*, Worsley had presented human society as corrupted by pride and custom, but his understanding of the spirit offered the hope of transcending this state. The spiritual centre in man gave him personality, and as such was the location of his desires for credit, power and esteem, and ultimately acquisitiveness and lust. However, man could attain spiritual perfection by considering 'what Spirit he entertaines into the bosome of him, to dwell and live & abide in him'.[50] The soul existed in different degrees of perfection, and it was necessary to 'separate the darkness from the light & to make the evening & the morning the first Day', an inner resurrection or reformation of the self. Corrupt society could be transcended by a communion of the spirits, uniting those 'that are reduced to a singleness of the truth & of the Light':

> Blessed are they whose centre union & rest is constantly in & with theire true roote & head. And blessed are they to whome the Lord hath & shall give a true & spiritual knowledg & discerning of theis things & of the great incomprehensible Misteryes that to attend them/ & are contained in them/ & to whom all this visible Worlds Power is nothing./ [51]

Here, Worsley discussed not only religion, but psychology, the metaphysical relationship between man and creation, and the nature of the true Church,

---

[47] Ibid.
[48] Ibid. HP 62/10/1B.
[49] Ibid. HP 62/10/2A.
[50] Ibid. HP 62/10/2B.
[51] Ibid.

as a spiritual union. By suggesting that living things could not move themselves he introduced a divine force as the final cause of movement in physical bodies, refuting materialist or mechanistic reductionism. However, rather than being a logical proof of the presence of the divine, Worsley's spiritology was intended principally to illuminate the inward struggle by which man could overcome his fallen and fragmented state, and attain perfection.

The search for divine perfection linked the sects of revolutionary England with the 'second reformation' of Alsted and Comenius, who hoped to see the *imago dei* restored to its original state, an internal reformation resembling a spiritual battle within the self. The fall of man, the divine sacrifice, the workings of grace and the resurrection could all take place within the individual, as could the millennial kingdom itself: 'as there are many Mansions prepared for us./ Soe perhap it is noe less true *that* there are many Mansions in us'.[52] This was the context in which Worsley wrote his letter to Robert Boyle in early 1659, claiming that death itself could be defeated.

Worsley's theology culminated in a spiritual communion, an alternative sociability which transcended the corrupt human world. In this light, Worsley's letter to Boyle appears as an attempt to reach him not just intellectually, but spiritually. We may speculate on how the famously scrupulous Boyle reacted to this approach.

In fact Worsley seems to have been aware of the religious objections his argument might provoke, and was at pains to demonstrate that it was not incompatible with Scripture's account of the origins of mortality in the fall. The author of this punishment, he explained, was not God, but the Devil, whose power was to 'alter the whole frame & Oeconomy of this our outward & humourall substance' and corrupt the body.[53] Physically, Satan wielded a power over the air, which brought corruption and death, 'by Rarefaction & Coagulation', the same atmospheric 'motions' which Worsley had considered in his 'Physico-astrologicall letter'. However, more important was the spiritual power by which the Devil was able to bring about spiritual death. Though physical mortality was introduced with Adam and Eve, the death of the spirit was repeated within each individual life thereafter, in the form of a struggle between light and darkness. Man had fallen from 'Paradyse & became changed in *the* very nature, Powers, principles & Operations of his life'.[54] But this did not 'extingvish that spirit in man that hath life in its roote', although darkness covered 'the face of this great & wide & indefinite Deepe … soule, minde, or spirit'. Recalling his discussion of the three 'centres' in man, Worsley described how the intellectual spirit was degenerated, unable to know even itself, indistinguishable from that of other creatures:

---

[52] Ibid.
[53] [Worsley] to [Boyle], *c.* late 1658–early 1659, HP 60/2/2B.
[54] Ibid. HP 42/1/32A.

The alpenetrating, Insanguinall indimensionall indissipable spirit of man not being able to oppose or resist in the meane time this inevitable motion or rotation of the spirit of the world together with the Periods & aspects of it upon her flesh nor yet able to defend this her wedded (Physikall & organicall) consort as not being recovered out of that state of weaknes & emasculatenes into which she is necessarily throwne by being subject to the Rule & light of the spirit of the world & of the flesh & to the light.[55]

If we recall that Worsley had described the intellectual centre in man as being in balance with the other centres, of gravity and respiration, here he seems to be suggesting that this attachment to the 'world spirit' was the cause of mortality. This was true both physically and spiritually, as man's fall into darkness had kindled 'a lust in the spirit of man to a union with the spirit of the world & with the outward light glory & splendor of it'.[56] But this spirit was 'fraile, brittle changeable & subject to all manner of motion & alteration', and man's lust to be united with it led to that 'constancy fixednes imortalitie (all which were & really are at the birth of every man hid in the roote of this his spirit) being utterly lost'.

However, it was possible for the spirit to overcome this darkness, and progress was possible through 'the severall Arts Invented, The multitudes of Lawes enacted & the subtility of that Policy & Government among men'. But the real victory of light over darkness would come from within. Worsley assumed 'that though all men come into the world alike darke, yet all men live not in the world so alike, some having raised & angelicall spirits while others are but Brutish & sottish'. Such elevation was a product of knowledge, acquired through 'labour, search, study & Travell', and God had 'afforded meanes for the improving, incouraging, & advantaging of him in his spirit & knowledge'.[57] Most important, God had promised 'to give wisedome, & to give his spirit to them that shall ask it'. Scriptural study showed that this was a promise of limitless 'light & knowledge', offering escape from 'the bondage, power, darknesse or naturall blindnesse of flesh & our sense by the light, power spirit wisedome of God'.

Whilst man's spirit, deceived by Satan, lusted for union with the world, it shared the condition of mutability and corruption of earthly objects, and the consequence was death. Therefore the only way to overcome death was to dissolve 'the lynk of lust or of unrighteousnes & sin in the roote of it which is the appetite'.[58] Fortunately, the spiritual power of Satan paled before that of God, and with his help the human spirit could be 'recovered into their true originall & pristine light':

As a state of darkenesse therefore is a state of weakenesse, so a State of light is a State of power. As a state of darkenesse & sense & brutishnesse

[55] Ibid. HP 60/2/2B.
[56] Ibid. HP 60/2/3A.
[57] Ibid. HP 42/1/33A.
[58] Ibid. HP 60/2/3B.

is a necessary & inevitable state of corruption & death, & cannot as wee acknowledge possibly be otherwise; so a state of light & exercise of power according to *the* spirit is a state of a life, or a state above *the* Power Reach or comprehension of death.[59]

Although death could literally be banished, Worsley did not anticipate this as resting on spiritual reflection alone. Ultimately, the causes of death were 'partly Physicall partly mysticall or Theosophicall'.[60] Man had to labour to achieve wisdom and enlightenment, through self-illumination and the study of nature, and Worsley's mention of 'the healing Water of an incorruptible fountain' reminds us of his scientific search for energy, that 'spermatical' liquid produced by nature to nourish all things. Divine and natural could never really be distinguished, however: the spirit was described naturalistically, and the study of nature would have divine ramifications.

What is striking about this letter is the ease with which Worsley moved from discussing a programme of Baconian medicinal reform which, one imagines, would have been welcomed by the soon-to-be founder member of the Royal Society, to a mysticism more to John Perrot's taste. No record of Boyle's response survives, but although he may have found its sentiments theologically suspect, we should note that in spite of his religious 'scupulosity' Boyle was relatively open to unorthodox opinions and influences, and was not so rigid a defender of Anglican orthodoxy as is sometimes suggested.[61] But there was undoubtedly a gulf between him and Worsley: at this point, the latter's spiritualism was at its zenith, and this would continue into 1659 when the breakdown of the Protectorate shattered the uneasy stability of the previous five years, creating a political vacuum which rival groups competed to fill. But whereas previously Worsley had questioned whether God's plan for England was clear, by now he was much more convinced that great changes were afoot, and his days of waiting appeared at last to be over.

Snares of the Devil

Man liberated from death would return to his pre-lapsarian state, a reformation of the individual which might be the basis of the reformation of the world. However, we have seen that Worsley's sceptical attitude to politics existed uneasily with any utopian pretensions, making him aware that the civil sword could threaten individual conscience, as Cromwellian rule

---

[59] Ibid. HP 42/1/33B.
[60] Ibid. HP 60/2/4A. The reference to 'theosophicall' causes suggests a Behemist influence, or perhaps Paul Felgenhauer's 'Theosophicall German treatise' from Hartlib's *Chymical and medicinal addresses*, referred to in chapter 5 above.
[61] For Boyle's attitude to religious unorthodoxy see Hunter, *Robert Boyle: scrupulosity and science*, 51–7.

seemed to demonstrate in its persecution of Quakers and Socinians.[62] We do not know if Worsley followed his patron Sir Henry Vane in calling for the separation of Church and State, but he did question whether civil authorities could suitably follow spiritual goals. In June 1655 Hartlib's German correspondent, the scholar Georg Horne, had written a letter calling for Protestants to unite against the papacy in a Holy War, 'While the English Fleet rides master vpon the Mediterranean Sea'.[63] Worsley's response is telling:

> For the Subiect of Dr. H. Letter, I doe a little stagger at, as not well vnderstanding the Composition of a Christiano Political War, not being as yet thoroughly convinced, that the way which the Lord has in his purpose determined for the subversion of Antichrist, is by a slaughter made of the Papists, or by an Oecumenical Councel & Confoederation of all the Protestants & their Princes. Yea I thinke, such Discurses to savor much more of Notion, & of a retired contemplative Speculation, then of a solid & sound judgment, even about the nature of Humane Actions.[64]

History showed 'the Vanity of such an Vndertaking', and the nation was 'in the darke, concerning the Councels of God'. In this state of transcendent doubt, Worsley counselled caution over 'such great & specious Ends', and advised 'following, rather then running, before the Voice of God in Providence'. This attitude upset John Dury, who had been advocating Protestant unity his whole adult life, often calling for a war against the papacy. He tersely advised that Worsley ('who has a good facultie of ripping vp deceitull & Politicall subtill practises of cunning men') devote his 'sharpe witte' to attacking the pope rather than his fellow Protestants, by which 'hee would serve God & the Commoncause at home, more advantagiously then I believe hee hath hitherto done in any of the employments'.[65] Dury was seemingly aware that he and Worsley were diverging in their attitudes to the Protectorate.

However, for most of the decade Worsley equivocated over opposing a regime which many saw as a betrayal of the 'good old cause'. He admired John Beale as a model of political impartiality, observing that 'those Persons are most successful in bringing forth of Generall good, ... are faithfull in the opportunities they have, though they seeme but small', in comparison with those who 'allwayes qvarrell with the present seasons & times'.[66] For most of the decade he was content to receive a state salary, but in 1658 Worsley became irrevocably alienated from the regime. His frustration centred on

---

[62] B. Worden, 'Toleration and the Cromwellian Protectorate', in W. J. Sheils (ed.), *Persecution and toleration* (Studies in Church History xxi, 1984), 199–233. See also J. Spurr, *English Puritanism, 1603–1689*, London–Basingstoke 1998, 114–30.
[63] G. Horne to Hartlib, 16 June 1655, HP 1/3/1A.
[64] [Worsley?] to [Hartlib], 1 Aug. 1655, HP 1/3/1B.
[65] Dury to Hartlib, 25 Aug. 1655, HP 1/3/3A–B.
[66] [Worsley] to Hartlib, c. Apr. 1657, HP 8/22/1A.

an attempt to finance Hartlib's old project of an Office of Address with the proceeds of Irish lands, which William Petty opposed.[67] This plan was launched in late 1656, during Worsley's extended visit to England, with William Rand's brother James fronting a petition to Cromwell on 25 December.[68] The committee appointed to consider this reported favourably, suggesting that the backers should be allowed to purchase £10–12,000-worth of debentures to finance the venture, subject to approval from the Lord Deputy and Council in Ireland.[69] Worsley was clearly organising the project behind the scenes in conjunction with Samuel Hartlib, Jr, supported by allies like Boyle; by December 1657 he claimed to have 'a considerable stock assigned by the donors', and things looked hopeful in January 1658 when the proposals were presented to the Irish authorities.[70] But, in February, he was warning that 'our affaire here is yet doubtfull'.[71] Worsley was soon complaining about his letters being opened under Petty's orders, and feared that Petty would take over the proposal for his own ends.[72] To avoid this Worsley turned to Dury, pleading that he personally stood to lose up to £800 if the plans did not go ahead.[73] But by June it was clear that the regime had no intention of offering support, the design having been 'privatly & by an unknowne hand obstructed'.[74]

As well as his personal antipathy to Worsley, Petty appears to have seen the revived Office of Address as a potential vehicle for Henry Cromwell's opponents.[75] Indeed, Colonel Sankey was involved, but despite this it is unlikely that there were any politically sinister motives in a venture supported by a moderate like Boyle.[76] However, Petty's suspicion encouraged Worsley to close ranks, stating that the venture had to be managed 'entirely among our selves, who understand the aimes, hearts, lives, ends, principles & Spirits one of another', naming Hartlib, Dury, Boyle, Sadler and Beale as trustees.[77]

---

[67] Barnard, *Cromwellian Ireland*, 229–34.
[68] Petition to Cromwell on the Office of Address, 25 Dec. 1656, HP 47/4/1. William and James's father, an apothecary also called James, had been an investor in the Irish adventure; his son James inherited his share in 1654: *CSPI*, *Adventurers*, 102.
[69] Committee report, HP 47/4/6.
[70] Worsley to S. Hartlib, Jr, 23/27 Jan. 1658, HP (Royal Society, Boyle letters 7.3, fo. 1v); Worsley to Hartlib, Jr, 29 Dec. 1657, included in Hartlib to Boyle, 7 Jan. 1658, *Boyle correspondence*, i. 248.
[71] Worsley to Hartlib, 10 Feb. 1658, HP 47/3/1A.
[72] Worsley to Hartlib, 23 Feb. 1658, ibid.; Worsley to Hartlib, 26 May 1658, HP 47/3/1B–2B.
[73] Worsley to Dury, 26 May 1658, HP 33/2/9.
[74] Worsley to Hartlib, 9 June 1658, HP 47/4/3B.
[75] Petty later noted (with tongue-in-cheek) the various means used to attack him in the late 1650s: 'Emissaries sent forth to all quarters from whence the least light was hoped; Letters dispatcht into all Corners of the Nation; a formal Office of Address erected': *Reflections*, 124.
[76] The subscribers to this venture apparently included Dr Thomas Clarges and Colonel Arthur Hill, certainly no radicals: see *ODNB*.
[77] Worsley to Hartlib, 26 May 1658, HP 47/3/2A.

Worsley was becoming ever more disillusioned with a regime which allowed someone like Petty to prosper at his expense, encouraging him belatedly to discover individual liberties against state power: 'If the state have a mind to set up such an Institution, let them doe it of their owne, & dispose it to their owne Ministers', he asserted, but 'If other men are willing to lay a foundation of so much good, let not the State hinder them by interposing among them; For in these things every man is free.'[78]

Worsley's political disillusion, his paranoia about Petty and his religious mysticism converged in 1658. He became increasingly concerned to ensure the support of his Hartlibian allies. In hyperbolical terms, Worsley offered himself to Hartlib 'as a sonne to be disposed of by you', promising to serve his wishes in the (increasingly probable) event of Hartlib's demise.[79] Such elevated piety was also prominent in Worsley's surviving correspondence with a newer acquaintance, the projector William Potter. Rather than taking an interest in his banking or engineering projects, Worsley took to offering Potter some rather pompous words of fatherly advice.[80] He cautioned Potter to recognise that his talents were 'from the Lord alone', and that 'the lesse you are knowne to men (expecially to those who onlÿ have the spirit of the world:) the lesse subject you will be to be deceived bÿ them'.[81]

In the light of his spiritual principles, personal relationships held an elevated significance. In his letter on the causes of death, Worsley hinted at the existence of a spiritual elect who would be used by God in his war against the Devil: 'That as he hath had his Venefici whom he hath instructed in this his art of poysoning incantation & sorcery soe the Lord & his Helias is about & will have their schoole of Candidati who shall instruct the world to avoid the snares of the Devill.'[82] By 1659 Worsley was quite attached to the prophecy of Elias Artista, whom Paracelsus had predicted would come forth to illuminate the world.[83] Worsley assured the ailing Hartlib that 'The Devill hath but a litle while & he Rageth', before 'the greate Elias & his ministery which is suddainly to suprize part of the world; Soe when he & his schoole fellowes of children are truly embodied in one society together, Satans power will never … deceive the world'.[84] Furthermore, Worsley claimed to have become 'acquainted with some that are really (at this present) of the said schoole of the said Elias Artist the greate'. Perhaps such hopes were behind an attempt by Worsley to exchange alchemical manuscripts with one 'Dr Floud', apparently a kinsman of the English mystical writer and promoter of the Rosicrucians, Robert Fludd, mentioned in Beale's letters to Hartlib

---

[78] Ibid.
[79] Worsley to Hartlib, 6 Jan. 1658, HP 33/2/7A.
[80] Worsley to Potter, 7 Apr. 1658, HP 39/2/62–3.
[81] Worsley to Potter, 20 Jan. 1658, HP 33/2/10, and 17 Nov. 1658, HP 26/33/6.
[82] [Worsley] to [Boyle], c. late 1658–early 1659, HP 60/2/4A.
[83] Young, Faith, 236–7.
[84] Worsley to Hartlib, 4 Feb. 1659, HP 33/2/16A.

in late 1658.[85] Beale longed to know Worsley's opinion of 'De adeptis, et R.C', but was himself wary of delving into magic, believing that Fludd had been 'iustly blameable for publishing soe much of those curious arts, which are dangerous & prohibited'.[86] Worsley certainly owned the edition of *The fame and confession of the fraternity of ... the Rosie Cross*, published in 1652 with a Sendivogian preface by Thomas Vaughan, as well as nine works by Fludd and six by his fellow mystic Michael Maier.

Although we can only speculate about whom Worsley meant by the 'candidati', he was more open about naming those oppressors who would be vanquished in the coming 'separation ... betwene the wheate & *the* chaffe'.[87] Following the failure of the Office of Address project, Worsley's outpourings against Petty became ever more apocalyptic as he warned that the Lord would bring his enemy 'if not to a timely & great Remorse, then to an eminent ruine. For it is no small stayne, Pride – crime & guilt that his soule hath contracted'.[88] Soon Worsley's apocalyptic anger would spread from Petty to the regime he served, as it began to unravel following the death of Oliver Cromwell.

The kingdom of the Lord

Worsley's pronouncements in those dramatic months were his most directly millenarian, and he was even confident enough to date the coming of the Lord to 1666 (a prediction shared by the potentially familist Elizabethan prophet 'TL', whose *A voyce out of the wildernes* of 1651 is in the *Catalogus*).[89] Even before then, 'Rotennesse and Corruption shall perpetually follow all *the* Councells plots, and designes of evill men' into oblivion.[90] His hopes were pinned on Sir Henry Vane, who was frequently accused of seeking to introduce a dictatorship of the saints.[91] But there is a disparity between Vane's evocation of the rule of the regenerate, and his simultaneous advocacy of liberty of conscience and the separation of Church and State. It appears that Worsley, who also 'privileged the spirit' in his politics, reconciled these positions by positing the role of the godly as destroying spiritual oppression, and creating the conditions where religious liberty would thrive:

[85] Beale to Hartlib, 7 Dec. 1658, HP 51/39–40. This was probably the same Dr Fludd whom Robert Child had visited in Maidstone in late 1650, and who apparently had a large collection of chymical books and manuscripts: 'Ephemerides', 1650, pt III, HP 28/1/68A–B; pt IV, HP 28/1/73A. See also Stubbs, 'John Beale, philosophical gardener', pt I, 482.

[86] Beale to Hartlib, 14 Dec. 1658, HP 51/41; 21 Dec. 1658, HP 51/52.

[87] Worsley to Hartlib, 20 Jan. 1658, HP 33/2/12B.

[88] Worsley to Hartlib, 14 July 1658, HP 47/3/4A–B.

[89] For 'T. L' see Lake, *Boxmaker's revenge*, 120–47.

[90] Worsley to Lady [Ranelagh?], 20 Apr. 1659, HP 33/2/13A.

[91] Parnham, 'Politics spun out of theology'.

And indeed so thinke *that* Darckenesse, Wickednesse, Oppression, evill, vnrightes lyes, falsehood, covetousnesse, Death, payne, misery, wayling, lamentation, Bondage, cruelty, deformity, disquiett and trouble: shall all of them have an end; shall all of them have an end together; And *that the* end of them all is really et truly already at hand. And to thinke, *that* after they are dead, they shall never rise againe to reigne any more for ever et ever, and to thinke, wee shall see the fullfilling of these things in part even our selves in these our dayes, I say all are no small Considerations to arme vs both with Patience et with Courage.[92]

Before this utopian state could commence, however, it was necessary to overthrow corruption, and for Worsley this was symbolised by William Petty, who was by then undertaking the survey of the adventurers' lands.[93] Henry Cromwell's enemies launched a concerted attempt to turn the adventurers against Petty throughout 1658, probably with Worsley's assistance.[94] Although Petty eventually succeeded in gaining the adventurers' support for his re-survey, some of the mud thrown at him had undoubtedly stuck.[95] In December Petty received news of 'a strange libell issued against him at Dublyn, with news of a great endeavour there to undoe him'.[96] This alleged that Petty had defrauded the army of thousands of pounds; the warning that in the forthcoming parliament 'he will receive his fatall stroake', was ominously prescient.[97] Henry Cromwell was soon pressured to investigate, forming a committee of seven officers including both Petty's ally Anthony Morgan, and his Baptist enemies Richard Lawrence and Sankey.[98] Accusations rumbled on over the winter, before the focus of attack switched back to London where Sankey formally charged Petty with corruption in Richard Cromwell's parliament, in March 1659.[99] Petty replied with a powerful speech on 21 April, but a day later the assembly was dissolved.[100]

Petty believed that 'his professed enemy' Worsley was supplying ammunition for Sankey's charges, and this appears to have been the case.[101] Worsley had been lying low on his estate in Queen's County over the winter, but

---

[92] Worsley to Lady [Ranelagh?], 20 Apr. 1659, HP 33/2/13A–B.
[93] See chapter 4 above.
[94] Worsley's involvement is hinted at by the fact that the initial attack on Petty's reputation, dated 12 May 1658, was directed to his former colleague on the Council of Trade, Alderman John Fowke. Petty alleged that he faced numerous libels when he visited London in May 1658 to negotiate with the adventurers: Petty, *Cromwellian survey*, 228–32.
[95] Ibid. 232–52.
[96] Ibid. 257.
[97] Ibid. 262.
[98] Ibid. 267.
[99] Ibid. 289–92.
[100] Ibid. 292–6.
[101] Ibid. 291, and *Reflections*, 76–7.

was called to Dublin by Sankey in the spring; a letter written in April reveals that he was expecting to leave for London imminently.[102] In the same letter Worsley thanked the recipient (perhaps Lady Ranelagh) for sending 'that Caracter of our truly Worthy et honorable frind Sir Harry vane, to whom I lately writt by Col Sankey', and the suggestion that the main leader of republican opposition to the Protectorate in England was in contact with one of Henry Cromwell's most intransigent opponents on the eve of the collapse of the regime, hints at a widespread conspiracy.[103] Petty later described his impeachment as motivated by 'Reason of State': by pulling him down, his enemies sought 'to pull down the Government it self', a plot of 'the Sectarian party'.[104] Meanwhile Fleetwood and the more radical wing of the army had been moving closer to the Protectorate's opponents since early 1659, culminating in the recall of the Rump Parliament and the forced retirement of Richard Cromwell in May.[105] Henry Cromwell acquiesced with this in July, and so the political reasons for Sankey's pursuit of Petty disappeared.[106] Nevertheless Sankey continued to harry his enemy, presenting parliament with his charges on 12 July, by which time Petty had lost all his public offices.[107] Petty responded by beginning his counterattack in print, although it was not until the Restoration that he felt safe enough to unleash his ruthless wit, with Worsley, Sancho Panza to Sankey's Don Quixote, bearing much of the brunt.[108] Hartlib must have wondered at what had become of two of his former protégés.[109]

'If Sir *Hierome* and *Worsly* both, should happen to cumber the Upper Bench, like *Minos* and *Radamanth*, upon my case', Petty wrote with the safety of hindsight in 1660, 'I should be terribly afraid of what so much conceited ignorance and intoxicating pride might bring upon mee.'[110] By then, he could confidently predict that 'no Revolution that can come; will advance that *Multiloquious* pair', but this was far from the case in the previous year, when Worsley could afford to hope that greater changes were afoot. The coming 'Kingdome of the Lord', he explained in April 1659, 'shall not bee yea and nay/ (as now while wee are all in Confusion et Babell) but yea et amen, that it shall be clearenesse et certainty to consider', bringing 'unity',

---

[102] Worsley to Lady [Ranelagh?], 20 Apr. 1659, HP 33/2/14A.

[103] Ibid. HP 33/2/13A.

[104] Petty, *Reflections*, 57, 85–7.

[105] R. Hutton, *The Restoration: a political and religious history of England and Wales, 1658–1667*, Oxford 1985, 35–40.

[106] Ibid. 41; Petty, *Cromwellian survey*, 301.

[107] Petty, *Cromwellian survey*, 302–6.

[108] Idem, *A brief of proceedings between Sr. Hierome Sankey and Dr. William Petty*, London 1659, and *Reflections*, 82.

[109] Hartlib was certainly aware of the conflict between Worsley and Petty: his papers contain a copy of Sankey's articles of impeachment, HP 55/12/1–2.

[110] Petty, *Reflections*, 59.

'Concord', and most of all 'peace' to the divided saints.[111] Thus Worsley could hope that soon 'every year shall be a new spring': little could he have known then that the republic was about to enter its bleak winter.[112]

Worsley arrived in London late in May.[113] The parliament recalled earlier in the month, led by a new Council of State including Vane and Fleetwood, had immediately set about purging the most untrustworthy Cromwellians from positions of influence, particularly in the army.[114] Worsley was one of those who benefited at their expense, and on 8 July he was nominated by parliament's committee of safety as commissary-general of musters for Ireland.[115] The following month the regime faced its first overt challenge, Sir George Booth's rebellion in Cheshire; Sankey, now the most senior officer in the Irish army, led a regiment to mop up the remnants of the rising at Chirk castle in late August.[116] Concerned at this sign of resurgent royalism, the army radicals became increasingly keen to assert themselves to parliament, most visibly with the menacing Derby petition of 22 September. Sankey was one of three officers who drafted this document, and the resulting confrontation led to Lambert's dissolution of the Rump on 13 October, and the formation of yet another government two weeks later.[117] There is little evidence of Worsley's activities at the time, and Hartlib complained that he had stopped visiting him. But Hartlib also reported that Worsley had been heard to say that 'if the parliament had sat four days longer, his head would have gone off', suggesting that he was involved in the army's machinations.[118] Both Vane and Sankey participated in the army-backed regime that succeeded the Rump, and so there is no surprise in finding that Worsley was also involved.[119] In an attempt to organise support for the regime, a general council of the army was summoned, and Worsley was elected to represent the Irish regiment of Colonel Brayfield, on 7 December, although this was in fact too late for him to attend the meeting.[120] Thus he remained in London, where in any case potentially more profitable opportunities were arising.

Just before its dissolution, parliament had opened up John Thurloe's farm

---

[111] Worsley to Lady [Ranelagh?], 20 Apr. 1659, HP 33/2/13B.
[112] It has been argued, however, that the restored Commonwealth was a successful and potentially enduring regime: R. Mayers, *1659: the crisis of the Commonwealth*, Woodbridge 2004.
[113] His arrival is mentioned in Hartlib to Boyle, 31 May 1659, *Boyle correspondence*, i. 357.
[114] Hutton, *Restoration*, 45.
[115] CSPD, 1659–1660, 13; A. Clarke, *Prelude to Restoration in Ireland: the end of the Commonwealth, 1659–60*, Cambridge 1999, 56–66.
[116] Clarke, *Prelude to Restoration*, 73.
[117] Ibid. 87–8.
[118] This comment was apparently made by Worsley to the Swedish ambassador, Lord Friesendorf, and was noted in Hartlib to Boyle, 22 Oct. 1659, *Boyle correspondence*, i. 378.
[119] Hutton, *Restoration*, 72.
[120] Clarke, *Prelude to Restoration*, 104–7.

of the Post Office, on 11 October 1659.[121] As well as being highly lucrative, this position formed an important part of Thurloe's intelligence network, and so control of it was politically important. Apparently Worsley took over Thurloe's farm on 25 December.[122] Some years later, in a petition to Charles II, he claimed to have contracted to hold the farm for seven years at £20,000 per year rent, £6,000 more than Thurloe had paid, for which he was still owed £1,600.[123] He also claimed to have advanced the revenue of the office by £6,000, but Worsley can have had little chance to make any real changes given the turbulent political situation. Since the army's dissolution of parliament, the republican cause had been fragmenting, and Monck was already beginning his march from Scotland. Thus there was little opposition when parliament returned at the end of December, expelling Vane and his regime.[124] Meanwhile, parliament ordered the Council of State to take the office of postmaster into its own hands, on 7 January, and call its holders to account.[125] Worsley's petition later complained that he had been expelled from the Post Office, 'contrary to your Majesty's declarations & intended Clemency ... by the violence of Soldiers'.[126] However, it is unlikely that he managed to hold onto the office until the Restoration, for on 21 January the Council of State issued a warrant for his arrest, and although his conformity was certified soon after, as an associate of the by-now discredited Vane Worsley was clearly out of favour.[127] By then news had arrived of the taking of Dublin castle by forces loyal to parliament, and Worsley had been named as one of six dangerous radicals, in a pamphlet justifying the action.[128] In March 1660 parliament dissolved itself; the next month, a new one met, and by May the Stuart monarchy was restored. England's Commonwealth had collapsed, leaving Worsley in the wilderness.

---

[121] J. W. M. Stone (ed.), *The inland posts (1392–1672): a documentary calendar of historical documents with appendixes*, London 1987, 121.

[122] Ibid. On 23 December Worsley purchased the Great Seal from Sir Archibald Johnston of Warriston, on behalf of Fleetwood: *The diary of Sir Archibald Johnston of Wariston*, III: *1655–60*, ed. J. Oglivie, Edinburgh 1940, 161, 164.

[123] SP 29/142, pt 2, fo. 150. The petition is undated, but is calendared under 1665: *CSPD, 1665–1666*, 168.

[124] Hutton, *Restoration*, 80–5.

[125] Stone, *Inland posts*, 121.

[126] SP 29/142, pt 2, fo. 150r.

[127] *CSPD, 1659–1660*, 568, 322.

[128] J. Bridge, E. Warren and A. Warren, *A perfect narrative of the grounds and reasons moving some officers of the army in Ireland to the securing of the castle of Dublin for the parliament*, London 1660, 4 (dated 23 Jan. by Thomason).

7

Navigating the Restoration, 1660–1669

The next meadow

For many former servants of the Commonwealth and Protectorate, the shock of the Restoration must have been as great as that of the regicide had been to royalists, twelve years earlier. For Worsley, this can only have been exacerbated by the fate of certain former patrons, notably Sir Henry Vane, executed on 14 June 1662. By then Sir Hierome Sankey had been excluded from the act of indemnity, and although he was never so prominent as to be in danger of suffering Vane's fate, Worsley too might have feared losing his lands and being barred from public employment. Fortunately, Worsley had not burned his bridges with the Boyle family, now rising in influence thanks largely to Lord Broghill, who became earl of Orrery as a reward for his role in the Restoration. Worsley apparently used this influential contact to ensure that his Irish estates were not confiscated, selling them 'at a high price' to Orrery's nephew Captain Robert Fitzgerald, before Orrery supported Worsley and Fitzgerald's petition to confirm the title, probably in December 1660.[1] Worsley's immediate financial future was therefore secured.

The attitude of the returning king gave some grounds for optimism, too. At Breda Charles had voiced his willingness to grant some liberty of conscience, and Worsley hoped that he might find room 'to walke in the Kings broad high way'.[2] If not, his intention was to 'step into the next meadow, where I may be perhaps a lesse offence to others, & meete with lesse opposition to my selfe'. At some point in 1660 Worsley retreated to his wife's home town of Dartmouth, and from that safe distance he corresponded with Hartlib and John Beale about the religious settlement being fashioned. Debates centred on the form of the restored Church, with Robert Boyle being one advocate of admitting Presbyterians and moderate Independents. Worsley's own distaste for strict religious discipline was shown when he declared himself to be 'almost of that Doctors minde that told those people that would have a May pole they should and those that would not should have none'.[3] At the same time, however, he scorned those 'who thinke lyturgy the best service

---

[1] *CSPI*, 1663–5, 472. Fitzgerald had been responsible for capturing the parliamentary commissioners, and sometime employers of Worsley, Miles Corbett and John Jones, during the seizure of Dublin castle in December 1659: Clarke, *Prelude to Restoration*, 110.
[2] [Worsley] to [Beale], *c*. May–June 1660, MS Add. 78685, fo. 103r.
[3] Worsley to Hartlib, 10 Sept, 1660, HP 33/2/15A.

they can performe to God', without 'any other fervour & zeale of spirit in their addresses vnto God'. Worsley's loyalties lay with another sort of worship:

> Those on the other hand who thinke that Lyturgy a little too pædagogicall for them. A forme into which they can no way cast the freedome Liberty fire and fervour of their owne spirits; They who desire and thinke it but reasonable to offer that service to God that is most sutable to him, according to the measure of that knowledge and discovery they have had of him./ If they shall for these reasons desire also to be freed and delivered from those weak (not to call them beggarly) Rudiments I know but little ground for any sober Christians to Censure them.

Beale had already written to Worsley with his hopes 'that the Porch or outward Courte of the Temple should be arched or enlarged wide enough to receive all Nations'.[4] The liturgical task, therefore, was to discover the most 'universall summons', and for this Beale turned to the apostolic, pre-Nicene Church: 'Is the new addition better than the old unquestionable simplicity? Is the language of these men better than the Inspiration of God?'[5] Worsley was similarly dismissive of that 'vaine flatt insipid and prolixe Tautology & Repetition as hath beene the too much Custome of this Age'.[6] But he avoided publicly becoming 'an Interested Party on eyther side', a stance which soon proved sensible.

Despite Charles's sentiments at Breda, the parliament elected in May 1661 was set on revenge, riding on a wave of reaction against dissent after Thomas Venner's Coleman Street Fifth Monarchist rising in January, which was followed by mass arrests of Quakers and Baptists.[7] Affiliation with the Boyles did not protect Worsley this time, and he was imprisoned in Newgate with other supposed members of 'this Rebellious and bloody Crew'.[8] This spell in confinement apparently did not last long, but Restoration England was becoming increasingly inhospitable to dissenters and former republicans. Fortunately for Worsley certain members of the new regime recognised that they might salvage some of the policies and rhetoric of the Commonwealth, including its commercial governance, something on which few were better informed than him.

In fact, the last year of the republic was one of commercial depression, somewhat undermining the supposed association between prosperity and

---

[4] Beale to Worsley, 29 Aug. 1660, Royal Society, Boyle letters, vol. 1, fo. 51r.
[5] Ibid. fo. 51v.
[6] Worsley to Hartlib, 10 Sept. 1660, HP 33/2/15A–B.
[7] R. L. Greaves, *Deliver us from evil: the radical underground in Britain, 1660–1663*, New York–Oxford 1986, 49–57; J. Coffey, *Persecution and toleration in Protestant England, 1558–1689*, London 2000; Spurr, *English Puritanism*, 129–30.
[8] *Londons glory, or, the riot and ruine of the Fifth Monarchy men*, London 1661, 15. Worsley's arrest was reported in W. Petty to J. Petty, 9 Jan. 1661, MS Add. 72850, fo. 21r.

republicanism.[9] The republican author of *The grand concernments of England ensured*, published that October, knew that support for a royal restoration was growing, due to 'a mistaken belief, *that Trade would thereby lift up its head*'.[10] In response, the author posed the rhetorical question 'What have the best of all their Majesties that ever Reigned in *England* done *for the encouragement of Trade?* If they had done any thing Material, *England* had been more bound to thank them then it is, but Trade in general hath been little befriended.'[11] Whether or not this was the case for Charles I his son's regime was willing to offer the hand of friendship to the commercial world, as symbolised by the motifs glorifying commerce adorning Charles's royal entry to London in 1661.[12] More palpably, the monarchy adopted some of the policies of the usurper regimes, allowing commercial patriots like Sir George Downing to transfer their allegiance with relative ease.[13] Having already established a privy council committee for trade and plantations in August 1660, the regime addressed a letter concerning trade to London's aldermen.[14] Unsurprisingly it courted the opinions of the chartered companies, which might be expected to rally around a return to the pre-Civil War commercial order, but equally it addressed 'the unincorporated Traders, for Spain, France, Portugal, Italy, and the West India Plantations', and thus the Council of Trade formed on 7 November included prominent colonial merchants amongst its sixty-two members.[15] Most notable were Cromwell's advisors, Thomas Povey and Martin Noell, whose enthusiastic lobbying on behalf of West Indian trade encouraged the crown to found a similarly large Council of Plantations.[16] The increasing importance attached to colonial trade for national prosperity was reflected when parliament passed the first of several navigation laws in September 1660, which ensured that the most important, 'enumerated' commodities, were taken to England before being re-exported.[17] Thus, although old cavaliers like Sir William Berkeley in Virginia were restored to power, they found themselves subjected to a more restrictive commercial regime than in 1651, ensuring that colonial trade would not drift back into the hands of the Dutch, or away from English custom farmers.[18]

Worsley has occasionally been included alongside Povey and Downing as

---

[9]   T&C, 66–8.
[10]   *The grand concernments of England ensured*, London 1659, 15.
[11]   Ibid.
[12]   B. Hoxby, 'The government of trade: commerce, politics, and the courtly art of the Restoration', *English Literary History* lxvi (1999), 591–627.
[13]   Ibid. 593; J. Scott, '"Good night Amsterdam": Sir George Downing and Anglo-Dutch statebuilding', *EHR* cxviii (2003), 351–2.
[14]   Andrews, *Committees*, 62–6.
[15]   Ibid. 65.
[16]   Ibid. 68–70.
[17]   Harper, *English navigation laws*, 50–60.
[18]   Bliss, *Revolution and empire*, 106–11.

one of the key thinkers behind these developments, based on a draft of the instructions of the new trade council being misattributed to his hand.[19] In fact, he was lying low in Dartmouth in 1660, and it is unlikely that anyone of influence would not have been amongst the eighty-two members of the two councils. Historians have been critical of these unwieldy bodies, and colonial and commercial affairs were soon back in privy council hands.[20] But the idea of a commercial council to fill the vacuum between Whitehall and the Exchange had not been abandoned, and would eventually give Worsley the opportunity to return to the administrative position he had held under the Commonwealth.

Worsley had to wait until 1668 for this, however, by which time the initial strength of royalist reaction had waned somewhat. In 1661 this was in full force, perhaps explaining why Worsley was apparently seeking a means to leave England for the relatively more tolerant New England. A chance to secure employment overseas arose on 18 September 1661, when John Winthrop, Jr, the governor of Connecticut and correspondent of Hartlib, arrived in London on a mission to secure a charter for his colony from the monarchy.[21] By then Worsley was edging back to London, living in Highgate but regularly travelling to his rented quarters in Blackfriars. Before Winthrop's arrival, Worsley had asked Hartlib to inform Winthrop that 'the Court are vpon sending a Governor unto new England', and that he should therefore secure 'some Interest' in Whitehall. To this end, Worsley directed Hartlib to put his name forward as one who 'hath much *the* eare of *the* Chancellor', adding that 'in reference to *the* Plantations he is privy to most Transactions'.[22] Hartlib faithfully repeated Worsley's immodest description of himself as 'a Civill man', expert 'in all things relating to publicke good Iust Lyberty of Conscience and any sort of ingenuus kinde of improvement', in a letter to Winthrop from 9 October, and soon afterwards they met.[23]

Hartlib also reported that Worsley was about to be sent as a royal agent to the plantations, but this might be another example of Worsley's tendency to inflate his importance when seeking employment or patronage.[24] The one piece of evidence connecting Worsley to Clarendon at this time is rather misleading, namely a self-justifying autobiographical account he wrote to Lady Clarendon in November 1661, 'to acknowledge that Countenance my Lord Chancellor hath beene pleased at all times hitherto to honor me

[19] This attribution was apparently first made in Brown, *Shaftesbury*, 131. The manuscript in question belonged to Thomas Povey: BL, MS Egerton 2395, fo. 268r.
[20] A. P. Thornton, *West-India policy under the Restoration*, Oxford 1956, 9; Andrews, *Committees*, 74–85.
[21] R. C. Black, *The younger John Winthrop*, New York–London 1966, 206–26.
[22] Worsley to Hartlib, c. Sept. 1661, HP 33/2/27A.
[23] Hartlib to Winthrop, 9 Oct. 1661, in 'Correspondence of Hartlib, Haak, Oldenburg and others of the founders of the Royal Society, with Governor Winthrop of Connecticut, 1661–72', ed. R. C. Winthrop, *Proceedings of the Massachusetts Historical Society*, Boston 1878, 215–16; Black, *Younger John Winthrop*, 215.
[24] Hartlib to Winthrop, 3 Sept. 1661, 'Correspondence of Hartlib', 214.

with'.[25] Evidently Worsley had become acquainted with Clarendon, perhaps through Robert Boyle, who was a member of the Council of Plantations.[26] However, the letter suggests that Worsley had been exaggerating his influence, prompting some 'suggestions' to Clarendon about Worsley's questionable past. His main slanderer was apparently Sir Charles Coote (now the earl of Monrath), whom Worsley condemned as a lukewarm defender of the Protestant interest in Ireland.[27] In his defence, Worsley presented a portrait of a career of political neutrality and devotion to 'publicke service', exploiting in the process the continuity between republican and royal navigation policy:

> I was the first sollicitour for the Act for the incouragement of navigation, & putt the first fyle to it, and after writt the Advocate in defence of it/ In Ireland I held the place of chiefe Clarke or Secretary to the Councell There; of Commissioner general for all the Revenew There: of Surveyor general for all the forfeited lands, and last of all of Commissary generall of the musters; In all which places, as I never tooke one farthing fee, or one farthing gratuity from any person, so I was never advantaged Twenty pound any way, above my bare sallary, and that moneyes I received out of the Publicke Threasury. [28]

Winthrop was apparently unconcerned by any allegations against Worsley, whom he took into his confidence, not as an advisor in New England, but to assist in settling the boundary dispute between Connecticut and its neighbour Rhode Island.[29] Boyle had been acting as an arbitrator between Winthrop and his rival claimant, Dr John Clarke, in their meetings with Clarendon in summer 1662, and in the following March Worsley was nominated by Winthrop to the committee which would resolve the dispute.[30] He signed the agreement reached on 7 April 1663, alongside another former Hartlibian, Sir William Brereton, with William Potter as a witness.[31] Winthrop left the relevant papers with Worsley following his departure to Connecticut soon afterwards.[32] Although this was not an official state position, this probably went some way towards restoring Worsley's reputation, and by November 1662 he was confident enough to write a certificate to

[25] Worsley to Lady Clarendon, 8 Nov. 1661, MS Clarendon 75, fo. 300r.
[26] For Boyle's work on this council see Jacob, *Robert Boyle*, 144–8.
[27] Worsley to Lady Clarendon, 8 Nov. 1661, MS Clarendon 75, fo. 300v.
[28] Ibid. fo. 300r.
[29] For the origins of the dispute see Black, *Younger John Winthrop*, 226–31.
[30] Ibid. 241; J. M. Sosin, *English American and the Restoration monarchy of Charles II*, Lincoln–London 1980, 100–2. See also Boyle to J. Winthrop, Jr, 28 Dec. 1661, *Boyle correspondence*, i. 472.
[31] 'Letters of John Winthrop Jnr 1626–7–75–6' (Collections of the Massachusetts Historical Society viii, 1882), 82–3.
[32] Ibid. 86. Several papers in Worsley's hand are in the Winthrop papers at the Massachusetts Institute of Historical Research Society (microfilm reel 7). See also Black, *Younger John Winthrop*, 242.

the duke of Albermarle on behalf of an old Baptist associate from Ireland, Samuel Goodwin, who was being held in the Tower 'upon suspition of holding Correspondencie with Colonell Ludlow'.[33] Worsley explained that he had recommended Goodwin to a merchant friend who was looking for a factor to reside in Barbados.[34] The Restoration had of course prompted a new wave of nonconformist emigration to the colonies, and Worsley's Barbadian connections would provide the opportunity for his next venture.

The senna project

Worsley's ascent in state service in the 1640s began with his saltpetre project. Two decades later he continued the scatological theme by turning to the production of an exotic laxative, senna, as a way to restore his credit. In 1663 he began to discuss his intention to cultivate senna in the plantations with certain Anglo-Irish patrons, namely Lady Ranelagh, her brother the earl of Burlington and Sir John Clotworthy, now the Viscount Massereene, as well as Sir William Brereton and his father-in-law Francis Lord Willoughby, governor of Barbados and the Leewards. Having received their encouragement, Worsley purchased a number of senna seeds to experiment with, and by June 1664 was able to show the results to Charles II, who promised to encourage the product once perfected.[35] Progress was disrupted by the outbreak of plague in the following year, which forced him to leave London for eight months, but not before he had sent samples to be planted by an agent in Barbados. By September 1666 he had received 'some of the senna ripe and cured', which he subjected to further trials.[36] Soon afterwards Worsley presented the king with a parcel, who received it 'not only pleasedly, but greedily, and much complimented its presenter'.[37] Having earned a similar response from the royal physicians, Sir Alexander Fraser and Dr Thomas Coxe, Worsley set about drafting a formal petition, apparently with Clarendon's advice.[38] By the time he petitioned the king, on 30 October 1666, Worsley had therefore gone to considerable lengths to ensure its success.

Worsley's petition cited the commercial benefits of cultivating senna, as well as other Turkish commodities.[39] Previous attempts to produce import-

---

[33] Goodwin's petition, SP 68, fo. 327r; Greaves, *Deliver us from evil*, 115.

[34] Worsley's certificate to George Monck, duke of Albermarle, on behalf of Samuel Goodwin, 1 Nov. 1662, SP 68, fo. 330r.

[35] Worsley to William, Lord Willoughby of Parnham, memorandum, 22 Jan. 1668, in 'Locke notebook', 263; Worsley, 'Severall reasons humbly tendered … for the encourageing of the plantation of senna', c. Mar. 1668, TNA, CO 1/20, fo. 283r.

[36] Lady Ranelagh to Boyle, 12 Sept. 1666, *Boyle correspondence*, iii. 235.

[37] Lady Ranelagh to Boyle, 18 Sept. 1666, ibid. 239.

[38] Worsley to Willoughby, memorandum, 22 Jan. 1668, 264.

[39] Petition for a senna patent, 30 Oct. 1666, CO 1/20, fo. 282r.

substituting goods in the colonies had suffered 'manifest Losse & miscarriage ... for want of due Regulation', particularly tobacco. Worsley could therefore justify his patent as a means to regulate this potentially valuable crop, which was previously only available from the Levant. However, Worsley denied that he was seeking a normal fourteen-year monopoly patent: instead, he requested a twelve-year 'lease' of a royal licence to plant senna, which would be used to regulate this commodity in the long term. Furthermore, its sale would be tightly regulated, and Worsley suggested that all senna imported from the colonies should be collected into a general store for inspection, before being sold at a comparable price to Alexandrian senna. The latter would only be admitted once the colonial stock had been sold, avoiding a glut in the market and the price-falls that had plagued tobacco.

As chapter 1 discussed, projects were seen as a controversial but potentially lucrative means by which to wed private finance and public authority. In the saltpetre project, public authority was vested in parliament, but by contrast in 1666 Worsley petitioned the crown to accept the 'Comoditie of Senna as properly belonging to your Majesty, & as your Majestys peculiar & Inherent Right', to be regulated 'as shall seem best to your Majestys Wisedome'. Worsley even offered to pay a rent, as 'Acknowledgement of your Majestys Sole Right in & to the said Commoditie'. Clarendon himself could hardly have offered a better depiction of the traditional royalist economic order, where the crown regulated commerce by prerogative right, contracting with its subjects to monopolise certain trades in return for concessions on a personal, rather than legislative, basis, a far cry, perhaps, from the rhetoric of public interest of the saltpetre project. However, despite its royalist bias, the senna petition was presented in largely similar terms to its civil war precursor, as an act of 'publick service'. A commodity like senna might belong to the monarch, but should still be regulated to serve the public good. Public power would be invested in Worsley acting simultaneously as a private individual and an agent of the state, a partnership justified because 'the plantation of any new Commodity within our plantations can never possible be expected unless undertaken by the Industry & Ingenuity of some private and perticuler persons'.[40] However, such initiatives involved much 'charge hazard Patience and Expence', and therefore required assurance that interlopers would not 'reap the equall benefitt of such an improvement': otherwise, it could not be 'rationally expected that any such undertakeing againe shall or will at any private mans charge be ever at any time attempted'.

By then Worsley had apparently become frustrated with the crown's failure to grant his patent: he was still awaiting a response from the attorney-general, George Palmer, in 1668, and in order to speed things up, sent an account of the project to William Lord Willoughby, who had succeeded his brother Francis as governor in Barbados.[41] Worsley also addressed a second

---

[40] Ibid. fo. 283v.
[41] Worsley to Willoughby, memorandum, 22 Jan. 1668, 263–5.

memorandum to Palmer, explaining how the project would not only improve the plantations, but would also reduce 'our expence of money into forraigne parts', and, by adding to the stock of colonial goods traded into England, would encourage shipping and settlement.[42] However, he was by now willing to accept a conventional patent, and accordingly Palmer reported favourably, leaving 'the other matters petitioned for' to parliamentary consideration. Finally a warrant for a fourteen-year patent was issued, on 12 August 1668, although (like the saltpetre project before it) there is no evidence that Worsley prosecuted these privileges.[43]

In fact, it seems that the project had fulfilled the same function as saltpetre had done, allowing Worsley to advertise his qualities to admiring patrons and politicians, particularly those who were on the rise since Clarendon's exit in 1667. This event was connected to the aftermath of the Anglo-Dutch War, which entailed commercial depression as well as a political shift: 'the crisis occasioned by the Second Dutch War and the fall of Clarendon opened the way for new adventurous policies', notably with regard to commerce.[44] Thus in 1668 Worsley found that there were both individuals willing to listen to his arguments about the importance of colonial trade, and a commercial situation which made it appear important to act on them.

For eight years before then Worsley had to survive without the state salary which had supported him throughout the 1650s. His ample earnings throughout that decade had provided for his attempted purchase of the Post Office farm in 1659, and the sale of his Irish lands probably compensated for any loss suffered from this venture, but he was still without an income. He seems to have waited until the mid-1660s before petitioning for compensation for losing the Post Office, in the meantime raising funds by selling telescopes to Beale and Winthrop.[45] For a more secure income, Worsley turned back to medicine, although he practised physic rather than surgery.[46] Senna was a medicinal plant, and he appears to have personally known the royal physicians who tested his samples, Fraser and Coxe, as well as the latter's namesake Dr Daniel Coxe, who held similar ideas about the life-giving propensities of salt.[47] Another minor acquaintance was the

---

[42] 'Severall reasons humbly tendered', c. Mar. 1668, CO 1/20, fo. 283r.

[43] CSPC, 1661–8, 604.

[44] Kelly, 'Introduction', to Locke on money, 5.

[45] The Post Office petition is at SP 29/142, pt 2, fo. 150. For telescopes see Beale to Hartlib, 14 Jan. 1662, HP (MS Add. 6271, fo. 10r); Winthrop to Worsley, 27 Oct. 1670, Winthrop papers, microfilm reel 9; D. Yeomans, 'The origin of North American astronomy: seventeenth century', Isis lxviii (1977), 416.

[46] He is described as 'Dr. in Physick' in the London visitation records of 1664: London visitation pedigrees, 1664, 154. A draft list of the membership of the 1672 Council of Trade and Plantations describes him as the doctor of the merchant Peter Buckworth: TNA, 30/24/49, fo. 106r.

[47] D. Coxe to Boyle, 7 Nov. 1666, Boyle correspondence, iii. 268. For Coxe's ideas see Clericuzio, Elements, principles and corpuscules, 154–61. See also Winthrop to H. Oldenburg, 12 Nov. 1668, 'Letters of John Winthrop Jnr', 136.

famed medical writer, Dr Thomas Sydenham, who apparently sent a paper in Worsley's hand to Beale, in 1665. The subject was an account of the feats of Valentine Greatrakes, the Irish 'stroker' who claimed the ability to heal by touch. It is no surprise to find Worsley's name associated with this *cause célèbre* of the 1660s given his spiritual and scientific convictions.[48] Worsley was probably the 'Doctor Worley' whose servant, John Hayes, suffered from a 'stoppage of stomack, and shortness of breathing', and who after being stroked by Greatrakes 'voided wind upwards in abundance, insomuch as he feared to be choked with the violence of it'.[49]

Greatrakes hoped to win the patronage of Robert Boyle, who by then had become a public celebrity and leading representative of the new science in England, embodied in the institution founded to promote it in an increasingly vibrant public arena, the Royal Society of London.[50] Despite the involvement of several of Hartlib's former correspondents, including Boyle, Beale, Oldenburg, Evelyn and Petty, Worsley was one of those excluded from this body and therefore rather marginalised from the intellectual life of Restoration England.[51] Many of his former Hartlibian allies fared less well in the 1660s, not least Hartlib himself, who finally died in 1662, bringing to an end a major source of information for Worsley. Of others, Dury never returned to England after 1661, Culpeper died in poverty in 1662 and William Rand followed shortly after, whilst the mentally troubled Sadler was drifting off into his mystical-exegetical utopia, *Olbia*.[52] However Worsley remained in contact with Boyle and his sister Lady Ranelagh, for example writing to the former about luminous wood from his refuge from the plague at Theobalds in Hertfordshire.[53] Worsley hoped that Boyle would help him find an investor for the senna project.[54] In fact, Boyle may personally have helped ease Worsley's financial problems. A letter to Boyle from Lady Ranelagh described how shortly after the great fire in September 1666 she had discussed with

[48] Beale to Boyle, 7 Sept. 1665, *Boyle correspondence*, ii. 522. This account was apparently given by one Lionel Beacher, 'sometime mayor of Biddiford'. Greatrakes visited England from January to May 1666: N. Steneck, 'Greatrakes the stroker: the interpretations of historians', and B. Kaplan, 'Greatrakes the stroker: the interpretations of his contemporaries', *Isis* lxxiii (1982), 160–77, 178–85; *ODNB*.

[49] This was reported in Dr Fairclough to Sir W. Smith, 5 May 1666, in V. Greatrakes, *A brief account of Mr Valentine Greatraks … in a letter addressed to the Honourable Robert Boyle Esq*, Dublin 1668, 71.

[50] For the Royal Society see Hunter, *Establishing the new science*; for the Restoration public sphere see S. Pincus, '"Coffee politicians does create": coffeehouses and Restoration political culture', *Journal of Modern History* lxvii (1995), 807–34.

[51] For the intellectual context see M. Hunter, *Science and society in Restoration England*, Cambridge 1981.

[52] This work is listed in Worsley's *Catalogus*.

[53] Boyle recorded this letter in his work diary: Worsley to Boyle, 30 Oct. 1665, *Boyle correspondence*, ii. 569. Boyle later included this information in his *Mechanical production of light*, introduced as 'from a certain learned doctor'. See also Oldenbury to Boyle, 20 Oct. 1664, *Boyle correspondence*, ii. 361.

[54] Lady Ranelagh to Boyle, 12 Sept. 1666, ibid. iii. 235.

Worsley the 'providence, that assisted to his preservation and that of his goods, which he probably enough thinks raised in value, as to that part of them wherein you have any interest, by the great consumption that has been of that sort of commodity, both at *Sion* college, and also in St. *Faith's* church'.[55] Two of Worsley's old haunts, Coleman Street and Fetter Lane, were half-destroyed by the conflagration, and so perhaps he was staying in one of these addresses.

The 'commodity' in question was evidently books, particularly Bibles, and it appears that Boyle owned a stake in Worsley's library, with the sum of £250 being mentioned in a deal which involved Sydenham as an inter-mediary.[56] After his death Worsley's huge library was auctioned, and given that he appears to have had no children, it is possible that some of the proceeds of this transaction went to Boyle, in return for money lent in the 1660s. The Restoration had slightly dented his book-buying abilities, but Worsley still managed to purchase ten of Boyle's works alongside those of several other natural philosophers. Many of these accorded with the Royal Society's agenda to render science useful through 'histories of trade', by authors such as John Evelyn and Christopher Merret. Publications associ-ated with the Royal Society included Thomas Sprat's *History of the Royal Society*, Henry Stubbe's attack on the institution, *Legends no histories,* and Joseph Glanville's defence, *Philosophia pia,* as well as volumes two to eight of the *Philosophical Transactions*. Medicine also continued to be a strong interest, with the Danish physician Thomas Bartholin the favoured author. The year 1661 saw the publication of a Hebrew translation of the New Testament by Worsley's associate William Robertson, yet another impris-oned nonconformist, and Worsley continued to collect works by Hebraists such as Buxtorf, and the orientalist Johann Heinrich Hottinger.[57] Thus we have some hints of his private interests in the post-Hartlib era, but much of our knowledge of this time relates to his public career, transformed by the political shift of 1668.

Imperial designs

The Restoration politician with whom Worsley is usually associated is Sir Anthony Ashley Cooper, Lord Ashley and from 1672 earl of Shaftesbury. However Worsley never attained the level of trust which John Locke did with this, or indeed any other, politician, instead offering advice to several leading 'Cabal' statesmen, including Lord Arlington and the duke of Buck-

[55] Ibid. iii. 234.
[56] Ibid. iii. 235.
[57] W. Robertson, *Testamentum novum hebraicum*, London 1661. For Worsley's acquaint-ance with Robertson see Hartlib to Worthington, 26 Aug, 1661, *Diary of John Worthington,* i. 365–6. For Robertson see chapter 1 above.

ingham. In late 1666 he had some meetings about commercial affairs with Viscount Conway, actually a supporter of Ashley's rival, Ormond, who described him as 'a person of great ingenuity' with 'great acquaintance among the Dutch merchants'.[58] His senna project also brought him to the attention of the king, with whom he discussed the production of what was fast becoming England's most valuable colonial staple, sugar.[59] Worsley suggested to Charles II 'how much of Import it might be to his affairs either to agree upon a Regulation of Sugars with the King of Portugall; or to take such an effectuall order … as that the Portugeez might be wholly discouraged and beaten out of the trade'.[60] He drafted a lengthy paper describing the second course of action with particular reference to Jamaica, possibly addressed to Buckingham in summer 1668.[61] Although Jamaica had escaped the ravages of the second Anglo-Dutch War, it remained vulnerable and underdeveloped.[62] Worsley was not alone in arguing that it was potentially the most profitable West Indian colony, but the case still needed to be made for persevering with its settlement.

In order to highlight the importance of sugar, Worsley turned once again to the persistent example of Dutch commercial might. Twenty years earlier he had noted that Amsterdam's prosperity was built on East Indian profits, and his opinion had not changed since then:

As the great & extraordinary power of the East India Company of Holland doth sufficiently appeare not onely in the standing Garrisons they maintaine, and in the Fleet they have been able upon all occasions to set forth in the East Indies; but in the warrs which they have at severall times waged with some of the most Puissant & Civilized Princes of these Countries soe the one single instance sheweth us not onely what a Nation, but even what a number of private persons (by agreeing togeather to make use of the

---

[58] Viscount Conway to Sir G. Rawdon, 27 Nov. 1666, in HMC, *Seventy-eighth report: manuscripts of the late Reginald Rawdon Hastings, esq., of the Manor House, Ashby de la Zouche*, ed. J. Harley and F. Bickley, ii, London 1930, 874.

[59] C. Bridenbaugh and R. Bridenbaugh, *No peace beyond the line: the English in the Caribbean, 1624–1690*, New York 1972, 69–100.

[60] Worsley to Lord Ashley, memorandum on 'The peculiar advantages which this Nation hath by the trade of our plantations', 14 Aug. 1668, TNA, 30/24/49, fo. 251v.

[61] Worsley, letter on Jamaican sugar addressed to duke of Buckingham, c. summer 1668, in 'Locke notebook', 215–19, 232–52. This is included along with other Worsley material and, although it is unsigned, it was certainly written by Worsley. On p. 237 he made the claim that the quantity of sugar currently imported into Europe was so great that a variation of its price by one farthing in the pound amounted to £40,000, which he repeated in his letter to Ashley of 14 August 1668 (fo. 224v), cited above. The paper also makes references to the Englishmen wishing to depart from Surinam (p. 242), which had been transferred to the Dutch in April 1668. Summer 1668 seems therefore a probable date. The recipient is assumed to be Buckingham because he is addressed as 'your Grace' throughout, and because Worsley wrote two more lengthy papers regarding Jamaica to the duke, in 1668–9.

[62] Thornton, *West-India policy*, 39–66.

advantages of trade) may if they will, doe; to render themselves considerable abroad in the World.[63]

Dutch success rested on the size of the 'Capitall Stock' invested in the trade,
combined with their military control over markets and trade routes.[64] Thus
they had been able to monopolise 'the trade of the Molluccoes, Ceylon, for
Japan' and elsewhere, eventually 'ingrossing into their own hands the sole
disposeing of a very fast Bulk of certain Comoditys'.[65] The East Indies were
strategically vital to the States General, who relied on customs, fines and
borrowing from the company. In fact, 'the upholding of the Company is soe
much the joint and united concerne of all the provinces that … there is not
a greater Cement … In all theire whole Government'.[66] This was because
the joint-stock status of the Dutch East India Company (VOC) allowed
non-merchants to invest and partake in its profits, so that 'the Interest of
the said Company is manifestlie linked or weaved with the Interest of the
whole Nation it selfe'.[67]

Worsley had not offered this eulogy to the VOC in order to promote its
English counterpart, however. Although this trade alone was sufficient to be
'a super-balance to all Christendome', it would be fruitless to challenge the
Dutch in their strongest arena.[68] As well as dominating this trade, Dutch
commercial power was supported by their herring fishery, clothing industry,
and Greenland and Russia trades.[69] Against this seemingly indomitable array
of assets, and given 'the great improbability … That we shall effectually
set upon the Fishing or that wee shall ever recover our Woolleen Manufacture', colonial trade was all that England had left to counterbalance the
Dutch.[70]

England's commercial future lay in the West, and not the East Indies,
therefore. But Worsley had analysed the power of the VOC not just as a
warning, but as an example of how to conduct the American trade, one
lesson being that 'the prudence even of private persons, when manageing of
trade justly and adventagiously for the good of the Common Interest; may
… rise, stengthen and increase even the Government it selfe which they
are under'.[71] It was in consortium with private merchants, therefore, that
the state should seek to advance colonial trade. This might suggest that
Worsley favoured the erecting of a trading company for the West Indies, as
Povey and Noell had argued for in the 1650s.[72] However, elsewhere Worsley

---

[63] Worsley to Buckingham, *c.* summer 1668, 'Locke notebook', 215.
[64] Ibid. 216.
[65] Ibid. 232.
[66] Ibid. 231.
[67] Ibid. 232.
[68] Ibid. 233.
[69] Ibid.
[70] Ibid. 235.
[71] Ibid. 218.
[72] Andrews, *Committees*, 53–5; Bliss, *Revolution and empire*, 68–70.

cited as a particular benefit of colonial trade the fact that it was not 'stinted to any Company'.[73] Rather, the form of regulation he had in mind centred on particular commodities, especially sugar, whose defence should be 'made an act & designe of State among us, As the improveing of the Cloth was formerly, or as the keeping up of the East India Trade & of the Monopoly of spice is now among the Hollanders'.[74] Worsley went on to calculate the quantity of sugar consumed in Europe (at least 20,000 tonnes yearly), and the amount of land necessary to produce this amount (4–5,000 acres), which Jamaica could easily provide.[75] West Indian sugar would sweep away its Brazilian rival, which was encumbered by high customs and confined to a company charging excessive freight rates. Despite their strong presence in the West Indies, neither the French nor the Dutch had made much progress in erecting sugar-works.[76] Only careful management was necessary in order 'to make us the sole Masters of Sugar to all the world'.[77]

Worsley's suggestions focused on granting privileges to encourage sugar cultivation on Jamaica, including the easing of taxes on planters, an expedient which had occasionally been granted throughout the 1660s.[78] Refined sugar was lighter and cheaper to ship than coarse, whilst too much raw sugar was being re-exported, only to be refined by foreigners, in the same way that the Dutch had traditionally finished English white cloths.[79] The state could also advance this trade by ensuring the removal of Dutch and French impositions on English sugar, if necessary by retaliation.[80] Worsley opposed the Guinea Company because their slaves cost more than those bought from the Dutch, but it would be better still to grant a patent for slave-trading on the River Corentyne, in Guiana, providing a cheap and convenient source.[81] With all these expedients taken care of, Worsley looked forward to the sugar trade amounting to £1,000,000 annually.[82]

A similar concern with the continued strength of Dutch shipping is demonstrated in another paper Worsley wrote from about this time on the herring fishery, which was published in slightly enlarged form in the 1690s, introduced as written by 'Person of great ingenuity and truth', who 'had spent some years and Hundreds of Pounds, in making himself master of this Craft,

[73] Worsley to Ashley, memorandum, 14 Aug. 1668, TNA, 30/24/49 fo. 222v.
[74] Worsley to Buckingham, c. summer 1668, 'Locke notebook', 235.
[75] Ibid. 237–9. Worsley in fact under-estimated the potential demand for sugar: imports to Europe from the West Indies rose from 10,000 tonnes *per annum.* in the 1660s to 24,000 tonnes by 1700: Clay, *Economic expansion and social change,* 169.
[76] Worsley to Buckingham, c. summer 1668, 'Locke notebook', 240–3.
[77] Ibid. 243.
[78] Ibid. 245; Bliss, *Revolution and empire,* 141.
[79] Worsley to Buckingham, c. summer 1668, 'Locke notebook', 246.
[80] Ibid. 251.
[81] Ibid. 244–5.
[82] Ibid. 251. This was overly optimistic: by 1686 sugar imports to London from the West Indies amounted to £586,528: N. Zahedieh, 'London and the colonial consumer in the late seventeenth century', *EcHR* xlvii (1994), 246.

by his Travels into *Holland*'.[83] This explained how Dutch commercial might was able to dominate the herring fishery (valued at £3,000,000 per year), contributing to that nation's 'Super Ballance'.[84] English efforts to launch a national fishery had largely failed due to 'the power of the Hollander to Under sell us', combined with a fixation on making London 'the Principal Scale, Seat, or Staple for the said Fishing Trade'.[85] Because of these adverse conditions, 'there can be no ground rationally to expect, That any Stock should for the future ever againe be raised to sett on foot the said Fishing out of the Contribution of ordinary and private persons'.[86] What was needed was 'the Express Authority of the Government', and Worsley suggested a council of directors to manage the affair under privy council supervision, being paid a premium from fishing profits as an incentive. The key, though, was to raise 'a Fund or Stock that may be both Annual and certain', although Worsley seemingly envisaged private funds being used along with monies raised from the salt duty, including foreign investment.[87]

Perhaps such papers brought Worsley to the attention of Ashley at this time.[88] Ashley was more involved in colonial and commercial affairs than any other Restoration statesman, and 1667–73 were his peak years.[89] Thus it comes as no surprise that Ashley asked Worsley to produce 'something for the restoring of our trade that might be as acceptable to the Nation as

---

[83] *A collection of advertisements, advices, and directions, relating to the royal fishery*, London 1695, 38. The paper was reprinted in *A third collection of scarce and valuable tracts, on the most interesting and entertaining subjects*, London 1751, 338–45. Contemporary manuscript copies entitled 'Some considerations with all humblenesse propounded to His Majestie about the herring fishing', are at MS Add. 28079, fos 201–2, and Institute of Historical Research, London, Coventry papers, vol. xii, fos 365–6. Patrick Kelly, however, suggests the date of 1663 for the paper: 'Dutch data in Locke's economic writings', *Locke News-letter* xxvi (1995), 137. See also J. R. Elder, *The royal fishery companies of the seventeenth century*, Aberdeen 1912, 94–5. The paper perhaps arrived in print via the mathematician and FRS John Collins, who served as a clerk under Worsley on the Council of Foreign Plantations and shared certain patrons such as Brereton. Collins became accountant to the revived Royal Fishery Company in 1676. See W. Letwin, *The origins of scientific economics: English economic thought, 1660–1776*, London 1963, 105–6, and for Collins's commercial opinions (including his model of a council of trade), *A plea for the bringing in of Irish cattel*, London 1680.

[84] MS Add. 28079, fo. 201r. This figure was cited in a paper presented to the Swedish general diet in 1746–7 entitled 'The Dutch gold-mine', later published in the Parisian *Journal oeconomique* and translated into English in a pamphlet, *Select essays on commerce*, London 1754, 299–302. This presumably explains why Worsley's estimate was quoted by no less a figure than Gabriel-Honoré de Riquetti comte de Mirabeau in his *Doubts concerning the free navigation of the Scheld claimed by the emperor*, London 1785, 115–16.

[85] MS Add. 28079, fo. 201r–v.

[86] Ibid. fo. 201v.

[87] Ibid. fo. 202r.

[88] Brown suggests that their acquaintance went back to the 1650s, but presented no evidence: *First earl of Shaftesbury*, 130.

[89] Ibid. 128–49; Haley, *Shaftesbury*, 227–64; Rich, 'Shaftesbury's colonial policy', 47–70.

... to his Majesty', which he did in the form of a paper dated 14 August 1668, two days after the warrant had been issued for his senna patent.[90] Entitled 'The peculiar advantages which this Nation hath by the trade of our plantations', this is the most well known of Worsley's Restoration papers: Arlington owned a copy, and Locke copied it into his notebook.[91] Here, Worsley persuasively argued that colonial trade was the only way to compensate for the decline of English cloth, an argument which, according to Kelly, probably influenced Locke's own political economy.[92]

This was principally because of the insulated commercial system which the navigation laws had created, which allowed the profits of its freight to be 'appropriated to ourselves & alone exclusive to all others'. A prevailing concern of the seventeenth-century discourse of trade was that it was possible to lose, as well as gain, by international trade, and Worsley's discussion shows how the development of colonial political economy was shaped by this perspective.[93] Colonies both produced commodities which could not be grown in England, and provided a market for English goods which were uncompetitive in Europe, enriching English merchants and producers alike. As prosperity increasingly came to be identified with population, colonies were accused of draining productive hands which would otherwise be used in domestic industry or agriculture.[94] But, Worsley argued, colonial emigration merely redistributed labour to where it could be most productive, so that 'it is the Empire of England likewise that is hereby rendered more August formidable & Considerable abroad'.[95]

Culturally, colonial trade avoided the need for merchants to work under the 'Customes & Lawes' of foreign nations, and thus 'contract an Interest & affection that is forreigne'. This attitude reflects a pervasive unease about the transnational status of the merchant, blameworthy for wasting the nation's stock in unprofitable trades, sacrificing the public good for his own private interests or, worse still, those of another nation.[96] The greatest advantage, though, was legal, creating a single trading community working under the same laws and thus achieving the long sought after dominion of the seas.[97] This allowed a more universal approach to commercial legislation

---

[90] Worsley to Ashley, memorandum, 14 Aug. 1668, TNA, 30/24/49, fos 221–7.

[91] Arlington's copy is probably that at Bodl. Lib., MS Rawlinson A478, fos 65–72. Another copy is in 'Locke notebook', 16–17, 158–71. The Rawlinson copy is printed, although not fully, in T&C, 533–7, without the author being attributed.

[92] Kelly, 'Introduction', to Locke on money, 10, 52–3.

[93] For a longer discussion of this theme see Leng, 'Commercial conflict'.

[94] See, for example, S. Bethel, An account of the French usurpation upon the trade of England, London 1679, 16; R. Coke, A discourse of trade, London 1670, 8–13; and C. Reynell, The true English interest, London 1674, 88–92.

[95] Worsley to Ashley, memorandum, 14 Aug. 1668, fo. 224r.

[96] A. Finkelstein, Harmony and the balance: an intellectual history of seventeenth-century English economic thought, Ann Arbor 2000, 24–5; Gauci, Politics of trade, 156–93.

[97] On the domination of the seas see D. Armitage, The ideological origins of the British empire, Cambridge 2000, 100–24.

than possible elsewhere. However, historically the plantations had not been managed to England's best advantage, creating a dangerous reliance on over-produced staples. As well as diversification, remedies included redistributing population southwards by encouraging emigration out of New England, 'the nursery of all unto the Rest of our plantations'.[98] To ensure the effectiveness of these reforms, a greater effort should be made to enumerate the benefits of the plantations to English trade.

Compiling such statistics would be one task of a colonial council. Worsley specified the fundamental defect in colonial government as a 'want of such an authority to whom all the plantations should in theire Customes & Govern-ments be subject unto'.[99] Colonial trade was by now of such significance that it demanded a council to itself, and this reflected Worsley's understanding of recent commercial history. Casting his mind back to the economic situation of his youth, when English cloth was exported into Holland itself, Worsley recalled how the decline of English drapery had been masked by gains made at the expense of warring Holland and Spain, in the Mediterranean and Iberia. But the Peace of Münster had shattered this false position, so that the Dutch, as he had warned at the time, became 'manifestly risen in theire trade beyond us and wee sensibly growne to a decay in our stock and our trade'.[100] The consequences were clear:

> the plantations considered in theire present state doe not more if soe much depend upon the interest of England, as the interest of England doth now depend upon them. For if the Ballence of our trade can now noe way be preserved or kept up without them It is not onely manifest how much we stand in need of them and how uncapable wee are at present to subsist without the trade of them; But equally manifest; that the very interest of this nation & of the trade of it is now changed, and vastly different from what it was forty years since.[101]

The 1668 Council of Trade

Worsley had no doubt that Europe had entered into a new commercial era, but whether this would enrich or enfeeble his nation was yet to be decided. England was surrounded by hostile rivals:

> For if our Neighbours have soe well considered the Consequence of trade as that they find if a new Monarchy be to be set up in the World It can be set up by no other way then by trade because not to be effected without a large Aggreagation of sea force Or if a Monarchy be to be hindered it can be noe other way prevented then either by getting into a Course of trade

[98] Worsley to Ashley, memorandum, 14 Aug. 1668, fo. 224r.
[99] Ibid. fo. 225r.
[100] Ibid. fo. 222r.
[101] Ibid. fo. 221v.

themselves & giving the highest Countenance & promotion that may be possible to it; Or by entring into consideration with others whose Interest leads them most principally to pursue it.[102]

Given this situation, England must either 'Lead a party & make our selves the formost in this great affaire', or else be forced 'to follow ... the interest of such who shall ... gett the start of us'. As well as diplomacy, reason of state called for rational and effective government of trade, and this was the subject of another paper written to Ashley. A Council of Trade was founded in October 1668, and so Worsley's 'Considerations about the Commission for Trade' was probably written around then.[103] This began by stating that 'the Interest of Commerce though formerly neglected is of late yeares Become an Expresse Affayre of State, as well with the French as with the Hollander and Swede'.[104] Following the Anglo-Dutch Wars, fought largely at sea, it was now clear that trade, more than territory, was the key 'toward an universall monarchy', that persistent spectre in the English imagination, explaining why the European nations had now made commerce 'their Interest & Government'. The only choice left to England was either to 'leade this great & generall Affayre of state; By making our selves the masters of Commerce or ... be Lead by it and humbled under the Power of them, that have the Ability Best to Rule it & Governe it'.[105]

Just as it had been twenty years before, the difficulty lay in finding the best way to conduct this government. 'Commerce As it is an Affayre of state', Worsley argued, was 'widely different from the mercantile part of it', which concerned purchasing the best goods, freighting ships, finding the best market and negotiating the best price.[106] Private interest was sufficient to guide the merchant, but it was much harder for the state to discern the public good. As a guide, Worsley listed ten fundamentals of commercial policy, beginning with 'the Publicke Countenancing our Merchants abroad ... As the proper stewards ... of the Publicke stocke Wealth & Interest of the nation'.[107] Partly this was a matter of upholding mercantile privileges abroad and opposing foreign taxes, but equally the state should ensure that English merchants dealt justly, and upheld the 'Credit' of exported manu-

---

[102] Ibid. fo. 225v.
[103] Worsley to Ashley, memorandum 'Some considerations about the commission for trade', c. 1668, TNA, 30/24/49, fos 86–9. The dating is suggested by Worsley's concluding remark, advising that in 'settling this Comision a second Time nothing be omitted that may rationally make it the more effectuall': fo. 88v.
[104] Ibid. fo. 86r.
[105] Ibid. On changing attitudes to universal monarchy see S. Pincus, 'The English debate over universal monarchy', in J. Robertson (ed.), A union for empire: political thought and the British union of 1707, Cambridge 1995, 37–62, and 'Republicanism, absolutism and universal monarchy: English popular sentiment during the third Dutch war', in G. M. MacLean (ed.), Culture and society in the Stuart Restoration, Cambridge 1995, 241–66.
[106] Worsley to Ashley, memorandum, TNA, 30/24/49, fos 86r–v.
[107] Ibid. fo. 86v.

factures. Care should be taken to ensure that exports were neither under-valued nor priced out of the market, with the same considerations being paid to imports. The state should encourage manufacturing innovation, whilst considering prudent means to 'putt a stop to any of the manufactures of our neighbours', especially those competing with English exports.[108] Ultimately, commercial policy was neither 'within the Prospect of the merchant', nor 'their Power Care or Consideration; And least of all in their Aime, when some of them are easily discerned to be expressely contrary to their privatt profitt or gayne'.

This was the rationale for erecting a mainly non-mercantile council of trade, which was free from 'the Intrigues & privat designes of merchants'.[109] Worsley recommended that 'The maior part may Consist of such of the Gentry of the nation whose Interest it may be to be more concerned; in the generality of the Trade of the nation and in the good of the management of if Then in the profitt of this or That perticular Trade which may possibly sway with the privat merchants.'[110] This, combined with the paternalist vision which Worsley presented of government as the nation's 'naturall Parent', protecting 'the good & wellfare of every perticular person', suggests a conservative attitude to the government of trade.[111] However, rather than suggesting a natural hierarchy of obedience and duty, Worsley evoked a harmony of private economic interests, in which the state 'doth obleige the Interest of all persons universally, to a hearty union & Concurrence with it, & to a yeelding of all possible duty & subiection to it'. Similarly, it was not the gentry's natural quality of leadership which justified this role in governing trade, but their status as the social group whose commercial interests were closest to the nation's as a whole, as opposed to the merchant who was likely to favour specific trades. Even so, Worsley stressed the need to limit the powers of a council, which should initially be probationary, to avoid its membership becoming a private cartel.[112]

Worsley's papers must have won him some admirers, for he was appointed to the new Council of Trade founded on 20 October 1668, with a salary of £200.[113] However, the composition of this body contradicted Worsley's advice, as it included a hefty mercantile contingent of perhaps nineteen out of forty-two members.[114] Worsley would have been happier with the detailed

---

[108] Ibid. fo. 87r.
[109] Ibid. fo. 87v.
[110] Ibid. fo. 88r.
[111] Ibid. fo. 87r–v.
[112] Ibid. fo. 87v.
[113] Kelly, 'Introduction', to *Locke on money*, 7; J. C. Sainty, *Office holders in modern Britain*, III: *Officials of the Board of Trade, 1660–1870*, London 1974, 19. The salary is ascertained by a warrant issued to Worsley for £200 on 15 December 1669, i.e. just over a year after the Council of Trade was formed: *CSPD, 1668–9*, 617. This order was confirmed by the Treasury on 23 Feb. 1670: *CTB, 1669–72*, 373.
[114] Andrews, *Committees*, 93; Thornton, *West-India policy*, 135.

instructions issued to the council, which included free ports amongst a wide range of subjects to be considered.[115] Worsley sent a copy to John Winthrop in Connecticut, requesting 'That if any thing do occurre to your Observation ... I may better enioy the Benefitt of it or rather not I But the nation it selfe'.[116] To Worsley, England and New England were part of the same nation therefore, but Winthrop was keen to distinguish the interests of his colony from those of the metropolis. Thus he was glad that 'many very weighty matters are conteined therein pointing at the publique good, & benefitt not only of the English people at home, but those also of the plantations abroad', but added as a caution that 'I hope God will guide your consultations for a generall advantage to the English aswell in their swarmes, as in the hives.'[117]

It appears that such an unwieldy council was ill-suited to achieve this, suffering from the same problems as its 1660 predecessor, and it fell into inactivity after 1670.[118] Despite this, Worsley was apparently a prominent member, and was amongst the signatories to the council's most important report, which led to customs officials being sent to the colonies to administer the oath requiring governors to promise to uphold the navigation acts, a notable example of metropolitan assertiveness.[119] Historians have seen the Council of Trade as less important than the committee summoned by the House of Lords in October 1669 to consider the decay of rents, but which also examined commercial depression more widely.[120] Worsley was the first of five members of the Council of Trade called to give evidence on 4 November.[121] He stressed that the fall in rents was a consequence of an adverse balance of trade, blaming 'The negligence of manufacture whereby the nation have lost their repute abroad'.[122] It was therefore necessary to encourage domestic manufacturing, especially of cloth, although as we have seen Worsley doubted whether English drapery could recover. The figure who dominated proceedings, however, was Josiah Child, who argued for the legal reduction of interest to 4 per cent.[123] Child was opposed by Silius Titus who argued that a forced cut would cause money to be 'called in', leading

---

[115] The instructions are printed in T&C, 524–8.
[116] Worsley to Winthrop, c. June 1670, Winthrop papers, microfilm reel 9.
[117] Winthrop to Worsley, 27 Oct. 1670, ibid.
[118] Roger North would later allege that the council was ruined by conflict between East India and Levant merchants, who comprised many of its leading members: Letwin, *Origins of scientific economics*, 24–5.
[119] Report dated 4 Dec. 1668, CSPC, 1661–8, 629–30; Andrews, *Committees*, 94–5; Thornton, *West-India policy*, 139. In a petition requesting that he be paid his overdue salary for his first year of employment, Worsley claimed that he had 'never been absent nor declined any command in the service': CSPD, Oct. 1668- Dec. 1669, 651.
[120] Letwin, *Origins of scientific economics*, 5–9. On perceptions of economic depression at the time see J. Spurr, *England in the 1670s*, Oxford 2000, 119–26.
[121] The minutes of the committee are printed in T&C, 68–79.
[122] Ibid. 69.
[123] Ibid. 71; Letwin, *Origins of scientific economics*, 7–8. Child's ideas were presented in his *Brief observations concerning trade, and interest of money*, London 1668. See also T. Keirn

to a shortage for lending. Worsley agreed that 'Interest of money [is] so necessary an appendix to all civil affairs', but he leaned to Titus' position, arguing that 'He that persuades the lowness of interest must show that there is sufficient for trade, for the rebuilding of London, for the nobility and gentry's use, and for his Majesty's occasion ... Where seed is made choice of and the land not manured and fitted for the seed, the crop must fail.'[124] Worsley thus subscribed to the opinion that lower interest rates would be a consequence, rather than a cause, of expanded trade. The committee actually went with Child, but a bill to cut interest was later rejected, partly thanks to Ashley's opposition; at the same time, Locke wrote his own paper which followed Worsley by favouring colonial trade as the means to bring in money naturally.[125]

Worsley would doubtless have preferred to serve on a council more focused on colonial trade, but occasionally such business did come its way, one example involving property rights in the aftermath of the second Anglo-Dutch War. Since its settlement by Europeans the New World had been plagued by disputes over property, conquest and sovereignty amongst the colonial powers, negotiated diplomatically between rival empires.[126] This particular one concerned the former English colony of Surinam, which had been founded in 1651 by Francis Lord Willoughby, and which had 4,000 settlers by 1663.[127] However, its proximity to Dutch and French settlements on the Guianan coast meant that Surinam was particularly vulnerable during the second Anglo-Dutch War, and was captured by Zeelanders on 6 March 1667.[128] The reasons given for this capitulation by the governor, William Byam, vividly attest to the precarious existence of colonial settlements caught up in inter-European disputes:

> To Conclude an universall and Continued sickness an imperfect halfe built Fort, the vast distance of our settlements an unable and devided people the Age, sickness, weakness, and Backwardness of many the Infedellity of more, the want of Ammunition, the Insolent disorders of our owne Negroes, The dayly expectation of the merciless French and the utter dispaire of any releife, were the Confluence of united Judgments, which our sinns had ripened, all concurring to Subject us under the yoake of our Enemies.[129]

and F. Melton, 'Thomas Manley and the rate-of-interest debate, 1668–1673', *JBS* xxix (1990), 147–73.

[124] T&C, 74.

[125] Kelly, 'Introduction', to *Locke on money*, 9–10, 52–4.

[126] For the importance of such inter-state negotiations to empire and state-building see E. Manke, 'Empire and state', in D. Armitage and M. Braddick (eds), *The British Atlantic world, 1500–1800*, Basingstoke 2002, 175–95.

[127] C. Goslinga, *The Dutch in the Caribbean and on the Wild Coast, 1580–1680*, Assen 1971, 421–5.

[128] Ibid. 396–400; J. A. Williamson, *English colonies in Guiana and on the Amazon, 1604–1668*, Oxford 1923, 177–84.

[129] Lieutenant-General William Byam's journal of Surinam, 1665–7, MS Sloane 3662, fo. 37r.

The colony had subsequently been recaptured and placed under a new governor, Major-General James Bannister, in October, but by then the Peace of Breda that ended the war had ceded Surinam to the Dutch, in exchange for New Amsterdam.[130] Bannister reluctantly surrendered the colony in April 1668, having done much to render it worthless. In retaliation, the Dutch government refused the remaining English settlers access to their property or the right to leave, which was enshrined in the treaty, and arrested Bannister.[131] Bannister's complaints reached the crown in October, and must have been directed to the Council of Trade then, for on 12 November its members advised that the articles of surrender had clearly been violated and the crown should intervene.[132] Bannister was eventually ejected from Zeeland in December, and so it was probably shortly after then that Worsley met with him on behalf of the Council of Trade, as its leading expert on colonial affairs.

Worsley produced a thorough account of the meeting, focusing on Bannister's understanding of the crucial fifth clause of the articles of surrender, which granted inhabitants the right to depart and sell their estates.[133] Their case rested on the terms of surrender, which confirmed their natural property rights:

> For as the Word power in the 5th Article, which is given to every of the said Inhabitants to sell that should at any time depart, can be understood no other power than that which naturally and doth of right result to every man from the plenary property which he himselfe hath in any thing (exclusive to all others) so this power to sell is not given but taken away, when he that is to sell may not have liberty to sell to whome he will.[134]

The Council of Trade thus supported Bannister's petition to the king, dated 5 May 1669.[135] This, and other complaints, produced a reply from the Grand Pensionary Johann de Witt, dated 2 July 1669, which fell under the consideration of Lord Arlington. Arlington had already received copies of some of Worsley's papers, whilst Worsley had previously advised his secretary, Joseph Williamson, on shipping matters.[136] Thus it was Worsley whom Arlington commissioned to answer the Dutch statesman.

De Witt argued that Surinam was possessed by the Dutch 'with all the

---

[130] Goslinga, *Dutch in the Caribbean*, 407.

[131] *CSPC, 1660–8*, 598–600.

[132] Ibid. 621, 623.

[133] Worsley's report on Surinam, probably presented to the Council of Trade, *c.* Jan. 1669, MS Rawlinson A478, fos 32–7 (copy belonging to Lord Arlington).

[134] Ibid. fo. 35r.

[135] Ibid. fo. 37r; *CSPC, 1669–74*, 21–2.

[136] See Williamson's notes, 2 Apr. 1669, *CSPD, Oct. 1668–Dec. 1669*, 260–1, 290–2. See also V. Barbour, 'Dutch and English merchant shipping in the seventeenth century', *EcHR* ii (1930), 273. On Williamson see A. Marshall, 'Sir Joseph Williamson and the conduct of administration in Restoration England', *HR* lxix (1996), 18–41.

rights and a Power unlimited of Superiority and Soveraignity', and therefore its inhabitants had no right to appeal to Charles II, or he to intervene in their affairs: if this rule was ignored, 'the whole world would bee
disturbed, and turned upside Downe'.[137] Worsley's answer praised de Witt's
'Maturenesse' and 'strength of Argument', which he described as 'De Jure
Grotium'.[138] As De Witt argued, the colonists' appeal threatened to introduce two competing sovereigns within the colony, and thus 'there could
never be any peace or any end put to the settlement of the soveraignty or
Dominion of them'.[139]

Worsley accepted that sovereignty was indivisible, remarking that the
alternative would be inconvenient for English rule in New Amsterdam.[140]
He therefore turned to means by which the crown could get round these
problems and intervene on behalf of the English remaining in Surinam.
Worsley conceded that the treaty had clearly stated that 'either party shall
keep & possesse for the future all such Lands, Places, & Colonies ... with
plenary Right of Soveraignty, property and possession'.[141] However, it had
equally enshrined the articles of surrender, which clearly provided for the
settlers' right to depart.[142] Worsley therefore argued that 'if the limitation
be not to be applyed to the soveraignty it must of necessity be applyed to
the possession & detention because beside these two things there is nothing
else before mentioned'.[143] The implicit conclusion was that the remaining
English settlers could therefore protest to Charles II on the issues of their
property and detention without compromising Dutch sovereignty, which
did not extend to these matters. Meanwhile Worsley asserted that England
retained a right to settle those parts of the Guianan coast which the Dutch
did not possess when the articles of surrender were signed. Worsley's neat
logic allowed him to demonstrate to Arlington his skill in interpreting inter-
colonial jurisdictional disputes, in a way which favoured English interests.

Worsley's respect for the Grand Pensionary's opinions seems to mark
a shift in his attitude to the Dutch, precipitated not by any decline in
their commercial power, but by the growing assertiveness of France under
Louis XIV and Colbert, particularly in the West Indies.[144] Worsley had already
complained to Ashley that 'while they pretent to peace they doe actually
make warr with us', through tariffs on English imports, and argued that it

---

[137] De Wit's discourse on Surinam, 2 July 1669, copied into a colonial entry book
concerning Surinam: CO 278/2, pp. 7–13 (quotes at pp. 7, 9).
[138] Worsley, 'Animadversions on my Lord de Wits paper presented to my Lord Arlington',
after 2 July 1669, in 'Locke notebook', 253. A copy is also entered at CO 278/2, 13–
19.
[139] 'Locke notebook', 256.
[140] Ibid. 260.
[141] Ibid. 259.
[142] Ibid. 258.
[143] Ibid. 260.
[144] Thornton, West-India policy, 127.

was 'farr better, to have noe trade at all & to be at open Warr with a nation; Then to have such an unequal peace or Comerce'.[145] Here we can see that shift from anti-Dutch to anti-French sentiment amongst many Englishmen, which has been discussed by Pincus.[146] Whilst Worsley apparently did not see it as so serious a commercial rival in the West Indies as the Dutch, he feared that through force France would come to dominate the Caribbean.

In fact, Louis's main target was the decaying Spanish empire, but Worsley recognised that this threatened England by upsetting the regional balance of power, and so advised upholding the Spanish empire as a bulwark in two papers for Buckingham. These centred on the controversial issue of the Jamaican privateers, who, despite the complaints of Spain, had been tacitly supported by the governor Sir Thomas Modyford throughout the 1660s.[147] This period saw much debate about whether to suppress these marauders in return for commercial concessions with the Spanish colonies, or to continue to use them in defence of that vulnerable colony. Worsley's problem was that, although he was in favour of a strategic alliance with Spain against France, he recognised the difficulty of suppressing the privateers, as well as the importance of the trade to Jamaica's economy.[148] Although Worsley believed that Jamaica's future lay in sugar, in the meantime necessity dictated supporting actions which could only be countenanced in the moral vacuum that existed 'beyond the line'.

Worsley's first letter on the subject, dated 18 December 1668, responded to Spanish complaints about Henry Morgan's recent raid on Porto Bello, which had provoked particular indignation given that England and Spain had signed a commercial treaty in May 1667.[149] Worsley acknowledged that the king's first instinct would be to suppress the perpetrators of this unauthorised attack, given his 'Inclination to Love to live quietly among his neighbours ... As preferring not only Justice and peace But good order and Governement before his profitt'.[150] However, this decision had wider strategic implications. Given that 'once a Theife and ever a Theife', it was unrealistic to hope that the privateers would lay down their arms. If they were forced to do so, the privateers were likely simply to switch their attention to English shipping and settlements. More worryingly, the 2,000 or so privateers would be sure to look for protection to some less scrupulous colonial

---

[145] Worsley to Ashley, memorandum, 14 Aug.1668, TNA, 30/24/49, fos 225v–226r.

[146] S. Pincus, 'From butterboxes to wooden shoes: the shift in English popular sentiment from anti-Dutch to anti-French in the 1670s', HJ xxviii (1995), 333–61.

[147] Thornton, West-India policy, 67–123.

[148] N. Zahedieh, '"A frugal, prudential and hopeful trade": privateering in Jamaica, 1655–89', Journal of Imperial and Commonwealth History xviii (1990), 154.

[149] Thornton, West-India policy, 97.

[150] Worsley to Buckingham, 'Considerations about the Jamaica privateers', 18 Dec. 1668 (also sent to other privy councillors including Lord Arlington and Sir Orlando Bridgeman), MS Rawlinson A478, fo. 61r (copy belonging to Arlington). There is a second copy in 'Locke notebook', 172–9.

governor, and given that the Dutch were 'a sober & Tradeing people', there was only one likely candidate: the French. This had already happened with regard to the 'Buckaneeres or Cow-Killers's of Hispaniola'. Thus, although Charles was likely to 'make great scruple' about tolerating privateers, 'Yett it followeth not therefore that the French will be of the same temper.'[151]

By focusing on the West Indies, Worsley argued, Louis could 'with farr less Charge & trouble to himselfe ... make himselfe the universall monarch of Christendome, then by any Attempts he can propound to himself upon Germany Millaume Flanders & Franche Comte'.[152] The privateers became a pawn in this power game played across the Atlantic, due both to their military power and the fact that 'a very Considerable number of persons alsoe doe live in Jamaica by the advantage of them'. In fact, the Treaty of Madrid of 1670 and the recall of Modyford saw the crown take a stricter attitude to privateers, but they continued to play an important role in Port Royal until its destruction in 1692.[153] Meanwhile Worsley wrote a lengthy sequel to his first letter, which had been circulated to Arlington and other statesmen, in February 1669. Again, Buckingham was the recipient, but Arlington and Ashley also received copies.[154] This time Worsley was much more explicit about French designs on Hispaniola, the strategic key to the Bay of Mexico, which only Jamaica stood in the way of.[155] France was likely to use the decaying Spanish empire as a stepping-stone before eventually challenging England, and so Worsley advocated a strategic alliance with the Spanish empire, England's traditional enemy in the Americas. This, in turn, might be the most effectual way eventually to suppress the privateers and settle Jamaica's long-term commercial future, and Worsley suggested that England and Spain enter into an American alliance.[156]

This, however, was no easy matter. As well as its grievance about privateering, Spain's long-standing refusal to recognise any English presence or trade in the West Indies was a stumbling block. Worsley proposed playing the one off against the other. The suppression of piracy, he suggested, should be a joint Anglo-Spanish enterprise, largely financed by the latter. This would also force the Spanish to finally recognise England's possession of the island seized from it in 1655.[157] Similarly, it would be fair compensation to allow Jamaica to monopolise trade into Spanish America, 'as may in some

---

[151] MS Rawlinson A478, fo. 62r.
[152] Ibid. fo. 61v.
[153] Zahedieh, '"A frugal, prudential and hopeful trade"', 156–7.
[154] Worsley to Buckingham, second 'large' letter on Jamaica, 24 Feb. 1669 (also sent to Ashley and Arlington), TNA, 30/24/49, fos 37–48 (Ashley's copy). Further copies are in 'Locke notebook', 180–214; MS Add. 11410, pp. 623–74. Worsley was still in touch with Buckingham in December 1669: A. Browning (ed.), *Thomas Osborne, earl of Danby and duke of Leeds, 1632–1712*, II: *Letters*, Glasgow 1951, 24.
[155] Worsley to Buckingham, 24 Feb. 1669, fo. 36v.
[156] Ibid. fo. 41v.
[157] Ibid. fo. 40v.

measure answer both to the kindness, trouble, and charge that his Majesty is likely to be put to'.[158] Jamaica had already benefited from illegally trading with Spanish colonies.[159] Worsley suggested cultivating Port Royal's role as 'the greatest seat of trade of any in the West Indies', as an 'express act and designe of State'.[160] This would be one aspect of a programme aimed at developing Jamaica's economy so that it could subsist without relying on the dubious benefits of plunder. The navigation system had placed colonial trade in an imperial straitjacket, requiring planters to rely on a limited number of traders and thus forcing down prices. However, Worsley did not simply see the plantations as a cash-cow for the metropolis, and his colonial political economy would compensate for this with other privileges.

These by now familiar concessions included free trade in slaves, along-side various customs immunities and royal encouragement for 'planting of any new Commodity in the said Island belonging to Turkey', presumably including senna.[161] More specifically, Jamaican chocolate should be exempt from paying any excise, whilst Jamaica should be given a colonial monopoly for the production of cacao nuts and pepper. The popularity of chocolate throughout Europe meant that it was 'ready & current money in all places', whilst in England the 'Common people' had already 'got the Taste of it and doe seeme much to Covett it'.[162] The irresistible appetite of Englishmen for luxuries could not be suppressed with sumptuary laws, and so it was necessary to ensure a plentiful supply of these commodities from a domestic source, or else be at the mercy of some foreign supplier.

These improvements would be secured by augmenting Jamaica's defences, presumably one of the responsibilities of the royal governor for the West Indies, whom Worsley suggested should be sent over in imitation of the French.[163] This last measure was not in fact adopted, but the interest with which statesmen received Worsley's papers is suggested by their wide circulation. Meanwhile, the Treaty of Madrid introduced an Anglo-Spanish rapprochement along the lines that he had suggested. However, the best indicator of the reputation Worsley was building is the path that his career would take after 1670 under Charles II although, as the final chapter shows, there would be a final twist in his long engagement in the service of the state.

[158] Ibid. fo. 41r.
[159] See N. Zahedieh, 'The merchants of Port Royal, Jamaica, and the Spanish contra-band trade, 1655–1692', WMQ 3rd ser. xliii (1986), 570–93, and 'Trade, plunder, and economic development in early English Jamaica, 1655–89', EcHR 2nd ser. xxxix (1986), 205–22.
[160] Worsley to Buckingham, 24 Feb. 1669, fos 41r–v.
[161] Ibid. fo. 47r.
[162] Ibid. fos 44v–45r.
[163] Ibid. fo. 40r.

8

Commerce and Conscience, 1670–1677

Colonial and commercial councils, 1670–3

Sometime before the summer of 1670 Benjamin Worsley moved to West-minster, residing in Tuttle Fields, 'right over against the Military Ground next to Mr William Brewers'.[1] Such proximity to the corridors of power was fitting, for on 30 July 1670 a Council for Foreign Plantations was formed under the presidency of the earl of Sandwich, with Worsley as assistant to the secretary Henry Slingsby, drawing a salary of £300.[2] The fact that this body was confined to ten members (although eight were added in 1671, including Buckingham), with nobles and gentlemen preferred to merchants, made it much closer to Worsley's ideal model than the 1668 council.[3] Its instructions, too, seem to owe something to the Worsley's advice, paying great attention to the rationalisation of imperial rule and the regulation of colonial production and trade.[4] In particular, they demanded increased oversight of colonial governors, which was acted upon by the council when drafting new instructions, and scrutinising colonial legislation.[5]

As well as dealing with the governors, the council's meetings (generally more than weekly) dealt with a wide range of matters, and were somewhat inundated with time-consuming petitions and complaints.[6] It is difficult to discern Worsley's voice in distinction from that of the council as a whole. One rare glimpse of his personal input was noted in the diary of another member, John Evelyn, which recorded that in February 1671 the council had 'entred upon enquiries about improving his Majesties American Dominions by *Silk, Galls, Flax, Senna* &c & considered how *Nutmegs* & *Cinamon* might be obtained, & brought to *Jamaica*, that Soile & Climat promising successe; upon this Dr. *Worsley* being called in spake many considerable things'.[7]

---

[1] Worsley to Winthrop, *c.* June 1670, Winthrop papers, microfilm reel 9. Worsley was named as commissioner for Westminster in an act to raise £1,238,750 supply for the crown in 1672. See *Statutes of the realm*, V: *1628–80* (1819), 752–82: URL: http://www.british-history.ac.uk/ date accessed, 6 Mar. 2007.
[2] Sainty, *Office holders*, 20–1. The president's salary was £700, with the other members being paid £500 each.
[3] Although Arlington and Ashley were not official members, they frequently attended as members of the privy council.
[4] Printed in Andrews, *Committees*, 117–26.
[5] Thornton, *West-India policy*, 141, 145–6; Andrews, *Committees*, 103–4.
[6] Andrews, *Committees*, 104–5; Bieber, 'British plantation councils', 102–6.
[7] *Diary of John Evelyn*, 567.

Doubtless the council would have made use of Worsley's experience when it drew up a commission for James Bannister finally to fetch the remaining English from Surinam, in November 1670, as well as when considering matters such as colonial sugar.[8] This commodity was included in the Subsidy Bill of November 1670, which became a subject of dispute between the Commons and Lords throughout 1671 over the appropriate level at which to tax white sugar exported from the colonies. Worsley wrote a paper on the subject for Sandwich, arguing in favour of granting privileges to promote colonial sugar refining, against the interests of English refiners.[9]

The death of Sandwich in 1672 led to a reorganisation whereby the council absorbed the defunct Council of Trade, under the presidency of Ashley (now earl of Shaftesbury and Lord Chancellor). Worsley was promoted to secretary, with a salary of £500.[10] John Locke was employed as his assistant, and the council represented the summit of Shaftesbury's colonial designs, although other statesmen such as Arlington remained involved.[11] An initial draft of the lengthy instructions is in Shaftesbury's papers, probably drafted by Shaftesbury and Locke, perhaps with recourse to Worsley's suggestions.[12] Accompanying this was a bold measure: the Declaration of Indulgence of 15 March 1672, giving breathing space to dissenters like Worsley.[13] These measures seemed to be taking the English state in a direction of which Worsley would have approved, but they came at a cost. In order to pursue the policy of indulgence, Charles II needed to free himself from reliance on parliament, and Worsley would not have welcomed the means he found to do so: alliance with France. Fiscal concerns were also behind the Stop on the Exchequer of 2 January 1672, much to the dismay of the London business community.[14] Meanwhile the Treaty of Dover led to a third Anglo-Dutch War, beginning on 13 March 1672, with the French this time as allies. Sandwich himself was an early casualty.

Thus the new Council of Trade and Plantations had from its beginnings to contend with the effects of another Dutch war, to add to the disastrous legacy of the last one. Fortunately, this time the Caribbean was not so intensive a theatre of conflict, although the first item of business the council had to deal with was a rumour, conveyed by Arlington, that the Dutch were

[8] Andrews, *Committees*, 133–4. Bannister's instructions are in the Colonial Entry Book concerning Surinam, CO 278/2, pp. 26–32. This mission did not settle the matter, however: see pp. 33–74.

[9] A copy of this paper, entitled 'The true state of the manufacture of sugar within our plantations, which requires all manner of incouragement', is in volume ten of Sandwich's journals, in private ownership. See F. R. Harris, *Edward Montagu 1st earl of Sandwich (1625–1672)*, ii, London 1912, 225–6.

[10] Sainty, *Office holders*, 23.

[11] Andrews, *Committees*, 106–7.

[12] TNA, 30/24/41, fos 120–3, printed in Andrews, *Committees*, 127–32.

[13] Spurr, *England in the 1670s*, 29.

[14] Ibid. 27.

preparing to attack Jamaica.[15] It could therefore basically continue the work of its predecessor, although now trade in general fell under its jurisdiction.[16] As secretary, Worsley was responsible for administering the council's business, recorded in his meticulously neat handwriting in an entering book.[17] One of his main tasks was to correspond with the colonial governors on the council's behalf, congratulating the governor of Jamaica Sir Thomas Lynch for his 'care for the wellfare of the said island, especially that you have endeavoured to remove that humour of Debauchery, that was got much into Creditt in the tyme of your Predecessor'.[18] Worsley seems to have been unconcerned about voicing his own opinions in these letters, questioning Lynch about Jamaican flora, which interested him 'as a Phisitian' with some 'Friendship and Intimacy with Mr Robert Boyle'. Another letter mentioned approvingly that the colony 'had near three times the trade this year that they had the last', noting with relief that they had had 'no manner of disturbance from the Dutch'.[19] Worsley was not alone in thinking the Dutch threat to Jamaica exaggerated: Lynch himself purported to be little 'troubled with the feare or Noyse of an invasion'.[20] However, he welcomed the council's letters as 'Blessings from Heaven, that are long look'd and long pray'd for, soe it is an extraordinary Comfort to the Inhabitants to thinke soe many Great men, and good Patriots are concerned for them'.[21]

The council could generally be relied on to speak on Jamaica's behalf, insofar as this was consistent with the imperial oversight that it was attempting to inaugurate. In Jamaica's case, this meant subjecting the colony's laws to intensive scrutiny, although only about seven of thirty-four acts signed by Lynch in May 1672 were successfully approved.[22] Perhaps this encouraged the council to pass an order formalising future assessment of colonial legislation.[23] Aside from Lynch, the only colonial governor with whom Worsley corresponded was William Lord Willoughby of Barbados. This was partly because the council was preoccupied with the supposed designs of the Dutch in the Caribbean, but equally it appears to have been less interested in mainland America than the more lucrative West Indies. Worsley would probably have shared this attitude; as he wrote to Willoughby, he had little doubt

---

[15] Journal of the Council of Trade and Plantations, 1672–4, Bodl. Lib., microfilm 496 (original copy possessed by the Library of Congress, Washington), 2–3.

[16] Andrews, *Committees*, 110–11.

[17] CO 389/5.

[18] Worsley to Sir T. Lynch, 2 Nov. 1672, CO 1/29, fo. 102 (calendared in *CSPC*, 1669–74, 424). See also 'Plantations journal, 1672–4', 3, 5, 7–8, and Worsley to Lynch, 30 Nov. 1672, CO 1/29, fo. 140r (*CSPC*, 1669–74, 439).

[19] Worsley to Lynch, 1 Jan. 1673, CO 1/30, fo. 1r (*CSPC*, 1669–74, 459).

[20] Lynch to Worsley, 6 Apr. 1673, CO 1/30, fo. 46r (*CSPC*, 1669–74, 479).

[21] Lynch to Worsley, 15 May 1673, *CSPC*, 1669–74, 490.

[22] Bieber, 'Plantation councils', 104; 'Plantations journal, 1672–4', 5, 27–8, 30–1, 44.

[23] 'Plantations journal, 1672–4', 38. Central oversight of colonial laws would become a source of conflict later in the decade, as Poyning's Law attempted to remove from colonial governors and assemblies the power to make laws: Bliss, *Revolution and empire*, 182–9.

that 'neere a 3d parte of the interest, Trade, & stock of this Nation doth at this time depend upon the safety of our southerne Plantations'.[24] Such sentiments encouraged the governor that he had 'a friend in the Councell to whome I dare presume to speak plaine English'.[25] The council had written to Willoughby to issue the same warnings as it had to Lynch, but Worsley's covering letter focused on the threat posed by England's ostensible ally, France. He therefore put it to Willoughby that should 'the French ... vigorously fall into the Spanish West Indyes; ... wee may have a worse Neighbour to deale with ... then wee have hitherto had of the Spaniard'.[26]

Ironically, just as French armies were marching through the Netherlands on England's side, the Council of Trade and Plantations was engaged in settling a dispute in the West Indies left over from the last war against France. The case in question was somewhat similar to that of Surinam, although on this occasion England had managed to regain possession of the colony on St Christophers through the Treaty of Breda, after it had been briefly held by the French with whom they shared the island. Worsley twice reported on the issue in February, giving a detailed assessment of the refusal of the French to comply with their treaty obligations, an affront to crown and subjects alike.[27] Worsley prepared the council's address, which after much revision was signed on 9 June.[28] This described the behaviour of the French as an insult to English sovereignty in the West Indies, and was backed up by a lengthy list of complaints about French behaviour, compiled by Worsley, which seemed to prove that his fears about Louis's aggressive ambitions in the West Indies were founded.[29]

The council's members would have been familiar with such a dispute from their experience on previous bodies, but now their responsibilities also included trade in general. This was a rather less clear area to supervise than the plantations, lacking state agents to work through as was the case with the colonial governors, and rendering the council rather reactive. Its approach can be demonstrated by one case involving manufacturing and commercial interests. On 14 January 1673 it heard a petition referred from the crown by a number of merchants styling themselves the Gambia Adventurers, who traded mainly in African redwood, which was imported for use in the cloth industry.[30] Their complaint involved the use of a rival dye-wood, sanders, imported from the East Indies and purchased by members of the Salters' Company who then sold it to clothiers, so that the Gambia trade was now 'allmost totally lost & Discredited'.[31] The adventurers argued that

[24] Worsley to Willoughby, 17 Dec. 1672, CO 1/29, fo. 175r (CSPC, 1669–74, 448).
[25] Willoughby to Worsley, 7 Mar. 1673, CO 1/30, fo. 34r (CSPC, 1669–74, 471).
[26] Worsley to Willoughby, 17 Dec. 1672, CO 1/29, fo. 175r (CSPC, 1669–74, 448).
[27] 'Plantations journal, 1672–4', 32, 35; CSPC, 1669–74, 466–7, 469.
[28] 'Plantations journal, 1672–4', 38–41.
[29] CO 389/5, 50–61. The signed report is at CO 1/30, fos 95–6.
[30] 'Plantations journal, 1672–4', 26. The petition is entered at CO 389/5, 47.
[31] 'Plantations journal, 1672–4', 29.

this was merely a poor quality substitute, and 'a great fraud to the Buier'. Like its 1650 predecessor, the council had been instructed to consider how manufactures could 'be truely made and manufactured at home', so they were duty bound to consider any case which might 'Discredit and prejudice' English industry.[32] Furthermore, sanderswood was currently only imported by the Dutch East India Company, in direct contravention of the Navigation Act.

In response, on 6 February, the council heard evidence from representatives of the Salters' Company, who complained that the adventurers tended to sell 'onely to two or three particular men', which inflated the price.[33] However, they did agree to purchase redwood instead of sanders if its price was reduced, which the adventurers agreed to providing that the Salters purchased at least 300 tonnes. This seemed to be a compromise pleasing to all groups, but the council's attitude changed on 18 February when representatives of the Dyers' Company reported the findings of a trial, which had concluded that sanderswood was as good as redwood.[34] This contrasted markedly with the conclusion of the Salters, who appear to have been deliberately attempting to force the Gambia Adventurers to cut the price of redwood. But the Dyers, who had to buy from members of the Salters' Company, were happy to use the cheaper substitute. The council's report of 14 April therefore concluded that rather than suppress the purchase of sanders, 'It deserves all Lawfull Encouragement from your Majestie to be Imported untill such tyme as Our East India Company can upon this Notice of its use, be able to furnish themselves a sufficient Quantety of it'.[35] The Gambia Adventurers must have regretted making their petition at all.

In this case the council had managed to settle the dispute fairly efficiently, but matters were not always so easily resolved, as was the case with a dispute involving the duties paid by English merchants to maintain the crown's consul at Venice, George Hayles, which took up time in no less than nine meetings in late 1672.[36] It can be difficult to discern a consistent policy of colonial or commercial government through such detail. Worsley had considered one responsibility of a trade council as arbitrating between rival parties involved in colonisation, but he can hardly have anticipated how time-consuming this would be. For example the petition of John Rodney, a former resident of Nevis, against the governor James Russell, was first read on 8 November 1672, but the council was only able to agree on a report on 23 June 1673, and in fact the affair would eventually outlive the council itself.[37] Bieber concluded that this council and its predecessor 'took

[32] Quoted in Andrews, *Committees*, 127; CO 389/5, 49.
[33] 'Plantations journal, 1672–4', 34.
[34] Ibid.
[35] CO 389/5, 50.
[36] The petition is included ibid. 32–3.
[37] 'Plantations journal', 6–7, 25, 36–7, 39–40, 43; CSPC, 1669–74, 429–31, 481–2; CO 1/29, fos 118–20; CO 1/30, fos 101–2.

a narrow view of their function and failed, with few exceptions, to develop any general colonial policy', but this perhaps underestimates the restraints the state faced in governing at a distance: Andrews's judgement, that they 'inaugurated a policy and system of control that was more comprehensive than any which had been put into practice by the previous boards', may be closer to the intent behind the council's deliberations, if not always their outcome.[38]

Worsley himself seems to have been nothing but diligent as secretary, although he was in the post for less than a year. His rise in the service of Charles II had been aided by the Declaration of Indulgence, but once this was withdrawn, Worsley was forced to reassess his position. Charles could not ignore parliament forever, and in March 1673 he was forced to submit to a Test Act. This had been intended principally to exclude Catholics from office, but its demands also provoked Worsley's 'solitary, exemplary resignation', as a dissenter.[39] Worsley announced his intention to quit as early as 23 June 1673, a few days after being granted payment for his work as assistant to the previous council, but his employers were happy to keep him in office until 13 September, when he formally resigned.[40] On that date the council gathered specially to hear Worsley explain his regret at being 'made wholly incapable of performing any further Duty to them ... because of some clauses in the late Act for the preventing the growth of Popery which Act though it concerned not him at all as a Papist, nor as one that scrupled his fidelity & Allegiance to his Majestie yet it doth effect him ... as one who in the controversy about the Lords Supper did dissent from the practice of the Church of England'.[41] In response the council ordered 'That it should be entred in their Journalls as a Testimony to their respects to him, that their Lordships had received a satisfaction in the Attendance of the said secretary upon them and that they did approve of his services to them'. Worsley's assistant, John Locke, was sworn in on 15 October 1673; in his first full session as secretary, the council was confronted with news that the Dutch had captured New York.[42]

In fact, the council's commission was withdrawn in December 1674, and even by then the dismissal of Shaftesbury had robbed it of its most important member.[43] Although over the previous four years this and the preceding council had attempted to put their mark on colonial governance, it may be doubted that they had fulfilled their ambitious instructions. A relative lack of authority was but one problem: perhaps more difficult to surmount were

---

[38] Bieber, 'Plantation councils', 106; Andrews, *Committees*, 102.

[39] Aylmer, *Crown's servants*, 121.

[40] *Letters addressed to Sir Joseph Williamson*, ed. W. D. Christie, i (Camden viii, 1874), 60–1, 67; *CTB, 1672–1675*, 173. In fact, the council seems to have been almost completely inactive over the summer months: 'Plantations journal, 1672–4', 43–5.

[41] 'Plantations journal, 1672–4', 46.

[42] Ibid. 47–8.

[43] Andrews, *Committees*, 111.

the considerable difficulties which the state faced when seeking to govern distant colonies and expanding commerce. Thus, the ambitious statements of imperial intent of advisors like Worsley may be dismissed as irrelevant to the actual practice of colonial and commercial governance, which plodded on reactively, changing only gradually as the powers of the state grew. Indeed, it is hard to see a handful of aristocrats gathered in a rented private room, wondering exactly what powers were held by the governor of Jamaica as His Majesty's vice-admiral in the West Indies, as amounting to the overarching supervision of an imperial state.[44] However, the councils of trade with which Worsley was involved represent a period of trial and error in which the state extended its supervision over the commercial and colonial world, haltingly because there was no clear blueprint for how to do so, but with increasing purpose. Throughout this period ambitions outstripped capability, but they were none the less instrumental in terms of setting out the future priorities of governing a commercial empire which would inform the foundation of the Board of Trade and Plantations of 1696, a body linked directly to the 1672–4 council by Locke's membership.[45]

Whether Locke still made use of the papers he had copied from his former supervisor is impossible to know, but together these form something of a corpus, representing Worsley's mature vision of colonial political economy. Most of these – the three papers to Buckingham on Jamaica, his letter to Ashley on the importance of colonial trade, and his answer to de Witt about Surinam – received relatively wide circulation as state papers, but Locke also included one of Worsley's addresses to Willoughby on the senna project, which was probably copied from his personal papers. Locke also included a report from the Council of Trade and Plantations discussing with statistical detail 'The state of Ireland in reference to trade', which Worsley was presumably mainly responsible for drafting, and which concluded with a call to unify the two nations.[46] Together, these amount to almost 30,000 words written on over 100 sides, and although unpublished, those who did see them were important figures in high office, establishing Worsley's importance in the development of colonial and commercial government over a period of twenty-three years.

The political economy of conscience

On 23 June 1673 William Bridgeman wrote to Sir Joseph Williamson concerning the governmental changes following the Test Act. Although the main casualty was the Catholic duke of York, Bridgeman's attention was

---

[44] The council posed this query on 9 January 1673: 'Plantations journal, 1672–4', 24.
[45] I. Steele, *Politics of colonial policy: the Board of Trade in colonial administration, 1696–1720*, Oxford 1968, 4–18.
[46] 'Locke notebook', 220–31.

drawn by the resignation of Benjamin Worsley, for this particular bureaucrat was 'not to bee so much as suspected as a Catholique, for I dare sweare he is far from it'.[47] His resignation raises certain questions. Having managed to transfer his allegiance to Charles II apparently with ease, why did Worsley's conscience suddenly trouble him in 1673? And, before then, how could he justify serving a regime which seemed so opposed to the political and religious principles that he had previously upheld?

However, this regime was no 'monolith of royalist and anglican reaction'.[48] In the 1660s, the staunchest supporters of a strong alliance between the church hierarchy and the monarchy sat in parliament, whilst the king himself was open to alternative strategies for governing religion. Whether Charles was motivated by Catholic sympathies or desire to gain greater independence from parliament is of less concern than the fact that he was willing to listen to former Cromwellians. Under Clarendon this tendency was contained, but his fall, and the rise of a number of ambitious courtier-politicians in his place, saw this change. Of those 'Cabal' ministers whom Worsley knew, Ashley and Buckingham were notable defenders of nonconformity, whilst Arlington's Catholic tendencies encouraged him to explore the possibilities of toleration. The years 1667–73 may have been the first 'crisis' of the restored monarchy, but this also presented an opportunity to remodel the Restoration settlement.[49] Worsley was one of those dissenters happy to benefit from this change of climate, and it is no coincidence that his return to state service spanned precisely these years.

The most questioned aspect of the Restoration settlement was the treatment of Protestant dissenters, a matter of conscience with ramifications about the nature of the confessional state and the national Church.[50] Those advocating liberty of conscience tended to emphasise the monarch's responsibility to defend the public good, protecting the material welfare of his subjects and ensuring that the nation was not plagued by conflicts over conscience. One such pamphlet began by wishing that 'we might study and debate how to advance the Glory, Riches and Power of this Nation', rather than argue over minor points of religion.[51] Prosperity united the nation, and the state's role was primarily to uphold this rather than to enforce any particular form of Protestantism. Thus the discourse of toleration became linked to the discourse of trade, and it is no coincidence that the late 1660s were a formative period for John Locke's views on both.[52] Liberty of conscience

[47] *Letters addressed to Sir Joseph Williamson*, i. 59.
[48] M. Goldie, 'Danby, the bishops and the Whigs', in T. Harris, Seaward and M. Goldie (eds), *The politics of religion in Restoration England*, Oxford 1990, 75.
[49] G. De Krey, 'The first Restoration crisis: conscience and coercion in London, 1667–73', *Albion* xxv (1993), 565–80.
[50] Idem, 'Rethinking the Restoration: dissenting cases for conscience, 1667–1672', *HJ* xxviii (1995), 53–83; Coffey, *Persecution and toleration*, 171–2.
[51] *A letter to a member of this parliament, for liberty of conscience*, London 1668, 3.
[52] J. Marshall, *John Locke: resistance, religion and responsibility*, Cambridge 1994, 49–62.

and improvement of trade were often seen as complementary, and perhaps this is why the 1668 Council of Trade was suspected by the duke of York of being a subversive strategy of Buckingham and Ashley to promote noncon-formity.[53] This body may not have posed any threat to the government, but York was right to see its formation as potentially part of an attempt to rework the Restoration settlement, supported by individuals who were rather too admiring of the policies of the English and Dutch republics.

Despite these republican associations, religious toleration was portrayed by its promoters as in the joint interest of the king and the nation.[54] Thus, Slingsby Bethel asserted that 'the *richest*, most *active*, *industrious*, *thriving* part of these Tradesmen' were the dissenters, and thus their persecution created 'a great hole in the *Trading-stock of the Nation*'.[55] Liberty of conscience, like trade, was 'not only the Common Interest of all the Nation, but especially of his Majesty', who could rely on the loyalty of those nonconformists whose religious rights he protected.[56] The state had no business in infringing on individual conscience, but it still had a duty to govern public religion and defend international Protestantism against absolutist popery. Those calling for liberty of conscience were vulnerable to accusations of being soft on Catholicism, and so writers like Bethel asserted their Protestant credentials, in the process adding a different dimension to their anti-popery. Protestant polemicists often used the popish counter-example as a 'negative image' to highlight what they believed should be the true religion, 'a symbolic means of labelling and expelling trends and tendencies which seemed ... to threaten the integrity of a Protestant England'.[57] Therefore by stressing the connection between Protestantism and prosperity, writers like Bethel also transformed the image of the popish nation, so that the 'notion of popery became a complex one, referring to all of the means by which human flour-ishing, both material and spiritual, was prevented'.[58] This inversion appeared in Bethel's *The world's mistake in Oliver Cromwell*, with its caricature of popish nations impoverished by parasitic clergy, idle friars and wasteful holidays.[59] Nor was this stereotype confined to polemical pamphleteers, being echoed in the Council of Trade and Plantations' 1673 report on Ireland.[60] Thus we

---

For Locke's mature arguments on toleration see his *A letter concerning toleration* (1689), ed. J. Tully, Indianapolis 1983.

[53] Letwin, *Origins of scientific economics*, 21–4. See also R. North, *Examen: or, an enquiry into the credit and veracity of a pretended complete history*, London 1740, 461–2; Andrews, *Committees*, 92–3.

[54] De Krey, 'Rethinking the Restoration', 60–3.

[55] S. Bethel, *Et à dracone: or, some reflections upon a discourse called Omnia à Belo comesta*, London 1668, 9–10.

[56] Idem, *Present interest of England stated*, 13.

[57] Lake, 'Anti-popery', 183.

[58] M. Goldie, 'The civil religion of James Harrington', in A. Pagden (ed.), *The languages of political theory in early-modern Europe*, Cambridge 1987, 200.

[59] Bethel, *World's mistake*, 17–18.

[60] 'Considerations relating to the improvement of Ireland the state of Ireland in refer-

see that during the toleration debates of the Restoration there developed 'a distinctly commercialist (and, one is tempted to say, proto-Weberian) account of how Protestant states are more prosperous than priestly ones'.[61]

Calls for toleration might appear as conspiratorial challenges to Charles II and the Restoration state by parliamentarians and radicals of the 1640s and '50s. However, political alignments had changed since then, and the case of the tolerationists actually relied on upholding the royal supremacy over the Church, against parliament and the clergy.[62] Meanwhile their vision of the patriot king ruling over a prosperous and happy nation had some appeal for Charles, who was not above courting nonconformists, if only from fear of subversion.[63] Arlington monitored dissenter opinion for the crown, and Worsley wrote to him about 'whether it would not tend greatly to the honour of our nation' to settle 'all our maine differences about Religion'.[64] Thus he flew the flag for Hartlibian irenicism, something shared by the so-called 'latitudinarians' often associated with the Royal Society. Worsley owned books by 'moderate divines' including John Wilkins, Edward Fowler, Edward Stillingfleet and John Tillotson, as well as another proponent of 'rational religion', Sir Charles Wolseley. Unlike the latitudinarians, however, Worsley was outside the national Church, and in late 1671 his name appeared in the notes taken by Joseph Williamson regarding nonconformist meetings. One mention concerned the notorious Captain Thomas Blood, who became Arlington's agent after his failed attempt to steal the crown jewels.[65] Blood complained that Worsley had endeavoured to 'ruin him with Lord Arlington', suggesting that they were rivals for Arlington's patronage.[66] Worsley also appears to have acted as a go-between for Arlington and two Scottish Presbyterians who arrived in London in late 1671.[67] Another acquaintance was the Quaker William Penn, with whom he had some unidentified business

---

ence to trade', report of the Council of Trade and Plantations, dated 25 March 1673, in 'Locke notebook', 220–31.

[61] Goldie, 'Civil religion of James Harrington', 221.

[62] Idem, 'Priestcraft and the birth of Whiggism', in N. Phillipson and Q. Skinner (eds), *Political discourse in early modern Britain*, Cambridge 1993, 225.

[63] For Charles's equivocation over dissenters see J. Miller, *Charles II*, London 1991, 154–7.

[64] Worsley to Lord Arlington, c. 1668–73, SP 29/143, fo. 55r; *CSPD, 1665–6*, 174. Although calendared under 1665, this letter was probably written when Worsley was serving on one of the councils of trade or plantations of 1668–73, because it mentioned the lack of a settled place for such a council to meet and requested that he be paid his arrears. For negotiations between representatives of the regime and the nonconformists see Miller, *Charles II*, 188–91.

[65] R. L. Greaves, *Enemies under his feet: radicals and nonconformists in Britain, 1664–1677*, Stanford 1990, 204–15; A. Marshall, 'Colonel Thomas Blood and the Restoration political scene', *HJ* xxii (1989), 561–82.

[66] Greaves, *Enemies under his feet*, 221; *CSPD, 1671–2*, 46.

[67] *CSPD, 1671–2*, 29; *CSPD, Charles II: addenda (1660–85)*, 342; Greaves, *Enemies under his feet*, 220–1.

relations pertaining to Ireland.[68] He was also known to two other high-profile advocates of toleration, Andrew Marvell and his patron Philip, Lord Wharton. In December 1671 Worsley corresponded with Marvell about a possible bride for Wharton's son Thomas, having heard about the heiress from his connections amongst the Devon nonconformists.[69] The efforts of those seeking Protestant toleration bore fruit in 1672, with the Declaration of Indulgence, which neutralised any potential radical threat which the third Anglo-Dutch War may have precipitated.[70] Worsley went on to enjoy a year of professional success: even Petty was forced to acknowledge that he was 'a person of very good qualification'.[71] But this did not last, and Worsley was an unintended casualty of the Test Act of 1673. The oath which this act required from officeholders was a scruple too far for him: it was also a restatement of the goals of the confessional state in defending religious uniformity, the first step back to Danby's rapprochement between crown and Church. This alliance held firm until 1678, and so when Worsley left state employment in 1673, it was for the last time.

By then Worsley was in his mid-fifties, and the last four years of his life are relatively obscure. Soon after his resignation orders were issued for Worsley to return official books and papers in his possession, which he seems to have held onto as a bargaining point when petitioning for payment.[72] However he remained respectable enough to provide assistance to another harassed dissenting associate, the Baptist publisher Francis Smith, who in 1674 was seeking compensation for having copies of a pamphlet, Henry Danvers's A treatise of Baptism, seized by the Stationers' Company.[73] Having

[68] The papers of William Penn, I: 1644–7, ed. M. Dun and R. Dun, Philadelphia 1981, 566. Worsley owned Penn's Quakerism a new nick-name for old Christianity, London 1672.

[69] Five letters from Worsley on this matter survive: MS Rawlinson letters 50, fos 123–33, 149. See J. Kent Clarke, Whig's progress: Tom Wharton between revolutions, Madison–London 2004, 41–8.

[70] Greaves, Enemies under his feet, 224.

[71] Petty to [?] Tomkins, 7 Dec. 1672, MS Add. 72858, fo. 57v. Petty was attempting to complete a business deal concerning Ireland with this Mr Tomkins, who was apparently a correspondent of Worsley's and hoped to involve him, which would have made for some interesting dealings.

[72] CSPD, 1673, 591; CSPC, 1669–74, 531; CSPC, 1674–5, 186; CSPC, 1675–6, 183. A treasury warrant was issued for the remainder of Worsley's salary to be paid on 21 December 1674: CTB, 1672–5, 579. However, this order was evidently not fulfilled for, on 5 October 1675, Worsley petitioned for payment: CTB, 1672–5, 339. Possibly Worsley submitted the remaining papers then, but as late as 1685 (eight years after his death) the government's auditor was attempting to contact him to account for the monies he had disbursed as secretary to the Plantations Council, as part of a general auditing of government revenue: CTB, 1685–9, 37. Worsley also issued a certificate for his clerks and officers confirming that they had not been fully paid, on 20 May 1674: CSPC, 1669–74, 582.

[73] T. J. Crist, 'Francis Smith and the opposition press in England, 1660–1688', unpubl. PhD diss. Cambridge 1977, 81–5. See also M. Knights, Politics and opinion in crisis, 1678–

been notified of 'this poore mans Case ... by some friends & some persons of Quality', Worsley wrote a certificate claiming that Smith was innocent of any seditious intent, and the victim of a vendetta by Samuel Mearne, a Warden of the Stationers' Company, perhaps enlisting Shaftesbury's support.[74] After this little more is heard of him until his death, some time between 25 August and 11 September 1677.

Robert Boyle for one mourned his friend of thirty years. Lady Ranelagh wrote to console him of the 'remove of our true, honest, and ingenious friends', Worsley and Henry Oldenburg, who died just before him, adding that 'they each of them in their way diligently served their generation, and were friends to us'.[75] Her epitaph was warm: 'they have left no blot upon their memories (unless their not having died rich may go for one) and I hope they have carried consciences or uprightness with them, and have made their great change to their everlasting advantage'. Worsley's death was marked more publicly in the following year, when his huge library was auctioned in one of the earliest of such events to take place in England. The possibility of Boyle's involvement in this is supported by the fact that Robert Hooke saw a copy of the catalogue at Boyle's house in January 1678, months before the auction began on 13 May.[76]

The size of the library was such that the auction, in a house on Paternoster Row, St Paul's, was still underway on 22 May, when Hooke visited.[77] The booksellers added the collections of two unnamed individuals, as well as a large amount of stock, but Worsley's share still comprised 1,857 books out of the total of 5,344, and was auctioned for more than £500.[78] Its contents reveal the owner's appetite for learning, as well as his eye for profitable investment, in particular numerous expensive Bibles. These included two versions of Brian Walton's *Polygotta* of 1657, fetching more than £18 between them, a fourteen-volume edition of the *Biblia maxima* published in Paris in 1660

81, Cambridge 1994, 160, 163, and G. Kitchin, *Sir Roger L'Estrange*, London 1913, 113–15. Copies of Danvers's text, and Francis Smith's *Symptoms of growth and decay in godliness*, London 1672, are in the *Catalogus*.

[74] Worsley's certificate to W. Bridgeman, 11 Feb. 1674, SP 29/360, fo. 277r. An account of the affair apparently by Smith is written in Worsley's hand at fo. 279.

[75] Ranelagh to Boyle, 11 Sept. 1677, *Boyle correspondence*, iv. 454–5.

[76] *The diary of Robert Hooke*, ed. H. Robinson and W. Adams, London 1968, 340.

[77] Ibid. 359.

[78] *Catalogus*. Many books were distinguished by the letters 'a', 'i' and 'u'. The 'a' category is the largest, comprising 2,712 books; the fact that this includes many duplications suggests that it is made up of the booksellers' stock. Those listed under 'i' and 'u' are smaller collections, comprising 570 and 205 books respectively: clearly individual collections. The category which fits most accurately with Worsley's interests is that without a letter, and the likelihood of this indeed comprising Worsley's collection is suggested by the presence of many of the specific books that he is known to have read or owned. The collection may be compared with that of a contemporary of his, Dr John Webster, whose library contained more than 1,500 works and was valued at approximately £400: *The library of Dr John Webster: the making of a seventeenth-century radical*, ed. P. Elmer, London 1986, 15.

by the Franciscan Jean de La Haye, which raised £33, and a Bible previously owned by Pope Sixtus V which was sold for £32 5s.[79] There was also a hefty presence of religiously heterodox literature ranging from Baptists and Quakers to Socinians, and both Latin and English versions of Isaac de la Peyrère's hugely controversial pre-Adamite work *Men before Adam*.[80] Unfortunately the owners of unbound pamphlets on many commercial, political and religious affairs, were not distinguished, but if Worsley owned a similar proportion of these as he did of the rest of the catalogue, then he would have been well-informed of the issues of his day.

Worsley died before the political crisis of 1678–83, when his sometime patron Shaftesbury led the attempt to exclude the duke of York from the succession.[81] However, it may be that he played a small role in these events, via some posthumously published writings. In December 1683 Robert Boyle received a letter from Benjamin Furly, the Amsterdam-based Quaker whose 'house was at the centre of the early Enlightenment', playing host to John Locke and Algernon Sidney amongst others.[82] Only a summary of the letter survives, noting its main subject as being 'Mr Worsleys Book'.[83] Although this may have referred to *The advocate* or *Free ports*, it is possible that Furly meant a more recent publication. One option derives from a note in a catalogue of the library of Robert Boyle's servant John Warr, in which a volume entitled 'An essay for reconciling differences among Christians', dated 1678, was described as 'Dr. Worsley's'.[84] The work which the catalogue's modern editor found to most accurately match this description was a short anonymous pamphlet, with a preface dated 13 July 1678, entitled *Christian unity exhorted to*. This pamphlet's combination of irenicism and spiritualism, and its stress on 'the difference between the Form and Power of Godliness', is indeed reminiscent of Worsley's piety.[85] Another alternative would be a book purchased from Worsley's collection, perhaps Philip Ayres's translation of the irenicist tract *The reuniting of Christianity* (1673). However, it seems that a pamphlet was in fact published under the specific title listed in Warr's collection, for a contemporary library catalogue noted a quarto

---

[79] This item, and the excellent collection of Bibles in general, was noted approvingly in a copy in the possession of the Bodleian Library: Whitmore, 'Dr Worsley being dead', 127–8.

[80] First published as *Pre-Adamitae*, Amsterdam 1655, and translated into English in 1656. See R. Popkin, *Isaac La Peyrère (1596–1676): his life, work and influence*, Leiden 1987, and W. Poole, 'Seventeenth-century preadamism, and an anonymous English preadamist', *Seventeenth Century* xix (2004), 1–35.

[81] For this crisis see Knights, *Politics and opinion*, and J. Scott, *Algernon Sidney and the Restoration crisis, 1677–1683*, Cambridge 1991.

[82] Marshall, *John Locke*, 331; J. Champion, *Republican learning: John Toland and the crisis of Christian culture, 1696–1722*, Manchester 2003.

[83] *Boyle correspondence*, v. 376.

[84] J. T. Harwood, *The early essays and ethics of Robert Boyle*, Carbondale–Edwardsville 1991, 253.

[85] *Christian unity exhorted to*, sig. A1v.

pamphlet from 1678 under this precise name.[86] Intriguingly, an eighteenth-century library catalogue also listed a quarto pamphlet from 1678 as 'Boyle's essay towards the reconciling of Differences among Christians'.[87] Should this elusive pamphlet be traced, we might know something more of Worsley's relationship to Boyle in his last years.

We are on more secure ground with another pamphlet of which Worsley was identified as author, this time by Richard Baxter in a pamphlet defending nonconformity published in 1681. Here, Baxter cited another work which 'hath strenuously handled the same chief matter for Scripture Sufficiency against unnecessary Impositions', which he identified as 'a posthumous book of Dr. *Worsleys* called, *The third part of the naked Truth*'.[88] The original *The naked truth* was published in 1675 by the 'maverick' Bishop Herbert Croft, calling for 'moderation, church reforms, and even comprehension, while undermining the case for regarding bishops as a separate order of the ministry'.[89] It had proved popular and controversial, encouraging others to publish sequels, although this one had little to do with the original text. It appears to have arrived in print due to the actions of Philip Cary, apparently Worsley's brother-in-law and the 'principal Anabaptist in Dartmouth'.[90] Cary deployed the agency of another Dartmouth nonconformist, the philosopher Richard Burthogge, in order to have this tolerationist pamphlet published by the radical publisher Richard Janeway in late 1681, although the two later fell out when Burthogge published an anti-Baptist work.[91]

[86] S. Brooke, *Catalogus librorum bibliothecae reverend. and eruditi viri D. Samuelis Brooke*, London 1681, 40. Another pamphlet with the same title but dated 1648 is also listed at p. 31.

[87] H. Turpin, *Catalogue of several thousand volumes*, London 1769, 13.

[88] R. Baxter, *A second true defence of the meer nonconformists*, London 1681, 11–12.

[89] J. Spurr, *The Restoration Church of England, 1646–1689*, New Haven–London 1991, 71–2.

[90] He is described as such in the biographical introduction to the works of the Dartmouth Puritan John Flavel, who argued against him in print: *The whole works of the Reverend Mr. John Flavel*, i, London 1701, unpaginated. A Philip son of William Cary was born in 1636 in the parish of St Saviours, Dartmouth; other children of a William Cary born before him were Marie, John and Sarah, although Lucy Cary's baptismal entry has not been found: parish registers of St Saviour, Devon Record Office, Dartmouth. It may be that this family had a track-record in radical religion: the Marie Cary born on 13 Jan. 1621 could conceivably be the celebrated Fifth Monarchist writer of the same name who was born in that year, a possibility strengthened by the fact that she shared a parish with Thomas Boone, to whom the Fifth Monarchist Cary dedicated a book. Boone was a member of the 1650 Council of Trade; the Fifth Monarchist Cary married a Rande, a family name which has of course appeared elsewhere in this book.

[91] Cary wrote to Burthogge on 8 September 1681 'about Perfecting the Printing and Publishing of a Book of Dr. *Worsley's*', as well as his views on adult baptism. See R. Burthogge, *Vindiciae paedo-baptismi, or, a confirmation of an argument lately emitted for infants baptism*, London 1685, 5–6. Burthogge printed his replies in *An argument for infants baptisme deduced from the analogy of faith*, London 1684, drawing an intemperate answer from Cary in *A disputation between a doctor and an apothecary*, London 1684. Worsley's

The pamphlet's subtitle described it as comprising 'some serious Considerations, that are of High Concern to the Ruling Clergy of *England, Scotland*, or any other Protestant Nation', along with 'A Discovery of the Excellency of the Protestant Religion as it stands in Opposition to Papistical Delusions'.[92] However the preface (by 'a Friend of the Author') stressed the pamphlet's secondary, anti-Catholic, purpose, suggesting that '*this very Discourse may prove to be such a Mirror or Looking-Glass, to as many of that Scarlet Generation … as will but give themselves leave seriously to look upon their own odious Pictures*'. In the context of 1681 this comment was clearly aimed at the Catholic duke of York, suggesting that the pamphlet was a contribution to the exclusion campaign. However, rather than railing against arbitrary monarchical power, the pamphlet itself actually appealed to the prince to wield his powers to rule religion with more authority and effect.

In previous years Worsley had advised the Restoration regime on how best to govern commerce, and *The third part of naked truth* deployed the same language of interest to analyse the government of religion. The pamphlet therefore began with a consideration of religion as a public affair, the author stating that he had 'for some time laboured and travelled with desire of Soul, to bring forth those things that have been given to me, which may tend to Peace and Unity'.[93] These ideals had been casualties of the religious wars following the Reformation, and 'the business of the Christian Religion is now a thing not capable to be separated from an Affair of State'. However, the Reformation had created difficulties for the Protestant prince, because 'the Prince having the Character or Repute only of a Secular Authority, hath not that immediate Influence upon Religion itself, or upon a Religious People, which the Clergy hath'. The dilemma for the Protestant prince therefore was to govern religion in the interests of the public, whilst accepting his limits as a secular power. This was made difficult not by the presence of religious diversity, but of a 'Ruling Clergy' who sought to monopolise the 'whole affair of Religion', as 'Persons not only of supposed sufficiency, but of supposed Conscience and Integrity'.[94] Whilst the royal supremacy might appear to augment the sovereign's power, clerical advice had frequently been 'very dangerous both To his Government, To his Safety, To his Honour, and to his Interest'.[95] This was because the clergy had their 'own interest' which was 'privately concerned' in maintaining their privileged status. History was littered with examples of princes who had been ruined by the misleading advice of their clergy, most recently in 'those things that happened at home even in our own Countey; which have drawn a Mourning Veil upon the

---

Catalogus included Burthogge's *Divine goodness explicated*, London 1671. On Janeway see Knights, *Politics and opinion in crisis*, 160.

[92] *The third part of naked truth*, London 1681.
[93] Ibid. 1.
[94] Ibid. 2.
[95] Ibid. 3.

Records of our Times'.[96] The lesson for the Protestant prince was clear: 'the committing of the Affairs of Religion and of the Church intirely to the Clergy without any check upon them is yet the more against the Interest of the Prince, because it layeth an express Temptation upon them, to Govern both the Church and Religion absolutely, and at their own Will'.[97]

The tract therefore called on the prince to exercise his erastian power over religion, like Thomas Hobbes blaming the clergy for dividing the nation. However, unlike Hobbes, who sought to eradicate the indeterminate influence of the spirit on political affairs through a monolithic state religion, this author constructed a vision of politics in which the prince defended the spirit against the incursions of the clergy, tolerating nonconformity. To demonstrate that dissent did not necessarily entail disloyalty, the author turned to the precepts of Protestantism itself. Fundamentally, the Reformation had initiated a 'restoration of the scriptures, in the Vulgar Tongue', which was the 'true glory' of Protestantism.[98] As a religion of the word, Protestantism demanded that Scripture be obeyed before any human authority, and no 'civil, outward, or temporal Account' could stand between the individual and God.[99] Any aspect of worship which was not clearly laid down in Scripture was voluntary and, as the Reformation itself demonstrated, 'a Church may Err, and may have Corruption in it', whilst 'Scripture cannot Err'.[100] Any Church which sought to 'constrain or exact an Obedience from her Members to her self, and to her own Authority as absolute', would therefore 'cease in her Principles and Practice to be Protestant'.[101]

It was at this point in the argument that The third part of naked truth discussed Catholicism, but not to emphasise the direct threat of a Catholic monarch. Rather, Catholicism was used as a negative example to shame the 'Ruling clergy' of England out of their persecuting ways. Worsley's Catalogus is full of conventional anti-Catholic literature, with recent examples by authors including John Tillotson, Thomas Wilson, Matthew Poole, Thomas Traherne, William Stanley and the rather more scurrilous Gregorio Leti. But he also owned numerous works of Catholic theology and devotion, and many Catholic editions of Bibles. These works conveyed the variety of contemporary Catholicism, encompassing Jesuits such as Suarez, Bellarmino, Maldonado and Possevino, alongside dissenting voices such as Cornelius Jansen, Blaise Pascal, Traiano Boccalini, Tommaso Campanella, Thomas White and Paulo Sarpi. More recently, Worsley owned works published in the 1660s by the Catholic controversialist John Sergeant, and by the Catholic author 'JVC' which sought to end 'the great combustion and broils

---

96   Ibid. 4.
97   Ibid. 5.
98   Ibid. 6.
99   Ibid. 8.
100 Ibid. 17.
101 Ibid. 18.

about religion here in England'.[102] This attitude contrasted with that of the Protestant Samuel Parker's anti-tolerationist *A discourse of ecclesiastical politie* (1670), which he owned along with attacks on it by John Owen and Andrew Marvell. At the very least, then, Worsley had the resources to draw a more complex understanding of the nature of popery than simply to equate the pope with the literal AntiChrist.[103]

In *The third part of naked truth*, Worsley presented the principal difference between Protestant and papist as being that, whilst the former obeyed Scripture before all other authorities, the latter 'takes the Authority of the Church for the whole Argument, or for the only Foundation of all his Obedience unto God'.[104] The persecution of dissent was an attempt to preserve this spiritual monopoly and impose an outward, hypocritical conformity, which was the essence of Catholicism. However, although Protestant reformers had broken from the papacy to avoid spiritual absolutism, persecution and hypocrisy, these popish characteristics had been adopted by many supposedly Protestant Churches, whose sin was therefore all the greater: 'MUST NOT these three things be MUCH MORE EVIL in a Protestant Church? … MUST NOT This Practice cast a manifest Blemish, and Reproach upon her own Reformation'.[105]

Rather than explicitly highlighting the danger of 'Popery and arbitrary government', as might be expected from a pamphlet written in 1681, here the main concern was with the popish behaviour of the Anglican Church, and the prince was called upon to put the clergy in their place. However, strict limits were placed on princely jurisdiction over religion: because the Protestant subject owed his obedience to God prior to any civil authority, '*all human Laws if they be inconsistent either with any of those common Principles that are writ in our Nature, (which are called the common Principles of Reason) or with anything that is expressly writ in the Word of God, They are null and void in themselves*'.[106] Despite this, the author was at pains to assert that religious and political dissent were separate: 'Non-obedience or Non-conformity to any of the said Laws, though it be in a sence voluntary, yet it is neither elective nor indeed truly or properly free, And therefore that such Non-obedience is not any the least breach of affection, Nor any the least forfeiture of a mans Duty to his Prince, or to the Government'.[107] The only way to resolve this potential clash between spiritual and civil allegiances, therefore, was for the civil magistrate to renounce any claim to govern the spirit:

---

[102] 'JVC', *Fiat lux*, London 1662; *Diaphanta*, London 1665.
[103] See A. Milton, 'A qualified intolerance: the limits and ambiguities of early Stuart anti-Catholicism', in A. F. Marotti (ed.), *Catholicism and anti-Catholicism in early modern English texts*, Basingstoke 1999, 85–115.
[104] *Third part of naked truth*, 16–17.
[105] Ibid. 19–20.
[106] Ibid. 14.
[107] Ibid. 15.

if the Law of the Church, or the Ruling Clergy, cannot in the matter of Worship any way compel or bind men to Obedience, farther or otherwise than as they apprehend it to be agreeable to *the Law of God*, or to *the Law of his Word*: Then neither can the Law of the Prince, or the Law of the Civil Government bind mens Consciences, in the matter of Worship, further or otherwise than the Law of the Church, *viz.* no otherwise, than as the said Law shall appear to them to be agreeable to Gods Law, which *is the Law of his Scripture or Word*, And consequently it can never be avoided by any Protestant Prince, but his Authority as relating purely to things Civil, with the Efficacy of it, must stand *upon one Rule*;

And his Authority as relating to things of Divine Worship, with the Efficacy of it, must necessarily and unavoidably stand *upon another Rule*.[108]

Religion as a public affair was distinguished from the religion of the spirit, which remained barred to the prince, and Scripture had clearly warned persecutors that Christ would '*cut them asunder and account them as Hypocrites*'.[109] Those advocating toleration, however, could also be accused of hypocritically calling for the indulgence of their own sect, whilst denying it to others when in power. The degree of toleration called for in *The third part of naked truth* is unclear: adherence to Scripture was seen as the common denominator of Protestantism and the only essential tenet of belief, but it was left unsaid as to whether this definition would have included Socinians, for example. Although he commended its demonstration of 'Scripture Sufficiency against unnecessary Impositions', Richard Baxter was uneasy with the absence of a further definition of orthodoxy, and added his own qualifications.[110] Thus the pamphlet was, perhaps deliberately, vague about the limits of Protestant conformity, but it did give the impression that any sort of persecution was the mark of a false Church. The case of Catholics was more problematic, however, as they could be portrayed as a civil threat. No comment was made in *The third part of naked truth* on whether Catholics should be excluded from toleration, but given the considerable lengths to which the author went to demonstrate the falsehood of their beliefs, it seems unlikely that they would have been afforded anything resembling religious 'rights'. However, Catholicism was not defined as a real, antiChristian presence, so much as the embodiment of an antiChristian spirit of persecution. The pamphlet was concerned much more with the ways in which this spirit infected Protestant Churches, than with the resurgence of Counter-Reformation popery.[111]

Worsley had long advocated a minimalist interpretation of Protestantism based on scriptural fundamentals and spiritual labour, and frequently warned

[108] Ibid. 9–10.
[109] Ibid. 27.
[110] Baxter, *Second true defence*, 12.
[111] For the latter see J. Scott, 'England's troubles: exhuming the popish plot', in Harris, Goldie, and Seaward, *Politics of religion*, 197–232.

180

against elevating any human institution above God. Likewise *The third part of naked truth* constructed a vision of politics which defended conscience, the cultivator of the spirit, and it is possible to read this text as Worsley's indirect advice to the king in the aftermath of the Test Act, hoping to encourage Charles II to return to his policy of indulgence. In the 1670s the domination of the crown by an episcopal elite, those 'twenty six Private persons' allied with Danby, was a much more conspicuous threat to dissenters than the possibility of a Catholic succession, and *The third part of naked truth* implicitly looked back to 1672 and not forward to the exclusion crisis.[112] The mid-1670s therefore seems a probable date of composition, coinciding with Shaftesbury and Locke's own anti-clerical, anti-Danby manifesto, *A letter from a person of quality, to his friend in the country*.[113] Worsley was politically pragmatic, supporting whoever could best offer toleration: had he lived into the exclusion crisis, he would surely have supported parliament, although he may equally have been amongst those dissenters like Richard Burthogge who rallied to James II when he issued his own declaration of indulgence.[114] Such was the fluid nature of political alignments in the Restoration, where any simple division between royalists and parliamentarians, or Whigs and Tories, was obscured by the complex politics of religion. This meant, too, that *The third part of naked truth* could be adapted to the circumstances of 1681.

'Popery and arbitrary government' were not the only spectres haunting this crisis: 'the pursuit of clerical power by the forcible imposition of unnecessary creeds' was also attacked.[115] Mark Goldie has shown the centrality of anticlericalism to the birth of Whiggism, arguing that 'the essence of the Whig struggle was to prevent the English churchmen building a Protestant popery', precisely the concern of *The third part of naked truth*.[116] Goldie has also shown that, rather than being an aspect of secularisation, this anticlericalism was 'grounded in an unfolding tradition of Christian reformism'.[117] Philosophically, the polemic against priestcraft was central to the early Enlightenment in England, again showing the continuing centrality of religious goals.[118] According to Goldie, anticlericalism, the Restoration toleration debate and the idea of civil religion were at the heart of 'the transformation of the Puritan into the Whig'; Worsley was neither, but it may be that the life of

[112] Ibid. 20. For Danby see Goldie, 'Danby, the bishops and the Whigs'.

[113] Marshall, *John Locke*, 85–7.

[114] M. Goldie, 'John Locke's circle and James II', *HJ* xxxv (1992), 557–86.

[115] Goldie, 'Priestcraft and the birth of Whiggism', 220.

[116] *Third part of naked truth*, 218.

[117] Ibid. 211. For the complexity of religious change in late seventeenth-century England see B. Worden, 'The question of secularization', in A. Houston and S. Pincus (eds), *A nation transformed: England after the Restoration*, Cambridge 2000, 20–40, and M. Knights, '"Meer religion" and the "church-state" of Restoration England: the impact and ideology of James II's declarations of indulgence', ibid. 41–70.

[118] As well as Goldie see Champion, *Pillars of priestcraft* and *Republican learning*.

this individual, who linked Sir Henry Vane to John Locke, tells us something of this shift.[119]

Water-stone of the wise

The third part of naked truth perhaps answers those questions noted earlier in this chapter, revealing that its author saw the malevolent influence of the 'ruling clergy' rather than the restored monarchy as the main threat to conscience; by distinguishing between civil and spiritual aspects of religion, and confining the prince to the former, the integrity of the spirit was preserved. Public power focused exclusively on worldly affairs, and so Worsley could serve the Restoration state with his conscience clean, as long as this state offered a bulwark against clerical persecution, as seemed to be the case until 1673. Thus Worsley was able to adapt his loyalties to the changing political climate, but in the process he appears to retreat further from the ideal of 'universal reform' which Charles Webster attributed to him. Perhaps Worsley now saw the millennium in purely spiritual terms, divorced from the corrupt 'spirit of the world'.

In the late 1650s Worsley's religion had become increasingly spiritualistic, but this was not confined to introspection, and for a time incorporated alchemical experimentation. After 1660 the evidence that Worsley continued to be interested in this subject is sparse. His 1670 letter to Winthrop, another practitioner, referred to certain alchemical 'Literature' which 'doth not advance so very fast as it did seem a while since to threaten that it would And yet there doth something Appear as if it were strugling for a Birth that may have a tendency of Blessing to *the* world'.[120] Winthrop responded to this tantalising reference with a series of questions, but no reply to him survives. This would be the disappointing end of the story, if it were not for the existence of a remarkable letter, written in Latin, and sent to Boyle on 25 August 1677 just a few weeks before Worsley's death was reported.[121] As the editors of Boyle's correspondence have noted, this appears to have been a valedictory statement in which Worsley reflected upon more than two decades of alchemical labour.

The letter began by reporting that 'after a great deal of expense, after suffering the greatest distress, and after almost countless, and extremely painful troubles', involving both reading books and 'investigating medicine', Worsley was at last 'master of the thing I sought'.[122] Worsley went on to exclaim 'And lo! I now present to you that most famous and truly metallic

---

[119] Goldie, 'Priestcraft and the birth of Whiggism', 215.
[120] Worsley toWinthrop, *c.* June 1670, Winthrop papers, microfilm reel 9.
[121] Worsley to Boyle, 25 Aug. 1677, translated in *Boyle correspondence*, v. 452–4. Ranelagh mentioned Worsley's death in her letter to Boyle, 11 Sept. [1677], ibid. 454–5.
[122] Ibid. 452.

oil, which is called the oil of the philosophers, and which is described under many other names.'

What, then, were the virtues of this substance? Firstly, Worsley described it as 'a living fountain (if there is any such thing) flowing indeed from the very lap of Nature herself, coming forth without any addition either of any menstruum', some sort of liquid form of the philosopher's stone, or as he termed it, 'the water-stone of the wise'. Furthermore, he claimed that 'this oil is that green oil of Paracelsus, which is said to contain the whole *crasis* of vitriol, and for that reason is not corrosive', adding that it was 'the cleanest, purest, and most penetrating in the whole world', and therefore 'the most incorrupt'.[123] Finally, it was a medicine, containing contrary properties of masculine and feminine, sun and moon, and sulphur and mercury.

Purity, incorruptibility and penetrability were traditionally key virtues of alchemical mercuries or elixirs, and clear signs of transmutational ability, but beyond this the precise composition of this exalted substance is obscure. However, we can explain the apparent meaning of some of its properties in terms of Worsley's earlier alchemical ideas. Worsley claimed that his success in producing his 'green oil' came only after 'tremendous patience; for although we have been by now involved with it for a period of twenty-two years without a break, nevertheless during that period of time it has been seen by me a mere three times, and only now have I completed it'. Whether Worsley had successfully performed that 'Phylosophicall putrefaction' which he highlighted twenty-two years previously, is unclear, but the reference to the oil being a 'living fountain', flowing from 'the very lap of Nature', suggests that this liquid was related to the 'pure and spermaticke substance' which he previously claimed was the life-giving property within all bodies.[124] If so, then no wonder he valued his discovery so highly, for when used as a medicine such a substance might indeed hold the key to defeating mortality, the possibility of which he had speculated about in another letter to Boyle.[125] Worsley concluded with 'a rare and amazing paradox ... namely, a man who is by no means rich, nevertheless has by virtue of this experiment both the right and the power of deciding on and adopting for himself an heir who will be rich beyond the riches of most men (if not kings), and who will be well instructed and equipped in medicine'.[126] Perhaps Worsley was choosing Robert Boyle, who had little need for material riches, as his alchemical heir.

If so, then Boyle did not have long to wait to claim his inheritance. The fact that Worsley died so soon after writing this valediction suggests that he may already have been ill, and looking to bring his alchemical labours

---

[123] Ibid. 453.
[124] Worsley to [Clodius], *c.* summer 1654, HP 42/1/26B.
[125] See his mention of 'the healing Water of an incorruptible fountain': [Worsley] to [Boyle], *c.* late 1658–early 1659, HP 60/2/4A.
[126] Worsley to Boyle, 25 Aug. 1677, *Boyle correspondence*, v. 454.

to some sort of meaningful conclusion. As Young has written, 'seekers of the stone' like Worsley, usually 'found what they were looking for because they defined their results in terms of what they were expecting to find'.[127] At least for minor practitioners, the importance of the various oils, elixirs and powders for which they made such fantastic claims lay not so much in their substantive effects, as in their ability to confirm a pre-conceived philosophy of the world. It is perhaps not too extravagant to suggest, therefore, that for Worsley the discovery of his 'green oil' represented more than just proof of his skills as an adept: it was a motif for faith itself, a metaphor for his search for certain knowledge of divine truth. Looking back on the turbulent years through which he had lived, which seemed so often to confound any search for divine meaning in changeable human affairs, here was a stable core of truth, embodied by this 'universal spirit'. However great the gulf between human and the divine might seem to be, Worsley had finally confirmed that the spiritual was indeed present in this corrupt world.

[127] Young, *Faith*, 172.

Conclusion

An experimental life

This book has considered the life of one individual within a variety of contexts, including the history of commercial and colonial policy, the development of experimental science, and the relationship between political and religious change, across locations ranging from London, Ireland and Amsterdam, to the global trade routes in which they were set. The conclusion will attempt to bring these strands together, but before doing so a brief reminder of Worsley's life is in order.

Chapter one opened with Worsley an apprentice surgeon in pre-civil war London, soon to depart for Ireland. Surgery furnished him with intellectual and technical skills, as well as an entrepreneurial ethos, which he deployed on returning to London in 1644, launching his saltpetre project. For promotional assistance, Worsley turned to Samuel Hartlib and his circle, adapting the project's ends to suit his new allies, for example in his imperialistic design, 'Proffits humbly presented to this kingdome'. In London, Worsley was introduced to a younger man also searching for a vocation, Robert Boyle, beginning a long relationship. During the late 1640s he drew closer to the Hartlib circle, acquiring a position of trust which allowed him to visit Amsterdam with their support in order to learn the art of alchemy. However, his lack of success led Worsley to become frustrated with the life of the projector, and he began to look for state employment instead. Thereafter, Worsley's interest in natural philosophy became less utilitarian, concentrating on theoretical and increasingly spiritual issues.

The product of Worsley's search for a state post was employment as secretary to the Council of Trade, from 1650 to 1651. Exploiting mercantile and political contacts, Worsley secured this position by demonstrating his knowledge of commerce, enlisting ideas which were part of a pre-existent discourse of trade in a way suitable to the new regime. This combination of continuity and innovation also marked the Commonwealth's commercial policy, which Worsley defended in two official pamphlets, *The advocate* and *Free ports*. Although the Council of Trade was not an unqualified success, Worsley's employment as its secretary enhanced his reputation, allowing him to be employed as surveyor-general in Ireland. However, his ascent stalled there, thanks to William Petty, and Worsley became increasingly disillusioned with Cromwellian rule. Intellectually, this was also a period of frustration, as Worsley struggled to uphold his sometimes extravagant claims to be pursuing a 'great work' in alchemy. The theories to which he adhered centred on identifying the 'spirit of life', and these proved particularly conducive to his spiritual reflections, under the influence of heterodox literature and religious radicals in the army. His relationship with the latter drew Worsley into opposition to Henry Cromwell's regime, culminating in his involvement with the parliamentary and military regimes which replaced the Protectorate.

The Restoration, therefore, threatened to cast Worsley back into obscurity. However, he proved remarkably successful at adapting to this new climate, partly because of the willingness of Charles II's government to adopt the commercial policies of the Commonwealth through its navigation acts and councils of trade. Worsley was able to regain his post as secretary to one of these bodies by adapting the ideas of the discourse of trade to the needs of this new regime, which proved to be similar to those of the Commonwealth. Once again, his career illustrates broader developments in commercial policy, as the state attempted to govern trade more proactively. This essentially secular conception of public power suited Worsley, who accommodated his spiritual convictions by distinguishing between the civil and spiritual spheres, a perspective shown in the pamphlet *The third part of naked truth*. Thus Worsley was able to serve the restored monarchy, as long as it offered a bulwark against clericalism. This ceased to be the case in 1673, when the Test Act forced Worsley's resignation, and he seemingly spent his last years honing his skills as an adept, before producing that cherished elixir which apparently confirmed his alchemical and spiritual beliefs. Thus by the time he died, in 1677, Worsley may perhaps have found contentment in knowing that his life's labours were not in vain.

The 'rediscovery' of Worsley as a historical actor was mainly the work of one historian, Charles Webster. How, then, does the Benjamin Worsley who has emerged in this study compare with the socially aware scientist and 'puritan ideologue' of *The great instauration*?

According to Webster, the various strands of Worsley's biography were brought together by 'universal reform', an ultimately spiritual ethic which nevertheless shaped his worldly goals: the saltpetre project, the Invisible College and the Navigation Act all had a part to play in elevating England to prosperity and power, and ultimately millennial perfection, made possible by the Puritan Revolution. This study, too, has noted a universalist ethos running through many of Worsley's activities, as he strove to become a 'universal scholar' and unite spiritual and natural knowledge. But this was matched by a strong sense of relativism, centred on the notion that human needs were driven by the force of 'interest', which could be in tension with such universal values. No such consistent programme as Webster's universal reform has emerged from this study. Instead we have seen much frustration and even contradiction in Worsley's life and activities, extending at times to his relations with other associates of Hartlib.

This has not been with the intent of denying the significance of the Hartlib circle in Worsley's life, or in the intellectual history of the period in general. Similarly, no attempt has been made to deny the reality of the Hartlib circle as a social and intellectual network constructed by Hartlib and animated by shared goals, although not all of those who deployed Hartlib's agency subscribed to all his aims. Worsley aligned himself with the Hartlib circle to a greater degree than many, wholeheartedly participating in its discussions, but these exchanges did not always lead to concord. We have seen this in Culpeper's disapproval of the nationalism of 'Profitts humbly presented', Worsley's disagreement with Dury regarding Georg Horne's anti-papal crusade, and above all his protracted battle with Petty, certainly the most damaging schism amongst Hartlib's *protégés*, and one which reveals something of the fate of universal reform in revolutionary England.

This was a dispute between two Englishmen who had come under the influence of 'the three foreigners' and their ideals. Hotson's study of the continental background of Hartlib, Dury and Comenius revealed their debt to a central European tradition of 'further reform', epitomised by Alsted, whose encyclopaedic universalism aimed at the reformation of society and learning in a way which prefigured the efforts of the Hartlib circle.[1] Here, reformation went hand-in-hand with the state-building aspirations of the godly princes of central Europe, an alliance of secular and spiritual goals which was reflected in 'Hartlib's enduring desire to use the state during the English Commonwealth and Protectorate, as an instrument for social, religious and intellectual change'.[2] However, there was another dimension to this 'second reformation', inward-looking and potentially in tension with orthodox Calvinism, and Hartlib, Dury and Comenius also transmitted this to Puritan England alongside the societal reformation focused upon in *The great instauration*.[3] Of these two dimensions of universal reform, we might expect Worsley, a civil servant who appreciated state power, to have prioritised state-sponsored reformation, but in fact his allegiances came to lie more with the internal reformation that would restore the fractured image of God in man.

Whilst Webster saw Worsley's religious aspirations as mainly directed outwards, into the reformation of the world, this study has revealed an intensely introspective spiritualism. Partly this reflected his encounter with the sects that blossomed in revolutionary England and Ireland, and nascent heterodoxies such as John Everard's perfectionism, but Worsley also drew on Hartlibian influences. Thus whilst he took from Everard the need to overcome the corrupt self, this could be achieved through a fusion of spiritual labour and learning similar to Comenius' *Pansophy*. Worsley in fact extended the limits of human perfectability by claiming that mortality itself

[1] Hotson, *Johann Heinrich Alsted*.
[2] M. Greengrass, 'Samuel Hartlib and international Calvinism', *Proceedings of the Huguenot Society* xxv (1993), 466.
[3] D. Čapková, 'The Comenian group in England and Comenius' ideal of universal reform', *Acta Comeniana* i (1970), 25–34.

could be overcome through embracing the spirit of the light, but immortality would not result from spiritual struggle alone. Worsley's spiritual principles absorbed more conventionally scientific goals, including medicine, alchemy and, above all, the search for energy, that 'universal spirit' of life.

Thus Worsley's natural philosophy was shaped by spiritual goals, but in a less utilitarian way than Webster suggested. Webster's overriding concern was to show that rather than precluding serious scientific research, the utopianism of Puritans like Worsley in fact encouraged it, as epitomised by the Invisible College. Because of the paucity of evidence, this putative organisation can no longer be afforded so central a place in the intellectual biographies of either Worsley or Boyle, however, leaving Worsley's role in the 'scientific revolution' uncertain. A case can still be made for Worsley exerting a more important influence on Boyle's natural philosophy than some accounts allow, but to suggest that this is the only way in which his scientific ideas are of interest is to do him an injustice. Primarily, Worsley was an adherent of alchemical theories about the energising properties of a philosophical salt, sal nitrum, best represented by the Polish adept Sendivogius. The role of alchemy and other occult arts in the scientific revolution is now well appreciated.[4] However, it is hard to discern any positive contribution which Worsley made to this, and at times he has appeared a rather frustrated scientist or adept. There was at times a gulf between his aspirations and achievements, perhaps suggesting that his natural philosophy warrants attention only as a footnote in the lives of his more successful acquaintances like Boyle or Starkey. In fact Worsley's example seems to show how the English scientific community as a whole was changing, as more sophisticated ideas and higher experimental standards began increasingly to relegate a part-time practitioner like him from scientific participant to consumer. Membership of the Royal Society might have allowed Worsley to avoid this, but his omission from this body rendered him marginal.

Thus Worsley was more or less forgotten as a scientist, until Webster rescued him from obscurity. The problems in Webster's account of the Invisible College should not condemn him to be forgotten once more, for Worsley still helps us understand the scientific culture of his period. For example, Worsley's uncertain reaction to Cartesianism was no means confined to an amateur scientist like him, and is illustrative of the way in which the acceptance of mechanism by English scientists entailed its redefinition.[5] Worsley's unease with mechanism, and his attachment to sal nitrum ideas, reflected a concern to locate the presence of the divine within the material. The

---

[4]   J. Henry, 'Magic and science in the sixteenth and seventeenth centuries', in Olby, Cantor, Christie and Hodge, Compendium to the history of modern science, 583–96; C. Webster, From Paracelsus to Newton: magic and the making of modern science, Cambridge 1982.
[5]   See M. Osler, Divine will and the mechanical philosophy: Gassendi and Descartes on contingency and necessity in the created world, Cambridge 1994, 222–36.

way in which Worsley blended scientific ideas with spiritual convictions shows how science was still a widely accessible cultural resource, yet to be monopolised by the professional scientist. For Worsley this culminated, quite literally, with his deathbed discovery of the 'green oil', an emblem of his faith in the physical reality of the spiritual, the only constant universal in an ever-changing world.

If this was a millenarian vision, it was one that looked inwards, not outwards. Although the presence of the millennium has loomed throughout this book, the meaning which Worsley afforded to it was not stable. Even at that apocalyptic zenith of 1651–2, Worsley questioned whether God's will for the Commonwealth was clear: this was a millennium continually deferred. In fact, the degree to which millenarianism offered a clear course of action even for Hartlib and Dury may be questioned, for the latter by the 1650s was also moving away from an overtly literal reading of biblical prophecies.[6] But whereas Dury feared that millenarianism could disrupt the political and religious order which the Commonwealth and Protectorate sought to establish, under Cromwell Worsley began to see the regime itself as the cause of this spiritual darkness. This did not lift until the end of the decade, when Worsley apparently began to expect the arrival of Christ's kingdom. However, even this was not literal millenarianism, but an imminent apocalypse, when AntiChrist would be defeated. Thus in 1659 his apocalypticism entailed the destruction of an ungodly regime, the Protectorate, more than the construction of a worldly utopia. Worsley probably saw this as preparing the way for the return of Christ by defeating persecution and allowing spiritual freedom, rather than creating a theocracy. He had already begun to describe the apocalypse in basically spiritual terms, as the victory of light over dark leading to spiritual perfection. The millennium would be the product of communion between like-minded spirits, made possible by the free pursuit of religious truth, rather than through direct political action.

Thus, after the Restoration, the political principle to which Worsley adhered after apparently abandoning any hostility to monarchy, was liberty of conscience. It would be wrong to see this as a repudiation of the goals of the Hartlib circle, for many of its members had been amongst the strongest defenders of toleration during the Revolution. However, this did not shake the commitment of Hartlib and Dury to the joint reformation of Church and State, imitating the central European second reformation.[7] But, in the

---

[6] K. Firth, *The apocalyptic tradition in Reformation Britain, 1530–1643*, Oxford 1979, 243–5. Joseph Mede-style millenarianism was not shared by all members of the Hartlib circle: for example Gabriel Plattes, author of the utopian 'manifesto' *Macaria*, condemned 'our hot Apocalyps men, and fierce expounders of Daniel, who are sure, in their owne conceit, that they have such divine revelations, that they cannot possibly be deceived': *A discovery of infinite treasure*, London 1639, sig. B2r.

[7] See, for example, [J. Dury], *Considerations tending to the happy accomplishment of Englands reformation*, London 1647.

course of the English Revolution, such a direct relationship between Church and State came to be challenged, particularly the authority of the state over conscience. William Petty's response was to deny (like Hobbes) that the spiritual had any place in politics, advising Henry Cromwell to focus on social order and material rule. Worsley reacted with hostility to this 'godless rule', but ultimately he too distinguished between the civil and the spiritual, confining the state to the former, not to deny the reality of the spirit, but to preserve its integrity.[8]

By refusing the state a role in advancing spiritual goals, Worsley moved a step away from universal reform. Partly this was a reaction to the developments of the English Revolution itself, but Worsley had already demonstrated a sense of relativism which existed uneasily alongside the universalism of Hartlib and Dury. Throughout this study we have seen Worsley evoke self-interest as the force which drove individual actions – he certainly never lost sight of his own, and the competitive ethos of the projector did not desert him. Worsley was not uncritical of self-interest, however, and the preface to *The advocate* portrayed apocalypse as the downfall of ambition and pride, the desires on which society and indeed commerce were built. Worsley was similarly sceptical about politics, an exercise of power rather than principle, and therefore invariably tending to corruption. Power also determined the course of international relations, and thus Worsley called for the aggressive defence of commerce by the state against its competitors, an economic nationalism potentially at odds with the Protestant internationalism of the Hartlib circle. Culpeper seems to have noticed that this subverted the utopianism of 'Proffits humbly presented', but in truth Worsley was never much of a utopian, unwilling to trust corrupt human institutions to advance spiritual goals. Although he evoked the identity of the spiritual and material in his natural philosophy, he retained an Augustinian sense of the gulf between this world and the next. Religion had to be purged of corrupt human additions which obscured the search for divine truth. Thus in politics the spiritual and the civil were ultimately incompatible, and Worsley drew a clear distinction between the authority of the prince over the two in *The third part of naked truth*.

Whilst Hartlib and Dury sought to transmit the ideals of the second reformation throughout the Protestant world, Worsley saw this world as divided into competing nation states; whereas the former aimed at a universal reformation of Church and State, Worsley's relativism led him to divorce the corrupt secular from the spiritual, elevating the reformation of the individual above that of society. To this extent his life reveals not so much the successes of universal reform in revolutionary England, as its diffusion into many smaller projects, and ultimately the spiritualism of a Restoration dissenter. However, if Worsley rejected the spiritual uses of state power in enacting reformation, he certainly embraced Hartlib's positive attitude

[8]   W. Lamont, *Godly rule: politics and religion, 1603–60*, London 1969, 136–43.

towards the state as an engine of social and economic transformation. When freed from confessional responsibilities, the state would be able to concentrate on advancing the sort of material goals which Worsley argued for throughout his career, as a state expert in the government of commerce.

Steven Pincus has recently argued that the English Revolution precipitated an upheaval in political culture, leading to the abandonment of the religious and universalist goals which informed early Stuart politics; thereafter, political economy was increasingly adopted as the interest of state.[9] Worsley's move away from the Protestant internationalism of the Hartlib circle to an economically driven understanding of national interest fits with this account. However, this study has been careful to show that this was part of long-term trends which predated the 1640s, and owed much to traditional, commonwealth ideals. Even before the seventeenth century these ideals had been remodelled in the face of expanded market activity, resulting in a new understanding of society as fundamentally competitive, and affording the state a greater role over economic affairs. The sixteenth century also saw the beginnings of commercial expansion, whereby English merchants began to travel farther afield, to the Levant, to the East Indies. Initially the state sought to cultivate these trades through company charters, but growing commercial complexity combined with economic crisis in the early Stuart period made this appear insufficient. The committee founded in 1622 marked the beginning of a period of experimentation with the conciliar government of trade, of which Worsley's career was a part. A key aim of these councils of trade was to emulate the major commercial power of the time, the United Provinces, by diversifying exports and markets, developing the carrying trade and becoming the 'warehouse of the world'.

By the time that parliament was recalled in 1640, therefore, it was faced with numerous calls to defend and advance trade, but no clear formula for how to do so. Given the historic association between parliament and free trade, the companies might have feared the worst, but mercantile allegiance was not so clear-cut as this suggests. Instead, following parliament's victory rival merchant groups were willing to compete for privilege from parliament, with the emerging colonial trades being particularly rich pickings. Brenner saw the 'new merchants' as representing a challenge to the traditional monopolistic regulation of commerce, but in their willingness to ally with the regime in return for exclusive privileges, their behaviour was not so different from that of the company merchants. Association with Maurice Thomson certainly aided Worsley's ascent in state service, but ultimately he posited himself as an impartial observer of commerce rather than mercantile mouthpiece. His position as secretary to the Commonwealth's Council of Trade was the first fruit of this strategy, and the creation of this body suggests

[9] S. Pincus, 'From holy cause to economic interest: the study of population and the invention of the state', in Houston and Pincus, *Nation transformed*, 272–98.

that the regime was indeed hoping to establish itself through commercial success.

In some ways the survey of the Council of Trade presented here has endorsed the more negative conclusions about its effectiveness. However, in ideological terms the significance of the Council of Trade, and the approach to governing commerce it represented, grew posthumously, contributing to a shift in the political language of interest of state, which increasingly prioritised commerce. Similarly, in terms of the content of commercial policy, the Commonwealth did impart a distinctive approach, characterised by the direct government of trade by the state, rather than the companies. The Navigation Act was the main product of this ethos, and Worsley's pamphlet *The advocate* its clearest exposition at the time. This act took over the defensive role of the companies by excluding foreign shipping, but it also had the more positive aim of expanding the nation's carrying trade, helping to create that 'universal magazine' which Worsley's other pamphlet, *Free ports*, envisaged. Although not a specifically republican ideology of trade, such goals reflected the priorities of the new regime seeking to establish itself in a hostile world and obsessed with proving its patriotic credentials, the ideal of the commonwealth brought into being. The legacy of the Council of Trade may be seen in a continuing tendency to associate republicanism with state-sponsored commercial progress, a tradition surviving even in the writings of a much later republican, Thomas Paine, for whom 'the true principle of the republic is thus, not self-sacrificing virtue, but intelligent public patronage'.[10]

However, any republican association did not prevent the restored monarchy from adopting a similar approach to governing commerce, allowing Worsley to resume his public career. Thus his senna project fulfilled a similar role to the saltpetre project, allowing Worsley to advertise his expertise in commercial affairs in a way which suited the monarchy. This project also signified the increasing priority which Worsley gave to colonial trade, which thanks to the Navigation Act allowed commercial expansion without compromising national independence, as Worsley argued in a series of papers issued to statesmen including Ashley, Buckingham and Arlington, and collected by Locke. Although the navigation system was aimed particularly against Dutch commercial power, Worsley increasingly identified a new threat to England's imperial status, France. Anglo-French rivalry in the Atlantic was for Worsley the conflict of rival empires, in which the old Spanish empire became a pawn, necessitating a reconfiguration of English diplomacy.

Once again, the vehicles for Worsley's career were the trade and plantation councils which he served from 1668 to 1673. However, if the imperial intent of these bodies became increasingly ambitious, their actual activi-

[10] D. Wootton, 'Introduction: the republican tradition: from commonwealth to common sense', in D. Wootton (ed.), *Republicanism, liberty, and commercial society, 1649–1776*, Stanford 1994, 39.

ties remained mired in detail, and this study has shown how much time was spent on such forgotten corners of empire as Surinam. These remind us that English, indeed European, imperialism was still a relatively insecure phenomenon in which vulnerable colonial outposts often clung to a precarious existence, caught up in inter-European conflicts. Similarly, the imperial oversight which the Council of Trade and Plantations attempted to institute remained relatively weak, and Worsley's ambitious programmes were often unfulfilled. The decision to discontinue the 1672 council and revert to privy council administration of commerce might suggest the failure of the councils of trade of the previous fifty years. However, it is more appropriate to see this period as one of experimentation, through which the future terms of governing England's commercial empire were set. In this, Worsley's career reflects larger developments which would doubtless have occurred without him; rather than being personally responsible for any innovation in commercial policy, he can be seen as merely repackaging commonplace ideas for the benefit of statesmen. However, his career has an importance that is more than simply illustrative: Worsley's particular strategy was to situate himself between the social elites that traditionally governed the nation, and the privately interested merchants who could not be trusted to govern themselves. In doing so, he identified his personal interests with those of the state, helping to create the 'functional space' for those permanent civil servants who would one day staff the imperial state that Britain became.

It would be wrong to see his career as marking the death of the confessional state and the birth of an imperial one, for to treat 'the state' as a single entity is to reify an imagined entity with many faces, whose role was contested.[11] The commercial state which Worsley evoked was an idealisation, therefore, but one which found more and more advocates throughout his lifetime. For supporters of toleration like Worsley, the main role of the state was to defend the material interests of its inhabitants through advancing trade, a nation united economically rather than confessionally. But for Worsley the same moral relativism which led him to desacralise the state and see it as an engine for material progress also justified the aggressive economic nationalism of the navigation system, the colonial domination and slave trade on which this relied, and the amoral conflict of rival empires which would be its legacy. A Europe dominated by relative, and not universal, values, pragmatism rather than religious idealism, would by no means be free from the bloodshed that had blighted the age of confessional conflict from which it emerged.

This study has sought to use an individual life to illuminate a historical period, based on the belief that biography allows us to appreciate the past in all its complexity. Like Worsley seeing through the microscope the infinite variety of God's creation, by subjecting his life to such microscopic observa-

---

[11] Braddick, *State formation*.

tion we can become as resistant to mono-causal explanations of historical change as he was of reductionist mathematical accounts of nature. But it might be argued that what this approach gains in understanding of the historical context, it loses in insight into the individual themselves. It is appropriate, therefore, to conclude by dwelling on Worsley himself.

Indeed, this is an interesting period to write biography, when perceptions of the self were in flux, from Hobbes's mechanistic interpretation of self-interested psychology and the 'economic man' of commercial discourse, to the desire of radical religion to extinguish the self and unite with God. We have also encountered the transformation of the self required of the alchemist, and the inner reformation which alchemical labour might help achieve. As this last example suggests, for Worsley and his contemporaries an understanding of the self hinged on resolving the paradoxical relationship between fallen man, corrupt and worthless, and man as the image of God, capable of redemption and even perfection.

Worsley, at times, assumed each of these guises. He boasted of his genius, his insight into the art of alchemy, only to express fears that he was an 'impostor', unable to achieve anything of worth. Religiously, Worsley veered between confidence that he had some great role to play in a divine plan, and doubt that God's will could be known by men at all. Although he expressed his absolute spiritual worthlessness and degeneracy, he none the less hoped to assume a state of divine enlightenment. But his understanding of the spirit decried worldly affairs as inherently corrupt, and Worsley frequently presented human nature as fundamentally self-interested, only to portray himself as a public spirit, pursuing his various projects for the public good. In a sense the experimental that appears in the title to this conclusion applies not just to science, or religion, but to experiments in the self.

In his programme of self-annihilation, John Everard wrote of the self as subject to many human desires, personified as 'Doctors', Doctor Pleasure, Doctor Honour, Doctor Reason and so on, schizophrenically tearing the individual apart. Only once a victorious Christ conquers and ultimately destroys this fragmented self is unity, and peace, restored.[12] Biography, too, often seeks to impose such a harmony on its subject, identifying an essential self, a stable mind directing life's journey, the particular subsumed into the universal. But this is to perpetuate the fiction of a Cartesian homunculus buried within the individual, guiding his actions, thinking his thoughts. It is not possible to unmask Worsley's many performances and reveal the actor behind them all: no such actor exists, or ever did. Perhaps this means that biography is just fiction; perhaps we should write just of discourses, and forget selves.[13]

---

[12] Everard, *Gospel treasures*, 66–71.

[13] See Rob Iliffe's contention about the supposed relationship between Isaac Newton's diverse intellectual activities, 'that an essentialised and psychologised "mind" should not be thoughtlessly invoked as the nescio quid that underpins the connectedness of

The self may be a creation, a fiction, but it is no less real for that: some-thing we need, something we use, something, it has been suggested, pre-linguistic, a feeling that the thoughts you have belong to you, before they are stored as memories and processed into an autobiographical story of self-hood.[14] But the self does not think: it is thought; not acted, but action. And this may serve as a defence of biography, for with its narrative struc-ture, conveying 'the changeableness of things', biography can evoke the transitory nature of self as continually rethought, not a stable mind but a process, always in the making, never made. We do not have access to this process itself, but we do have the traces that it left and these can be assembled and validly related with the knowledge that they were part of the same story of the self. Despite the contradictions, the paradoxes, the many gaps, Worsley is more than a face in the sand. This study has not attempted to reduce his personality to one overriding impulse or ambition, but rather to suggest a complex and in many ways ambiguous character. But if there is a metanarrative, it is of the tension between the forces of interest and spirit, the struggle to accommodate both within one self. Worsley has been described as 'evidently a man of considerable charm, with an acute brain and eclectic imagination', and without disputing this, it is fair to say that he did not always cover himself in glory.[15] Although maintaining some consistency of conscience, safeguarding the spirit from the corrupting force of interest, in a sense this involved renouncing moral responsibility for non-spiritual matters. Confident to the point of arrogance but contorted by self-doubt, striving for recognition and yet never fully stepping into the public light, Worsley absorbed and responded to the paradoxes of his age. It has been astutely suggested that 'his ultimate skill was survival', and if so, then perhaps Benjamin Worsley captures as well as any of his contemporaries the turbulence of his times, and the infinite capacity for creation of those who endured them.[16]

his work': 'Abstract considerations: disciplines and the incoherence of Newton's natural philosophy', *Studies in History and Philosophy of Science* xxxv (2004), 451.

[14] A. Damasio, *The feeling of what happens: body, emotion and the making of consciousness*, London 2000.

[15] Young, *Faith*, 218.

[16] R. Zaller, 'Benjamin Worsley', in R. L. Greaves and R. Zaller (eds), *Biographical dictionary of British radicals in the seventeenth century*, Brighton 1982, ii. 342.

Bibliography

Unpublished primary sources

Boston, USA, Massachusetts Institute of Historical Research
Winthrop papers, microfilm reels 7, 9

Exeter, Devon Record Office
Parish registers of St Saviour, Dartmouth

Ipswich, Suffolk Record Office
Aldeburgh borough records, EE1/P4/9, answer to Council of Trade

London, British Library
MSS Add. 2858, 4106, 5138 (includes papers on free ports), 11410 (papers on Jamaica), 28079, 72850, 72858 (William Petty's letterbooks), 78685 (John Evelyn's letterbook)
MS Egerton 2395 Thomas Povey's papers
MS Landsdowne 821 Henry Cromwell's letterbook
MSS Sloane 427, 648, 3662 Surinam papers

London, Corporation of London Record Office
Records of the court of aldermen, rep. 58 (1645–7)

London, Guildhall Library
Company of Barber-Surgeons, register of admissions, MS 5265/1 (copy held on microfilm)
Company of Barber-Surgeons, court minute books, volume v, MS 5257/5 (copy held on microfilm)

London, Institute of Historical Research
Coventry papers, vol. xii, Longleat house (copy held on microfilm)

London, The National Archives
C 24/812, pt 2 Chancery depositions
CO 1/20, 29, 30 Colonial papers
CO 278/2 Surinam entry book
CO 389/5 Council of Trade and Plantations entry book
SP 18/16
SP 28/210 Book of orders of Kent committee of sequestrations
SP 29/142, pt 2, 143, 360
SP 68
30/24/41, fos 120–3 Instructions to the 1672 Council of Trade and Plantations

30/24/49 Shaftesbury papers on trade and colonies

London, Royal Society
Boyle letters, vol. 1, 7

Oxford, Bodleian Library
MS Clarendon 75
MSS Rawlinson A473, A478
MS Rawlinson, letters 50
'The 1661 notebook of John Locke' (microfilm 77)
Journal of the Council of Trade and Plantations, 1672–4 (microfilm 496; original
copy possessed by the Library of Congress, Washington)

Letters, publications and selected other writings by Benjamin Worsley

[Unless otherwise stated, copies and extracts are in scribal hand. Where several
copies exist, the one used in the text is listed first. Some petitions calendared in
the state papers and cited in the text are not included. Question marks denote
uncertain authorship.]

1645
Petition to House of Lords for release from prison, 30 Mar.
Entered in *LJ* vii. 401

Certificate on behalf of Sir George Wentworth, 29 May
Copy entered into the book of orders for the Kent committee of sequestrations,
TNA, SP 28/210, fo. 71r

1646
Treatises, 'Propositions in the behalfe of the kingdome concerning salt-peter' and
'Motions to the City', c.1646
Copy, HP 71/11/8–11; further versions, HP 71/11/14–15; HP 71/11/12–13

Treatise, 'About the poore advertisements', c.1646
Copy, HP 15/2/5–6; second copy, HP 15/2/3

?Treatise, 'A newe waie for the making of salt peeter and maintaining the poore',
c.1646
Copy, HP 53/26/7. Probably associated with the saltpetre project

?Treatise, 'An exact discovery of the charge and damadge to the kingdome in the
making of salt peeter', c.1646
Copy, HP 53/26/3. Probably associated with the saltpetre project

?Untitled treatise on poor relief and saltpetre, c.1646
Copy HP 53/26/1; second copy, HP 12/136–7. Probably associated with the saltpetre project

?Untitled treatise on poor relief and saltpetre, c.1646
Copy HP 53/26/2. Probably associated with the saltpetre project

?Treatise, 'Divers services involvd into one benefitiall to the whole kingdome',
c.1646
Copy, HP 53/26/6; alternative version, HP 53/26/4–5. Probably associated with
the saltpetre project

?Treatise, 'An estimate of the greate quantitie of corne that pigeons doe spoyle
and destroye in the countie of Cambridge', c.1646
Copy, HP 25/3/4; further copies, HP 25/3/5; HP 66/24/1–2. Printed as 'An estimate made some years ago, of the great destruction of corn by the multitude of
pidgeon-houses', in Hartlib, *Samuel Hartlib his legacie*, 225–7. Probably associated with the saltpetre project

?Memorandum, 'A memorandum and caution concerning the observations and
animadversions about saltpeter', c.1646
Copy partly by S. Hartlib, HP 39/1/24. Probably associated with the saltpetre
project

Treatise, 'Proffits humbly presented to this kingdome', c.1646
Copy, HP 15/2/61–4; further copies, HP 25/3/7–10; HP 53/32/1

Petition to House of Lords for saltpetre project, 21 Nov.
Entered in *LJ* viii. 574

1647
Letter to J. Hall, 16 Feb.
Copy with alterations by Hartlib, HP 36/6/3–8; second copy HP 36/7/2. (Answer
to a letter from Hall, 5 Feb. 1647, HP 36/6/1–2, 36/7/2–3)

1648
Letter to Hartlib 14 Feb.
Copy, HP 36/8/1–6

Letter to Hartlib, 4 May
Two extracts, HP 71/15/1, HP 71/9/2

Letter to Hartlib, [18] May
Extract, HP 71/15/2

Letter to [Hartlib], 26 May [1648]
Extract, Royal Society, Boyle letters 7, no. 50, fos 1v–2v. See also Hartlib,
'Ephemerides', summer 1648, HP 31/22/18B

Letter to Hartlib, 1 June
Extract by Hartlib, HP 71/9/2–3

Letter to Lady Ranelagh, c. June
Extract included in Hartlib, 'Ephemerides', summer 1648, HP 31/22/14B

Letter to Hartlib, 22 June
Copy, HP 42/1/1–2; second copy HP 8/27/1–14

Letter to Hartlib, 27 July
Copy, HP 42/1/1–2; further copies, HP 8/27/1–14; partial copy, BL, MS Sloane
649, fos 50r–52r

Letter to Hartlib, c. Sept.
Original, attached to a letter from J. Sadler to Hartlib, HP 46/9/22

1649
?Letter to Hartlib, 19 Mar.
Extract, HP 53/35/2A

Letter to Hartlib, 18 May
Extract sent to R. Boyle, Royal Society, Boyle letters 7.1, fos 1r–2v

Letter to Hartlib, 1 June
Extract sent to Boyle, Royal Society, Boyle letters 7.2, fos 1r–2v

Letter to W. Petty, 15 June
Copy, HP 8/50/1–2

Letter to Hartlib, 22 June
Original, HP 26/33/1–3

Treatise, 'Of the destilling or drawing of spirits some animadversions', c. summer
Original, HP 26/33/9–10

Letter to J. Dury, 27 July
Original, HP 33/2/18–19. Adapted by Dury as 'A memorandum of the Virginian
    plantation', HP 33/2/22

Letter to [Hartlib], 3 Aug.
Original, HP 33/2/1–2

?Letter to Hartlib, 10 Aug.
Extract by Hartlib, HP 43/35–6

Letter to Dury, 17 Aug.
Original, HP 33/2/3–4

Letter to W. Strickland, c. Aug./Sept.
Copy by Worsley, HP 61/8/1–3

Letter to ?Hartlib, c. Sept.
Extract by Hartlib, HP 33/2/20–1

1650
Letter to C. Dymock, 15 Mar.
Copy by Hartlib, HP 62/2. Worsley is co-signer with Boyle, Sadler, Dury, Hartlib
    and Henry Robinson: possibly never sent

Treatise, 'Further animadversions about Virginia', c.1650
Original, HP 61/6/1–2, highly damaged

?Treatise, 'The ends of forraigne or out land trade stated and asserted', c.1650–1
Copy, HP 66/1/1–2, with alterations by Worsley. Not previously identified

1651

Letter to [Hartlib], *c*. spring 1651
Printed in Hartlib, *Samuel Hartlib his legacie*, 105–6. See also Hartlib, 'Ephemerides', 1651, pt I, HP 28/2/7B

The advocate: or, a narrative of the state and condition of things between the English and Dutch nation, in relation to trade, London 1651, 1652
Two editions, published by William Dugard by authority of the Council of State

1652

Free ports, the nature and necessitie of them stated, London 1652
Two editions, published by William Dugard by authority of the Council of State

Letter to Hartlib, 24 Nov.
Extract by Hartlib, HP 61/7/9B. Printed in Hartlib, *The reformed Virginian silkworm*

1653

Treatise, 'Observations about saltpetre', *c*. May
Copy, HP 39/1/11–12. See Newman and Principe, *Alchemy tried in the fire*, 240

Letter to Lady [Ranelagh?], 29 July 1653
Original, BL, MS Add. 4106, fos 224–5

Letter to Hartlib, *c*. late 1653
Extract quoted in letter, Hartlib to Boyle, 28 Feb., *Boyle correspondence*, i. 155

1654

Letter to Hartlib, 16 May
Four separate extracts: HP 66/15/1–4, partly printed in Hartlib, *Samuel Hartlib his legacie*, 217–19, entitled 'A philosophical letter concening vegetation and the vauses of fruitfulness'; HP 70/8/1; HP 70/7; further extract printed in Hartlib, *Samuel Hartlib his legacie*, 248

Treatise, 'De nitro theses, quædam', *c*. May
Copy by Hartlib, HP 39/1/16–20

Letter to Hartlib, *c*. May/June
Extract printed in Hartlib, *Samuel Hartlib his legacie*, 250

Letter to Hartlib, 28 June
Three extracts by Hartlib: HP 39/1/15; HP 70/8/1; HP 70/7

Letter to F. Clodius, *c*. summer
Copy by Dymock, HP 42/1/26–7

?Letter to ?Hartlib, *c*. autumn
Extract, HP 42/1/38–9

Letter to ?countess of Leicester, 27 Sept.
Copy, HP 65/15/1–4. Original part of the Sidney collection, addressed apparently to the countess of Leicester, wife of the earl of Leicester. Printed in HMC, *De L'Isle and Dudley*, vi. 496–8

Letter to [Hartlib], 31 Oct.
Extract, HP 42/1/3–4

Letter to Hartlib, 29 Nov.
Extract, HP 42/1/3–4

1655
?Letter to Hartlib, 18 Apr.
Extract, HP 26/41/1–2

?Letter to Hartlib, 1 Aug.
Extract, HP 1/3/1–4

?Letter to ?Hartlib, 14 Feb. 1655/6
Copy, HP 42/1/5–6

1656
?Letter to Hartlib
Extract, HP 26/58/1–2

1657
Letter to H. Cromwell, 17 Mar.
Original, BL, MS Landsdowne 821, fo. 352

?Letter to Hartlib, c. Apr.
Copy entitled 'a phytologicall letter', HP 8/22/1–4

Letter to Hartlib, c. July
Copy, HP 26/56/1–4; second copy, HP 26/56/5–8. Printed in R. Boyle, *The general history of the air* (1692), as 'Of celestial influences or effluviums in the air'; Latin translation by Nicolas Mercator, HP 42/1/18–25. See Clericuzio, 'New light', 236–46

?Note to Hartlib concerning the prophecy of John Perrot, c. late 1657
Original, HP 26/28/5. Although written in Worsley's hand, possibly this is a copy of a note addressed to Worsley, rather than by him. Included with a copy of Perrot's prophecy, HP 26/28/4, an account of his journey in Worsley's hand, HP 26/28/3, and a copy of Perrot to Worsley, 10 Sept., HP 26/28/1–2

Letter to Hartlib, 14 Oct., with a 'Problema physico-astrologicum'
Two extracts: HP 42/1/9–10, entitled 'Physico-astrological letter' by Hartlib; HP 42/1/7–8, entitled 'Vniversal Learning' by Hartlib. Copy of the enclosed 'Problema', HP 42/1/16–17

Letter to Boyle, 14 Oct.
Printed in *Boyle correspondence*, i. 242

Letter to Hartlib, 20 Oct.
Copy entitled 'Dr Worsly's physico-astrological letter', HP 42/1/11–12. Further copies, HP 42/1/9; HP 33/2/5

Letter to S. Hartlib, Jr, 29 Dec.
Extract quoted in letter, Hartlib to Boyle, 7 Jan., printed in *Boyle correspondence*, i. 248

Letter to Hartlib, 29 Dec.
Extract quoted in letter, Hartlib to Boyle, 7 Jan. printed in *Boyle correspondence*, i. 248

1658
?Letter to Hartlib, *c*. Jan.
Extract sent by Hartlib to J.Pell, BL, MS Add. 4279, fo. 48r

Letter to Hartlib, 6 Jan.
Original, HP 33/2/7–8

Letter to W. Potter, 20 Jan.
Copy, HP 33/2/10, enclosed in letter to Hartlib of same date

Letter to Hartlib, 20 Jan.
Original, HP 33/2/11–12

Letter to Hartlib, Jr, 23/27 Jan.
Extract, Royal Society, Boyle letters 7.3.1B; shorter extract, HP 47/3/1–4

Letter to Hartlib, 10 Feb.
Extract, 47/3/1A

Letter to Hartlib, 23 Feb.
Extract, 47/3/1A

Letter to Potter, 7 Apr.
Copy, HP 39/2/62–3

Letter to Hartlib, 14 Apr.
Extracts quoted in letter, Hartlib to Boyle, 27 Apr., *Boyle correspondence*, i. 267

Letter to Hartlib, 5 May
Two extracts: HP 47/3/1A-B; second extract quoted in letter, Hartlib to Boyle, 13 May, *Boyle correspondence*, i. 270–2

Letter to Hartlib, 26 May
Extract, HP 47/3/2A–B; quoted in letter, Hartlib to Boyle, 1 June, *Boyle correspondence*, i. 278–80

Letter to Dury, 26 May
Copy, HP 33/2/9. Extract, HP 47/3/1B–2B

Letter to Hartlib, 9 June
Extract, HP 47/3/3B–4A

Letter to Hartlib, 23 June
Extract, HP 47/3/4A

Letter to Hartlib, 14 July
Extract, HP 47/3/4A–B

?Letter to [Hartlib?], 28 July 1658
Extract, HP 15/8/19

Letter to [Hartlib], 8 Sept.
Copy entitled 'Of spirits' by Hartlib, HP 62/10/1A–2B

Letter to Potter, 17 Nov.
Extract with corrections by Hartlib, HP 26/33/6

Letter to ?Boyle, c. late 1658–early 1659
Two extracts: HP 42/1/28–33; HP 60/2/1–4. Printed in *Boyle correspondence*, i. 301–18

1659
Letter to Hartlib, 4 Feb.
Extract, HP 33/2/16–17

Letter to Lady ?Ranelagh, 20 Apr.
Extract, HP 33/2/13–14

1660
Letter to J. Beale, c. May–June
Copy, BL, MS Add. 78685, fos 103–4, sent to John Evelyn by Hartlib in a letter dated 23 June 1660 (letter bound in Royal Society Library, copy of Hartlib's *A designe for plentie*). Another copy, BL, MS Sloane 427, fos 65–6

Letter to Hartlib, 10 Sept.
Original, HP 33/2/15

1661
Letter to Hartlib, c. Sept.
Extract quoted in letter, Hartlib to J. Worthington, 24 Sept. *Diary of John Worthington*, 43–4

Letter to Hartlib, c. Sept.
Original, HP 33/2/27

Letter to Lady Clarendon, 8 Nov.
Original, Bodl. Lib., MS Clarendon 75, fos 300–1

1662
Certificate to George Monck, duke of Albermarle, on behalf of Samuel Goodwin, 1 Nov.
Original, TNA, SP 68, fo. 330r

1665
Petition to the king for post office money, c.1665
Copy, TNA, SP 29/142, pt 2, fo. 150

Letter to Boyle, 30 Oct.
Entered into Boyle's work diary and printed in *Boyle correspondence*, ii. 569

1666
Petition to the king regarding senna, 30 Oct.
Copy, TNA, C 1/20, fo. 282

1668
Memorandum to William, Lord Willoughby of Parnham, on the senna project, 22 Jan.
Copy in 'Locke notebook', 263–5, entered under 'Sena'
Treatise, 'Severall reasons humbly tendered to the Honourable the Attorney Generall for the encourageing of the plantation of senna by a pattent or by an act of parliament', c. Mar.
Copy, TNA, CO 1/20, fo. 283

Letter to ?duke of Buckingham on Jamaican sugar, c. summer 1668
Copy in 'Locke notebook', 215–19, 232–52, entered under 'Jamaica'

Treatise, 'Some considerations with all humblenesse propounded to his majestie about the herring fishing', c.1668
Copy, BL, MS Add. 28079, fos 201–2. Second copy, Coventry papers, vol. xii, fos 365–6, Longleat house (microfilm in possession of the Institute of Historical Research). Printed in *A collection of advertisements, advices, and directions, relating to the royal fishery*, London 1695, 38–48, and *A third collection of scarce and valuable tracts, on the most interesting and entertaining subjects* London 1751, 338–45. The date is assumed from a reference to recent wrongs done by the Dutch and to a treaty with that nation. Patrick Kelly, however, suggests the date of 1663 for the paper: 'Dutch data', 137

Treatise, 'Some considerations about the Commission for Trade', c.1668, addressed to Sir Anthony Ashley Cooper, Lord Ashley
Original, TNA, 30/24/49, fos 86–9 (Shaftesbury papers)

Treatise, 'The peculiar advantages which this nation hath by the trade of our plantations', 14 Aug., addressed to Ashley
Copy with corrections by Worsley, TNA, 30/24/49, fos 221–7 (Shaftesbury papers); second copy, probably sent to Lord Arlington, Bodl. Lib., MS Rawlinson A478, fos 65–72. Further copy in 'Locke notebook', 16–17, 158–71, entered under 'Plantations'

Letter to the duke of Buckingham, entitled 'Considerations about the Jamaican privateers', 18 Dec.
Copy with alterations by Worsley, MS Rawlinson A478, fos 61–2, probably sent to Arlington. Further copy in 'Locke notebook', 172–9, entered under 'Plantations' and entitled 'A copy of my first letter to the duke of Buckingham about the privateers communicated alsoe to my Lord Keeper, Lord Arlington, and some others of his majesties privy councell'

Letter to Arlington, c.1668–73
Original, TNA, SP 29/143, fo. 55. Calendared under 1665, CSPD, 1665–6, 174

1669
Report on Surinam, probably presented to the Council of Trade, c. Jan.
Copy probably owned by Arlington, MS Rawlinson A478, fos 32–7

Letter to Buckingham, entitled '2d large letter about Jamaica', 24 Feb. Copy with corrections by Worsley, TNA, 30/24/49, fos 37–48 (Shaftesbury papers). Further copies in 'Locke notebook', 180–214, entered under 'Jamaica'; BL, MS Add. 11410, 623–74, dating from the eighteenth century

Treatise, 'Animadversions on my Lord de Wits paper presented to my Lord Arlington', after 2 July.
Copy in 'Locke notebook', 253–62, entered under 'Surinam'; copy entered in the entering book for Surinam, TNA, CO 278/2, 13–19. The paper by Johann de Witt, the Dutch grand pensionary, was written on 2 July, TNA, CO 278/2, 7–13

Petition to the king on overdue payments, c.1669
Calendared in CSPD Oct. 1668–Dec. 1669, 651

1670
Letter to J. Winthrop, Jr, c. June
Original, Massachusetts Institute of Historical Research, Winthrop papers, microfilm reel 9

1671
Paper for Edward Montagu, earl of Sandwich, entitled 'The true state of the manufacture of sugar within our plantations, which requires all manner of incouragement', c.1671
Included in volume ten of Sandwich's journals, in private ownership (not consulted for this monograph): Harris, Edward Montagu, 225–6

Letter to A. Marvell, 27 Dec.
Original, MS Rawlinson, letters 50, fos 123–4

1672
Letter to Marvell, 1 Jan.
Original, MS Rawlinson, letters 50, fos 126–7

Letter to Marvell, 3 Jan.
Original, MS Rawlinson, letters 50, fos 129–30

Letter to Marvell, 20 Jan.
Original, MS Rawlinson, letters 50, fos 132–3

Letter to Philip, Lord Wharton, 12 Jan.
Original, MS Rawlinson, letters 50, fos 149–50

Letter to Sir Thomas Lynch, governor of Jamaica, on behalf of the Council for Trade and Plantations, 2 Nov.
Copy, TNA, CO 1/29, fo. 102; calendared in CSPC, 1669–1674, 424

Letter to Sir James Russell, on behalf of the Council for Trade and Plantations, 12 Nov.
Calendared in CSPC, 1669–1674, 430

Letter to Colonel George Duke, on behalf of the Council for Trade and Plantations, 29 Nov.
Calendared in *CSPD*, *1672–1673*, 213–14

Letter to Lynch on behalf of the Council for Trade and Plantations, 30 Nov.
Copy, TNA, CO 1/29, fo. 140; calendared in *CSPC*, *1669–1674*, 439

Letter to Sir Joseph Williamson, on behalf of the Council for Trade and Plantations, 3 Dec.
Calendared in *CSPD*, *1672–1673*, 239

Letter to Lynch on behalf of the Council for Trade and Plantations, 9 Dec.
Calendared in *CSPC*, *1669–1674*, 442

Letter to Willoughby, governor of Barbados, on behalf of the Council for Trade and Plantations, 17 Dec.
Copy, TNA, CO 1/29, fo. 175r; calendared in *CSPC*, *1669–1674*, 448

1673
Letter to Lynch on behalf of the Council for Trade and Plantations, 1 Jan.
Copy, TNA, CO 1/30, fo. 1; calendared in *CSPC*, *1669–1674*, 459

Report to the Council for Trade and Plantations on St Christophers, 18 Feb.
Calendared in *CSPC*, *1669–1674*, 466–7

Report to the Council for Trade and Plantations on St Christophers, 9 June
Copy, TNA, CO 389/5, 55–61

1674
Certificate to W.Bridgeman on behalf of Francis Smith, 11 Feb.
Original, TNA, SP 29/360, fo. 277

1677
Letter to Boyle, 25 Aug.
Printed and translated in *Boyle correspondence*, v. 452–4

1681
Pamphlet, *The third part of naked truth*, London 1681
Published by Richard Janeway. Probably written 1673–7. For identification see chapter 8

Published primary sources

Official publications
Acts and ordinances of the Interregnum, ed. C. H. Firth and R. S. Rait, London 1911
Calendar of state papers, domestic series (1651–73), ed. M. A. Everett Green, F. H. Blackburne Daniell and F. Bickley, London 1877–1939
Calendar of state papers, domestic series, Charles II: addenda (1660–85), ed. F. H. Blackburne Daniell and F. Bickley, London 1939

Calendar of state papers relating to Ireland (1633–65), ed. H. Mahaffy, London 1901–7

Calendar of treasury books (1669–89), ed. W. Shaw, London 1908–23

Calendars of state papers, colonial series (1574–1676), ed. W. N. Sainsbury, London 1869–96

The journals of the House of Commons

The journals of the House of Lords

Historical Manuscripts Commission

HMC, *Fourteenth report: manuscripts of the marquis of Ormonde*, i, London 1902

HMC, *Sixty-third report: manuscripts of the earl of Egmont*, i, ed. S. C. Lomas, London 1905

HMC, *Seventy-seventh report: manuscripts of Lord de L'Isle and Dudley preserved at Penshurst Place, Kent, VI: Sidney papers, 1626–1698*, ed. W. A. Shaw, London 1966

HMC, *Seventy-eighth report: manuscripts of the late Reginald Rawdon Hastings, esq., of the Manor House, Ashby de la Zouche*, ed. J. Harley and F. Bickley, ii, London 1930

Other published sources

Alumni dublinenses: a register of the students, graduates, professors and provosts of Trinity College in the University of Dublin (1593–1860), ed. G. D. Burtchaeli and T. U. Sadlier, Dublin 1935

Boyle, R., 'Memorialls philosophicall beginning in the New Year 1649/50', Royal Society, Boyle papers 28, pp. 309–12. Transcription online at http://www.bbl.ac.uk/Boyle/date accessed, 7 Jan. 2002

Browning, A. (ed.), *Thomas Osborne, earl of Danby and duke of Leeds, 1632–1712, II: Letters*, Glasgow 1951

A calendar of the court minutes etc. of the East India Company, 1644–1649, ed. E. B. Sainsbury, Oxford 1912

A calendar of the court minutes etc. of the East India Company, 1650–1654, ed. E. B. Sainsbury, Oxford 1912

A census of Ireland, circa 1659, ed. S. Pender, Dublin 1939

A collection of the state papers of John Thurloe, vi, ed T. Birch, London 1742

'Commonwealth state accounts, 1653–56', ed. E. MacLysaght, *Analecta Hibernia* xv (1944), 227–321

'Correspondence of Hartlib, Haak, Oldenburg and others of the founders of the Royal Society, with Governor Winthrop of Connecticut, 1661–72', ed. R. C. Winthrop, *Proceedings of the Massachusetts Historical Society*, Boston 1878

The correspondence of Robert Boyle, ed. M. Hunter, A. Clericuzio and L. Principe, London 2001

The diary and correspondence of Dr John Worthington, ed. J. Crossley, i (Chetham Society xiii, 1847)

The diary of John Evelyn, ed. E. S. Beer, London 1959

The diary of Robert Hooke, ed. H. Robinson and W. Adams, London 1968

The diary of Sir Archibald Johnston of Wariston, III: 1655–60, ed. J. Oglivie, Edinburgh 1940

'Gleanings from the Irish Council-Books of the times of the Commonwealth and the Cromwells', in S. Urban, *The Gentleman's Magazine* xxxvi (1851), 569–73

The Hartlib papers: electronic edition, 2nd edn (Sheffield: HR Online, 2002)

The inhabitants of London in 1638 (1931). URL: http://www.british-history.ac.uk/ date accessed, 22 Sept. 2006

Letters addressed to Sir Joseph Williamson, ed. W. D. Christie, i (Camden viii, 1874)

'Letters of John Winthrop Jnr 1626–7–75–6' (Collections of the Massachusetts Historical Society viii, 1882)

'The letters of Sir Cheney Culpeper (1641–1657)', ed. M. Braddick and M. Greengrass, in *Seventeenth-century political and financial papers* (Camden, 5th ser. vii; Camden miscellany xxiii, 1996), 105–402

The library of Dr John Webster: the making of a seventeenth-century radical, ed. P. Elmer, London 1986

Locke, J., *A letter concerning toleration* (1689), ed. J. Tully, Indianapolis 1983

London visitation pedigrees, 1664, ed. J. B. Whitmore and A. W. Hughes Clarke (Harleian Society xcii, 1940)

London will abstracts, ed. J. B. Whitmore, London 1961

The memoirs of Edmund Ludlow, 1625–72, i, ed. C. H. Firth, Oxford 1894

Oster, M. (ed.), *Science in Europe, 1500–1800: a primary sources reader*, Basing-stoke–New York 2002

The papers of William Penn, I: *1644–7*, ed. M. Dun and R. Dun, Philadelphia 1981

The parish registers of St Mary Aldermary, London, 1558–1751, ed. J. S. Chester (Harleian Society Registers v, 1880)

Petty, W., *History of the Cromwellian survey of Ireland, A.D. 1655–6, commonly called the 'Down Survey'*, ed. T. C. Larcom, Dublin 1851

Physicians and irregular medical practitioners in London, 1550–1640: database (2004). URL: http://www.british-history.ac.uk/ date accessed, 29 June 2005

Registers of St Olave, Hart Street, London, 1563–1700, ed. W. Bannerman (Harleian Society Registers xlvi, 1916)

Statutes of the realm, V: *1628–80* (1819), 752–82: URL: http://www.british-history.ac.uk/ date accessed, 6 Mar. 2007

Stone, J. W. M. (ed.), *The inland posts (1392–1672): a documentary calendar of historical documents with appendixes*, London 1987

Thirsk, J. and J. P. Cooper (eds), *Seventeenth century economic documents*, Oxford 1972

The works of the honourable Robert Boyle, ed. T. Birch, 2nd edn, London 1772

The works of Robert Boyle, ed. M. Hunter and E. Davis, London 1999

Contemporary books and pamphlets

Battie, J., *The merchants remonstrance*, London 1644

Baxter, R., *A second true defence of the meer nonconformists*, London 1681

Bethel, S., *Et à dracone: or, some reflections upon a discourse called Omnia à Belo comesta*, London 1668

———— *The world's mistake in Oliver Cromwell*, London 1668

———— *The present interest of England stated*, London 1671

—— *An account of the French usurpation upon the trade of England*, London 1679

Bridge, J., E. Warren and A. Warren, *A perfect narrative of the grounds and reasons moving some officers of the army in Ireland to the securing of the castle of Dublin for the parlament*, London 1660

Brooke, S., *Catalogus librorum bibliothecae reverend. and eruditi viri D. Samuelis Brooke*, London 1681

Brugis, T., *The discovery of a projector*, London 1641

Burthogge, R., *An argument for infants baptisme deduced from the analogy of faith*, London 1684

—— *Vindiciae paedo-baptismi, or, A confirmation of an argument lately emitted for infants baptism*, London 1685

Carter, W., *Englands interest by trade asserted*, London 1671

Cary, P., *A disputation between a doctor and an apothecary*, London 1684

Chappel, S., *A diamond or rich jewel*, London 1651

Child, J., *Brief observations concerning trade, and interest of money*, London 1668

Christian unity exhorted to, London 1678

Coke, R., *A discourse of trade*, London 1670

A collection of advertisements, advices, and directions, relating to the royal fishery, London 1695

Collins, J., *A plea for the bringing in of Irish cattel*, London 1680

Defoe, D., *An essay upon projects*, London 1697

de la Court, P., *The interest and political maxims of the Republick of Holland and West-Friesland*, London 1702

de Mirabeau, Gabriel-Honoré de Riquetti, comte, *Doubts concerning the free navigation of the Scheld claimed by the emperor*, London 1785

du Rohan, Henri, duc, *A treatise of the interest of the princes and states of Christendome*, London 1641

Dunmore, J. and R. Chiswell, *Catalogus librorum ... instructissimarum bibliothecarum tum clarissimi doctissimique viri D. Doctoris Benjaminis Worsley*, London 1678

[Dury, J.], *Considerations tending to the happy accomplishment of Englands reformation*, London 1647

Dymock, D., *A discovery for new divisions, or, setting out of lands*, London 1653

Everard, J., *Some gospel-treasures opened*, London 1653

Flavel, J., *The whole works of the Reverend Mr. John Flavel*, i, London 1701

Fortrey, S., *Englands interest and improvement*, 2nd edn, London 1673

Gardner, R., *Englands grievance discovered, in relation to the coal-trade*, London 1655

Gassendi, P., *The mirrour of true nobility and gentility: being the life of the renowned Nicolaus Claudius Fabricius Lord Peiresk*, trans. W. Rand, London 1657

The grand concernments of England ensured, London 1659

Greatrakes, V., *A brief account of Mr Valentine Greatraks ... in a letter addressed to the Honourable Robert Boyle Esq*, Dublin 1668

Hartlib, S., *The necessity of some nearer conjunction and correspondency amongst evangelicall Protestants*, London 1644

—— (ed.), *The reformed Virginian silk-worm*, London 1652

—— (ed.), *Chymical and medicinal addresses*, London 1655

—— (ed.), *The reformed commonwealth of bees*, London 1655

———— (ed.), *Samuel Hartlib his legacie of husbandry*, 3rd edn, London 1655

The Impartial Scout

Jenner, T., *Londons blame, if not its shame*, London 1651

Jessey, H., *The exceeding riches of grace advanced by the spirit of grace*, London 1647

Johnson, T., *A discourse consisting of motives for the enlargement and freedome of trade*, London 1645

Keymer, J., *A cleare and evident way for enriching the nations of England and Ireland*, London 1650

A letter to a member of this parliament, for liberty of conscience, London 1668

Londons glory, or, the riot and ruine of the Fifth Monarchy men, London 1661

Maddison, R., *Great Britains remembrancer, looking in and out*, London 1654

North, R., *Examen: or, an enquiry into the credit and veracity of a pretended complete history*, London 1740

Parker, H., *Of a free trade*, London 1648

Peter, H., *Good work for a good magistrate*, London 1651

Petty, W., *A brief of proceedings between Sr. Hierome Sankey and Dr. William Petty*, London 1658

———— *Reflections on some persons and things in Ireland*, London 1660

[Petyt, W.], *Britannia languens, or a discourse of trade*, in *Early English tracts on commerce*, ed. J. R. McCulloch, Cambridge 1856

Plattes, G., *A discovery of infinite treasure*, London 1639

Potter, W., *The key of wealth*, London 1650

———— *The trades-man's jewel*, London 1650

———— *Humble proposalls to the honorable the Councell for Trade*, London 1651

The proceedings at the Council for Trade, between the Muscovia Company, monopolizers of the trade to Green-Land, and others, adventurers thither, for a free-trade, London 1652

Reynell, C., *The true English interest*, London 1674

Roberts, L., *The treasure of trafficke, or a discourse of forraigne trade*, London 1641

Robertson, W., *The second gate, or the inner door to the holy tongue*, London 1654

———— *Testamentum novum hebraicum*, London 1661

Robinson, H., *Englands safetie in trades encrease*, London 1641

———— *Briefe considerations, concerning the advancement of trade and navigation*, London 1650

———— *Certain proposals in order to the peoples freedome and accomodation*, London 1652

Select essays on commerce, London 1754

Sendivogius, M., *A new light of alchymie*, trans. J. French, London 1650

Severall proposals for the generall good of the Commonwealth, London 1651

A third collection of scarce and valuable tracts, on the most interesting and entertaining subjects, London 1751

Turpin, H., *Catalogue of several thousand volumes*, London 1769

Violet, T., *The advancement of merchandize*, London 1651

———— *Mysteries and secrets of trade and mint-affairs*, London 1653

[von Frankenburg, Abraham], *Clavis apocalyptica: or, a prophetical key*, London 1651

Secondary sources

Andrews, C., *British committees, commissions, and councils of trade and plantations, 1622–1675*, Baltimore 1908
—— *The colonial period of American history*, IV: *England's commercial and colonial policy*, New Haven 1938
Appleby, J., *Economic thought and ideology in seventeenth-century England*, Princeton 1978
Archer, I., 'Material Londoners?', in Orwin, *Material London*, 174–92
Armitage, D., *The ideological origins of the British empire*, Cambridge 2000
Ashton, R., *The city and the court, 1603–1643*, Cambridge 1979
Aylmer, G., *The state's servants: the civil servants of the English Republic, 1649–1660*, London–Boston 1973
—— *The crown's servants: government and civil service under Charles II, 1660–1685*, Oxford 2002
Barbour, V., 'Dutch and English merchant shipping in the seventeenth century', *EcHR* ii (1930), 261–90
Barnard, T. C., 'Lord Broghill, Vincent Gookin and the Cork elections of 1659', *EHR* lxxxviii (1973), 352–65
—— 'Planters and policies in Cromwellian Ireland', *P&P* lxi (1973), 31–69
—— 'The Hartlib circle and the origins of the Dublin Philosophical Society', *IHS* xix (1974–5), 56–71
—— 'The Hartlib circle and the cult and culture of improvement in Ireland', in *SHUR*, 281–97
—— *Cromwellian Ireland: English government and reform in Ireland 1649–1660*, 2nd edn, Oxford 2000
Beer, G., *The old colonial system, 1660–1754*, New York 1912
Bieber, R. P., 'The British plantation councils of 1670–4', *EHR* xl (1925), 93–106
Billings, W. M., *Sir William Berkeley and the forging of colonial Virginia*, Baton Rouge 2004
Black, R. C., *The younger John Winthrop*, New York–London 1966
Bliss, R., *Revolution and empire: English politics and the American colonies in the seventeenth century*, Manchester 1990
Boas, M., *Robert Boyle and seventeenth-century chemistry*, Cambridge 1948
Bono, J., *The word of God and the languages of man: interpreting nature in early modern science and medicine*, I: *Ficino to Descartes*, London–Madison 1995
Bottigheimer, K., *English money and Irish land: the 'Adventurers' in the Cromwellian settlement of Ireland*, Oxford 1971
Braddick, M., *State formation in early modern England*, Cambridge 2000
Brenner, R., 'The civil war politics of London's merchant community', *P&P* lviii (1973), 53–107
—— *Merchants and revolution: commercial change, political conflict, and London's overseas traders, 1550–1653*, Cambridge 1993
Bridenbaugh C. and R. Bridenbaugh, *No peace beyond the line: the English in the Caribbean, 1624–1690*, New York 1972
Brooks, C., 'Apprenticeship, social mobility and the middling sort, 1550–1800', in J. Barry and C. Brooks (eds), *The middling sort of people: culture, society and politics in England, 1550–1800*, Basingstoke–London 1994, 52–83

Brown, L. F., *The first earl of Shaftesbury*, New York–London 1933

Buck, P., 'Seventeenth-century political arithmetic: civil strife and vital statistics', *Isis* lxviii (1977), 67–84

Butterfield, K., 'Puritans and religious strife in the early Chesapeake', *Virginia Magazine of History and Biography* cix (2001), 5–36

Canny, N., *Making Ireland British, 1580–1650*, Oxford 2001

Čapková, D., 'The Comenian group in England and Comenius' ideal of universal reform', *Acta Comeniana* i (1970), 25–34

——— 'Comenius and his ideals: escape from the labyrinth', in *SHUR*, 75–91

Carlton, C., *Going to the wars: the experience of the English civil wars, 1638–1651*, London 1992

Champion, J., *The pillars of priestcraft shaken*, Cambridge 1992

——— *Republican learning: John Toland and the crisis of Christian culture, 1696–1722*, Manchester 2003

Clarke, A., *Prelude to Restoration in Ireland: the end of the Commonwealth, 1659–60*, Cambridge 1999

Clay, C., *Economic expansion and social change: England 1500–1700*, II: *Industry, trade and government*, Cambridge 1984

Clericuzio, A., 'A redefinition of Boyle's chemistry and corpuscular philosophy', *Annals of Science* xlvii (1990), 561–89

——— *Elements, principles and corpuscules: a study of atomism and chemistry in the seventeenth century*, Dordrecht–Boston–London 2001

——— 'New light on Benjamin Worsley's natural philosophy', in *SHUR*, 236–46

Clucas, S., 'The correspondence of a XVII-century "chymicall gentleman": Sir Cheney Culpeper and the chemical interests of the Hartlib circle', *Ambix* xl (1993), 147–70

Coates, B., *The impact of the English Civil War on the economy of London, 1642–1650*, Aldershot 2004

Coffey, J., *Persecution and toleration in Protestant England, 1558–1689*, London 2000

Cogswell, T., 'England and the Spanish match', in Cust and Hughes, *Conflict in early Stuart England*, 107–33

Como, D., 'Predestination and political conflict in Laud's London', *HJ* xlvi (2003), 263–94

——— *Blown by the spirit: Puritanism and the emergence of an antinomian underground in pre-civil-war England*, Stanford 2004

Conquest, R., 'The state and commercial expansion: England in the years 1642–1688', *Journal of European Economic History* xiv (1985), 155–72

Cook, H., *The decline of the old medical regime in Stuart London*, Ithaca–London 1986

Cooper, J. P., 'Economic regulation and the cloth industry in seventeenth-century England', *TRHS* 5th ser. xx (1970), 73–99

——— 'Social and economic policies under the Commonwealth', in G. Aylmer (ed.), *The Interregnum: the quest for settlement, 1646–1660*, London 1972, 121–42

Corcoran, T., *State policy in Irish education, AD 1536 to 1816*, Dublin 1916

Corfield, P., 'Economic issues and ideologies', in C. Russell (ed.), *The origins of the English Civil War*, London-Basingstoke 1973, 197–218

Coughlan, P., 'Natural history and historical nature: the project for a natural history of Ireland', in *SHUR*, 298–317

Cramsie, J., 'Commercial projects and the fiscal policy of James VI and I', *HJ* xliii (2000), 345–64

Craven, W. F., *The southern colonies in the seventeenth century, 1607–1689*, Baton Rouge 1949

Cunningham, A., 'Thomas Sydenham: epidemics, experiment and the "Good Old Cause"', in French and Wear, *Medical revolution*, 164–90

Curry, P., *Prophecy and power: astrology in early modern England*, Cambridge–London 1989

Cust, R. and A. Hughes (eds), *Conflict in early Stuart England: studies in religion and politics, 1603–1642*, London–New York 1989

Dailey, B. R., 'The visitation of Sarah Wight: holy carnival and the revolution of the saints in civil war London', *Church History* lv (1986), 438–55

Damasio, A., *The feeling of what happens: body, emotion and the making of consciousness*, London 2000

Davis, J. C., *Utopia and the ideal society: a study of English utopian writing, 1516–1700*, Cambridge 1981

——— 'Against formality: one aspect of the Puritan Revolution', *TRHS* 6th ser. iii (1993), 265–88

Davis, R., 'English foreign trade, 1660–1700', in W. E. Minchinton (ed.), *The growth of English trade in the seventeenth and eighteenth centuries*, London 1969, 78–98

Debus, A., *The chemical philosophy: Paracelsan science and medicine in the sixteenth and seventeenth centuries*, New York 1977

——— *Man, nature and the Renaissance*, Cambridge 1978

De Krey, G., 'The first Restoration crisis: conscience and coercion in London, 1667–73', *Albion* xxv (1993), 565–80

——— 'Rethinking the Restoration: dissenting cases for conscience, 1667–1672', *HJ* xxviii (1995), 53–83

Donagan, B., 'The casualties of war: treatment of the dead and wounded in the English Civil War', in I. Gentles, J. Morrill and B. Worden (eds), *Soldiers, writers and statesmen of the English Revolution*, Cambridge 1998, 114–32

Drayton, R., *Nature's government: science, imperial Britain, and the 'improvement' of the world*, New Haven–London 2000

Dunlop, R., *Ireland under the Commonwealth*, ii, Manchester 1913

Edwards, P., *Dealing in death: the arms trade and the British civil wars*, Stroud 2000

Elder, J. R., *The royal fishery companies of the seventeenth century*, Aberdeen 1912

Elmer, P., 'Medicine, religion and the Puritan Revolution', in French and Wear, *Medical revolution*, 10–45

Farnell, J. E., 'The Navigation Act of 1651, the first Dutch war, and the London merchant community', *EcHR* 2nd ser. xvi (1961–2), 439–54

Finkelstein, A., *Harmony and the balance: an intellectual history of seventeenth-century English economic thought*, Ann Arbor 2000

Firth, K., *The apocalyptic tradition in Reformation Britain, 1530–1643*, Oxford 1979

Fix, A., *Prophecy and reason: the Dutch collegiants in the early enlightenment*, Princeton 1991

Foster, A., 'Church policies of the 1630s', in Cust and Hughes, *Conflict in early Stuart England*, 193–223

Frank, R. G., *Harvey and the Oxford physiologists: a study of scientific ideas and social interaction*, Berkeley–Los Angeles 1980

Freist, D., *Governed by opinion: politics, religion and the dynamics of communication in Stuart London, 1637–1645*, London 1997

French, R. and A. Wear (eds), *The medical revolution of the seventeenth-century*, Cambridge 1989

Garber, D., 'Soul and mind: life and thought in the seventeenth century', in D. Garber and M. Ayers (eds), *The Cambridge history of seventeenth-century philosophy*, i, Cambridge 1998, 759–93

Gauci, P., *The politics of trade: the overseas merchant in state and society, 1660–1720*, Oxford 2001

Goblet, Y. M., *La Transformation de la géographie politique de l'Irlande au XVIIe siècle*, Paris 1930

Goldie, M., 'The civil religion of James Harrington', in A. Pagden (ed.), *The languages of political theory in early-modern Europe*, Cambridge 1987, 197–222

———— 'Danby, the bishops and the Whigs', in Harris, Seaward and Goldie, *Politics of religion*, 75–105

———— 'John Locke's circle and James II', *HJ* xxxv (1992), 557–86

———— 'Priestcraft and the birth of Whiggism', in N. Phillipson and Q. Skinner (eds), *Political discourse in early modern Britain*, Cambridge 1993, 209–31

Goslinga, C., *The Dutch in the Caribbean and on the Wild Coast, 1580–1680*, Assen 1971

Greaves, R. L., *Deliver us from evil: the radical underground in Britain, 1660–1663*, New York–Oxford 1986

———— *Enemies under his feet: radicals and nonconformists in Britain, 1664–1677*, Stanford 1990

Greene, J. P., *Peripheries and center: constitutional development in the extended polities of the British empire and the United States, 1607–1788*, Athens, GA–London 1986

Greengrass, M., 'Samuel Hartlib and international Calvinism', *Proceedings of the Huguenot Society* xxv (1993), 464–74

———— M. Leslie and T. Raylor (eds), *Samuel Hartlib and universal reformation*, Cambridge 1994

Griffiths, P., *Youth and authority: formative experiences in England, 1560–1640*, Oxford 1996

Gunn, J. A. W., *Politics and the public interest in the seventeenth century*, London–Toronto 1969

Guerlac, H., 'The poet's nitre', *Isis* xlv (1954), 243–55

Hair, P. E. H. and R. Law, 'The English in western Africa', in N. Canny (ed.), *The Oxford history of the British empire*, I: *The origins of empire*, Oxford 1998, 241–63

Haley, K. H .D., *The first earl of Shaftesbury*, Oxford 1968

Hardinge, W. H., 'On manuscript mapped and other townland surveys in Ireland of a public character, embracing the Gross, Civil, and Down surveys, from 1640 to 1688', *Transactions of the Royal Irish Academy: Antiquities* xxiv (1873), 1–118

Harper, L. A., *The English navigation laws: a seventeenth-century experiment in social engineering*, New York 1939

Harris, F. R., *Edward Montagu 1st earl of Sandwich (1625–1672)*, ii, London 1912

Harris, T., P. Seaward and M. Goldie (eds), *The politics of religion in Restoration England*, Oxford 1990

Harwood, J. T., *The early essays and ethics of Robert Boyle*, Carbondale–Edwardsville 1991

Haycock, D. B., *Immortal flesh: a modern history of longevity*, forthcoming 2008

Henry, J., 'Magic and science in the sixteenth and seventeenth centuries', in Olby, Cantor, Christie and Hodge, *Companion to the history of modern science*, 583–96

——— 'Boyle and cosmical qualities', in M. Hunter (ed.), *Robert Boyle reconsidered*, Cambridge 1994, 119–38

Hill, C., 'A bourgeois revolution?', in J. G. A. Pocock (ed.), *Three British revolutions: 1641, 1688, 1776*, Princeton 1980, 109–39

——— *The century of revolution, 1603–1714*, 2nd edn, London 1980

——— 'The place of the seventeenth-century revolution in English history', in C. Hill, *A nation of change and novelty: radical politics, religion and literature in seventeenth-century England*, London–Chicago–Melbourne 1993, 19–37

Hinton, R. W. K., *The Eastland trade and the common weal in the seventeenth century*, Cambridge 1959

Horsefield, J. K., *British monetary experiments, 1650–1710*, London 1960

Hotson, H., *Johann Heinrich Alsted, 1588–1638: between Renaissance, Reformation, and universal reform*, Oxford 2000

Houston, A., '"A way of settlement": the Levellers, monopolies, and the public interest', *HPT* xivi (1993), 381–420

——— and S. Pincus (eds), *A nation transformed: England after the Restoration*, Cambridge 2000

Howell, R., *Newcastle Upon Tyne and the Puritan Revolution*, Oxford 1967

Hoxby, B., 'The government of trade: commerce, politics, and the courtly art of the Restoration', *English Literary History* lxvi (1999), 591–627

——— *Mammon's music: literature and economics in the age of Milton*, New Haven–London 2002

Hughes, A., *The causes of the English Civil War*, Basingstoke–London 1991

——— *Gangreana and the struggle for the English Revolution*, Oxford 2004

Hunter, M., *Science and society in Restoration England*, Cambridge 1981

——— *Establishing the new science: the experience of the early Royal Society*, Woodbridge 1989

——— *Science and the shape of orthodoxy: intellectual change in late seventeenth-century Britain*, Woodbridge 1995

——— *Robert Boyle, 1627–1691: scrupulosity and science*, Woodbridge 2000

Hutton, R., *The Restoration: a political and religious history of England and Wales, 1658–1667*, Oxford 1985

Iliffe, R., '"Jesus Nazarenus legislator": Adam Boreel's defence of Christianity', in S. Berti, F. Charles-Daubert and R. Popkin (eds), *Heterodoxy, Spinozism, and free thought in early-eighteenth-century Europe*, Dordrecht–Boston–London 1996, 375–96

——— 'Abstract considerations: disciplines and the incoherence of Newton's natural philosophy', *Studies in History and Philosophy of Science* xxxv (2004), 427–54

Israel, J. I., *Dutch primacy in world trade, 1585–1740*, Oxford 1989

——— 'England's mercantilist response to Dutch world trade primacy, 1647–1674', in S. Groenveld and M. Wintle (eds), *State and trade: government and the economy in Britain and the Netherlands since the Middle Ages*, Zutphen 1992, 50–61

——— *The Dutch Republic: its rise, greatness, and fall, 1477–1806*, Oxford 1995

——— *Radical Enlightenment: philosophy and the making of modernity, 1650–1750*, Oxford 2001

Jacob, J. R., *Robert Boyle and the English Revolution: a study in social and intellectual change*, New York 1977

James, M., *Social problems and policy during the Puritan Revolution*, London 1930

James, S. R., 'A list of surgeons in practice in London and its suburbs in 1641', *Bulletin of the History of Medicine* xix (1946), 282–90

Jenner, M., '"Another epocha"? Hartlib, John Lanyon and the improvement of London in the 1650s', in *SHUR*, 343–56

Kaplan, B., 'Greatrakes the stroker: the interpretations of his contemporaries', *Isis* lxxii (1982), 178–85

Katz, D. S., *Philo-semitism and the readmission of the Jews to England, 1603–1655*, Oxford 1982

Keil, I., 'Technology transfer and scientific specialization: Johann Wiesel, optician of Augsburg, and the Hartlib circle', in *SHUR*, 268–78

——— *Augustanus Opticus: Johann Wiesel (1583–1662) und 200 Jahre Optisches Handwerk in Augsburg*, Berlin 2000

Keirn, T. and F. Melton, 'Thomas Manley and the rate-of-interest debate, 1668–1673', *JBS* xxix (1990), 147–73

Kelly, P. H., 'Introduction', to *Locke on money*, ed. P. H. Kelly, Oxford 1991, 1–109

——— 'Dutch data in Locke's economic writings', *Locke Newsletter* xxvi (1995), 119–40

Kelsey, S., *Inventing a republic: the political culture of the English Commonwealth, 1649–1653*, Manchester 1997

Kent Clarke, J., *Whig's progress: Tom Wharton between revolutions*, Madison–London 2004

Kepler, J. S., *The exchange of Christendome: the international entrepôt at Dover, 1622–1651*, Leicester 1976

Kilroy, P., 'Radical religion in Ireland', in Ohlmeyer, *Ireland from independence to occupation*, 201–17

Kitchin, G., *Sir Roger L'Estrange*, London 1913

Knights, M., *Politics and opinion in crisis, 1678–81*, Cambridge 1994

——— '"Meer religion" and the "church-state" of Restoration England: the impact and ideology of James II's declarations of indulgence', in Houston and Pincus, *Nation transformed*, 41–70

Kukla, J., 'Order and chaos in early America: political and social stability in pre-Restoration Virginia', *American Historical Review* xc (1985), 275–98

Lake, P., 'Anti-popery: the structure of a prejudice', in Cust and Hughes, *Conflict in early Stuart England*, 72–106

———— '"A charitable Christian hatred": the godly and their enemies in the 1630s', in C. Durston and J. Eales (eds), *The culture of English Puritanism, 1560–1700*, Basingstoke 1996, 145–83

———— *The boxmaker's revenge: 'orthodoxy', 'heterodoxy' and the politics of the parish in early Stuart London*, Stanford 2001

Lamont, W., *Godly rule: politics and religion, 1603–60*, London 1969

Laslett, P., 'John Locke, the great recoinage, and the origins of the Board of Trade, 1695–1698', *WMQ* 3rd ser. xiv (1957), 369–402

Leng, T., 'Commercial conflict and regulation in the discourse of trade in seventeenth-century England', *HJ* xlviii (2005), 933–54

Leslie, M., 'The spiritual husbandry of John Beale', in Leslie and Raylor, *Culture and cultivation*, 151–72

———— and T. Raylor (eds), *Culture and cultivation in early modern England: writing and the land*, Leicester 1992

Letwin, W., *The origins of scientific economics: English economic thought, 1660–1776*, London 1963

Lindley, K., *Popular politics and religion in civil war London*, London 1997

Little, P., 'The Irish "Independents" and Viscount Lisle's lieutenancy of Ireland', *HJ* xliv (2001), 941–61

Loades, D., *England's maritime empire: seapower, commerce and policy, 1490–1690*, Harlow 2000

McLachlan, H. J., *Socinianism in seventeenth-century England*, Oxford 1951

Macpherson, C. B., *The political theory of possessive individualism*, Oxford 1962

Maddison, R. E. W., *The life of the honourable Robert Boyle*, London 1969

Malcolm, N. and J. Stedall, *John Pell (1611–1685) and his correspondence with Sir Charles Cavendish: the mental world of an early modern mathematician*, Oxford 2005

Manke, E., 'Empire and state', in D. Armitage and M. Braddick (eds), *The British Atlantic world, 1500–1800*, Basingstoke 2002, 175–95

Marshall, A., 'Colonel Thomas Blood and the Restoration political scene', *HJ* xxii (1989), 561–82

———— 'Sir Joseph Williamson and the conduct of administration in Restoration England', *HR* lxix (1996), 18–41

Marshall, J., *John Locke: resistance, religion and responsibility*, Cambridge 1994

Mayers, R., 'Real and practicable, not imaginary and notional: Sir Henry Vane, *A healing question*, and the problems of the Protectorate', *Albion* xxvii (1995), 37–72

———— *1659: the crisis of the Commonwealth*, Woodbridge 2004

Miller, J., *Charles II*, London 1991

Milton, A., 'A qualified intolerance: the limits and ambiguities of early Stuart anti-Catholicism', in A. F. Marotti (ed.), *Catholicism and anti-Catholicism in early modern English texts*, Basingstoke 1999, 85–115

———— '"The unchanged peacemaker"? John Dury and the politics of irenicism in England, 1628–1643', in *SHUR*, 95–117

More, E., 'Congregationalism and the social order: John Goodwin's gathered church, 1640–60', *Journal of Ecclesiastical History* xxxviii (1987), 210–35

Muldrew, C., *The economy of obligation: the culture of credit and social relations in early modern Europe*, London–Hampshire 1998

Newman, W., 'Newton's *Clavis* as Starkey's *Key*', *Isis* lxxviii (1987), 564–73

———— *Gehennical fire: the lives of George Starkey, an American alchemist in the scientific revolution*, Cambridge, MA. 1994

———— and L. Principe, *Alchemy tried in the fire: Starkey, Boyle, and the fate of Helmontian chymistry*, Chicago–London 2002

O'Hart, J., *The Irish and the Anglo-Irish landed gentry*, Dublin 1969

Ohlmeyer, J. (ed.), *Ireland from independence to occupation, 1641–1660*, Cambridge 1995

Olby, R., G. Cantor, J. Christie and M. Hodge (eds), *Companion to the history of modern science*, London–New York 1990

Ormrod, D., *The rise of commercial empires: England and the Netherlands in the age of mercantilism, 1650–1770*, Cambridge 2003

Orwin, L. C. (ed.), *Material London, ca. 1600*, Philadelphia 2000

Osler, M., *Divine will and the mechanical philosophy: Gassendi and Descartes on contingency and necessity in the created world*, Cambridge 1994

Parnham, D., 'Politics spun out of theology and prophecy: Sir Henry Vane on the spiritual environment of public power', *HPT* xxii (2001), 53–83

Paster, G. K., 'Purgation as the allure of mastery: early modern medicine and the technology of the self', in Orwin, *Material London*, 193–205

Peacey, J., *Politicians and pamphleteers: propaganda during the English civil wars and Interregnum*, Aldershot 2004

Pelling, M., 'Medical practice in early modern England: trade or profession?', in W. Prest (ed.), *The professions in early modern England*, London 1987, 90–128

———— *The common lot: sickness, medical occupations and the urban poor in early modern England*, London–New York 1998

———— *Medical conflicts in early modern London: patronage, physicians, and irregular practitioners*, Oxford 2003

———— and C. Webster, 'Medical practitioners', in Webster, *Health, medicine and mortality*, 165–235

Pestana, C. G., *The English Atlantic in an age of revolution, 1640–1661*, Cambridge, MA. 2004

Petry, Y., *Gender, Kabbalah and the Reformation: the mystical theology of Guillaume Postel (1510–1581)*, Brill 2004

Pincus, S., ' "Coffee politicians does create": coffeehouses and Restoration political culture', *Journal of Modern History* lxvii (1995), 807–34

———— 'The English debate over universal monarchy', in J. Robertson (ed.), *A union for empire: political thought and the British union of 1707*, Cambridge 1995, 37–62

———— 'From butterboxes to wooden shoes: the shift in English popular sentiment from anti-Dutch to anti-French in the 1670's', *HJ* xxviii (1995), 333–61

———— 'Republicanism, absolutism and universal monarchy: English popular sentiment during the third Dutch war', in G. M. MacLean (ed.), *Culture and society in the Stuart Restoration*, Cambridge 1995, 241–66

———— *Protestantism and patriotism: ideologies and the making of English foreign policy, 1650–1668*, Cambridge 1996

———— 'Neither Machiavellian moment not possessive individualism: commercial society and the defenders of the English Commonwealth', *American Historical Review* ciii (1998), 705–36

———— 'From holy cause to economic interest: the study of population and the invention of the state', in Houston and Pincus, *Nation transformed*, 272–98

Poole, W., 'Seventeenth-century preadamism, and an anonymous English preadamist', *Seventeenth Century* xix (2004), 1–35

Popkin, R., *Isaac La Peyrère (1596–1676): his life, work and influence*, Leiden 1987

—— 'Hartlib, Dury and the Jews', in *SHUR*, 118–36

—— *The third force in seventeenth-century thought*, Leiden 1992

—— *The history of scepticism from Savonarola to Bayle* (1960), Oxford 2003

Principe, L., *The aspiring adept: Robert Boyle and his alchemical quest*, Princeton 1998

—— and W. Newman, 'Some problems with the historiography of alchemy', in W. Newman and A. Grafton (eds), *Secrets of nature: astrology and alchemy in early modern Europe*, Cambridge, MA 2001, 385–431

Raylor, T., 'Samuel Hartlib and the commonwealth of bees', in Leslie and Raylor, *Culture and cultivation*, 91–129

Rich, E. E., 'The first earl of Shaftesbury's colonial policy', *TRHS* 5th ser. vii (1957), 47–70

Sacks, D. H., 'Parliament, liberty, and the commonweal', in J. H. Hexter (ed.), *Parliament and liberty from the reign of Elizabeth to the English Civil War*, Stanford 1992, 85–121

—— 'The countervailing of benefits: monopoly, liberty, and benevolence in Elizabethan England', in D. Hoak (ed.), *Tudor political culture*, Cambridge 1995, 272–91

Sainty, J. C., *Office holders in modern Britain*, III: *Officials of the Board of Trade, 1660–1870*, London 1974

Sargent, R. M., *The diffident naturalist: Robert Boyle and the philosophy of experiment*, Chicago–London 1995

Schilling, H., *Religion, political culture and the emergence of early modern society: essays in German and Dutch history*, Leiden 1992

Schuster, J., 'The scientific revolution', in Olby, Cantor, Christie and Hodge, *Companion to the history of modern science*, 217–40

Scott, J., *Algernon Sidney and the English Republic, 1623–1677*, Cambridge 1988

—— 'England's troubles: exhuming the popish plot', in Harris, Goldie, and Seaward, *Politics of religion*, 197–232

—— *Algernon Sidney and the Restoration crisis, 1677–1683*, Cambridge 1991

—— *England's troubles: seventeenth-century English political instability in European context*, Cambridge 2000

—— '"Good night Amsterdam": Sir George Downing and Anglo-Dutch statebuilding', *EHR* cxviii (2003), 334–56

—— *Commonwealth principles: republican writing of the English Revolution*, Cambridge 2004

Scott, W. R., *The constitution and finance of English, Scottish and Irish joint-stock companies to 1720*, ii, Cambridge 1910

Scott-Luckens, C., 'Propaganda or marks of grace? The impact of the reported ordeals of Sarah Wight in revolutionary London, 1647–52', *Women's Writing* ix (2002), 215–32

Shapin, S., *A social history of truth: civility and science in seventeenth-century England*, Chicago–London 1994

—— and S. Schaffer, *Leviathan and the air-pump: Hobbes, Boyle, and the experimental life*, Princeton–Oxford 1985

Shapiro, B., 'Latitudinarianism and science in seventeenth-century England', in Webster, *Intellectual revolution*, 286–316

———— *Probability and certainty in seventeenth-century England*, Princeton 1983

Shirren, A., '"Colonel Zanchy" and Charles Fleetwood', *Notes and Queries* cxcviii (1953), 431–5, 474–7, 519–24

Simmington, R., 'Introduction' to *The civil survey, AD 1654–1656*, Dublin 1931, pp. iii–x

Simms, J. G., 'The civil survey, 1654–6', *IHS* ix (1955), 257–61

Slack, P., *From reformation to improvement: public welfare in early modern England*, Oxford 1999

Smith, N., *Perfection proclaimed: language and literature in English radical religion, 1640–1660*, Oxford 1989

———— 'Exporting enthusiasm: John Perrot and the Quaker epic', in T. Healy and J. Sawday (eds), *Literature and the English Civil War*, Cambridge 1990, 248–64

Sosin, J. M., *English American and the Restoration monarchy of Charles II*, Lincoln–London 1980

Speck, W., 'Britain and the Dutch Republic', in K. Davids and J. Lucassen (eds), *A miracle mirrored: the Dutch republic in European perspective*, Cambridge 1995, 173–95

Spurr, J., *The Restoration Church of England, 1646–1689*, New Haven–London 1991

———— *English Puritanism, 1603–1689*, London–Basingstoke 1998

———— *England in the 1670s*, Oxford 2000

Steele, I., *Politics of colonial policy: the Board of Trade in colonial administration, 1696–1720*, Oxford 1968

Steneck, N., 'Greatrakes the stroker: the interpretations of historians', *Isis* lxxiii (1982), 160–77

Stewart, R. W., *The English ordnance office: a case-study in bureaucracy*, Woodbridge 1996

Strauss, E., *Sir William Petty: portrait of a genius*, London 1954

Struik, D., *The land of Stevin and Huygens*, Dordrecht 1981

Stubbs, M., 'John Beale, philosophical gardener of Herefordshire', *Annals of Science* xxxix (1982), 463–89 (pt I); xlvi (1989), 323–63 (pt II)

Supple, B., *Commercial crisis and change in England, 1600–1642: a study in the instability of a mercantile economy*, Cambridge 1959

Thorndike, L., *A history of magic and experimental science*, VIII: *The seventeenth century*, New York 1958

Thornton, A. P., *West-India policy under the Restoration*, Oxford 1956

Thirsk, J., *Economic policy and projects: the development of a consumer society in early modern England*, Oxford 1978

Tolmie, M., *The triumph of the saints: the separate churches of London, 1616–1649*, Cambridge 1977

Trevor-Roper, H., *Religion, the Reformation and social change*, London 1967

Tuck, R., *Philosophy and government, 1572–1651*, Cambridge 1993

Turnbull, G., *Hartlib, Dury and Comenius: gleanings from Hartlib's papers*, London 1947

Wear, A., *Knowledge and practice in English medicine, 1550–1680*, Cambridge 2000

Webster, C., 'Water as the ultimate principle of nature: the background to Boyle's Sceptical Chymist', *Ambix* xiii/2 (1966), 96–107

—— 'English medical reformers of the Puritan Revolution: a background to the "Society of Chymical Physicians"', *Ambix* xiv (1967), 16–42

—— 'New light on the Invisible College: the social relations of English science in the mid-seventeenth century', *TRHS* 5th ser. xxiv (1974), 19–42

—— *The great instauration: science, medicine and reform, 1626–1660*, London 1975; 2nd edn, Oxford 2002

—— 'Alchemical and Paracelsan medicine', in Webster, *Health, medicine and mortality*, 301–34

—— *From Paracelsus to Newton: magic and the making of modern science*, Cambridge 1982

—— 'Benjamin Worsley: engineering for universal reform from the Invisible College to the Navigation Act', in *SHUR*, 213–33

—— (ed.), *The intellectual revolution of the seventeenth century*, London–Boston 1974

—— (ed.), *Health, medicine and mortality in the sixteenth century*, Cambridge 1979

—— 'Worsley, Benjamin', in C. S. Nicholls (ed.), *Dictionary of national biography: missing persons*, Oxford 1993, 722–3.

Weinstein, R., 'London at the outbreak of the Civil War', in S. Porter (ed.), *London and the Civil War*, Basingstoke–London 1996, 31–44

Wheeler, S., 'Four armies in Ireland', in Ohlmeyer, *Ireland from independence to occupation*, 43–65

Whitmore, J. B., 'Dr. Worsley being dead', *Notes and Queries*, 28 Aug. 1943, 123–8

Williams, A. R., 'The production of saltpetre in the Middle Ages', *Ambix* xxii (1975), 125–33

Williamson, J. A., *English colonies in Guiana and on the Amazon, 1604–1668*, Oxford 1923

Wilson, C., *Profit and powe: a study of England and the Dutch Wars*, 2nd edn, The Hague 1978

—— *England's apprenticeship, 1603–1763*, 2nd edn, London–New York 1984

Withington, P., *The politics of commonwealth: citizens and freemen in early modern England*, Cambridge 2005

Wojcik, J., *Robert Boyle and the limits of reason*, Cambridge 1997

Woolrych, A., *Britain in revolution, 1625–1660*, Oxford 2002

Wootton, D., 'Introduction: the republican tradition: from commonwealth to common sense', in D. Wootton (ed.), *Republicanism, liberty, and commercial society, 1649–1776*, Stanford 1994, 1–41

Worden, B., *The Rump Parliament, 1648–1653*, Cambridge 1974

—— 'Toleration and the Cromwellian Protectorate', in W. J. Sheils (ed.), *Persecution and toleration* (Studies in Church History xxi, 1984), 199–233

—— 'The question of secularization', in Houston and Pincus, *Nation transformed*, 20–40

Wrightson, K., *Earthly necessities: economic lives in early modern Britain, 1470–1750*, London 2002

Yates, F., *Giordano Bruno and the hermetic tradition*, London 1964

—— *The Rosicrucian enlightenment*, London–New York, 1972

Yeomans, D., 'The origin of North American astronomy: seventeenth century', *Isis* lxviii (1977), 414–25

Young, J. T., *Faith, medical alchemy and natural philosophy: Johann Moriaen, reformed intelligencer, and the Hartlib circle*, Aldershot 1998

Young, S., *The annals of the Barber-Surgeons of London*, London 1890

Zahedieh, N., 'The merchants of Port Royal, Jamaica, and the Spanish contraband trade, 1655–1692', *WMQ* 3rd ser. xliii (1986), 570–93

——— 'Trade, plunder, and economic development in early English Jamaica, 1655–89', *EcHR* 2nd ser. xxxix (1986), 205–22

——— '"A frugal, prudential and hopeful trade": privateering in Jamaica, 1655–89', *Journal of Imperial and Commonwealth History* xviii (1990), 145–68

——— 'London and the colonial consumer in the late seventeenth century', *EcHR* 2nd ser. xlvii (1994), 239–61

Zaller, R., 'Benjamin Worsley', in R. L. Greaves and R. Zaller (eds), *Biographical dictionary of British radicals in the seventeenth century*, Brighton 1982, iii. 342

Unpublished theses

Crist, T. J., 'Francis Smith and the opposition press in England, 1660–1688', PhD diss. Cambridge 1977

Kelly, P. H., 'Locke on money: an edition of John Locke's three pamphlets on money published in the 1690s', PhD diss. Cambridge 1975

Man, Y., 'English colonization and the formation of Anglo-American polities, 1606–1664', PhD diss. Johns Hopkins 1994

Sharp, L. 'Sir William Petty and some aspects of seventeenth-century natural philosophy', DPhil diss. Oxford 1977

Index

alchemy, 27, 95, 97, 182–4; *sal nitrum* 'school', 25–6, 97–103, 109–10, 183, 188; spiritual, 38, 112–14, 119

Alsted, Johann Heinrich, 6, 7, 123, 124, 127, 187

Amsterdam, 37–8, 41–8, 115, 175

Andrews, Thomas, 51

Arlington, Henry Bennet, 1st earl of, 147, 152, 158, 161, 164, 170, 172

Arminianism, 47

Artista, Elias, 132

Ashe, John, 60

Ashley Cooper, Anthony, *see* Shaftesbury, 1st earl of

Ashmole, Elias, 107

astrology, 105–7

astronomy, 41, 105

Augustus, prince of Anhalt, 44

Aurelius, Marcus, 46

Ayres, Philip, 175

Bacon, Francis, 25; Baconianism, 3, 28, 32, 104, 106, 110

banking, 68–9

Bannister, James, 158, 164

Baptists, 20, 33, 120, 139, 173, 175, 176; in Ireland, 87, 93, 134, 143

Barbados, 49, 50, 57, 103, 143, 165

Barber-Surgeons' Company, 14, 19–20

Bartholin, Thomas, 147

Battie, John, 61

Baxter, Richard, 176, 180

Beale, John: religious beliefs, 122, 139; and Worsley, 104, 107, 111, 131, 133, 138–9, 145, 146; Worsley's respect for, 130

Ben Israel, Menassah, 45

Bennet, Henry, *see* Arlington, 1st earl of

Berkeley, Sir William, 50, 56, 57, 59, 140

Bethel, Slingsby, 171

Birch, Thomas, 2, 4

Blaeu, Johann, 41

Blood, Thomas, 172

Boate, Arnold, 19, 22, 32

Boate, Gerald, 19, 22, 25, 29, 33, 90

Böhme, Jacob, 44, 120, 125

Bohun, countess of, 15

Bontius, Jacob, 114

Boone, Thomas, 60, 176 n. 90

Boreel, Adam, 38, 44–5

Boswell, Sir William, 37

Bourne, Nicholas, 75

Boyle, Richard, *see* Cork, 1st earl of

Boyle, Richard, *see* Burlington, 1st earl of and 2nd earl of Cork

Boyle, Robert, 99, 101, 142; correspondence with Worsley, 2, 27, 114–17, 127–9, 182–3; and George Starkey, 71, 95–6, 102; and the Invisible College, 4, 26–8, 32, 188; *Of the vsefvlnesse of natural philosophy*, 29, 105; possible investment in Worsley's library, 146–7, 174; religious beliefs, 32–3, 34, 129, 138; scientific activities and ideas, 27, 95, 98, 108–11, 112, 146; and Worsley, 1, 39, 89, 92, 96, 131, 165, 174, 175–6

Boyle, Roger, *see* Broghill, Baron, and 1st earl of Orrery

Bradshaw, John, 50

Brereton, Sir William, 142, 143

Bridgeman, William, 169

Brocard, James, 43

Broghill, Roger Boyle, Baron, 1st earl of Orrery, 87, 89, 138

Brooke, Robert Greville, 2nd Baron, 22, 26, 124

Browne, Sir Thomas, 47

Bruno, Giodarni, 46

Buckingham, George Villiers, 2nd duke of, 147–8, 160, 161, 163, 170, 171

Burlington, Richard Boyle, 1st earl of and 2nd earl of Cork, 143

Burroughs, Jeremiah, 120

Burthogge, Richard, 176, 181

Butler, James, *see* Ormond, 1st duke of

Buxtorf, Johann, 147

Byam, William, 157

Cartesianism, 42, 106, 112, 188. *See also* Descartes, René

Cary, Lucy, 89, 138

Cary, Mary, 120, 176 n. 90

Cary, Philip, 176

Challoner, Thomas, 60, 64

Locke, John (*cont.*)
164, 168; Worsley's papers compiled
by, 2, 152, 169
London, 14, 16–17, 20, 22, 26, 34,
140; Coleman Street, 20, 34, 139;
corporation, 23–4, 69, 74, 140; Great
Fire (1666), 146–7; Great Plague
(1665), 143; medical marketplace,
14–15; religion, 17, 20, 32, 33
Louis XIV, king of France, 159, 161, 166
Ludlow, Edmund, 93, 143
Lull, Ramon, 124
Lushington, Thomas, 47
Lynch, Sir Thomas, 165

Maddison, Sir Ralph, 60, 65, 73
Maier, Michael, 133
Malynes, Gerald de, *see* de Malynes,
Gerald
Marcgraff, Georg, 43
Marvell, Andrew, 173, 179
Massereene, Sir John Clotworthy,
Viscount, 143
Mayow, John, 109
Mearne, Samuel, 174
Mercator, Nicholas, 105, 107
Merchant Adventurers, *see* trade and
merchants
merchants, *see* trade and merchants
Merret, Christopher, 71, 147
Methwold, William, 61, 66
Milton, John, 50, 70
Modyford, Sir Thomas, 160–1
Monck, George, 1st duke of Albermarle,
142
Monrath, Sir Charles Coote, 1st earl of,
85, 90, 142
Montagu, Edward, *see* Sandwich, 1st earl
of
Montagu, Richard, 47
More, Henry, 31, 41
Morgan, Sir Anthony, 83, 84, 134
Morgan, Henry, 160
Moriaen, Johann, 6, 38, 39, 40, 41, 44, 46,
71, 99

navigation acts: Restoration, 140, 152,
156, 162, 167; (1651), 2, 8, 36, 54, 59,
60, 65, 70, 74–7, 79, 192
Neale, Sir Paul, 41
Netherlands, *see* Dutch Republic
New England, 141, 153, 156
Nicholas of Cusa, 120
Niclaes, Hendrik, 120

Noell, Martin, 51, 140, 149
Norimbergius, Johann Eusebius, 43
Nuysement, Jacques de, *see* de Nuysement,
Jacques

Oldenburg, Henry, 146, 174
Ormond, James Butler, 1st duke of, 18,
148

Paine, Thomas, 192
Palmer, George, 144–5
Paracelsus, 97, 110, 112, 124, 132, 183;
Paracelsianism, 25–6, 97, 106
Parker, Henry, 62
Patient, Thomas, 120
Peiresc, Nicolas-Claude Fabri de, 25
Pell, John, 6
Penn, William, 172
Pennoyer, William, 51
Pergens, Jacob, 39
Perrot, John, 121–2, 129
Peter, Hugh, 62
Petty, Sir William: Irish career, 80, 82,
83–8, 120, 134; political attitudes and
activities, 81, 87–8, 93, 131–3, 134–5,
190; scientific activities and interests,
39, 96, 146; and Worsley, 1, 2, 30, 39,
72, 84–8, 90, 96, 118, 173, 187
Peyrère, Isaac de la, *see* de la Peyrère, Isaac
Physicians, College of, 14
Piso, Willem, 43
Postel, Guillaume, 46
Potter, William, 68–9, 132, 142
Povey, Thomas, 140, 149
privateers, 160–2
projects, 20–1, 39, 40, 97, 144
prophecy, 122–3
Pruvost, Peter le, *see* le Pruvost, Peter
Purchas, Samuel, 25
Puritanism, 3, 5, 6, 17, 26, 72
Pym, John, 22

Quakers, 44, 121–2, 130, 172, 175

Ramsay, David, 40
Rand, James, 131
Rand, William, 25, 47, 71, 131, 146
Randall, Giles, 120
Ranelagh, Katherine Jones, Viscountess:
household, 26, 72; intellectual
activities, 26, 32; visits Sarah Wight,
33; and Worsley, 26, 89, 92, 135, 143,
146–7, 174
Regius, Henricus, 42